THE ANARCHIST INQUISITION

THE ANARCHIST INQUISITION

ASSASSINS, ACTIVISTS, AND MARTYRS IN SPAIN AND FRANCE

MARK BRAY

ISBN 978-1-84935-514-8
Audiobook-ISBN 978-1-84935-538-4
Library of Congress Control Number: 2023935632

AK Press   AK Press
370 Ryan Avenue #100   33 Tower Street
Chico, CA 95973   Edinburgh, EH6, 7BN
USA   Scotland
www.akpress.org   www.akuk.com
akpress@akpress.org   akuk@akpress.org

The addresses above would be delighted to provide you with the latest AK Press
catalog, featuring several thousand books, pamphlets, audio and video products, and
stylish apparel published and distributed by AK Press. Alternatively, visit our websites
for the complete catalog, latest news and updates, events, and secure ordering.

Cover design by Henry Sene Yee
Cover photographs (clockwise from top left): mugshots of Pedro Vallina,
Bernard Harvey, Jesús Navarro, and Fermín Palacios. Archivo General de
la Administración, Asuntos Exteriores, Embajada en Paris, 5858.

Printed in the United States of America on acid-free, recycled paper

For Senia

Is it wrong to strike down the bloodthirsty tiger whose claws are tearing at human hearts, whose jaws are crushing human heads?

—Michele Angiolillo, 1897

CONTENTS

ACKNOWLEDGMENTS

My mentor, Temma Kaplan, had so many brilliant ideas lying around back in 2009 that she gave me one she had decided not to pursue herself: an analysis of anarchism and human rights in *el proceso de Montjuich*. For that idea, which became the kernel of this book, and for being an intellectual inspiration I send her my deepest appreciation. Thank you also to Melissa Feinberg, Jochen Hellbeck, and John Merriman, for their in-depth feedback and patience with my narrative-driven inclinations. This project was made possible with funds from the Fulbright Fellowship, the Mellon Dissertation Fellowship, the Center for Cultural Analysis at Rutgers University, and various grants from Rutgers. Thank you to Cornell University Press and Emily Andrew who believed in me and this project when we first discussed it in 2017. Thank you to the many scholars and comrades who took time to help me on my research journey: Chris Ealham, Eduardo González Calleja, Ángel Herrerín López, José Antonio Piqueras, Joan Casanovas, Antoni Dalmau, Ellison Moorehead, Belinda Davis, Sergio Higuera Barco, John-Erik Hansson, Jorell Meléndez-Badillo, Constance Bantman, Fabien Delmotte, Alejandro Gomez del Moral, Kevin Grant, Manel Aisa, Miguel Pérez, and the anonymous reviewers of my manuscript. Thank you to my caring and supportive parents, my wonderful sister Emily, and my little boys Xavi and Omar. And to Senia, the love of my life, without you this book, and everything else, would be unimaginable. ("It was a moment like this, do you remember?")

THE ANARCHIST INQUISITION

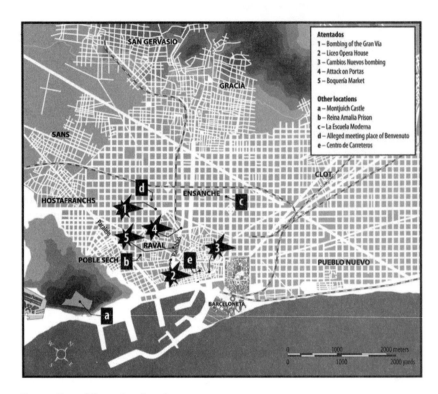

MAP 1. Turn-of-the-century Barcelona

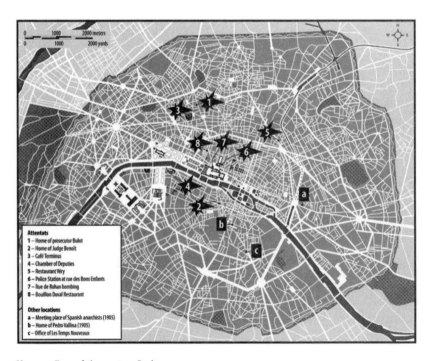

MAP 2. Turn-of-the-century Paris

Introduction
Two Children of Modernity

Among the vast brood begotten by modernity, two of the most quarrelsome siblings were the congenial "human rights" and the miscreant "terrorism." True, the birth of the latter occurred in defense of the former—at least, if we are to believe the arguments put forth by Maximilien Robespierre and his Committee of Public Safety during the French Revolution's Reign of Terror, when modern political terror emerged. Nevertheless, human rights and terrorism—two of this book's main themes—pursued starkly different paths over the following centuries. While the parentage of human rights was widely recognized as it became perhaps *the* modern political concept par excellence, that of "barbaric" terrorism was called into question as it wreaked havoc around the world. That is the basic story we are told. But apart from debates over the proper definitions, origins, and terminology of these phenomena, is there reason to question it?

The anarchists of the turn of the twentieth century have figured prominently in the story of terrorism. As the assassins of kings, presidents, and prime ministers on both sides of the Atlantic, they have been considered "the first global or truly international terrorist experience in history."[1] In the 1890s the French Third Republic and the Spanish state were besieged by an unprecedented wave of "propaganda by the deed" (an anarchist euphemism for attacks on symbols of oppression) that seemed to threaten the very foundation of civilization for many elites. As the century drew to a close,

1

dynamite ripped through packed theaters and cafés in Barcelona and Paris while explosives rained down on legislators in the French Chamber of Deputies. Both states responded to the anarchist threat with indiscriminate mass arrests, the passage of anti-anarchist laws, executions, and deportations. In 1896 the stakes were raised when a bomb killed twelve participants in a Corpus Christi procession in Barcelona. Predictably, the Spanish state responded by arresting even more radicals (possibly as many as seven hundred) and passing an even harsher law against anarchism that curtailed speech and political association. One need only think of the relationships between 9/11, the Patriot Act, and Abu Ghraib to grasp the familiar story of terrorism provoking states to curtail rights in the alleged interest of security. But whereas earlier rumors of torture in Spanish prisons had failed to exceed the level of scattered murmurs, this time allegations of sleep deprivation, starvation, and genital mutilation in the dungeons of the infamous Montjuich Castle overlooking Barcelona developed into a transnational chorus of outrage. Indeed, the repression and torture of anarchists and other radicals had failed to generate popular support for their plight in the early 1890s. Yet the Spanish government's "atrocities" during what came to be known as *el proceso de Montjuich* in Spain—termed the "revival of the Inquisition" by activists—and the Cuban War of Independence triggered a successful transnational campaign across Europe and the Americas "in the name of the rights of humanity" from 1896 to 1900. This campaign served as a model and inspiration for another five similar transnational campaigns against the repression of anarchists in Spain over the next decade.[2] On first glance this appears to be a story of human rights sweeping in to clean up the mess made by anarchism, perceived by many—then and now—to be terrorism incarnate.

But there are two main reasons to rethink this one-dimensional rendition. First, anarchists were not only bombers; they were also human rights activists who played key roles in organizing turn-of-the-century transnational Spanish prisoner campaigns among others such as the campaign to liberate Captain Alfred Dreyfus in France. Second, some anarchists were both. That is to say, anarchists such as Pedro Vallina, Charles Malato, and Francisco Ferrer were active organizers against "the revival of the Inquisition in Spain" *and* admitted, or very likely, plotters of acts of propaganda by the deed. Could doe-eyed human rights and maleficent terrorism have been in on it together? Or is dynamite a disqualification for admission into the realm of human rights?

This book is a narrative history that explores these and other questions by guiding the reader through conspiratorial backroom anarchist meetings in Paris, ominous torture chambers in Barcelona, a presidential assassination in Lyon, and anti-torture demonstrations in London and beyond. Based on research in twenty-five archives and libraries in Spain, France, England, the Netherlands, and the United States, it explores the interrelations between anarchist propaganda by the deed and the development of human rights activism by following influential figures such as Teresa Mañé i Miravet and Joan Montseny i Carret, Catalan anarchist schoolteachers turned human rights organizers, or Charles Malato, a French anarchist Dreyfusard imprisoned for the attempted assassination of the Spanish king, through key events of the tumultuous turn of the twentieth century. This book navigates overlapping worlds of transnational activism and intrigue across Europe and the Americas to illustrate how the feuding siblings of human rights and terrorism may have shared more of a family resemblance in a rapidly globalizing world than one might expect.

The Porous World of Transnational Anarchism

The anarchist ability to orchestrate transnational human rights campaigns (and/or acts of propaganda by the deed) flowed from their ideological cosmopolitanism and the geographically transnational nature of their movement at the turn of the century. Anarchism—an anti-hierarchical, anti-electoral form of revolutionary socialism—rejected nationalism, though some anarchists supported national liberation in Cuba or Korea, for example, or retained elements of national identification that were arguably at odds with their professed values.[3] Instead, anarchists advocated for a world without borders organized through free federations of worker-controlled enterprises exchanging goods and services based on the principles of mutual aid rather than market demand. Their ardent opposition to state, capital, and nation earned them the animus of their governments who increasingly began to deport them by the end of the century if they had not already fled repression, as in the case of many Russian anarchists.

Though intended to curb anarchism, deportations pushed anarchists to put their internationalist principles into practice as they forged new networks of resistance abroad. With the failure of attempts to create more formal international organizations in the 1870s and 1880s, turn-of-the-century anarchist networks usually revolved around prominent figures. Many were newspaper publishers who bridged the chasm between anarchist movements back home and exiles abroad through their papers and correspondence and frequently forged bonds between migrant anarchist communities in "nodal cities" such as London, Paris, Buenos Aires, New York, Havana, Alexandria, and Paterson, New Jersey.[4]

Exiled anarchists sparked the pivotal campaign against the torture and repression of anarchists incarcerated in Montjuich Castle in Barcelona (1896–1900), which set the stage for five more Spanish solidarity campaigns over the next decade. Among these exiled anarchist campaigners were the Cuban-born engineer Fernando Tarrida del Mármol, who fled Barcelona to Paris and then London after his release from Montjuich Castle, and the Catalan anarchist lay teacher Joan Montseny, who was deported with twenty-seven other prisoners to Liverpool before he eventually made his way to London and then Paris. Several years later, the Andalusian medical student Pedro Vallina played a key role in the 1904 transnational campaign to liberate the Alcalá del Valle prisoners after he fled to Paris to avoid charges of insulting the Spanish army. Anarchists like Vallina often arrived abroad with addresses and letters of introduction plugging them into local revolutionary milieus that revolved around places of radical sociability, such as editorial offices, anarchist clubs, and union halls.[5] Writing on the experience of turn-of-the-century German immigrant anarchists in New York City, Tom Goyens argues that such meeting places "assume, for anarchists, a much more important role in the running and conception of the movement" than for the socialists of the era because they "shun official channels and deny the legitimacy of bourgeois institutions."[6]

The cement that formed networks out of otherwise disparate spaces of anarchist sociability that were often divided by linguistic barriers included shared celebrations, such as May 1st or the commemoration of the martyrs of Haymarket or the Paris Commune; overlapping ideological disputes and convergences; and the key role of influential movement figures. "International militancy was therefore very much an elite phenomenon, which trickled down and was taken up by less famous individuals," argues Constance Bantman.[7] Although many Spanish anarchists never participated in the "elite phenomenon" of transnational migration, through their correspondence, publishing, and activism, such "sedentary anarchists" helped build the transnational movement without necessarily crossing borders.[8] Many economic historians have termed the global influences of this period the first era of globalization. Stretching from the middle of the nineteenth century to the start of the First World War, this era of unprecedented market integration, migration, and informational exchange reached its "high water mark" from 1870 to 1914.[9] The increased use of the telegraph and innovations in print technology allowed for the global dissemination of world events in newspapers with rising circulations. Anarchists took full advantage of this growing transnational media environment, even if most anarchist periodicals were ephemeral.

Among the most enduring fixtures in turn-of-the-century anarchist publishing was the Montseny-Mañé family publishing enterprise behind the theoretical journal *La Revista Blanca* and its newspaper corollary, *El Suplemento de
la Revista Blanca*, later renamed *Tierra y Libertad*.[10] According to his daughter
Federica Montseny, who would become an influential leader of the anarcho-
syndicalist CNT during the Spanish Civil War and paradoxically (for an anarchist) the first woman to become a government minister in Spanish history,
Joan Montseny was the "genius creator" of the family publishing enterprise,
while his wife, Teresa Mañé, was the indefatigable administrator.[11]

Yet Mañé, who usually published under the pseudonym Soledad Gustavo,
was a prolific writer, editor, and translator in her own right. She penned
pioneering articles on anarchist feminism, free love, anarchist theory, and
orchestrated the 1900 campaign to liberate the prisoners of Jerez de la Frontera.[12] Mañé and Montseny named their journal after *La Revue Blanche*, a
bohemian Parisian journal that was ardently supporting Captain Dreyfus
and publishing Fernando Tarrida del Mármol's accounts of torture in Barcelona's Montjuich Castle. The decision by Mañé and Montseny to name their
new journal after a republican rather than anarchist periodical speaks to their
desire to engage with a wider world of writers and readers than much of
the anarchist press offered. It also suggests that sometimes we fail to grasp
the social and political complexities of turn-of-the-century anarchism if we
speak exclusively in terms of an anarchist movement or an anarchist diaspora in transnational contexts. Anarchist activists in transnational hubs like
London and Paris, as well as in cities like Madrid or Barcelona that played

FIGURE 1.   Joan Montseny and Teresa Mañé. Íñiguez, *Enciclopedia historica*, 1983 and 1989.

similar roles during low tides of repression, shared places, ideas, symbols, and personal networks with a wide range of republicans, socialists, freethinkers, Freemasons, neo-Malthusians, lay educators, nationalist revolutionaries, and others.

Anarchists and radical or federal republicans shared anti-clerical, anti-monarchist, and insurrectionary values, but they also shared a past. This is part of the story of the "second anarchist generation" in Spain, of anarchist women and men whose parents had been federal republicans, as in the case of Teresa Mañé, or had been politicized as republicans in their youth before adopting anarchism, like Francisco Ferrer, or simply swam in the anarcho-republican milieu of workers' centers, *ateneos*, taverns, Masonic lodges, and other similar places, like Pedro Vallina, whose mentor, Fermín Salvochea, had been a republican mayor of Cádiz before embracing anarchism.[13] While workers may have flowed back and forth between anti-authoritarian and socialist unions in Spain, on the level of ideas and their personification in prominent movement figures, anarchists shared more with anti-establishment republicans than with Pablo Iglesias's Socialist Party.[14] Socialists played a much greater role in the Spanish prisoner campaigns outside of Spain.

It was this transnational network of anarchists and their allies, functioning through platforms like the Ligue des Droits de l'Homme in France or the Spanish Atrocities Committee in Britain, that orchestrated the Spanish prisoner campaigns of the turn of the century. Anarchists may have instigated the campaigns, but they relied on the support of republican editors like Alejandro Lerroux in Madrid or Henri Rochefort in Paris to reach a broader audience. Certainly, anarchists forged this appeal to "all men of heart" in conjunction with their allies out of necessity.[15] Ideally the transnational anarchist movement would have simply launched their long-desired revolution and demolished the walls of the prisons themselves in the process of establishing a postcapitalist society rather than depoliticize their propaganda in a broad coalition. But especially with the movement in Spain in retreat, anarchists had little choice but to put aside that which separated them from potential allies if they truly aimed to liberate their comrades (though some anarchists opposed this strategy). In the interest of establishing broad coalitions of support, one could characterize the anarchist strategy of depoliticizing their rhetoric into phrases about defending "humanity" as what Richard Griffiths has called "clan languages" or "stock languages" to consolidate activist group identity and demonize their enemies. Just as "truth and justice" became one of the rhetorical symbols of the French Dreyfusards, appeals to "humanity" bridged the political gaps that otherwise separated Spanish prisoner activists on both sides of the Atlantic and seemed to endow their cause with a foundation in basic ethical truth.[16] Together, anarchists and their allies claimed the mantle of "public opinion" on behalf of an aggrieved humanity against conservative forces that often disdained public opinion as ephemeral caprice as opposed to deep-seated "national conscience."[17]

The use of this clan language not only allowed Spanish prisoner activists to reach allies across ideological lines; it also situated the campaign to liberate the Montjuich prisoners and those that followed it within a broader era of transnational activism in the name of the "rights of humanity" that included opposition to the oppression of czardom; outrage against Ottoman abuses of Greeks, Cretans, Bulgarians, and Armenians; protests against Spanish colonial atrocities in Cuba and the Philippines; the Dreyfus affair in France; indignation at hacienda slavery in Mexico; resistance to lynching in the US South; and the movements against the "new slaveries" in the Congo Free State, Portuguese West Africa, and the Putumayo jungle of South America.[18] In general, the network of anarchists and their allies behind the Spanish prisoner campaigns had little ideological or personnel overlap with the largely British network of evangelicals, merchants, and avowedly apolitical humanitarians behind the campaigns against the "new slaveries" in Africa and elsewhere. Whereas the Spanish prisoner network could trace much of its anti-clericalism and radicalism to the French Revolution, the "new" anti-slavery network owed its reformist, apolitical brand of activism to the campaign against chattel slavery in the Americas earlier in the century. Unsurprisingly, the Spanish prisoner campaigns had far more overlap with the campaign against oppression in Russia, evident in the shared membership between the Spanish Atrocities Committee and the Society of Friends of Russian Freedom, the Dreyfus affair, and opposition to Spanish atrocities in Cuba and the Philippines.

Anarchism and Human Rights

Scholars differ over whether these turn-of-the-century movements should be considered examples of "human rights," a contested term whose common usage only emerged in the twentieth century, and/or "humanitarianism," a far less controversial label that was commonplace in the nineteenth century. Popular understandings of these terms posit that human rights activism aims to establish rights to prevent suffering in the future, while humanitarianism focuses on alleviating suffering in the present. Yet distinctions between these two types of activism maintain their form more easily in terms of twentieth-century organizational outlooks and prerogatives—in comparing Amnesty International to the Red Cross, for example—than they do in terms of nineteenth- and early twentieth-century campaigns that often freely blended elements that had yet to be firmly solidified.[19]

Although the exact phrase "human rights" was used rarely (though more often than one might expect), I argue that the Montjuich campaign and those that followed it were, in fact, human rights campaigns (and perhaps also humanitarian campaigns). The validity of my argument, and all others in the debate over human rights periodization, comes down to the question of definition. What are / were human rights? Which definition is most useful? Following Lynn Hunt, who situates the origin of human rights in the Enlightenment and the revolutions of the late eighteenth century, I define human rights as those that are considered natural, equal, and universal.[20] Drawing on the rich political legacy of the French Revolution, the "rights of humanity" defended by Spanish prisoner activists were thought to exist independently of the laws of states or the origins or status of those who invoked them. Following Samuel Moyn, I define human rights as those that transcend state sovereignty.[21] Yet whereas Moyn argues that rights only began to transcend the state in the 1970s, I argue that such a transcendence occurred at the turn of the twentieth century with the Montjuich campaign and its successors (and to varying degrees with some of the other campaigns of the era). The Spanish prisoner activists did not frame their arguments in terms of the laws of Restoration Spain or even in terms of reforming the country's judicial system. The Montjuich campaign consistently presented an appeal for rights beyond the Spanish state.

"Even the most internationalist late-nineteenth-century socialists," Moyn argues, "were not able in the end to escape the gravitation of state and nation."[22] But what about the anti-state and (largely) anti-nationalist anarchist movement? As I have argued elsewhere, anarchists not only participated in campaigns that transcended the state; as theorists who sought to incorporate the revolutionary potential of classical liberal individualism into their vision of class warfare, they were the only political tendency to promote a vision of human rights against the state.[23] Joan Montseny and other anarchists argued that the "written laws" of the state were always "opposed to natural laws" that anarchists upheld.[24] The French anarchist Jean Grave elaborated on the vast array of universal rights that such "natural laws" were thought to entail: "to satisfy one's hunger is a primordial right that takes precedence over all other rights and stands at the head of the claims of a human being. But anarchy embraces all the aspirations and neglects no need. The list of its demands includes all the demands of humanity. . . . Indeed, every being has a right not only to what sustains life, but also to whatever renders it easy, enlivens it, and embellishes it."[25] Therefore, the strategic use of the rhetoric of the "rights of humanity" on the part of anarchists does not mean that such language contradicted underlying anarchist values. Nor does it mean that their conception of human rights was identical to those held by their liberal, republican, or socialist allies or that it directly caused the modern human rights movement of recent decades.

Though the era between the abolition of slavery and the establishment of the United Nations has been largely overlooked in the history of human rights, by including the turn of the twentieth century we gain insight into an alternate trajectory of transnational rights advocacy that was short-circuited by the political transformations and carnage of the two world wars. By incorporating into human rights history trajectories that died out, we can better understand how notions of universal rights beyond the state are, in fact, portable concepts that can coexist with and within a wide variety of politics and other "utopias." Rather than unraveling human rights genealogy, we can understand the turn of the twentieth century and the 1970s as eras of heightened globalization when similar transnational discourses of universal rights came to the fore. In comparing the "depoliticized new humanitarianism of human rights" of the 1970s and Victorian "moral campaigns" of the nineteenth century, Stefan-Ludwig Hoffman argues similarly. "Contemporary historians of human rights," he argues, "have more to learn from the history of the long nineteenth century than they realize."[26]

Human Rights *and* Terrorism?

Anarchists as human rights activists? No doubt such a proposition pricks the sensibilities of some readers. But anarchists as human rights activists *and* so-called terrorists? Beyond the pale? We will see, but first, the challenge of language. Terrorism is notoriously difficult to define, as scholars have formulated over 250 different definitions.[27] Nevertheless, one reason to use the term in this study is that, in addition to phrases like "propaganda by the deed" or "attack" (*atentado* in Spanish, *attentat* in French), many anarchists and their enemies described anarchist bombings and assassinations as "terrorism" or "terror." "To white terror," an 1893 anarchist pamphlet proclaimed, "we will respond with red terror."[28] For pro-dynamite anarchists, class war was terror; the only question was, "Which side are you on?" Yet insurrectionary advocates of propaganda by the deed were a minority within the anarchist movement, and only a small fraction of their ranks ever picked up a bomb. In 1908, in response to a proposed anti-terrorism law, Barcelona anarchists launched a "campaign against the two terrorisms: that of the iron bombs that dynamiters explode in the streets and that of the legal bombs that the government throws to kill" the lower classes.[29] As the framing of this campaign suggests, the anarchist movement was well aware of how the word "terrorism" was used by the press and politicians to demonize terror from below while normalizing terror from above.

This tendency has persisted not only in how states frame terrorism (as violence perpetrated exclusively by "sub-national groups or clandestine agents," according to the US Department of State) but by many scholars who view "state terrorism" as "a square circle."[30] Since the term "terrorism" "has the illocutionary force of moral censure, repudiation or outright condemnation," its nearly exclusive application to violence from below bears significant political consequences.[31] In the aftermath of September 11, 2001, the field of critical terrorism studies was born to bring "state terrorism" into the picture among other goals.[32] Richard Jackson, one of the field's leading scholars, argues that "although terrorism can never be adequately defined due to its unstable ontological status," scholars ought to use the term to avoid "marginalising their views and their access to power."[33] Yet I argue that it is absurd to hope that critical scholarship will ever succeed in fundamentally altering the state's strategic discursive deployment of the rhetoric of terrorism to delegitimize violence from below and normalize it from above (or at most apply the term to antagonistic authoritarian regimes). I join scholars who consider terrorism to be a "failed paradigm" that should be discarded (along with the paradigm of "extremism") in favor of a broader, more nuanced, and less normatively charged analysis of violence from above and below.[34] Although we can certainly highlight the importance of advances in communications technologies in differentiating the modern terrorist from the premodern assassin,[35] we can discuss this and other related historical transformations without using language that empowers state violence. Therefore, although the term "terrorism" was used to refer to anarchist violence, this book uses other popular terms of the era, such as propaganda by the deed, *atentado*, or *attentat*, to describe anarchist attacks instead.

In an effort to push back against earlier work that portrayed anarchism as inherently terroristic, recent scholars of anarchism have strongly emphasized that only a small minority of anarchists ever detonated bombs. While this corrective has been necessary, less frequently do such scholars acknowledge that between the pro-dynamite insurrectionaries and the staunchly anti-dynamite anarchists (who were largely focused on labor organizing) there existed at the turn of the century a vast gray area of anarchists, revolutionaries, and working-class people who showed varying degrees of sympathy for acts of propaganda by the deed on a case-by-case basis depending on the targets chosen and the methods used in the *attentat*. The case of the famed Russian anarchist geographer Peter Kropotkin is emblematic of this tendency. After wholeheartedly supporting propaganda by the deed as a method of revolution in 1880, Kropotkin shifted by 1891 to argue that "an edifice built upon centuries of history cannot be destroyed by a few kilos of explosives."[36] Nevertheless, privately he still sympathized with what he perceived to be the "desperation" of Santiago Salvador's 1893 bombing of the Liceo Theater in Barcelona and supported more targeted attacks like the assassination of the French president in 1894 or the Spanish prime minister in 1897.[37] Kropotkin was far from alone in this regard.

Although some anarchist pacifists like the German Gustav Landauer supported the Spanish prisoner campaigns, generally speaking the opinions of most of the anarchist campaigners seem to have existed in the broad gray area between ardent insurrectionism and a universally anti-dynamite position. For while anarchist campaigners and their allies usually did not directly call for the death of King Alfonso XIII (though sometimes they did), they routinely wielded the specter of retaliatory *atentados* to pressure state officials to release imprisoned anarchists. The looming threat of reprisals for inaction was the fourth element, along with press campaigns, public meetings, and broad transnational coalitions, in what I call the Montjuich template of resistance that informed the strategies behind the next five Spanish prisoner campaigns that followed in its wake: those in favor of the Jerez de la Frontera prisoners of 1892 (1900–1901), the Mano Negra prisoners of 1882 (1902–3), the Alcalá del Valle prisoners of 1903 (1903–4 and 1908–9), and the two Francisco Ferrer campaigns (1906–7 and 1909). While it is impossible to ascertain the exact effectiveness of such threats, after the Montjuich campaign and Michele Angiolillo's 1897 assassination of Prime Minister Cánovas del Castillo, correspondence between government officials evinced grave concern that unwarranted repression could provoke a new spiral of retaliation. That caution influenced instances over the next decade where repression could have reached the level of *el proceso de Montjuich* (1896–1900) but did not.

Yet anarchist campaigners went further than simply warning state officials of the lamentable potential of a "desperate" act of vengeance in the event of their inaction. For example, in 1904 a committee of Spanish, French, and German republicans and anarchists in Paris published a short-lived newspaper called *L'Espagne inquisitoriale* that promoted the transnational campaign to liberate the Alcalá del Valle prisoners while also advocating propaganda by the deed *as part of the campaign*. Joaquín Miguel Artal, who had attempted to assassinate Prime Minister Maura to avenge the Alcalá del Valle martyrs, was featured prominently on the cover of the paper's third edition.

FIGURE 2. *L'Espagne inquisitoriale*, September 1904. International Institute for Social History.

L'Espagne inquisitoriale considered its veneration of figures like "the sublime Angiolillo," who assassinated Prime Minister Cánovas del Castillo, to be in the service of its participation in the "indignant clamor of all of humanity" in support of the Alcalá del Valle prisoners.[38] According to Joan

Montseny, the Spanish Atrocities Committee, which was the main engine of the Montjuich campaign in Britain, secretly funneled money into an unsuccessful plot to assassinate the queen regent of Spain.[39]

Did anarchist efforts to organize plots to deprive monarchs and politicians of what could be considered the most basic right of all, the right to live, contradict their professed advocacy of that very same right for all? In 1905 the longtime anarchist militant and former Montjuich prisoner Anselmo Lorenzo published the influential *El banquete de la vida*, which argued that "the limitation of life" by the oppression of the upper classes pushed the "disinherited" to "affirm their right to live." But Lorenzo also clarified that "the right to live . . . is only denied to man when he attempts to justify absurdity and iniquity, and violated when he exploits and tyrannizes."[40] Similarly, the Italian anarchist Errico Malatesta argued that "the oppressed are always in a state of legitimate self-defense, and have always the right to attack the oppressors."[41] An agenda item for an 1892 Parisian anarchist meeting encapsulated how many anarchists viewed the paradoxical duality of survival under capitalism: "The right to existence with its consequences. (The right to theft and murder)."[42] These remarks demonstrate that for many anarchists the oppressive actions of tyrants and exploiters invalidated their right to live and to enjoy bodily security. From the perspective of many anarchists, there was no inherent contradiction in the notion of assassinating a brutal leader in the name of the "rights of humanity."

Nonviolence is generally taken as a foundational pillar of the concept of human rights. In the 1970s, for example, Amnesty International would not help victims of state repression, such as the East Timorese resistance to Suharto, because of their utilization of violence in self-defense.[43] But if the Declaration of the Rights of Man and Citizen was born out of the storming of the Bastille, the phrase "human rights" came out of the Second World War, and the NATO invasion of Kosovo and the Iraq War were justified on human rights grounds, then the association between the two may not be so straightforward. Granted, scholars who follow Moyn's periodization would exclude examples before the 1970s, and one could argue that the justification of violence on human rights terms is simply a perversion of the concept. But even human rights activists who profess nonviolence turn to state violence when they call for human rights violators to be prosecuted or for the United Nations to send soldiers to prevent atrocities. The prevalent association between human rights and nonviolence really reflects the degree to which the notion of human rights has been subsumed into a liberal human-rights-ism that portrays violence as the antithesis of justice while naturalizing and obscuring the routine state violence of all but the most brutal countries.

Despite the pacifistic self-image that human rights advocates have constructed for themselves in recent decades, notions of human rights have always coexisted with violence. The discourses of "human rights" and "terrorism" actually function very similarly in that their shared demonization of exceptional instances of violence implicitly serves to legitimize and ultimately invisibilize routine state violence. But whereas many human rights activists and moderate nineteenth-century campaigners like E. D. Morel of the Congo campaign have downplayed other atrocities or everyday wrongs in the interest of drawing attention to their cause célèbre, anarchists and other radical campaigners sought to use their campaigns to indict larger systems of injustice. At a London protest meeting against torture in Montjuich Castle, Kropotkin argued that actually "everywhere, where there is a prison there is torture"—a notion that has gained currency in recent years with the growth of the prison abolition movement.[44] This maximalist vision of prison abolition is anathema to the "minimalist, hardy utopia" of modern human rights.[45] In this book I demonstrate how this was not always the case. By analyzing the ideas and activism of the anarchists and their allies who advocated striking down the "enemies of humanity," we gain a greater understanding of how concepts of natural, equal, universal rights have coexisted with revolutionary maximalism, political violence, and a wide variety of other "utopias."[46] Then again, perhaps the "fiction of moral autonomy from politics" that governs modern human rights simply provides cover for human rights to implicitly legitimize the "utopia" of liberal capitalist hegemony, the allegedly apolitical violence of incarceration, and the maximalist aspirations of the modern surveillance state.[47]

The Ethics of Modernity

Appeals to the "rights of humanity" or the "humanitarian" reduction of suffering struck a chord with Western audiences because of a broader discursive shift that occurred moving into the second half of the nineteenth century that produced what I call the ethics of modernity: the popular belief that Western society had achieved the elevated moral status that was considered to be a necessary corollary of modern civilization. Enlightenment conceptions of historical progress premised on the capacities of human rationality and ingenuity to mold society had for many years been associated with aspirations toward a corresponding moral advancement grounded in a kind of empathetic sensibility. The ethics of modernity came into being once much of the West considered that quest completed. "Despite commonplace assumptions about the Enlightenment," Susan Maslan argues, "the primary qualification for inclusion within the category of the human was the capacity to feel, not the capacity to reason."[48] Indeed, a "passion for compassion," as Hannah Arendt phrased it, reshaped the ethical landscape during this period.[49] As Michael Barnett argued, "The revolution in moral sentiments and the emergence of a culture of compassion is one of the great unheralded developments of the last three centuries. . . . The alleviation of human suffering became a defining element of modern society."[50] Contemporaries such as Oscar Wilde were aware of this dynamic, as is evident in the quip offered by Lord Henry in Wilde's 1890 classic *The Picture of Dorian Gray* that "the nineteenth century has gone bankrupt through an over-expenditure of sympathy."[51] This heightened ethical sensibility was reflected in the development of penitentiaries and greater concern for the welfare of prisoners and the mentally ill, the disfavor shown toward the abuse of children and animals, and the declining utilization of corporal punishment such as flogging in the military, among other examples. Lynn Hunt argues that new forms of novel reading in the eighteenth century promoted empathetic sensibilities by encouraging readers to identify with the situations of their protagonists.[52]

The Catalan anarchist Joan Montseny was particularly attuned to the power of literary sentimentalism in the pursuit of justice. By the time he died in exile in France in 1942, Montseny had published twelve novels, ninety-nine novellas, and countless articles as Federico Urales. The work that Montseny considered to be his greatest—and the one whose title captured his self-perception—was *Mi Don Quijote*. The novel's protagonist asks: "Is it easier to rouse the people through sentiment than through ideas?"[53] Montseny certainly believed so. As a former Montjuich prisoner, his intellectual persona continually sought to elicit what he perceived to be an eminently human emotional response to atrocities by presenting himself as a witness of suffering, such as that experienced by freezing Filipino prisoners in Montjuich Castle, or by taking on their voices in his Montjuich play *El Castillo maldito*.[54] Lynn Festa's warning that "sentimentality produces hierarchy and difference as much as it creates reciprocity and likeness" was certainly evident in these campaigns, since British or French support for imprisoned Spanish anarchists often represented "declarations of a superior stock of humanity" on their part as contrasted with Spanish "backwardness."[55] Nevertheless, the campaign writings of Urales and his allies successfully used sentiment to merge the two rhetorical motifs of the Spanish prisoner campaigns, and others like them, at the turn of the twentieth century: personification through the figure of the intellectual and gruesome accounts of torture, often from survivors themselves, coupled with images of torture implements and the wounds they generated. Though in theory Spanish anarchists retained the legal rights of subjects, particularly in the wake of the 1896 bombing of a Corpus Christi procession in Barcelona, politicians, judges, and wardens depoliticized and dehumanized anarchists and their alleged crimes in order to bypass corrupt and unequally applied legal safeguards. In so doing, they systematically sought to reduce these "beasts, more ferocious than those of the virgin jungles," to what Giorgio Agamben terms "bare life."[56] It was when anarchists had been almost reduced to "the abstract nakedness of being human and nothing but human," as Arendt phrased it, that their largely depoliticized corporeality redeemed their suffering bodies.[57] After all, "there is something terribly morbid," Wilde's Lord Henry remarks, "in the modern sympathy with pain."[58]

Sentimental appeals to alleviate the suffering and respect the rights of others succeeded, when they did, because the ethics of modernity were so widespread that they were shared, or at least publicly respected, even by many of the political actors who were most antagonistic to the rights of man or humanitarianism. Even the conservative La Época of Madrid appealed to the values of the ethics of modernity in lambasting the 1893 bombing of the Gran Vía as violence that "fills the country with great fear . . . that makes social life impossible, hoping to drag us back to a state of barbarism unimaginable even in primitive times."[59] Subsequently, activists made the same argument against state torture pulling "civilization" backward. As opposed to eighteenth-century debates over the institution of slavery, for example, where the gulf that separated the avowed principles of abolitionists and advocates of enslavement was wide, by the turn of the twentieth century the conflict was not over the ethical question of whether slavery or torture was acceptable but rather over the factual question of whether these practices had occurred at all. The core of the ethics of modernity was publicly accepted by almost everyone across the ideological spectrum, and so, rhetorically, politics became a matter of situating oneself in the best position to champion those widely shared values. Unethical conduct, whether anarchist bombings or state torture, was unworthy of modernity and even risked dragging civilization back into a state of barbarism—a societal regression that Charles Darwin considered possible.[60]

The "ethics of modernity" entails the perspective that ethics can only be truly achieved in their fullest sense once a society surpasses "savagery," "barbarism," or any other "backwards" stages of human prehistory to reach "modernity." This analysis undergirded the civilizing mission by lending it a scientific veneer. Therefore, the concept of the ethics of modernity points to the sense of moral self-satisfaction that many in the Western world had developed by the late nineteenth century by comparing what they saw as their ethical enlightenment to the "backwardness" of earlier centuries. The ethics of modernity came into being as the West started to consider the task of transcending its past cruelties to be finished and therefore imagined that the stage of advanced civilization had been attained. The ethics of modernity represented the finale of a story about internal redemption for the West and the shift toward a greater emphasis on another about external redemption. Both humanitarian or human rights campaigns and imperial civilizing missions were products of this shift in the guiding narrative of the West. For the purposes of our inquiry, it is less important that Europeans considered "barbarians" to be immoral than it is that they considered immorality to be "barbaric." The terror that allegations of atrocities elicited in Europeans was grounded in popular anxieties about the distance between "civilization" and "barbarism." The "backwards" peoples of the world were not seen as simply less capable; they were thought to be living in the past.

Most turn-of-the-century European (and plenty of non-European) anarchists embraced the framework of the ethics of modernity and the predominant conception of modern scientific "progress" that accompanied it. Certainly, the overwhelming majority of anarchists were staunch anti-imperialists who critiqued the abuses as well as the very essence of empire.[61] Yet frequently the burning desire to stoke the flames of revolution among a given newspaper's readership in the metropole led to greater foci on abuses closer to home at the expense of a more sustained focus on atrocities being perpetrated in imperial contexts, which were easily the gravest occurring on the planet at the time. Moreover, to borrow framework from Edward Said's *Orientalism*, the European anarchist rejection of *manifest* imperialism masked an underlying embrace of a *latent* imperialism.[62] In other words, despite their rejection of explicit empire, most European anarchists embraced much of the new intellectual and scientific work that underpinned the imperial project even if they conceived of this embrace as working against religious superstition and promoting the emancipation of humanity.

This tendency to embrace elements of the predominant European imperial outlook was evident in the tendency of Spanish prisoner activists to use the popular conception of the "savage" against their enemies in the Spanish government. "What difference is there between a savage and a so-called civilized European?" José Prat asked. "None . . . The moral foundation of our civilization is as savage as possible."[63] Similarly, Charles Malato argued that "the odious governments who condemn the innocent to such moral tortures perhaps believe themselves to be superior to the black cannibals of central Africa!"[64] Rather than challenge the racist category of the "savage," anarchist and non-anarchist campaigners used prevalent Western disgust with "savagery" to shame elites into action and everyday people into active support for their movements.

"Part I: The Propagandist by the Deed" explores the outburst of anarchist propaganda by the deed in France and Spain in the early 1890s through the stories of figures such as Ravachol, Émile Henry, Paulino Pallás, and Santiago Salvador. Although their bombs provoked mass arrests and the passage of anti-anarchist laws in both countries, popular outrage against state repression did not materialize. As the French state de-escalated its response to propaganda by the deed, "Part II: *El Proceso de Montjuich*" examines how the Spanish state amplified its repression and use of torture in the wake of the 1896 bombing of Cambios Nuevos in Barcelona, thereby triggering a groundbreaking transnational campaign in the name of the "rights of humanity." Michele Angiolillo's assassination of Spanish prime minister Cánovas represented a pivotal moment in the blurring of the lines between campaigning for "humanity" and striking down the "enemies of humanity." "Part III: The Shadow of Montjuich" analyzes the influence of the Montjuich campaign on the development of five similar Spanish prisoner campaigns over the next decade. Through the written word and through dynamite they raised the stakes of unleashing another anarchist inquisition.

PART I

*The Propagandist
by the Deed*

CHAPTER 1

"With Fire and Dynamite"

As the blaring of the Bourbon trumpeters marching down the Gran Vía in Barcelona on September 24, 1893, faded into the shouts and *vivas* of the throngs of ebullient onlookers, General Arsenio Martínez Campos sat comfortably atop his steed reviewing an oncoming squadron of lancers. From the balconies above, heads tilted to get a glimpse of this unusual spectacle of military grandeur in celebration of the fiestas of the Virgin of Mercy.[1] Martínez Campos later recounted, however, that at 12:30 p.m., merely a half hour into the day's festivities, he was "contemplating with satisfaction the military spirit and good demeanor of our lancers, when at the instant they passed in front of me I was surprised by a very powerful detonation accompanied by a large cloud of smoke, running and shouting." Since the general was "a little hard of hearing," he assumed there had been an accidental artillery explosion, but instants later he heard, and felt, another blast that knocked him off his horse.[2]

Moments earlier, a municipal officer noticed a man push out of the crowd onto the street and advance toward Martínez Campos. While the officer "was asking himself what this subject was up to," the man hurled two Orsini bombs at Martínez Campos. They exploded at the feet of his horse, mutilating the animal but only slightly injuring the general. Two nearby generals received minor contusions, but a civil guardsman had his leg blown off and died shortly thereafter. The bombing caused one death and sixteen injuries, some quite severe, such as that of a spectator who had her leg amputated.[3]

The explosions and screams triggered a wave of frenzied panic. "The multitude, crazy, blind, ran in opposite directions knocking over everything, falling here, smashing into benches, trees, clogging up doorways and stores forming legitimate human mountains."[4] "Some of the soldiers remained immobile and stupefied. Others broke formation as if they were ready to run. Others, here and there, as if ripped by panic, pointed their rifles at the people."[5] But rather than take advantage of the chaos to escape, right after the explosion the bomber threw his cap in the air, shouting, "¡Viva la anarquía!" and stood still as the police seized him.[6] His name was Paulino Pallás Latorre, and he had just unleashed the first major *atentado* (attack) in a series of shootings, stabbings, and explosions that would earn Barcelona the reputation of "the city of bombs" over the next decade and a half.

As part I explores, however, bombings did not only occur in Barcelona. Both France and Spain experienced their own wave of assassinations and explosions in the early 1890s. With each new spectacle of dynamite, politicians and journalists across the political spectrum demonized anarchists as subhuman monsters who threatened to turn back the clock on the "progress" of "civilization" in accord with what I call "the ethics of modernity." Media dehumanization paved the way for physical dehumanization as both states carried out mass arrests and passed harsh anti-anarchist legislation that expanded state repression well beyond anarchism. Such measures provoked little popular outcry. Yet whereas the French state would pull back on escalating repression by mid-decade, its Spanish counterpart would only escalate its brutality over the coming years, thereby provoking a groundbreaking transnational campaign against the "revival of the Inquisition."

Not long after his arrest, the police, who previously knew nothing of Pallás, paid a visit to his cramped apartment in the working-class neighborhood of Sans outside of Barcelona. There they found his pregnant wife Àngela, their three young children, his widowed mother, and his fifteen-year-old brother living together in a "modest room."[7] His wife claimed that she knew nothing of the bombing; earlier that morning Pallás had left home simply telling her he would return later in the evening. According to his later testimony, Pallás went into Barcelona and ate a meal at a *taverna* near the Mercado de San Antonio before continuing up Montjuich mountain to a cave, where he dug up two bombs he had previously buried wrapped in cotton to protect them from the humidity. He claimed to have acquired the bombs from an Italian anarchist named Francesco Momo (a convenient story since Momo had accidentally blown himself up the previous March). After unearthing the small

FIGURE 3.   Paulino Pallás. *La Campana de Gracia*, September 30, 1893.

spherical explosives, Pallás wrapped them in handkerchiefs, rested them in his sash, and set off for the military parade.[8]

In the Pallás home, the police found a laminated lithograph portrait of the Haymarket martyrs, anarchist pamphlets and periodicals, and a copy of Kropotkin's *The Conquest of Bread*.[9] Pallás had wholeheartedly embraced anarchism, but he had only done so a few years earlier. The son of a stonecutter, Pallás was born in 1862 in Cambrils, a small coastal village outside of Tarragona. In his youth, he learned to be a typographer and lithographer, but he had trouble finding consistent work. To supplement his income, he sometimes sang in the choir that performed *Els hugonots* at the Liceo Theater on La Rambla in Barcelona. Considered to be generous and altruistic by those who knew him, Pallás was said to have adopted "authoritarian socialism" in the late 1880s before moving his family to Argentina to find employment.[10] The Pallás family were among the nearly 1.5 million people who journeyed from Spain to the former colony of Argentina between 1871 and 1914.[11]

In Buenos Aires, and then Rosario de Santa Fe, Pallás immersed himself in the diverse, multilingual world of Argentine revolutionary politics, regularly attending discussion groups and increasingly making a name for himself as an orator at public events such as International Workers' Day on May 1, 1890. He met the famed Italian anarchist Errico Malatesta, then living in Argentina, who influenced Pallás's shift toward anarchist communism. Continually in search of work, the penniless Pallás traveled to São Paulo, an important hub for the nearly 200,000 Spaniards who migrated to Brazil from 1887 to 1903. There he sought work at a local Italian café frequented by Spaniards and Catalans, though to no avail. The following year the family relocated to Rio de Janeiro.[12]

Eventually Àngela had to return to Barcelona after receiving word of the passing of her father. Paulino followed her in the spring of 1892. With the inheritance from her deceased father, they opened a cloth shop before Pallás left the enterprise for more stable employment at a printing workshop, but he was fired for his political activities. He is then said to have spent some time in Paris, where he would have been influenced by the frenzy whipped up by the soon-to-be-legendary French anarchist bomber Ravachol (the subject of chapter 3), since, on his return in the fall of 1892, Pallás helped publish an anarchist periodical in Sabadell bearing his name (*Ravachol*).[13] In the months leading up to the bombing, Paulino and Àngela seem to have spent most of their time working from home on their Singer sewing machines. Neighbors also explained to reporters that Pallás rarely spoke of politics and that his poor wife did not know he was an anarchist, something she even affirmed herself. However, she did in fact identify with anarchist ideas but most likely denied it out of fear.[14]

The day after the bombing, before there was time to clean up the hats, canes, umbrellas, and shredded fabric that still littered the intersection of Gran Vía and Muntaner, the journalistic panic and politicking had already begun.[15] Politicians and commentators from across the political spectrum demanded that the government mete out harsh repression on the anarchists whose crimes were commonly described in the press as an affront to humanity that turned back the clock on civilization. The conservative *La Época* of Madrid wrote that anarchist violence "fills the country with great fear . . . that makes social life impossible, hoping to drag us back to a state of barbarism unimaginable even in primitive times."[16] In the Madrid liberal daily *El Impar-cial* it was the "barbarous anarchists that are the shame of humanity."[17]

The Liberal and Conservative Parties dominated Restoration Spain after the destruction of the short-lived First Republic in 1874. Though differences existed between the two parties, they prioritized the stability of the liberal monarchy against the ultramontane Carlists on the right and republicans and the workers' movements on the left. Together they established the *turno pacífico*, a system to alternate in power every two years through electoral fraud perpetrated by local bosses called *caciques* who adjusted vote totals in exchange for political favors. This system would start to falter over the coming years as differences between the two parties expanded, but in 1893 Conservatives, Liberals, and even republicans called for the harsh repression of anarchists—though their arguments entailed very different political conclusions. The Conservative press argued that repression must target what they saw as the root of the threat: the uncontested spread of anarchist ideas and associations. The editors of *La Época* argued that there have always been those born with the criminal germ, but in the past they were "without mutual solidarity," so their crimes were "hidden in shadow. . . . It was reserved for our century, this new . . . progress of criminality, as much in its methods as in its systematic organization." The solution, therefore, was to crush the ability of those predisposed to crime to associate or propagate their ideas, but according to the editors:

> Modern Governments have remained apathetic, conceding to theoretical anarchism the same prerogatives and liberties that the most noble and holy ideas deserve to enjoy. The result of this weak tolerance has been all of these horrors. . . . In the Spanish Parliament there has been no shortage of orators who have declared the legitimacy of anarchist ideas, as long as they remain *purely* in the realm of theory. "Liberty— they said—has a correction for its deviations in liberty itself"; and armed with the phrase . . . they thought they had resolved the dreadful problem [of the anarchists]. The recent events of Paris, Madrid, and Barcelona have been necessary to prove the ridiculous nature of such garrulous language. . . . Today all tolerance of the anarchists should be gravely censured. . . . It is necessary, in addition, to persecute without rest and without compassion those who espouse anarchist ideas. Their secret sessions, their meetings, their periodicals, their libels are outside of the law.[18]

Conservative critics considered the Gran Vía bombing to be definitive proof that Liberal tolerance for free speech inevitably ended with carnage. Like the anarchists themselves, ironically enough, Conservatives argued that even theoretical anarchist ideas would over time catalyze social upheaval. Social defense, they claimed, required the government to jettison its liberal commitment to civil liberties and distinguish between constructive and destructive ideas. The Liberal Party mouthpiece, *El Imparcial*, cautioned against repressive laws: "If there are police deficiencies in Barcelona then this is something that should be disclosed to the *ministro de la Gobernación* with the governor of Barcelona, but to hope to charge liberal methods with the blame for these crimes which are committed under all governments, and one could even add with more frequency when the means of command are tighter, is to hope for the impossible, because it would be the same as hoping that a few coercive laws would cure what an absolutist government and a real police army in Russia haven't been able to cure." If the methods of czarism, the most repressive government on the continent, actually augmented bombings and assassinations, the Liberals argued, then abandoning civil liberties and shutting down newspapers would risk exacerbating the problem. Simply enhancing repression at the expense of liberties would not work, but, as *El Imparcial* was quick to point out, neither would turning in the other direction toward a republic since anarchist violence was "a social form from which neither monarchies nor republics are exempt."[19] In response, the republican *El País* claimed that anarchist violence would disappear under a republic: "The republicans would make the ferocious intransigence of anarchism useless from the moment they facilitate a legal path for the rational just demands of the working classes. If the Republic translated into laws all or the greater part of the aspirations of the workers . . . what purpose would dynamite bombs have anymore? The Republic isn't only law and justice. The Republic is peace."[20] The only way to stop more bombs from exploding, the republicans argued, was to resolve the social issues that turned poor people into enemies of the state. They promised that a future republic would be up to the task. Conveniently, they ignored the prickly problem of explaining why the French Third Republic was struggling through its own wave of propaganda by the deed.

Regardless of public debate over the proper response to the bombing, the police wasted no time in rounding up between eleven and twenty suspected accomplices the next day, before reaching sixty arrests shortly thereafter.[21] Inspector Tressols and his agents targeted labor leaders, "suspicious" foreigners, those suspected of involvement in past bombings, and known anarchists, such as the influential anarcho-communists Martín Borrás and Emilio Hugas.[22] According to the police, Pallás had joined a small anarchist group known as Benvenuto that met regularly at a pub on Calle de la Diputación, literally around the corner from the site of Pallás's bombing.[23] As Ángel Herrerín López notes, taverns were places of "informal sociability" where anarchists could converge to hatch plots without arousing suspicion, especially in times of repression.[24] Allegedly Pallás and his comrades took this path when they plotted the Gran Vía bombing five days earlier.[25]

While the police were discovering and/or fabricating this information, Pallás sat in a cell in the Atarazanas barracks at the end of the Rambla awaiting trial. While in his cell, he was said to have told the guards, "I am an anarchist and they will kill me; but someone will avenge me."[26] Five days later, Pallás, wearing brown corduroy pants and a blue shirt, was escorted into the courtroom of the Atarazanas barracks "with serenity" by a group of soldiers and sat down opposite the judge. Immediately, Pallás started to fidget with the caps of the inkwells on the table in front of him, seemingly disinterested in everything going on around him. When the judge asked, "To what political society does the prisoner belong?" Pallás responded, "To none, I am an individualist," affirming his opposition to organized association. In the center of the room, packed with eager journalists, rested fragments of Pallás's bomb, a box of pistons, his black sash, and some anarchist papers. The judge asked when he developed the idea to attack the general, and he responded that it was in 1874 when Martínez Campos led the coup that restored the Bourbon monarchy at the expense of the fragile First Spanish Republic. Pallás feared that Martínez Campos's recent appointment as captain general of Catalonia would allow him to unleash brutal repression on the region.[27]

Pallás was very concerned about his legacy, clarifying that he could have escaped but "didn't want to in order to avoid being called a murderer." He also explained that he wasn't interested in what society thought of him: "[I am not] afraid of, or concerned about, the judgment of this stupid, hypocritical, and evil society, but rather because I don't want my children to be considered children of a murderer, but rather children of an honorable man, who gave his life for a cause, that perhaps wrongly he thought the best, but that in good faith he gave his blood thinking that he was doing a service for humanity."[28] Pallás recognized that many people, especially those who upheld the existing society, would denigrate his actions. He was not troubled by that, but he was desperate to clarify to both his critics and supporters that he acted in good faith based on his conscience and that he willingly gave his life for the advancement of "humanity." Beyond political differences about the military or capitalism, Pallás sought to communicate the purity of his motivations.

Although Pallás refused to be represented by an attorney, military authorities appointed one on his behalf. The lawyer spoke of Pallás's poverty and portrayed him as a good father and husband whose industrious personality led him to seek work in South America. He continued to plead for clemency for his client, claiming that he suffered from a "psychiatric affliction," but as he argued that Pallás had repented, his client shook his head "energetically" in disagreement, causing the judge to send him out of the courtroom. When the prosecutor called for the death penalty, Pallás shouted, "¡Aprobado!" (approved), demonstrating his agreement with the requested sentence. Pallás was so frustrated with his lawyer that during the closing arguments he alternated between attempting to speak over him and simply laughing over his remarks, causing the president of the Council of War to silence him continually. At the very end, when it was customary to beg for a pardon, Paulino said, "I don't repent; I don't want a pardon." Pallás started to explain that his only regret was failing to kill the general, but he was cut off and the Council of War ended the trial. Outside, his mother and his wife were sobbing with their "stunned" children next to the barracks.[29]

Pallás was sentenced to death by firing squad to be carried out at Montjuich Castle, an ominous mountaintop edifice overlooking the city beside the sea. That night he was placed in a carriage and escorted up the mountain by a squadron of forty infantrymen. The next day his sorrowful family came to visit Pallás in his cell. After signing his sentence, he solemnly affirmed: "Signing this death sentence, I sign that of my prosecutors! This fulfills the law of Talión: an eye for an eye and a tooth for a tooth." Republican deputies also visited Pallás in the chapel to explain their plans to push for a pardon, but Pallás rejected their proposal, saying that "ideas are stronger than walls and real anarchists should die defending their cause." However, Pallás used the opportunity he had before the republican deputies to ask them to make sure that after his death his head would be studied by a phrenologist to prove that he wasn't crazy, and that after the examination his head would be placed in a museum while the rest of his remains were given a civil burial. On another occasion, he requested that he be allowed to give the order of "Fire!" to the soldiers of his firing squad, that the coins he had in his pocket be melted down and their residue thrown in the air, and that his clothing also be put on display in a museum. None of his requests were granted.[30]

While republicans and Masons were pushing for a pardon, anarchists around the city were taking the opportunity to foment a climate of fear and retaliation leading up to Pallás's execution. Anonymous posters were put up around Barcelona threatening the authorities if Pallás were executed and anonymous threats were mailed to a number of "distinguished people," such as the director of *El Noticiero Universal*. The British ambassador to Spain wrote that the bombing and its aftermath "caused a deep impression in Madrid, where the feeling of security is never very strong."[31] Anarchist proclamations and pamphlets called for "war to the tyrants! The blood of Pallás should run mixed with that of the captain general. *¡Viva la anarquía!*" Anarchists were called on to arm themselves with gasoline, dynamite, knives, or any weapons at their disposal for the day of the execution since "governments impose terror with hunger and rifles, the anarchists have to impose it themselves with fire and dynamite." To "white terror," one anarchist wrote, "we will respond with red terror. We will avenge Pallás."[32]

CHAPTER 2

Propaganda by the Deed and Anarchist Communism

In early 1877 Italian anarchists Errico Malatesta, Carlo Cafiero, and their comrades concocted a simple plan to catalyze revolution through guerrilla warfare. Armed with old rifles and accompanied by approximately one hundred anarchist comrades, they planned to "rove about the countryside for as long as possible, preaching [class] war, inciting social brigandage, occupying small towns and leaving them after having accomplished whatever revolutionary acts we could, and to proceed to that area where our presence would prove more useful."[1] If the impoverished Italian countryside contained the kindling of social upheaval, maybe it just needed a spark? To that end, Malatesta and Cafiero set off into the Matese mountains with the former Russian artillery officer turned revolutionary Sergei Kravchinskii (known as Stepniak). Stepniak, who had been a member of the socialist Circle of Tchaikovsky in the early 1870s with Kropotkin, met Malatesta in the Balkans while fighting alongside the Slavs against Ottoman forces a year earlier.

Their plans began to unravel before they were even set in motion. Preemptive arrests reduced an intended band of one hundred down to twenty-six. Police surveillance spurred the conspirators to launch their foray into the mountains a month early, before the heavy snow deposited during the winter had melted. Moreover, Malatesta and Cafiero were the only southerners in the group who could even communicate to the locals in their dialect. Adorned with red and black cockades, the guerrillas managed to wreck local public record offices, burn official documents, and break tax-collecting devices in several villages, thereby gaining the approval of some villagers. Yet while a chain reaction of social revolution did not materialize, a force of twelve thousand soldiers did. After trudging through the snowy mountains for a little under a week, the anarchists eventually surrendered without resistance.[2]

Though the misadventures of Malatesta, Cafiero, Stepniak, and their comrades amounted to little, the politics behind their attempted insurrection emerged at the intersection of two important developments: the economic philosophy of anarchist communism and the strategy of propaganda by the deed. Both emerged in the wake of the 1876 death of the Russian ex-aristocrat Mikhail Bakunin (1814–76), the most influential figure in the development of anarchism. Although Pierre Joseph Proudhon (1809–65) was the first to describe himself as an anarchist and center his critique on the oppressive nature of the state, his market-based economic program and distaste for class struggle stood in stark contrast with Bakunin's socialist revolutionism. Bakunin essentially infused Marx's critique of capitalism with Proudhon's anti-statism to develop an anarchism that was anti-hierarchical, decentralized, completely opposed to private property and market-based exchange, and focused on fomenting a popular class war that would abolish capital and the state. Yet Bakunin held on to Proudhon's perspective that workers should receive the integral product of their labor according to the maxim "From each according to his abilities, to each according to his productivity." To distinguish his ideas from Marx's "authoritarianism," Bakunin called his economic theory "collectivism." Anarchism, Bakunin said, was simply "Proudhonism, greatly developed and taken to its ultimate conclusion."[3] Furthermore, although Bakunin famously quipped, "The passion for destruction is at the same time a creative passion," he saw anti-authoritarian unionism and mass action as the keys to revolution rather than isolated, individual reprisals against symbols of oppression.[4] This was evident in the fact that the heavily Bakuninist Spanish anarchist movement emerged in 1870 as the strongest faction in the labor organization Federación Regional Española (FRE), the Spanish section of the International Workingmen's Association (IWMA) known as the First International.[5]

Toward the end of his life, however, a number of Bakunin's disciples and comrades started to rethink elements of his thought. On his death, any reluctance to offend the aging revolutionary faded, and two influential and interrelated theoretical innovations in anarchist doctrine emerged over the next few years: anarchist communism (or anarcho-communism) and propaganda by the deed. In the late 1870s the foundational theories of anarchist communism developed among Bakunin's former comrades in the Swiss Jura Federation, including the Italian Benevento revolutionaries Errico Malatesta, Carlo Cafiero, and Andrea Costa; the French geographer Élisée Reclus; and the Russian anarchist émigré Pyotr Kropotkin.[6] As opposed to the collectivist focus on building a postcapitalist society that would provide the worker with the integral product of their labor based on their level of production, the anarchist communists shared Marx's final goal of a society where remuneration would follow Louis Blanc's famous 1839 slogan, "From each according to his abilities, to each according to his needs."[7] From the communist perspective, in order to create a truly just society, it was essential to disentangle one's productivity in the workplace or the economy from their ability to survive. As the influential Mexican anarchist Ricardo Flores Magón phrased it, "A man is free, truly free, when he doesn't need to rent out his arms to anyone in order to lift a piece of bread to his mouth."[8]

In 1880 the term "anarchist communism" was formally adopted at the congress of the Jura Federation, marking the point when this new doctrine had surpassed collectivism throughout most of Europe, except in Spain, where it would not win out until the turn of the century. Since collectivism privileged the quantitative production of the workforce, as opposed to the more holistic communist emphasis on the equality of the dispossessed, it was much stronger in Spain where anarchists maintained their dominance in the labor movement, as opposed to the rest of Europe, where socialists were often pushing their anti-authoritarian competitors to the margins. Given the growing distance between anarchism and labor, it is no surprise that many in the movement started to question the ability of unionism to bring the revolution. As early as 1873, at the Geneva Congress of the Anti-Authoritarian International, almost everyone was highly pessimistic about the general strike except the Spanish delegate.[9]

At the 1876 Berne Congress of the International, the Italian delegates, including future Benevento rebels Malatesta and Cafiero, advocated the "insurrectionary deed" as a substitute for increasingly institutionalized trade unionism, yet the majority of the delegates backed the Belgians who pushed for the union struggle. Their attempted rebellion in the Matese mountains was an effort to follow through on their arguments about promoting ideas through action. As their comrade Costa phrased it, the idea was to transition from peaceful propaganda of ideas to "clamorous and solemn propaganda of insurrections and barricades."[10]

Months later, the French anarchist doctor Paul Brousse, who had listened to Malatesta and Cafiero argue for the "insurrectionary deed" at the Berne Congress, used his position as temporary editor of the *Bulletin de la Fédération Jurassienne* to publish an article titled "Propaganda by the Deed" that the usual editor James Guillaume would have opposed. Yet by "propaganda by the deed" Brousse simply meant putting ideas into action. The original concept was about actively and collectively creating revolutionary situations rather than waiting for them to emerge. For Brousse, the Paris Commune was the epitome of propaganda by the deed.[11] Shortly thereafter, though, the term "propaganda by the deed" started to develop its long-standing association with the kinds of isolated, individual attacks on symbols of oppression, such as Pallás's bombing of the Gran Vía, that would come to identify the anarchist with the shadowy bomb thrower in the global popular imagination.

As early as 1866, Dmitri Karakozov attempted to shoot the Russian czar Alexander II as an attempt to carry out what he described as "factual propaganda." In contrast to the premodern regicide who sought to replace one ruler with another, Karakozov became the first "terrorist" in history, according to historian Claudia Verhoeven, because he targeted Alexander as a symbol. Karakozov explained, "I cannot but feel sorry that I made an attempt on the life of a ruler like Alexander II, but it was not at him that I shot; I took action against the emperor in him—and this I do not regret." Although it is unclear whether this specific act influenced later anarchists, Karakozov's desire to target symbols of oppression to unleash popular fury at the empire prefigured many important aspects of propaganda by the deed.[12]

In 1878 Russian revolutionary Vera Zasulich continued Karakozov's legacy by shooting and wounding the infamously brutal General Trepov, governor of Saint Petersburg. In *Underground Russia*, his influential exposé on the hidden Russian revolutionary underworld, Stepniak, who later that very same year returned to Russia and assassinated the Saint Petersburg chief of police, wrote that Zasulich's act "gave to Terrorism a most powerful impulse. It illuminated it with its divine aureola, and gave to it the sanction of sacrifice and of public opinion."[13] Overall, 1878 saw an astounding proliferation of assassination attempts across Europe. In February a bomb exploded in Florence at the funeral for King Victor Emmanuel II, and later in the year more bombs exploded in Florence and Pisa before the failed attempt of Giovanni Passannante to assassinate Umberto I in Naples.[14] Also that same year, Max Hoedel and Karl Nobiling each made attempts on the life of Kaiser Wilhelm I, and Juan Oliva y Moncasi attempted to assassinate King Alfonso XII of Spain.[15] This wave of assassination attempts culminated with the successful attack on Czar Alexander II in March 1881 by the organization Narodnya Volya. Years later, Kropotkin recounted how in the early 1870s his underground revolutionary Circle of Tchaikovsky, founded by future Narodnya Volya assassin Sophia Perovskaya, had been committed to promoting a mass movement and had been so opposed to assassinations that they even stopped a would-be assassin who came to Saint Petersburg to kill Czar Alexander II.[16] By the early 1880s, however, Stepniak, Perovskaya, and Kropotkin had wholeheartedly embraced propaganda by the deed. Kropotkin considered it to be a method of "revolutionary education," and in *Le Révolté* he published an article calling for "permanent revolt in speech, writing, by the dagger and the gun, or by dynamite," written by former Benevento rebel Carlo Cafiero.[17]

Although the assassins of this era were not anarchists, the dynamism of their actions convinced many anarchists of the exponential potential of an individual or a small group to drastically arouse society with a single bold act. At an international anarchist congress in London in the summer of 1881, months after the assassination of the czar, an interpretation of propaganda by the deed in terms of individual or small group attacks on power was agreed on as an important strategy of the movement. From this point onward, the individualist version of propaganda by the deed dominated the earlier popular insurrectionary interpretation. The congress was attended by a wide variety of influential anarchists, including Malatesta, Kropotkin, and the German devotee of dynamite, Johann Most.[18] Most had been a Social Democratic representative in the Reichstag until Bismarck's anti-socialist law of 1878 forced him to flee to London, where he became an anarchist advocate of propaganda by the deed. Inspired by the explosive attacks of the Irish Fenians and the assassination of the czar, Most published *The Science of Revolutionary Warfare* in the mid-1880s after emigrating to the United States. He wrote that recently invented dynamite was "a genuine boon for the disinherited, while it brings terror and fear to the robbers [i.e., capitalists]."[19]

In some cases, the police were eager to provoke an incendiary, yet ineffectual, application of propaganda by the deed. For example, a key factor behind the adoption of propaganda by the deed at the 1881 anarchist congress was the enthusiasm of several provocateurs including Serraux, the alias of an agent of the Parisian Prefecture of Police.[20] Months earlier, Serraux had been behind the 1880 creation of the first French anarchist newspaper after the Paris Commune, *La Révolution sociale*. The paper was masterminded and funded by the prefect of police as a way to "place Anarchy on the payroll" and have direct knowledge of the movement.[21] Jean Grave sensed that Serraux was a spy, but prominent anarchists Louise Michel and Émile Pouget were tricked into collaborating on the paper.[22] Kropotkin described *La Révolution sociale* as "of an unheard-of violence; burning, assassination, dynamite bombs—there was nothing but that in it."[23] Serraux opposed plans to attack the Banque de France or the Prefecture of Police and redirected the group toward the far more harmless target of the statue of Thiers, though their bomb failed to harm the statue.[24] Historian Walter Laqueur argues that such police funding and instigating was quite common among incendiary revolutionary papers in the 1880s and 1890s.[25]

One of the most important incidents in the history of propaganda by the deed occurred on May 4, 1886, when a bomb was thrown into a group of two hundred police officers entering Haymarket Square in Chicago to shut down a protest against the previous day's deadly police attack on a demonstration for the eight-hour day. When the bomb exploded, the police opened fire on the crowd, and some workers, wary of being shot at as happened the day before, returned fire. Seven officers were mortally wounded and about three times as many workers lay dead. Although the identity of the bomber was never discovered, eight anarchists, mainly German immigrants, were charged with the bombing without evidence. Four were executed, one committed suicide, and three were given long prison sentences. The fate of the "Haymarket martyrs," as they came to be known, was a pivotal moment in the popularization of anarchist propaganda by the deed and the legacy of anarchist martyrdom. Over the coming years, the memory of their illegitimate executions would play a central role in anarchist and socialist May Day demonstrations, but their forced martyrdom was of a very different kind than that of the self-professed anarchist bomber who sacrificed his life for "the idea."[26]

In Spain, however, propaganda by the deed developed in response to a significantly different set of factors. As opposed to many other European anarchists who attempted to respond to the growth of reformist social democratic electoral action and unionism, Spanish anarchists developed their early theory and practice of propaganda by the deed in response to harsh state repression that made legal resistance impossible. After the destruction of the first Spanish Republic and the restoration of the Bourbon monarchy in 1874, the FRE (the Spanish section of the IWMA) was declared illegal, and thousands of republicans, socialists, and anarchists were forcibly relocated to remote corners of the Spanish Empire. In response, the FRE started to create a "secret revolutionary organization" with "an executive nucleus of vengeance" to coordinate "committees of revolutionary action" inspired by the long nineteenth-century tradition of clandestine cell-based organizing and secret societies.[27] At the 1877 congress of the Anti-Authoritarian International in Verviers, the Spanish delegate González Morago argued for a version of propaganda by the deed inspired by the Russian nihilists as a method of self-defense.[28]

When the Liberal Party gained power and legalized political association in 1881, an irreconcilable split had developed between the advocates of mass unionism and propaganda by the deed, fracturing the FRE. Determined to create a legal labor organization free from the influence of propaganda by the deed, anarchist unionists formed the Federación de Trabajadores de la Región Española (FTRE) in 1881 in an effort to return to the tactics of the early FRE. Although the FTRE stated that it would respond to violent bourgeois efforts to impede its progress with force, it emphasized, "We will never achieve our aspirations by violent or criminal methods." By 1882 the federation boasted a membership of 57,934, two-thirds of which were from the southern province of Andalusia. Although the FTRE did its best to cover up the insurrectionary decisions of the London Congress, by the second Congress of the FTRE in Seville in 1882, the insurrectionary line reemerged. In part, this reflected the ongoing tension within the movement between urban, skilled industrial workers who tended to favor legal methods and the unskilled rural membership in the impoverished, rural region of Andalusia. In the 1870s the Spanish agricultural economy was increasingly susceptible to fluctuations in the global market, culminating in waves of conflict across Andalusia, Extremadura, and the Levant toward the end of the decade. Even after the return of civil liberties, bread riots spurred on by a historically disastrous year for cereal production were confronted with cavalry charges and mass arrests.[29]

The most dramatic episode of this era took place in 1882–83 when authorities blamed a series of murders in the Andalusian town of Jerez de la Frontera on a shadowy, clandestine anarchist group called Mano Negra. Historians disagree about the existence of Mano Negra, but police fabrication or not, it was certainly used as a pretext to repress the FTRE in the region.[30] Ultimately, nine were executed, hundreds arrested, and dozens deported for their alleged involvement in Mano Negra. Combined with the more general repression of the FTRE, by mid-1883 more than two thousand militants had been arrested amid accusations of torture and suicides in prison. Convinced that a massive "Black International" was behind the murders, General

Polavieja asked for special anti-anarchist laws, but such laws would not materialize for another decade, as we will see shortly.[31] Yet unlike later episodes of widespread repression, there was no public outcry on behalf of the Mano Negra or FTRE prisoners. It was not until 1902 that activists would organize a campaign for their liberation in the wake of the Montjuich campaign, as I explore in chapter 11.

The increasingly moderate FTRE attempted to distance itself from the Mano Negra saying that they had never "been party to robbery, arson, kidnapping or assassination" and that they had never had anything to do with any group "whose object is the perpetration of common crimes."[32] The director of *La Revista Social*, the Madrid-based FTRE organ, even tried to convince his comrades not to argue for the innocence of those arrested until the ruling of the court.[33] Eventually, the eagerness of the FTRE to distance itself from the kinds of everyday tactics of insurrection and illegality that campesinos felt forced to turn to in repressive circumstances alienated much of the federation's rural base. Over time, groups in favor of insurrection and propaganda by the deed, such as Los Desheredados (The Disinherited), were purged by the federation or left voluntarily.

This conflict was aggravated by the development of anarchist communism starting in the mid-1880s. Although anarchist communist ideas had spread to major cities such as Barcelona and Madrid by the start of the decade, the power of collectivism, as promoted through the FTRE, and the relative isolation of Spain from the most up-to-date currents of European anarchist thought delayed the doctrine's development below the Pyrenees. The first public defense of anarchist communist ideas was made by the shoemaker Miguel Rubio at an FTRE regional congress in Seville in 1882. A year later, a small anarchist communist nucleus developed in the Barcelona suburb of Gracia around the shoemaker Martín Borrás and the tailor and typographer Emilio Hugas (who would be among the first arrested immediately following the bombing of the Gran Vía ten years later). In large part, their interest in anarchist communism stemmed from the fact that their French language skills enabled them to read Kropotkin's anarchist communist *Le Révolté* published out of Geneva. At a time when most sections in the region supported the FTRE federal commission against the insurrectionary minority, the Gracia shoemakers' section dissented and put forward a proposal to counteract the "bureaucratic centralism" of the federal commission.[34]

By 1885, Borrás and Hugas had helped create the first explicitly anarchist communist group in Spain, Grupo de Gracia. By 1887, communist currents spread faster with the translation of Kropotkin's writings on the subject, spearheaded by the Anarchist Communist Library of Gracia, and the first anarchist communist newspapers *La Justicia Humana* (1886) and *Tierra y Libertad* (1888–89), also published by the Grupo de Gracia.[35] Propaganda by the deed fit well with anarchist communism because just as the communist economic vision shifted emphasis away from the quantifiable production of workers to the well-being of the dispossessed as a whole, propaganda by the deed emerged as a broad, flexible vision of resistance beyond the constraints of the workplace. Anyone could pick up a knife or follow a simple dynamite recipe and change history.

Although anarchist communism would be heartily adopted by organizationally minded twentieth-century anarcho-syndicalists, in the 1880s and 1890s anarchist communists tended to be opposed to formal organization beyond the small affinity group of eight to twelve *compañeros*, and fully committed to any tactic, no matter how destructive, that could eat away at structures of power. For example, *Ravachol*, the anarchist communist paper that Pallás worked on prior to his bombing, argued that organization "is the principle obstacle to the revolution: it uproots from the daily struggle considerable quantities of men, who bury within it their freedom of thought, to work and to judge for themselves; it breaks their power, it kills individual initiative, and it makes them uselessly serve as instruments."[36] As opposed to anarchist labor leaders who spent a significant amount of time embroiled in meetings and polemics, the anti-organizational anarchist communists called for immediate action. They argued that if even a small fraction of the thousands of union members that existed in Spain took up arms, the revolution could be possible. Yet the bureaucratic unions stifled the spontaneous initiative necessary for revolution. In a similar vein, the first issue of the anarchist communist *La Justicia Humana* argued, "We are illegalists, that is, not believing that with the help of laws made by and in the benefit of our exploiters, can we arrive at the social revolution. . . . We are not advocates of organizing the working classes in a positive sense; we aspire for a negative organization. [We are] anarchists in every expression of the word without forming a manageable body. . . . We believe this should be by groups, without statutes."[37] From the anti-organizational communist position, large labor federations were "always propelled by hidden bosses" that turn members into "dues machines" and curb "all initiative," leaving the organization a "school of laziness."[38] Instead, anarchist communists saw the revolution as resulting from a buildup of individual and small-scale acts of resistance that would trigger mass revolt, as was evident in an article from *La Controversia* from Valencia: "In the social world each great revolution is fertilized and determined by an infinite number of isolated or partial rebellions that are the immense accumulation of the forces necessary to transmit movement to the final action."[39]

The FTRE finally collapsed in 1888. Although other labor federations with varying degrees of anarchist influence were formed in its wake, the center of gravity of Spanish anarchism shifted toward cultural centers, cafés, clubs, *ateneos*, newspapers, and informal groupings into the 1890s.[40] As the federation fell apart, anarchist propaganda by the deed escalated. Elsewhere in Europe, the 1880s saw very few acts of anarchist propaganda by the deed despite the rhetorical storm that accompanied the theory, but many bombs exploded in Spain over the course of the decade. Such attacks usually related to a particular, local ongoing struggle or conflict where workers targeted their bosses or police officials. There were also several attacks on employers' associations, such as the 1886 bombing that injured five bosses.[41] By carrying out such a public attack with broad, national symbolism transcending his specific circumstances, Pallás's *atentado* marked an important development in the history of Spanish propaganda by the deed.

Unsurprisingly, the contours of the debate over Pallás's actions in anarchist circles followed the familiar collectivist/communist debate. José Llunas's satirical, Barcelona-based, anarchist paper *La Tramontana* represented the collectivist position. Llunas was a veteran of both the FRE and the FTRE and had been harshly criticized for his collectivist stance on the Mano Negra affair a decade earlier.[42] His paper continued the traditional collectivist disdain for propaganda by the deed, writing that they were "repulsed at *dinamiterisme*" and that there was an "incongruency between this method and genuinely and rationally anarchist ideas." *La Tramontana* speculated that Pallás may have turned to propaganda by the deed as a spectacular form of suicide. It also warned that "the execution of Pallás will foment *dinamiterisme* much more than if his sentence were commuted. . . . Pallás, executed, will have admirers like a saint."[43] In contrast, the anarchist communist *La Revancha* from Reus reveled in Pallás's martyrdom and characterized his act as one "of reparatory justice, an act purely regenerative and highly human" (as opposed to the press, which characterized propaganda by the deed as monstrous and inhuman). A common argument made by the defenders of propaganda by the deed was that it was hypocritical for monarchists and capitalists to be horrified at the collateral damage of bombings when their own military operations and exploitative economic systems have killed so many more: "To achieve our objective, we employ and we will employ every method of violence that we need . . . but we'll never cause as many victims as you have caused in the course of the centuries, and you still cause with your whims in [the Spanish colonial possession of] Melilla and in the workshops and factories of the towns and cities."[44]

Anarchist communists refused to shy away from violence when their adversaries had piled up so many bodies. Pallás echoed this point himself in his letter to *El País* when he wrote that reading the newspaper articles about his bombing "has made me feel like vomiting; I have turned away from them in horror with a nauseated stomach. They are indignant, horrified, frightened of my crime: they, who celebrate the massacres of Olot, of Cuenca and of a thousand others with lewd orgies . . . When will anarchism have the number of victims that these ferocious white-collar bandits have?"[45] Pallás and his fellow defenders of propaganda by the deed argued that capital and the state produced unparalleled violence that was obscured by their mystifying legitimacy. In their eyes, the only reason they were singled out as violent was that their *atentados* occurred beyond the sanctifying parameters of the state's monopoly on the legitimate use of force. *La Controversia* attacked the "disgusting conduct" of the collectivist *La Tramontana*, whose director, José Llunas, "call[ed] himself an anarchist." Yet despite their differences, anarchist periodicals on both sides of the debate joined in creating subscriptions for the Pallás family, while the dynastic papers opened subscriptions for the family of the dead civil guardsman.[46]

However, beyond the sectarian conflict, some started to realize that Pallás's *atentado* was different from earlier bombings insofar as it catapulted the figure of Pallás into popular consciousness as the epitome of what I call the "propagandist by the deed." As strange as it may sound, Pallás was actually the first bomber to be apprehended in the history of Barcelona propaganda by the deed, even though forty-six explosions had occurred, in addition to more than twenty additional bombs that the police discovered (or planted), since 1884.[47] Since Pallás gave himself up without fleeing and eagerly confessed to the bombing, he managed to embody the ethos of the individual bomber whose "bravery" and martyrdom transcended the act itself. As *La Tramontana* noted, "Pallás, obscure, unknown Sunday morning, by the afternoon was almost a . . . celebrity." Pallás fueled "the popular fantasy . . . of those who suffer in misery, and see in him an avenger of their punishments and an *entire character* who has boldly defied all of the powers that sustain the present state of things; they admire that valor, that temerity, they love that suicide that made him a hero. . . . They raise him to the category of martyr, searching for his portrait and guarding it carefully and finally erecting altars to him in their heart, for being the only one before them truly worthy of adoration."[48] Many within the angry, destitute lower classes of Barcelona transposed their dreams and desires onto Pallás's single suicidal act of complete defiance. His *atentado* and subsequent indifference about his fate had struck such a chord that instead of simply being the man behind the bomb, the bomb came to be seen as the epitome of the man, "an *entire character.*" Pallás had become the first in Spain to shift the focus from *propaganda* by the deed to the *propagandist* by the deed and present an ascetic image of pure revolutionary sacrifice. Yet he was not the first anarchist to self-consciously construct this image. The first man to project the identity of the "propagandist by the deed" was the namesake of Pallás's newspaper, the "violent Christ," Ravachol.[49]

CHAPTER 3

The Birth of the Propagandist by the Deed

Ravachol. A "violent Christ" whose explosive deeds were set to verse. A name turned into a threatening verb meaning "to explode." A legendary symbol of uncompromising war against the bourgeoisie. The original propagandist by the deed (anti-)celebrity who inspired Paulino Pallás and many others in the anarchist pantheon of martyrdom and triggered a cycle of bloody attacks on elite Parisian society. Homage and repulsion would follow the death of Ravachol, but in 1891 he was simply an unknown anarchist. On May 1 of that year, however, two dramatic events occurred that set Ravachol on a collision course with the French state.

First, in Fourmies, a town of fifteen thousand in northern France, an ongoing textile strike culminated in a march of several hundred that was gunned down by soldiers wielding (recently invented) machine guns as it made its way into a local square. Some of the young demonstrators threw rocks at the soldiers, who opened fire killing nine and injuring over thirty. The same day in Paris, a group of anarchists was marching toward Clichy when they were confronted by the police. A gunfight ensued when the police chased them into a nearby bar to seize their red flag. Most of the anarchists escaped, but three were apprehended by saber-wielding gendarmes. At the police station, they were beaten, deprived of water, and denied medical care. Charles Malato described their treatment as "an outrage upon humanity." Although one anarchist was subsequently acquitted, his comrades received what were considered to be exceptionally harsh sentences of three to five years in prison. Some of the surviving Fourmies workers were also imprisoned.[1]

With the support of his anarchist comrade Charles Simon, known as "Cookie," Ravachol decided to take vengeance. He may also have been eager to dissuade accusations of being a police informant that stemmed from his 1891 murder of Jacques Brunel, an old man thought to be hoarding riches. As it turned out, the rumors were true, and Ravachol and his accomplices walked away with 15,000 francs. He would later explain his actions by saying, "If I killed, it was first of all to satisfy my personal needs, then to come to the aid of the anarchist cause, for we work for the happiness of the people."[2] Although it is unclear exactly how all of that money was used, Ravachol did use some of it for political ends, as we will see shortly. Nevertheless, the murder tarnished Ravachol's reputation in the eyes of anarchists when it was publicized a year later. Ravachol and his accomplices were arrested when they returned to Brunel's house several more times in search of additional hidden treasure. Suspicion of Ravachol being an informant developed when he managed to escape police custody while his accomplices remained behind bars.[3]

Ravachol defended his actions by arguing that the poor had to rob the rich "to escape living like brute beasts" and that "to die of hunger . . . is cowardly and degrading. . . . I preferred to turn contrabandist, coiner of counterfeit money, and murderer."[4] Indeed, much of Ravachol's life had been a struggle against being reduced to a bestial existence. Born François Koenigstein near the industrial town of Saint-Chamond in 1859, Ravachol had a Dutch millworker father who was said to have regularly abused his mother before leaving her in a state of dire poverty with her four children. She worked in a raw silk factory when she could, but she had to send her children out onto the street to beg for their survival. The young boy, who at some point started going by his mother's maiden name, Ravachol, went to school until the age of eleven despite continual taunting for his ragged clothing. Around the time that a fever killed his sister, young Ravachol was freezing in the mountains working as a herder without adequate shoes. Later he worked in mines and textile workshops, but in one instance he had to quit because he was not allowed any time to eat or use the toilet during his entire shift.[5] A man "of good and muscular figure, with an energetic, proud expression of face, a well-formed forehead, and deep-set, resolute eyes," according to Malato, Ravachol went to Lyon in search of work after three years as a dyer's apprentice.[6] He embraced anarchism around the same time that Eugène Sue's *The Wandering*

Jew led him to renounce religion. Later, still supporting his mother and siblings, Ravachol occasionally played the accordion at local festivals to earn a little money.[7] That not sufficing, he also stole chickens. Later, he dabbled in counterfeiting, smuggling alcohol, and even grave robbing when he opened the coffin of a countess, discovering, to his disappointment, nothing more than decaying flesh and flowers.[8]

With little to lose as he hid from the police to evade murder charges, Ravachol and Cookie hatched a plot to avenge the Fourmies workers and the Clichy anarchists. To that end, on the night of February 14, 1892, they stole thirty kilograms of dynamite from a quarry southeast of Paris. Two weeks later, a bomb went off at an upper-class restaurant on rue Saint-Dominique, which heightened tensions amid calls for reprisals even though it caused only minor damage. It is unknown whether this bombing was directly connected with the dynamite heist, but we know that on March 7 in a Saint-Denis warehouse Ravachol and Cookie constructed a bomb made of fifty dynamite cartridges and iron shards packed into a pot, which they intended to detonate at the Clichy police station. Since it was too difficult to get close to the station, especially given the rumors circulating that it was a prime target, they decided to go after Judge Benoît, who had convicted the Clichy anarchists. Cookie scouted out his house on boulevard Saint-Germain in advance, then on March 11 Ravachol, Cookie, and their accomplices took a tram into Paris. A woman comrade hid the bomb under her skirt as they passed through the customs barrier surrounding the city before leaving it with the three men. Ravachol, armed with two pistols, entered Benoît's building and lit the fuse on the second floor in the middle of the building, since he didn't know exactly where the judge lived, and ran out. He hit the sidewalk as the bomb exploded, causing minor injuries for one person but leaving Judge Benoît unscathed in his fifth-floor apartment.[9]

Days later, around the same time as the anarchist cabinetmaker Théodule Meunier detonated a dynamite cartridge outside of the Lobau barracks, shattering the windows of Saint-Gervais church, Ravachol and Cookie were constructing another bomb. Intended for the Clichy prosecutor Bulot, this bomb was more than twice as powerful as the first. Although information from an informant led to the arrests of Cookie and another accomplice on March 17, Ravachol had already left home, taking the bomb with him. Ten days later, he set off the new bomb in Bulot's building on rue de Clichy, injuring seven, but not Bulot, who was out at the time. Afterward, he went to eat at Le Véry restaurant. When his waiter started to complain about military service, Ravachol, no doubt ebullient about his recent attack on the French state, preached to him about anarchism. Not terribly concerned with maintaining a clandestine existence, Ravachol returned to the very same

FIGURE 4.   Mugshot of Ravachol. Photo from Creative Commons.

restaurant three days later where the same waiter, who had noticed that a scar on his recent customer's hand matched the description of the bomber, notified the police, who arrested him. Though Ravachol didn't have time to pull out his revolver or use his sword cane, it still took ten cops to finally

capture him. Some anarchists were so shocked at Ravachol's apparent impru-
dence that they refused to believe that the police had arrested the real Ravachol. Instead, *L'Agitateur* suggested that the man who had been arrested was
merely the "opera-bouffe Ravachol."[10]

Despite his capture, the cycle of revenge continued. The day before Ravachol's trial, Théodule Meunier, who had recently bombed the Lobau barracks, went to visit Le Véry restaurant with one of his comrades from an
anarchist affinity group of cabinetmakers known as the Flat Feet. When
they arrived at the restaurant, they went up to the counter, where Meunier
set down a suitcase. Shortly thereafter, the two left and a concealed bomb
exploded killing two, including the owner, Monsieur Véry.[11] The next day,
April 26, the trial of Ravachol and his accomplices began amid swirling
rumors of revenge and a mounting wave of hysteria that increasingly scared
away foreign tourists. Soldiers protected the courtroom in the Palace of Justice, and police stood guard around the jury and judge. Across the courtroom, the prosecutor Bulot took on the task of condemning the men who
had attempted to kill him. In his testimony, Ravachol stated that his goal was
to avenge the Clichy anarchists who had been abused and "not even given
water to wash their wounds." He sought "to terrorize so as to force society
to look attentively at those who suffer."[12] In the course of the proceedings,
witnesses affirmed that Ravachol had provided the wife of one of the Clichy
anarchists with money and clothing for her children.[13] When asked whether
he had aided Ravachol, Cookie famously affirmed, "Absolutely!" The two of
them received sentences of life in prison with hard labor since their bombs
had failed to take life.

The next month, however, Ravachol was condemned to death at a second
trial in Montbrison for his earlier murder and other charges. He calmly told
the judges, "I have made a sacrifice of my person. If I still fight, it is for the
anarchist idea. Whether I am condemned matters little to me. I know that
I shall be avenged."[14] On hearing his sentence, he shouted, "Vive l'anarchie!"
On July 11, 1892, Ravachol walked to the guillotine defiantly shouting the
"Song of Père Duchesne." As a priest walked toward him, he shouted,
"I don't care about your Christ. Don't show him to me; I would spit on him!"
Shortly thereafter the falling blade interrupted his attempt to scream, "Vive
la révolution!"[15]

Ravachol's death triggered an unprecedented wave of homage and martyr
worship for a man previously unknown to the French Left. "I admire his
valor, the goodness of his heart," Elisée Reclus proclaimed, "[and] I am one
of those who see in Ravachol a hero gifted with a rare greatness of soul."[16]
Several songs eulogized this anarchist avenger, including "Les Exploits de

Ravachol" and a new anthem of class resentment, "La Ravachole," which was sung to the tune of the popular revolutionary song "Carmagnole."[17]

Octave Mirbeau described Ravachol as "the peal of thunder to which succeeds the joy of sunlight and of peaceful skies."[18] Oscar Wilde was so fascinated by this mysterious French bomber that he visited Ravachol's body after his death.[19] His exploits became such a popular phenomenon that the verb *ravacholiser*, meaning "to blow up," came into vogue and was even used as a potent threat.[20] For example, an anonymous group from "the school of Ravachol" mailed a threatening letter to a wealthy property owner saying, "We are going to Ravachol you."[21] In fact, the Archive of the Prefecture of Police in Paris has nearly three thousand threatening letters from 1892 filling three boxes.[22] Most were sent to targets considered to be class enemies around the city with signatures like "the avengers of Ravachol," "the *compagnons* of Ravachol," or simply "Dynamite." This concerted attempt to capitalize on Ravachol's bombings to broaden the scope of bourgeois horror succeeded to the point where affluent Parisians hesitated to go out to high-class restaurants or theaters and landlords were reluctant to rent apartments to magistrates.[23] The cycle of reprisals had accelerated to such a point that judges and police officers were walking targets for anarchist avengers. The prosecutor Bulot exclaimed, "Really! The profession of judge is becoming impossible because of the anarchists!"[24]

In his "Eulogy for Ravachol" the novelist Paul Adam wrote that "his benevolence, his disinterest, the vigor of his actions, his valor before irremediable death, exalt him to the splendor of legend. In these times of cynicism and irony, a saint has been born to us." As Adam astutely noted, the death of Ravachol the man was necessary for the birth of Ravachol the legend, a "Christ" who became the "renovator of the essential sacrifice," and whose death, Adam noted, "will open an era."[25]

And "open an era" it certainly did. Ravachol, and even more importantly the construction of his posthumous legendary status, marked the transition from "propaganda by the deed" to "the propagandist by the deed" in anarchist history. Whereas in the 1880s the focus of anarchist propaganda was the (often potential) attack on the bourgeoisie itself, given the lack of exemplary martyrs "of the deed," Ravachol came to be understood as the act incarnate in human flesh. He was not someone who simply put aside some time to strike a single blow at a tyrant before going on with his life; he was interpreted by his sympathizers as someone who selflessly transformed himself into a weapon of popular vengeance committing himself fully to continual assaults on oppression until either he or the state collapsed. As opposed to the Haymarket martyrs, who professed their innocence until the end, Ravachol's open embrace of his deeds established the prototype of the anarchist avenger and set the mold for Paulino Pallás a year later. Subsequently a litany of individual portraits would populate the canon of anarchist martyrs "of the deed" alongside that of the original protagonist of dynamite himself.

If, as historian Fred Inglis claims, the modern notion of celebrity "combines knowability with distance,"[26] then we can see how the popular mystique of the "propagandist by the deed" fostered the ability of many within the Spanish and French lower classes to identify with the class origins, experiences, and resentments of men like Ravachol or Paulino Pallás while the explosive act maintained an insurmountable gap with their sympathizers. For as much as many readers undoubtedly fantasized about carrying out similar acts of class vengeance against the guardians of wealth and privilege, almost none of them would ever actually risk it all to follow through. That expanse between fantasy and tragically sacrificial reality generated the element of transcendence at the core of appeal of the propagandist by the deed. In his eyes, and the eyes of his sympathizers, he burst through the mundane constraints of an oppressive everyday existence to strike a blow at the heart of elite society and thereby sacrifice himself on behalf of those who could not or dared not. This tantalizing combination of knowability with distance points to the fact that anarchist propagandists by the deed could be included among the earliest international (anti-)celebrities with explorers, artists, and other figures.[27] The saga of the propagandist by the deed sold newspapers by epitomizing the collision between two hallmarks of late nineteenth-century journalism: sensational news and the human interest story.[28] While the spectacular act drew readers into the daily construction of the anarchist's biography, the tales of personal destitution, depression, and determination that popular newspapers cobbled together to drag out the journalistic marketability of an *atentado* for an extra week or two endowed a bombing or assassination attempt with a humanizing narrative element. Yet although the "propagandist by the deed" emerged out of the same individualistic and sensational mass media developments as the celebrity, another model of "knowability with distance" came from the personal incarnation of God in the form of Jesus Christ. Catholicism informed the cultural and metaphorical worlds of late nineteenth-century France and Spain even among anti-clerical radicals. Spanish anarchist propagandists were referred to as "apostles of the idea," Pallás would come to be thought of as a sort of anarchist saint, and, as we have already seen, Ravachol came to be known as a "violent Christ." Therefore, the propagandist by the deed was the hybrid product of the modernity of media-fueled political violence and celebrity and older popular religious and political traditions.

The degree to which Ravachol's actions were recognized as a turning point was evident in comments from the Spanish foreign minister in April 1892, a month after Ravachol's bombings. Although Barcelona had experienced forty-six explosions prior to the Gran Vía *atentado*, the minister wrote that "in Spain, without doubt, the contagion has not arrived to such an extreme that the assertion could be ventured that *atentados* will occur among us such as those that . . . are committed in other places."[29] Likewise, in June 1892 Llunas, the director of *La Tramontana*, published a letter in *El Liberal* in response to Ravachol speculating about the possibility of a Spanish equivalent: "I don't know if there could be in Spain, above all, an anarchist of good faith who thinks that they can do something worthwhile in favor of their ideas in particular and the working class in general, exploding bombs. . . . What I do know is that if we had one all other anarchists would have the unavoidable obligation of bringing them out of their error making them see, beyond the repulsive and abominable nature of the method, how counterproductive it would be for their ideals."[30] In 1892 the notion of an anarchist propagandist by the deed figure seemed remote if not impossible despite the detonation of a significant number of bombs in Spain over the previous years. After Pallás, such questions were no longer posed in the hypothetical.

However, it is essential to note that the birth of the identity of the propagandist by the deed occurred when the consensus in international anarchist circles around the efficacy of propaganda by the deed was deteriorating. For example, although Kropotkin had advocated for propaganda by the deed in the 1880s, by the early 1890s he had become much more skeptical. Regarding Ravachol, Kropotkin was especially harsh about his earlier robberies and murders writing at the time that his actions "are not the steady, daily work of preparation, little seen but immense, which the revolution demands. This requires other men than Ravachols. Leave them to the fin-de-siècle bourgeois whose product they are."[31] Yet once his bombings had elevated his stature, Kropotkin's *La Révolte* called for vengeance and wrote that his earlier actions "made it seem like he had acted for his own personal interest, but the acts accomplished subsequently present the affair in a different light, and certainly force us to modify our appreciation."[32] Although Kropotkin was increasingly pessimistic about the ability of propaganda by the deed to bring the revolution, he maintained solidarity with anarchists whom he saw as striking back against oppression. His opinion seems to have been similar to that of Charles Malato, who said that although Ravachol's actions "far from sufficed to bring about a desirable transformation of society . . . we did not think we had a right to insult a man, however dubious his deeds might be, who seemed to have acted from conviction and disinterestedness, and who was about to pay the penalty with his head."[33] Such hesitation about the larger strategic question would eventually expand, but in the early 1890s the immediacy of dynamite vengeance was intoxicating for many.

A police informer squeezed into a packed crowd calling for revenge for the recently convicted Ravachol at the Salle du Commerce in late May 1892. The Parisian police were increasingly concerned about the intoxicating effects of Ravachol's mystique. The informant took copious notes as the first speaker said, "Let's steal, kill, and dynamite—all means are good in order to get rid of this scum!" Next, a short, thickset man with brown hair and sideburns stepped up and began to laud Ravachol, arguing that all that was needed was for more and more people to imitate his example. If bombings such as his had been duplicated for fifteen days, this fiery orator argued, "we would have been masters of the situation." He concluded by shouting, "Death to those who govern! Death to the bourgeoisie!" Then, pulling out what appeared to be a dynamite cartridge, he added, "Here are our weapons, what we need to blow up the bourgeoisie! Death to those bandits."[34]

The informer recognized him as Fortuné Henry, a Parisian anarchist who wrote a pamphlet around this time titled "Ravachol, an Anarchist? Absolutely!" (the exclamation in reference to Cookie's famous testimony). Two days later, the police knocked on the apartment door of Fortuné's younger brother, Émile Henry, who would soon follow in Ravachol's footsteps. Both brothers were out at another meeting, so the police called a locksmith and entered the apartment to find a loaded revolver with a box of bullets and anarchist papers and pamphlets, including an Italian article about bomb making. The next morning, they arrested Émile Henry and his brother after they came across his address in Émile's letters. Humorously, Fortuné told the police that rather than saying, "Here is our weapon, dynamite," he had in fact shouted, "Here are our arms . . . , the pen [with which we] write down our thoughts." Both were released shortly thereafter.[35]

Their father, Sixte-Casse Henry, who also went by Fortuné, fought on the Parisian barricades in 1848 as a republican, and after becoming a socialist and joining the IWMA, he was elected to the leadership of the Paris Commune in 1871 representing the tenth arrondissement. Disguised as a painter, Fortuné the elder managed to escape the repression of the Commune and fled to Barcelona with his wife and his small son Fortuné. While working as a miner, the elder Fortuné's wife gave birth to Émile in 1872 in Pueblo Nuevo just outside of Barcelona (but part of the city today). Eventually the Spanish government confiscated the family's property after Fortuné Henry the elder was accused of participation in the burgeoning Catalan anarchist movement, so the family returned to France after the amnesty of the Communards in 1879.

As the boys grew older, Émile Henry got a scholarship to an elite school and distinguished himself as "an excellent pupil in every way, very intelligent, hardworking, and docile."[36] Unlike his older brother Fortuné, who was developing into the firebrand that police informants would witness years later, Émile Henry was described as quiet, sensitive, and introspective. By the age of nineteen he seemed to be destined for a middle-class, professional life of a very different sort from that of Ravachol or Paulino Pallás. Over the coming years, however, his outlook drastically shifted. He briefly dabbled in spiritism and spent a short stint as a socialist before following his brother down the path of anarchism around 1891 or 1892. Reflecting on this transformation, Émile recounted that until 1891 he had believed in "the present morality" based on ideas "of country, family, authority, and property," but he then concluded that the ruling class "has appropriated everything, robbing the other class not just of the sustenance of the body but also the sustenance of the mind."[37]

As the frenzy of Ravachol's bombings and arrest captivated the country in the spring of 1892, Émile Henry stopped by the cellar offices of the artistic anarchist newspaper L'Endehors hoping to get involved. Over the following months he grew close with several of the most prominent Parisian anarchists such as Félix Fénéon, Sébastien Faure, and Charles Malato. Malato introduced Henry to a new small action-oriented anarchist group. Not long after, he became one of their most active members. Malato remembered that Henry would often stay up all night with his comrades and then go straight to work. At first Henry opposed the actions of Ravachol, arguing that "such acts do us the greatest harm with the masses. . . . A real anarchist . . . goes and strikes his particular enemy down; he does not dynamite houses where there are women, children, workmen, and domestic servants."[38] But over time his thinking changed. During this period Henry worked at a cloth company where he was fired after his boss found anarchist writings in his desk, including an article on reversal bombs that exploded when they were turned over or rattled.[39]

Émile Henry established himself in anarchist circles and ingratiated himself with the editor of L'Endehors, Zo d'Axa, who was so impressed with Henry's "constant obsession . . . to work for anarchism" that he named him the temporary director of the paper when d'Axa fled to London after being charged with insulting the authorities in the repressive aftermath of the arrest of Ravachol. As Fortuné Henry continued to publicly call for the dynamite demolition of the houses of the bourgeoisie, his brother used the pages of the paper he came to control to defend Ravachol and refute those who questioned propaganda by the deed.[40]

Although the legend of Ravachol took hold in Italy, where one anarchist paper went so far as to argue that from then on "whoever fails to present themselves as a revived Ravachol does not deserve to be called comrade," Malatesta, the most prominent Italian anarchist and former Benevento insurrectionary, was not so enthusiastic. In an interview with *Le Figaro* in 1892, Malatesta explained that he agreed with some of Ravachol's actions but strongly opposed those that could have injured the innocent and abhorred his murder of the wealthy hermit.[41] After all, Malatesta originally supported propaganda by the deed not as an individualistic exaltation of isolated explosions but as a strategic emphasis on popular collective action. In August 1892 Malatesta published an article in *L'Endehors* called "A Little Theory" that attacked the anarchist glorification of violence and seeming disregard for injuring the innocent and argued that anarchists should never go beyond "the limit determined by necessity." Instead, he argued that anarchists should act like surgeons who only make incisions where necessary and should act from love rather than hate. He wrote that "hate does not produce love, and by hate one cannot remake the world."[42] Émile Henry penned a reply arguing that Malatesta's position contradicted anarchists' respect for autonomy and restricted the right of the individual to act of their own initiative. This concern for larger groups or even standards of conduct constricting autonomy was at the core of the anti-organizational impetus that came to distinguish "insurrectionist" from "mass" anarchism.[43] Although both Henry and Malatesta were anarchist communists, Malatesta's position reflected the more organizational direction that most anarchist communists would pursue into the twentieth century, while Henry's arguments reflected the essence of late nineteenth-century anarchist communist anti-organizational thought. Henry asked, "Should the future Ravachols before joining the fight submit their projects for acceptance to the Malatestas self-appointed as grand jury to judge the appropriateness of these acts?"[44] "To those who say, 'hate does not give birth to love,'" Henry expounded, "I reply that it is love, human love, that often engenders hate."[45]

That same month a strike broke out in Carmaux, north of Toulouse, pitting rural miners against the Carmaux Mining Company. Over the previous months, the company had laid off workers and reduced wages as demand declined. The miners went on strike. Henry monitored the strike closely as it carried on over the following months. He left *L'Endehors* and worked as an unpaid watchmaker's apprentice to learn how to make a timer for explosives, according to the police who were observing him. An undercover reported that he was secretly practicing with an alarm clock in his apartment. When the strike collapsed on November 3, 1892, Henry was livid. He blamed the union leadership and parliamentary socialists who had supported the strike in the press for being "fancy speakers" who stifled class struggle and potentially violent responses to the company's offensives.[46]

Instead, Henry had resolved "to add to the concert . . . a voice that the bourgeoisie has already heard, but which they believed stilled with the death of Ravachol, that of dynamite." The "golden calf [of the bourgeoisie] would shake violently on its pedestal, until the final blow knocks it into the gutter and pools of blood." Shortly after learning of the defeat of the Carmaux strike, Henry started constructing a reversal bomb by inserting ten dyna-mite cartridges into an iron pot and adding potassium chlorate and sodium. The chemicals would mix when the pot was turned. He bought a metal pen case and filled it with mercury fulminate to transform it into a detona-tor. The next day he visited the Paris headquarters of the company to see whether the bomb would injure "unfortunates." Since the only people he saw coming and going seemed to be bourgeois, he was satisfied with the target. "The entire bourgeoisie," Émile reasoned, "lives from the exploita-tion of the unfortunate, and all of it should pay for its crimes." Moreover, if the police ended up taking the bomb away, "either I will kill the rich or I will kill the police!"[47]

On the morning of November 8, 1892, Émile Henry left his job working for a decorative sculptor on the pretext of completing errands for his boss. He used the opportunity to take a carriage to the Carmaux Company's office with the bomb carefully balanced on his lap. Henry set the package down in front of the door to the company office. About fifteen minutes later, a company official noticed the package and had the office cashier examine it. He unwrapped newspaper to find a gray cast iron pot whose lid was attached with a cloth strip fastened to the handle. Thinking this was a suspicious deliv-ery, he had the concierge take it outside and set it down on the sidewalk by the back entrance of the building. A small crowd noticed white powder oozing out of the pot. Eventually the police took the strange object back to the station on rue des Bons-Enfants. Three officers carried the heavy pot up the stairs and set it down on a table a little less than forty minutes after Henry delivered it. Two minutes later it exploded.[48] One officer's legs were blown off, and a sergeant was shivering face down in a pile of wreckage, his gray flesh exposed through his shredded uniform. An inspector's face had been destroyed and his leg mangled. The walls were splattered with blood, the floor caved in, and human remains dangled from the light. Overall, the bomb killed five including an office boy from the mining company and the police secretary.[49]

The authorities had no idea who had delivered the bomb. Although the Henry brothers were on their initial list of 180 suspects, after they searched Émile's apartment, they found nothing to implicate him and removed his name from their list. Nevertheless, Émile Henry fled to London, where according to Zo d'Axa, "isolation compounded the dense sadness of the fog."[50] Eventually Émile Henry would return to Paris and, inspired by Pallás's bombing of the Gran Vía, unleash an even more terrifying attack.

The night before his execution, Paulino Pallás barely ate. On the morning of October 6, he was led out of Montjuich Castle to be shot. As he crossed the plaza, Pallás sang an anarchist hymn, and as he approached the site of the execution, he started to hear shouts of "¡Viva la anarquía!," "¡Viva la dinamita!," and "¡Viva la venganza!" (vengeance) from workers who were dispersed by soldiers.[51] Once Pallás reached the firing squad, he kneeled with his back to an infantry regiment that opened fire.

Overall, five to six thousand people trekked up the mountain along the road guarded by infantry units and two additional cavalry squadrons to attend his 9:00 a.m. execution, "especially vendors of portraits and biographies of Pallás." In fact, lithographic portraits were "produced profusely" and sold at so many kiosks in Barcelona that the day after the execution the police went around confiscating them. As *La Tramontana* had written, Pallás had come to epitomize the aura of the selfless avenger of the people as no Spanish anarchist had before. Over twenty thousand people came to visit his grave prompting authorities to station a guard there for fear that his corpse would be exhumed.[52]

Shortly before the fatal shots were fired, Pallás shouted, "The vengeance will be terrible!" A month later Barcelona would learn just how terrible it would be.

CHAPTER 4

Introducing the "Lottery of Death"

A little over a month after the execution of Paulino Pallás atop nearby Montjuich mountain, much of the anxiety that had plagued Barcelona elites had begun to fade. Things seemed to be gradually returning to normal. Certainly, the early November explosion of the *Cabo Machichaco* transporting dynamite to the port of Santander that killed 590 people renewed the pervasive fear of explosives, but at least it was accidental. For some, the opening of the winter season of the opera at the Liceo Theater must have been a welcomed diversion from dynamite. This was especially true for the wife and two daughters of General Martínez Campos, the target of Pallás's bombing, who filed into the near-capacity crowd of four thousand to experience Rossini's *William Tell* on the rainy evening of November 7, 1893.[1] "In the theater were the most florid, the most brilliant of the bourgeoisie," "the most select of Barcelona society," "a very distinguished crowd," who applauded and whistled for several hours until two Orsini bombs cascaded from the fifth floor of the balcony into the crowd below toward the end of the second act.[2] After a relatively quiet explosion, the theater quickly filled with a dense cloud of gray smoke emanating black rays. At first, the audience and musicians applauded, thinking the noise was part of the show, but once reality set in, the singers and orchestra froze in horror. Instantly, panic gripped the screaming, frenzied mass of terrified theatergoers as they formed an "avalanche of human flesh," trampling each other and crashing

55

into the seats in a desperate rush to the exit.[3] Moments later, the groans and screams of the injured and maimed rose above the general cacophony. Artists, singers, dancers, and extras in full costume "hallucinating from terror" pushed through the spectators onto the street.[4]

The authorities arrived soon thereafter followed by stretchers from the military hospital of the Atarazanas barracks and priests hurrying to administer last rites. On entering the theater, they found a "mountain of cadavers" surrounded by a vast puddle of blood extending across several rows.[5] For many it was too late for the priests. The journalists who arrived took care to note every gory detail of each corpse in the macabre scene, noting what they were wearing and detailing their fatal injuries. One of the Orsini bombs exploded on impact, shattering seats and sending hundreds of splinters and metal shards into the air, which injured even spectators in the upper rows. The bombing killed twenty people, more than the total number of deaths caused by anarchist propaganda by the deed in the world over the previous thirty years. Estimates of the number injured range between twenty-seven and thirty-five.[6] Had it not been for the malfunctioning of the second Orsini bomb, which did not explode, the totals would have been higher.[7] The injured were rushed to nearby pharmacies, medical facilities, and especially to Santa Cruz Hospital around the corner (today the Biblioteca de Catalunya). Fortunately for the injured, the audience was packed with doctors.[8]

News of the explosion spread rapidly, causing "people with family members in the theater [to run] through the streets terrified."[9] When they arrived, friends and family pressed up against the door of the theater trying to find their loved ones.[10] The overwhelmed police arrested an Italian marble worker and a French baker who had been detained for previous bombings.[11] A local jeweler who had the fortune to emerge from the theater unharmed returned home to find that someone had taken advantage of the police focus on the chaos of the Liceo bombing to rob his jewelry store down the street from the theater.[12] Not only did the police miss the jewel heist, but in their chaotic efforts to arrest the first suspicious people they could get their hands on, they failed to notice that the real author of the *atentado* was under their nose the entire time. Amid the wailing wounded, sobbing relatives, frenzied police, and curious passers-by, the anarchist Santiago Salvador Franch stood back and reveled in the panic unleashed by his inauguration of what one paper called the "lottery of death."[13]

The sequence of events that led up to Santiago Salvador's bloody *atentado* can be traced back to his introduction to the tumultuous underworld of

Catalan anarchism in the years after the Bourbon Restoration. In 1881, at the age of sixteen, Salvador fled a world of poverty and violence in the Aragonese countryside to search for a new life in Barcelona. As an alienated, isolated teenager trying to find his way in the big city, Salvador got a job as a domestic servant and started to read anarchist periodicals sold at the kiosks on La Rambla. Representing the most complete break possible from his ultramonarchist, Catholic upbringing, anarchism appealed greatly to the young servant. Years later, he settled in Barcelona permanently when he married Antònia Colom i Vicens in 1891. While Salvador was working at a tavern and selling wine, his wife gave birth to a daughter in November 1892. Around this time, he heard about "one of the best orators" of the anarchist movement named Paulino Pallás, the eventual bomber of the Gran Vía. Salvador later recounted, "I went to listen to him, I liked him a lot, we became friends, and together we read the writings that he got and the ones that I had. From that point onward my only *compañeros* were those who sustained the idea; I didn't go to other places than those that we used for meetings, nor did I have interests other than reading and discussing." During this period, Salvador supposedly joined Benvenuto, Pallás's affinity group, though Salvador's name was never mentioned during Pallás's trial.[14]

Salvador closely followed the final days of his *compañero* Paulino Pallás. He recounted, "The death of Pallás produced a terrible effect in me and, to avenge him, as a tribute to his memory, I developed the goal of committing an act that would frighten those who had delighted at his death and believed that now they had nothing to fear; I wanted to disillusion them and also enjoy it myself. I didn't think a lot nor did I vacillate; I fulfilled my duty. I only pondered the method to achieve it so that it would make a lot of noise."[15] And so, on November 7, 1893, Salvador left home with two Orsini bombs and one peseta that his wife had given him to buy some salt. Although regular admission to the Liceo was two pesetas, seats on the fifth floor were only one peseta. Salvador paid the cheaper price of admission and entered through a side door.[16] Toward the end of the second act, Salvador threw the bombs into the crowd below. After the explosion, he filed out with the confused theatergoers: "On the street, I stayed near the Theater for a long time, very close to where the police allowed the transients and the curious, letting me slip between circles where they were making commentaries on what had happened. . . . I saw the authorities and the priests enter the Liceo. . . . How frightened are the bourgeoisie!"[17]

Not especially concerned about his safety, the next day Salvador took a victorious stroll throughout the city and met with some anarchist *compañeros* to brag about his triumph. "They seemed quite stunned," Salvador recounted, "and even desirous of getting rid of me. What a lack of character! What a lack of courage! I, without hesitation, have offered my life in the benefit of human progress."[18] On his way home that evening, he did not pass by any more theatergoers since all Barcelona theaters shut down in mourning.[19] When he arrived, he told his wife what he had done, causing her to sob uncontrollably.[20] Nevertheless, Salvador was proud of his act and eager to read as many accounts of the bombing as he could get ahold of in the daily papers. "I wanted to know everything they said and all that they wrote 'about the Liceo.' What fear, what panic among the bourgeoisie! The truth is that my 'blow' caused a colossal surprise, making 'the mood tumble' in society."[21]

What Salvador found in the papers was that just as journalists described Pallás's *atentado* as inhuman, they decried the Liceo bomber(s) as "monsters in human form" with the "instincts of a hyena, the hatreds of a savage," "without any human vestige," who are causing "a regression of hundreds of years in human civilization."[22] Dynastic and republican journalists argued that the "instinctive cruelty" of the bombers, who were immediately assumed to be anarchists, was evident in their decision to target "innocent" people in a cross-class setting.[23] The notion that the bomber had targeted the Liceo because of the class character of the audience, or the suggestion that Barcelona was marked by class conflict at all, were unfathomable considerations for the press. *La Vanguardia* imagined Barcelona as "eminently democratic, where everyone works and toils during the day, and where the particular *fiestas* and receptions, that can mark a certain isolation of the classes, are celebrated only rarely, [so] there is a need for a general center. . . . All of Barcelona goes to the Liceo. The barriers that in other cities can separate the different classes of society don't exist in our capital."[24] The press made a strong effort to erase class stratification, emphasizing that cries of protest came "from all social classes, from the man of the pueblo and the gentleman."[25] Yet the fact that such arguments were made before the identity or motives of the bomber had been identified suggests that underneath the rhetoric, journalists sensed that the Liceo bombing was an attempt to strike a blow at a "bourgeois" crowd. Calculated or not, an *atentado* against such an anonymous crowd was seemingly without precedent. "In the lamentable gallery of voluntary *atentados* against human life, nothing is known that equals [this] despicable and horrible killing," *El País* argued. "The Irish dynamiters blow up the tower of London, Westminster palace, buildings of the enemy state; the nihilists put dynamite in the imperial palace. Still to none of the criminal fanatics of anarchism had it occurred that it was permissible to kill spectators of a theatrical function for the honor and glory of their cause. . . . Pallás was in the infancy of crime. It was yesterday and it seems like a century has passed."[26] For *El País* and most other papers, attacks against clearly defined political opponents in London and Saint Petersburg were at least intelligible if no less reprehensible. Yet killing "random" people made more "political" crimes seem tame. Similarly, *La Correspondencia de España* added, "Crime is always crime, but up until here these odious conspiracies . . . had as their target elevated personalities like in Russia; magistrates who had participated in famous trials like in France; a leader in the army or men of state like in Spain, and all of them, warned of the risk, can take precautions. . . . What has not been seen before . . . [is] a kind of lottery of death."[27] Against the specter of anarchist violence targeting an entire class of society, the press promoted the unwavering assertion that in its randomness and the indisputable innocence of its victims, the Liceo bombing had ushered in the unprecedented phenomenon of the "lottery of death." Critical terrorism scholar Timothy Shanahan describes such attacks that target specific groups of people, but not particular individuals within those groups, as being "strategically indiscriminate."[28]

Fearing the inability of the authorities to squelch the anarchist threat, *La Vanguardia* asked, "Where will we end up if we allow tigers to roam free in the heart of society?"[29] But *La Dinastía* rejected the notion that the "pleasure of making damage" of the "dynamiter" had parallels in the animal world: "Nature itself with its blind impetuses of instinct does not offer even in the irrational an example of such cruelty. The lion, the tiger, only attack when threatened by hunger or by danger; the scorpion and the asp only bite when provoked; only the dynamiter searches for contact with those who have not offended him personally."[30] Anarchists were coming to be seen as not only inhuman but even unnaturally malignant. Regardless of whether anarchists were considered animals or worse, they were certainly considered a force external to society waging a "war, not against a politics, nor against a social order, but rather against the entirety of humanity."[31] The government, legal system, and police were all seen as impotent before this perverse threat without precedents "in the annals of crime."[32]

As in the aftermath of the Gran Vía bombing months earlier, the Liceo bombing prompted political clashes over the limits of free speech and political association in Spain. In that vein, the conservative *La Dinastía* blamed the development of the anarchist threat on "utopian democratic principles." The author continued, "In their shadows and under the protection of these strange liberties, schools of criminals called meetings have grown and spread whose civilizing idea is to destroy everyone as in the heart of Africa, as in the most savage countries; even worse."[33] Conservatives argued that political liberties disarmed the state before its most ruthless adversaries whose heinous violence was identical to the "savage" aggression of Africans. And just as the "savage" violence of Africans rendered them unfit to enjoy the same rights as Europeans under prevailing imperial logic, so too did bombings banish anarchists from the realm of modern rights considerations. Such arguments were part and parcel of the prevailing Western notion that I call the "ethics of modernity," which asserted that those who attacked the moral standards of modern civilization were inhuman threats to progress.

The conservative solution was to remedy the excess of rights that gave birth to the anarchist menace while depriving anarchists of all rights since their "inhumanity" made them unworthy of the privilege. *La Dinastía* argued that broad civil liberties provided fertile ground for the growth of the anarchist menace: "Those who a few years ago laughed at anarchist publications and meetings, supposing that liberty was the valve to ease the hatreds of these madmen, should start to change their criteria before the destroyed cadavers of the calle de Cortes and the Liceo theater. If we were *fusionistas* or republicans and as such had confidently defended the freedom of propaganda, we would publicly confess our error and we would search for the remedy in another system."[34] Anarchist explosions were considered to be the logical conclusion of liberalism and a definitive refutation of the republican position. In response, the republican *El País* argued that such a bombing would not occur "under a republican or revolutionary regime. It appears after nineteen years of restoration. . . . What is the mission of the monarchy according to its advocates? To conserve order, defend social interests. Valiant defense!"[35] If the underlying rationale for the return of the monarchy was the preservation of safety and security, then for the republicans, the bombings demonstrated the uselessness of such an anachronistic institution.

The conservative solution to this dangerous excess of liberties was to enact powerful anti-anarchist legislation or, if that failed, to organize any form of social defense that would treat the anarchists like the inhuman monsters they were thought to be. Even more than after the bombing of the Gran Vía, "'Special laws against anarchism!' [was] the general cry, and no one dare[d] to oppose such a measure."[36] A powerful article indicative of the elite, conservative reaction to the Liceo bombing called "Inside or Outside the Law" published in *La Dinastía* argued that if a special anti-anarchist law were not enacted, "honorable men will have to move beyond the law," suggesting paramilitary or extralegal solutions.[37] Reflective of the strong influence of English-language scientific research across the continent, some conservatives justified their proposals in Darwinian terms: as the epitome of "El *struggle for life*" (retaining the original English phrase) waged against anarchism.[38] For society to adhere to natural law and defend itself from this inhuman menace, it was necessary, conservatives argued, to wield the full force of the law against anarchism. Yet this would not contradict the liberal principles of the monarchy since laws and rights were "for men, not for bloody wild beasts." "If [the anarchists] are not men, if they are wild beasts, then they deserve to be treated as wild beasts and not as men. . . . They have to be persecuted and exterminated without waiting for them to commit one of their horrendous crimes."[39] According to the conservative press, it was not an infringement on the rights of Spaniards to deny the "right to murder," which did not "fit in our century of laws and rights."[40] The rhetorical dehumanization of anarchists paved the way for their physical dehumanization by framing the issue as a question of popular survival that transcended debates about the legitimate scope of rights, which were only fit for "men." Referencing the racist murders of African Americans in the post-emancipation southern United States, one letter to the editor of *La Correspondencia de España* called for "proceeding *á la americana* and applying to all of them the law of Lynch," since they threatened "our women and children."[41] Pressure was mounting for Barcelona authorities to stem the tide of dynamite before the upper class set out to do it themselves.

In some cases, this pressure took concrete form as in a letter to the editor of *La Dinastía* that argued for the creation of a private "secret police" that the "wealthy classes" would fund to destroy anarchism. "The hour has arrived," the author argued, "when the wealthy classes search for an effective method to protect themselves . . . and to be able to counterattack force with force and cunning with cunning." Momentum for a secret police force developed to the point where the proposal was endorsed by the Employers' Association, Barcelona elites, conservative papers such as *La Dinastía* and *Diario de Barcelona*, and even the republican *La Publicidad*. Only the republican *El Diluvio* feared that a secret police force would "commit abuses" against opposition groups.[42]

For many, it was clear that something had to be done to rectify the woeful state of Barcelona security forces. As late as 1896, the Barcelona police force had only 193 officers for a population over 400,000, while Madrid had 1,500. Around the same time London had 14,000 police, and Paris had 16,000 municipal police and 9,000 agents.[43] But the problem went deeper than numbers. The day after the bombing, a special French commissioner in Barcelona filed a report on the state of law and order in the city, stating that "the anarchist element, which is very numerous and very powerful in

Barcelona, isn't sufficiently monitored." The failure of the "poorly recruited, poorly directed, poorly paid" police to consistently monitor anarchists was exacerbated by the fact that whenever control of the government changed, the new party would "fire the police chiefs that served the preceding minister" and reinstall their political allies.[44] The only training afforded to Spanish police was a massive manual with 226 articles, yet literacy was rare. When this system of replacing the police force every few years was abolished in 1908, and all officers were required to take competency exams, most failed. Civil governors were authorized to dispose of police personnel as they desired. Given the clientelistic relationship between the political parties, civil governors, and the police, many officers collected paychecks without working.[45]

Something had to change. Or at least local officials had to make an effort to appease the upper-class fear of spiraling into chaos. To that end, General Martínez Campos, still recovering from the shock of his family's near-death experience, had a telegraphic conference call with the interior minister and the minister of war about how to respond to the seemingly perpetual threat of anarchist dynamite. The call reflected the tensions between force and restraint and military versus civil authority that would plague the Spanish state over the coming years. After congratulating the general on his family's fortunate survival, the minister of war proposed "the declaration of a state of war [*estado de guerra*] in the province of Barcelona or in the entire Principality; the only effective method, for the moment, that occurs to me to bring the guilty before military tribunals and energetic regulation." Yet Martínez Campos replied, "You can't adopt states of war except when the civil authority is impotent. I already know that now it is almost impotent before anarchism, because the organization of this sect makes it almost invulnerable; but . . . I think military prosecutors are less appropriate for discovering these plots. Ordinary civil jurisdiction would work better and doubly so here where the military prosecutors are almost useless. In my judgment it would be a scandal before Europe to declare a state of war." Bypassing the civil legal system was not only less effective, Martínez Campos argued; it also ran the risk of tarnishing Spain's international image of liberal monarchism. While he opposed trying to fuse the case of the Liceo bombing to the Gran Vía bombing without evidence, he suggested that the Cortes pass an anti-anarchist law that would bring before military tribunals not only those accused of committing *atentados* but also those who instigated them or possessed explosives in order to "tranquilize opinion, which is excited and horrified."[46] While it was important to crush anarchism, Spanish officials that were attuned to broader European opinion did not want to overreact by declaring a state of war, thereby projecting weakness, especially in the context of ongoing military operations in Morocco.[47] Yet in order to quell the powerful demand for repression, General Martínez Campos, and eventually the government as a whole, decided to legislate military courts for the adjudication of anarchist crimes, despite doubts as to their efficacy, and suspend constitutional guarantees.

In late November 1893 the notorious general Valeriano Weyler was called back from his post as the captain general of the Philippines to be the new captain general of Catalonia. The youngest man of the era to achieve the rank of general for his role in putting down the Cuban rebels in the Ten Years' War, Weyler had made a name for himself as a counterinsurgency specialist. He had helped defeat the 1863 popular revolt, aided by Haiti, in the Dominican Republic against its reincorporation into the Spanish Empire, returned home to Spain to put down the Carlist rising of the 1870s, and most recently distinguished himself as the merciless persecutor of the Filipino resistance.[48] The Spanish government hoped that his experience putting down uprisings at home and abroad could inform a successful strategy to root out clandestine anarchist networks.

In addition to installing Weyler as captain general of Catalonia, the government also implemented a number of administrative reforms to streamline police and judicial operations. For example, the minister of government issued an ordinance in December 1893 creating indexes of anarchist suspects in each province, and judges across Spain were instructed to mete out harsher sentences for apologists of anarchism.[49] The civil governor created a register of foreigners living in Catalonia, initiated deportations, and worked with French authorities to prevent anarchists from crossing the porous border. Yet their collaboration was not without obstacles. In December 1893 the Spanish requested permission to deport nine anarchists to France, but the French would only take the three that were French nationals, returning six Italians. Subsequently the Spanish simply stopped asking.[50] Over the coming years, tensions around anarchist deportations sparked several international incidents, as we will see. At the same time that the Spanish government tried to slip deported anarchists through the French border, in late 1893 they were trying to win the approval of French and other European governments for their "project for common international action for the repression of anarchism." Although Portugal and Austria-Hungary said they would sign on, unfortunately for the Spanish initiative France and Great Britain turned them down, dooming the project.[51] Not only did Britain lack a domestic anarchist threat that was sufficiently threatening to cause alarm, the British also distrusted the potentially authoritarian results of an international anti-anarchist accord.

In a confidential note, the Foreign Office's Earl of Rosebery explained to the British ambassador to Spain that part of the Foreign Office's unease with an international anti-anarchist accord was that "it was not easy to draw a clear line between Anarchism and other forms of more or less extreme opinion."[52] Increasingly, the British were concerned that such measures would provide carte blanche for continental repression.

The mayor of Barcelona eventually acceded to mounting pressure and created a secret anti-anarchist police force. Led by a lieutenant of the civil guard and staffed with former members of local police forces, this new secret force participated in a massive roundup of known or suspected anarchists. Yet as there were no new *atentados* over the coming months, the funding for the new secret police was gradually reduced until it faded out of existence in the spring of 1894.[53] It would not be the last of its kind. Spurred on by the Jesuits and the recently formed Parents' Association of Catalonia against Immorality, which informed the authorities about local "indecency," the police carried out many more arrests than they had after the bombing of the Gran Vía.[54] Whereas by mid-November there had been twenty-six arrests following the Pallás *atentado*, by March 1894 at least 415 were arrested for the Liceo bombing.[55] Prisoners were packed into Montjuich Castle, the Reina Amalia prison in the Raval neighborhood of central Barcelona, and the prison of the Atarazanas barracks; others were held aboard a ship brought into the port to house the overflow of suspected accomplices.[56] Ironically enough, José Llunas, the vehemently anti-*dinamiterisme* director of the anarchist collectivist newspaper *La Tramontana*, was among those arrested.[57]

Two days after the bombing, a massive public funeral procession left from the patio of the Santa Cruz Hospital around the corner from the Liceo in the pouring rain. The procession was led by mounted scouts of the municipal guard followed by children from the provincial House of Charity holding candles and by clergy in mourning habits with raised crosses. It turned right down La Rambla navigating "human rivers" of mourners who uncovered their heads, despite the downpour, as it passed. Streetlights were adorned with black crepe paper and black hangings extended down from the balconies of La Rambla's buildings. After the clergy passed, altar boys, military bands, and individual coaches for each of the deceased lavishly covered with flower arrangements moved slowly down La Rambla. Next came "distinguished personalities of commerce, industry, and banking," and later there was a contingent with doctors, the civil governor, the mayor, Martínez Campos, and other officials.[58] The police were on high alert as the procession headed down the street toward its culmination at the gigantic monument to Columbus by the sea. Given the fear and uncertainty swirling through the city and the high profile of many in the funeral procession, some feared that it would be another anarchist target. And with good reason, since that morning Santiago Salvador, predicting the prestigious turnout to the much-anticipated funeral, went to "ask for more bombs from 'my *compañeros.*' They told me they didn't have any, but I am convinced that they just didn't want to give them to me. . . . Always fear! Isn't it true that there is a lack of men of my courage?" Nevertheless, Salvador filtered into the massive crowd to witness the aftermath of his *atentado.* "From the highest point I could reach on the Columbus monument I saw how they said goodbye to their grief. What a 'magnificent' occasion to throw more bombs! All of the most important authorities together!"[59] But without more explosives all he could do was watch, imagine, and rejoice inwardly at the destruction he had wrought.

More than a year had passed since the French anarchist bomber Ravachol etched the blueprint for the "propagandist by the deed": the anarchist avenger personality who devoted his life, often in a literally sacrificial sense, to violently dismantling systems of oppression. Perhaps, given the recent commotion generated by the bombings of the Gran Vía and Liceo over the previous months, many hoped that propaganda by the deed had migrated across the Pyrenees. Boulangists and other protofascist elements on the French Far Right were not among them. In fact, Far Right forces made overtures to anarchists in the early 1890s in an effort to destabilize the Third Republic, though significant collaboration never materialized. While most of the parliamentary left supported the republic, enemies on the extraparliamentary left and the far right stalked the fledgling state.[60]

One such enemy carried out his own "strategically indiscriminate" attack on November 13, 1893.[61] A nineteen-year-old anarchist shoemaker named Léon Léauthier decided to "strike the first bourgeois that comes along." Not knowing who his victim was, Léauthier stabbed Rista Georgevitch, the plenipotentiary minister of Serbia in Paris, as he dined at the Bouillon Duval restaurant in Paris. Georgevitch survived and Léauthier turned himself in to the authorities soon thereafter.[62] The anarchist Sébastien Faure, who would soon take an active role in the Dreyfus and Spanish prisoner campaigns and knew Léauthier personally, argued that his act was "very beautiful and very useful. Very beautiful, because it is a brilliant manifestation of the revolt that rumbles in the breast of the miserable classes, because it is courageously independent; very useful because it has, perhaps, had the gift of making the wealthy reflect and inspire the terror of reprisals among them."[63]

A month later, on December 9, 1893, an unemployed anarchist named Auguste Vaillant threw a small bomb into the French Chamber of Deputies from the second row of the public gallery.[64] During his later testimony, Vaillant explained that he was "tired of leading this life of suffering and cowardice."[65] As a child, he was an apprentice for a pastry cook but was fired for stealing brioche. His gendarme father abandoned him at the age of ten, and his aunt discarded him when he was twelve. Vaillant found work here and there in a sawmill, in a leather shop, and as a shoemaker, but more frequently in order to survive he had to steal and beg, for which he was arrested four times. Later he worked in a quarry in Algeria before heading to Argentina in 1890 to participate in an exploratory project on the Pilcomayo River. In Argentina Vaillant sought refuge from "the pains of civilization . . . [and] rest in the shade of the palm trees [while studying] nature. [But] there even, more than elsewhere, I have seen capital come, like a vampire, to suck the last drop of blood."[66] Disillusioned and destitute in Argentina, Vaillant returned to France in 1893 and lived with his new bride and their baby in Montmartre. Once the editor of *L'Union Socialiste*, Vaillant became intoxicated by his neighborhood's robust anarchist milieu and shifted his loyalties from socialism to anarchism.[67] As he struggled to feed his family working at a leather workshop in the Parisian suburb of Saint-Denis, Vaillant developed links with local anarchist groups, such as the Independents and the Equals, and met prominent figures in the movement, such as Jean Grave and Sébastien Faure.[68]

Though many historians have argued that the bomb that Vaillant carried into the Chamber of Deputies in December 1893 hidden in an oval tin box was rather weak, in fact as the historian Jean-Paul Brunet details, the metal shards it sprayed into the air caused several serious and near-fatal injuries. The president of the Chamber has been famously quoted as nonchalantly remarking, "*Messieurs*, the session continues" after the explosion, but this famous quip occurred after a twenty-minute delay.[69] Vaillant explained during his testimony, "I preferred to injure a large number of deputies rather than kill a few. . . . If I had wanted to kill, I would have put bullets [in the bomb]. I put nails, so I wanted to injure."[70] However, had the bomb reached the floor of the assembly rather than exploding in midair, fatalities would have been likely.[71] A police inspector later claimed that authorities had learned of Vaillant's intentions in advance through an informant who was instructed to provide Vaillant explosive materials that were specially constructed in the Prefecture's lab to be loud but innocuous in order to heighten the demand for harsh anti-anarchist legislation.[72] Yet Brunet convincingly argues that the case for direct police involvement in the *attentat* is "absurd."[73]

Although anarchists usually debated the merits of every *attentat*, no one publicly critiqued Vaillant. Malato explained this, writing that "his deed was accomplished with such clearness and precision of purpose, was so free from all ambiguous or painful consequences, that we all joined in a chorus of praise."[74] In contrast, the prominent socialist Jules Guesde described the bombing as "just monstrous. It's the act of a madman. Those who do this aren't just beyond the law, they are beyond humanity."[75] Conscious of the impact that his *attentat* would produce in the press, Vaillant went to take a photograph of himself the week before the attack that his comrades seem to have sent to the press.[76] Like Paulino Pallás in Spain and the Russian revolutionary Karakozov before him, Vaillant noted in his journal the day before the bombing, "I don't feel any hatred against those who will fall tomorrow." His action was not about the individual politicians but about taking a step to "hasten the advent of the new era."[77] At his trial, he argued that "massacres" were necessary for the success of the French Revolution, and that it was hypocritical to criticize him for his bombing, considering "the dead and wounded of Tonquin, Madagascar, Dahomey, adding thereto the thousands, yes millions of unfortunates who die in the factories, the mines, and wherever the grinding power of capital is felt. Add also those who die of hunger, and all this with the assent of our Deputies. Beside all this, of how little weight are the reproaches now brought against me!"[78] Several months after the bombing of the Chamber of Deputies, Auguste Vaillant's trial concluded amid general curiosity about whether President Sadi Carnot would condemn him to death. A petition in the Chamber of Deputies beseeching the president to spare the life of the bomber gathered sixty signatures, while Vaillant's daughter wrote a letter to Carnot's wife on behalf of her father.[79] An article in *Le Parti socialiste*, which earned its author two years in jail and a fine of 1,000 francs, argued that if Carnot "coldly" chose death for Vaillant, "there won't be a single man in France to complain for him, if one day he has the small inconvenience of seeing his carriage blown to bits by a bomb."[80] The likelihood of reprisals was enhanced by anarchist posters plastered onto the Arc de Triomphe, saying, "The bourgeoisie will be victims of anarchist vengeance if they touch Vaillant's head. *Vive l'anarchie!* Death to the bourgeoisie! *Vive Ravachol! Vive Vaillant!*"[81] Undeterred by the prospect of retribution, Carnot sentenced Vaillant to death. It was the first time in nineteenth-century France that someone had been sentenced to death without having killed anyone. French officials wanted to send a strong message. When he learned that he would die,

Vaillant cried out. *"Vive l'anarchie!* My death will be avenged."[82] As the date of the execution approached, the usual rumors of anarchist plans to bomb the execution or assassinate the executioner swirled throughout Paris. Yet the guillotine dropped at dawn on the gray, cloudy morning of February 5, 1894. Over the coming months, Vaillant's grave received so many visitors that politicians started to complain.[83]

While Spanish deputies were still debating special anti-anarchist legislation, days after Vaillant's *attentat* French lawmakers wasted no time in enacting the first two of what would become three anti-anarchist laws known pejoratively as the *lois scélérates*, or "villainous laws." The first law targeted writers who sympathized with assassinations, bombings, arson, or any kind of illegal violence in addition to antimilitary sentiments. Those convicted faced one to five years in jail and fines of 100 to 3,000 francs. The second law targeted all "formal or informal associations . . . which prepare or commit crimes," essentially outlawing anarchism by reducing it to criminality.[84] A police report critiqued the law for "only respond[ing] imperfectly to the nature of anarchist procedures" in its targeting of anarchist associations. Instead they believed that the planning of propaganda by the deed "is always an isolated work in [anarchist] houses."[85] Since there was no evidence to suggest that the *attentats* were originating from associations, socialists and radicals started to fear that the contours of the laws were so nebulous that their scope would extend beyond anarchists to dissidents in general.

Meanwhile, as the *lois scélérates* were being passed, Émile Henry returned to Paris for good after spending the past year bouncing back and forth across the English Channel following his bombing of the police station on rue des Bons-Enfants in Paris. While living in London in the winter of 1892–93, Henry had developed a reputation among the predominantly migrant London anarchist scene of Soho and Tottenham Court Road as a dedicated advocate of dynamite. In part, this was the result of his incessant bragging about having been the true author of the *attentat* of the rue des Bons-Enfants. Yet many weren't so quick to believe this brash, young French exile. The radical journalist Henri Rochefort, living in exile in London since 1889 because of his role in the Boulanger Affair, wrote, "Well! Although he was the son of a former member of the Commune, he was so little in touch with the anarchist party that nobody believed his story, and it was greeted either as a young man's boasting, or else as an imaginative romance invented to get money out of those who might be stupid enough to credit it. I recollect Malato saying to me one day—'There is a fellow going all over London saying that he is the author of the Rue des Bons-Enfants explosion; he is evidently taking people in.'" Not only did Henry brag about what he had done, he promised to unleash more destruction on Paris in the future. Very quickly, therefore, Henry became a polarizing figure among the Italian, Russian, German, French, Jewish, and other migrant anarchists in London. While the anti-dynamite *fraternistes* thought he was "insane," he was given a warm welcome at the Autonomy Club, an insurrectionary anarchist hub founded by Germans in 1886 with a portrait of Ravachol on the wall. There, Henry met the French insurrectionary group Free Initiative, which wrote screeds against anarchists who opposed propaganda by the deed.[86]

After his wealthy aunt turned down his request for 500 francs to start a business in early 1893, Henry went to Brussels, where he claimed to have taken an active role in one of the many small bands of workers that roamed the city smashing shop windows as part of the general strike called by the Belgian Workers' Party on April 11, 1893, to demand universal manhood suffrage. He even claimed to have fired a pistol in the conflict. When the Belgian police came looking for him at his hotel, Henry left for Paris in time for the annual demonstrations of May 1. Yet even back in Paris, police suspicion was growing. Undercover agents started to piece together his authorship of the bombing of rue des Bons-Enfants, and some friends offered to sell him out.[87]

By the fall of 1893, Émile Henry was gripped by developments in Barcelona. Referring to a conversation that he had with Henry the day after the Liceo bombing, the French anarchist Charles Malato recounted that "the bombs of Barcelona hypnotized him: the only thing he thought of was to strike a blow and die. 'Today is the anniversary of the dancing-lesson,'" Henry pointed out in reference to his police station bombing. "He grew in his own eyes," Malato recalled. "He said to himself that his *rôle* of destroying angel had only just begun." Émile Henry was ready to resume his personal assault on the bourgeoisie. As his friend Charles Malato phrased it, Henry sought to "answer terrorism by terrorism."[88]

CHAPTER 5

"There Are No Innocent Bourgeois"

At 6:00 a.m. on the morning of January 1, 1894, suspected anarchists across France woke up to police banging on their doors. A coordinated campaign of hundreds of searches for explosive materials or writings "establishing affiliation to a criminal (anarchist) association" led to more than two hundred arrests over two months in the most intense wave of state repression the country had witnessed since the fall of the Paris Commune more than twenty years earlier.[1] The police were said to have planted evidence where none existed, though little was necessary to justify detention. On the street, they prohibited kiosks from selling anarchist papers and eventually shut down many including *Père Peinard*, whose director, Émile Pouget, fled to London, and *La Révolte*, whose director, Jean Grave, was arrested.[2] Previously "the measures taken by the government against anarchy have had an individual and momentary character . . . [but] for the first time [anarchists are] viewed as a whole." Since the anarchists "declare a bloody war against the civilized world," *Le Temps* was comfortable "even ignor[ing] what these home searches turn up [because] that is not the essential point. What has struck public opinion, and reassured it at the same time, is the practical demonstration that the new legislation against the anarchists will not be a dead letter."[3] Indeed, by wielding the indiscriminate power of the new anti-anarchist *lois scélérates*, the commissioner of police sought to make sure that 1894 was nothing like the cacophonous 1893.

Such hopes would not come to fruition, as we will soon see. For unbeknownst to authorities, Émile Henry had clandestinely crossed the English Channel in late 1893 to witness "the formidable repression."[4] Certainly some socialist politicians spoke out against the mass arrests, and the Parisian intelligentsia organized a strongly worded petition signed by 120 artists and intellectuals including Paul Gauguin, but little resistance developed.[5] The minister of the interior delighted in this state of affairs, applauding how the government "had thrown terror into the anarchist camp." Henry was aghast at how the anarchist had been turned into "a wild beast to be hunted everywhere while the bourgeois press . . . demands its extermination." And so, having taken the minister's words as "a challenge," Henry "waited only for the right moment" to reprise his role as anarchist avenger and "hunt the hunters."[6]

Days after Vaillant's execution, Émile Henry started to flesh out a plan of attack in conversations with his anarchist comrade Louis Matha, who had spent time with him in exile in London. Henry decided to target a space of bourgeois leisure like the opera or an upscale restaurant. Matha tried to talk him out of it, but on February 11, 1894, Henry told him, "Your friendship bothers me," and on the 12th, he didn't show up for their regularly scheduled discussion. That evening, Henry carried a package wrapped in brown paper and string around with him as he visited several Parisian cafés dressed in tattered black pants with a white shirt, a black tie, and a vest. Café de la Paix and Café Américain were too empty, but Café Terminus was filling up so he ordered a beer and a cigar. After a while, he got up and rushed toward the door seemingly attempting to avoid paying for his drink. But then he turned back and threw his bomb into the dining room. It hit the chandelier and crashed to the floor near the orchestra, bursting with metal shards in every direction, mortally wounding one person and injuring about twenty.[7]

As the bomb left his fingers, Henry bolted out the door. Unlike Paulino Pallás, Henry was not ready for his martyrdom just yet. He dashed down the street as a waiter shouted, "Stop him, stop him!" Henry's plan was to head to the Gare Saint-Lazare to take a train out of town, but he was pursued by an office worker who happened to be outside the café. Soon, a waiter and a railroad worker joined the pursuit. Henry pulled out a pistol and fired at the waiter, grazing him, as they passed by a policeman who was alerted to the situation. Next, a barber dashed out of his shop with his shaving brush. When Henry turned and shot the barber, the shots alerted two ticket inspectors at the station who also took off after him. As the policeman seized

Henry, he shot the officer in the chest, although his life was saved rather serendipitously by his thick wallet. Henry shot at him two more times, grazing his arm and narrowly missing his face, before one of the ticket inspectors hit him on the head. After a fishing-tackle merchant entered the fray, Henry was eventually subdued. As a crowd formed around him, Henry shouted, "Bunch of pigs! I would kill you all!" and "The more bourgeois who get killed the better."[8]

Although initially he refused to reveal any information about himself, claiming that his name was "Breton," Henry eventually confessed to both the bombing of the Café Terminus and the police station on the rue des Bons-Enfants. In his cell, he was curious as to how many victims his *attentat* had caused and, like Ravachol, only regretted that there were not more. He explained that he had not targeted certain people in particular "but rather the entire bourgeoisie, of which the former was only a representative."[9] In vain Henry tried to convert the two guards in his cell to anarchism. He explained to them that he had sought to avenge Vaillant.[10] He wrote a letter to his mother explaining his decision and encouraging her to be proud of him, or at least not distraught at what he had done. He wrote, "You know me and can say to them that the real criminals are those who make life impossible for anyone with a heart, those men who uphold a society in which everyone suffers."[11] Apparently, Henry also tried to console his mother by assuring her of the possibility of the arrival of the social revolution before his trial; many practitioners of propaganda by the deed genuinely believed that a few strategically targeted explosions could tip the social balance toward revolution.

In addition to writing an anarchist treatise, Henry passed his time reading Herbert Spencer, Alexandre Dumas, Darnaudeau's *Les Nihilistes*, and three novels by Émile Zola, including *Germinal*.[12] An epic tale of perseverance and resistance during a strike in a small mining town in the 1860s, Zola's *Germinal* (1885) became one of the most popular novels among anarchists in the late nineteenth century for its vivid portrayal of everyday class war and its cryptic depiction of the Russian nihilist-anarchist character Souvarine. Henry underlined the line "Begin then by letting me blow up the prison where you perish."[13] Many anarchist journals and affinity groups named themselves after Zola's work, which was also a spring month in the French revolutionary calendar. His favorite, however, was Dostoevsky's *Crime and Punishment*.[14] It is not hard to envision Henry imagining himself as a kind of Raskolnikov.

While in prison, Henry met some legendary figures in the history of French law enforcement and criminology. Over the coming days, he was interrogated by Prefect of Police Louis Lépine and inspected by Alphonse Bertillon, head of the anthropometric department.[15] Lépine was given command of the prefecture in 1892 in response to the first waves of anarchist propaganda by the deed. Although the police responded to the *attentats* of Ravachol, Vaillant, and Henry with mass arrests, Lépine, inspired by the British police, started to believe that effective, long-term policing required developing a favorable public image for the force and positive relations with the community. Unlike his European contemporaries, Lépine came to argue that prevention, rather than repression, was the key to maintaining order and crushing anarchism since mass arrests only prolonged cycles of retaliation. Over time, Lépine instituted a much more selective hiring process for officers and administrators paired with state-of-the-art training, including modern crowd control.[16]

Émile Henry was also brought into the anthropometric department where Alphonse Bertillon measured his head and body, including the lengths of his extremities and digits. Bertillon had developed a pioneering system of physical measurements and descriptions to scientifically quantify and identify criminals. This system, which the prefecture had used since 1883, came to be known as bertillonage or *portrait parlé* (spoken portrait) when applied to the face. Bertillon's examinations were seen as decisive in connecting Ravachol to his earlier crimes, and the growing field of criminal anthropology played an important role in disseminating the rhetoric of the inhuman, atavistic anarchist.[17] Bertillonage had spread throughout the Americas, North Africa, and India, and after 1898 it started to spread across much of Europe, except the Balkans, although by 1901 Scotland Yard switched to fingerprinting.[18] In 1895 it was instituted in Barcelona.[19]

Unsurprisingly, Henry's *attentat* compounded the panic and alarm that had developed over the previous years. Given the regularity of anarchist bombings, conservatives started to fear that men like Henry were indicative of a new generation of rebellion produced by France's modern secular educational system. Others feared that this violence reflected the generation born in the wake of the Commune (one journalist wrote that Henry had been conceived during the Commune, thereby predetermining his later actions).[20] Foreshadowing the Dreyfus affair, which would begin only months later, *Le Soleil* described Henry as "a materialist and atheist . . . the natural product of our Judeo-Freemason society, of our frivolous and corrupt society, without beliefs, ideals, and faith."[21] This internal anarchist enemy seemed to be chewing away at the very foundations of the republic. Octave Mirbeau lamented that "a mortal enemy of anarchism could not have done better than Émile Henry when he hurled his inexplicable bomb in the midst of tranquil and anonymous people who had come to a café to drink a beer before going to bed."[22] Charles Malato, who knew Henry fairly well, said, "I entirely share Octave Mirbeau's appraisal: the act of Émile Henry, who is nevertheless an anarchist of the utmost intelligence and great courage, has above all struck anarchy. . . . I approve of all violence that . . . strikes the enemy, not that which strikes blindly. . . . To the masses—who have the right to go to the café—we should throw ideas rather than dynamite."[23]

Although Malato was sympathetic to propagandists by the deed who targeted elites, such as Pallás and Vaillant whom he "admired without reserve," he "declar[ed] an absolute lack of enthusiasm" for those who attacked more indiscriminately.[24] Over the coming days, the police were on high alert guarding major hotels and monuments. At one theater, the scenery fell over, triggering pandemonium. Reports of small bomb-shaped objects proliferated, with just enough of them actually containing explosives to keep the police on edge. In fact, four hours after learning of Henry's *attentat* (and well before he had revealed his identity or address), a group of his friends went to his home and took away his leftover dynamite, picric acid, fulminate, and other explosive materials representing enough to construct twelve to fifteen new bombs.[25]

On April 27, 1894, Émile Henry sat across from the prosecutor Bulot, whom Ravachol had attempted to blow up years earlier, as his trial commenced. The throngs of journalists and curious high-society spectators were enthralled with this well-dressed, highly educated anarchist as he casually shrugged and smiled his way through the description of his charges. Henry readily admitted his actions and seemed to derive pleasure in correcting the police's description of events. They said the bomb was hidden under his belt, but he pointed out that it was actually in his overcoat pocket since "I wasn't going to unbutton my pants in the middle of a café!" When he was asked whether he wanted to kill as many as possible as an act of vengeance for Vaillant, Henry joyously referenced Cookie's famous declaration and said, "Absolutely." He was very flattered that the judge said his bomb-making skills were those of "a veritable artist."[26]

A medical expert argued that Henry was mentally ill, possibly as a result of the typhoid fever he endured as a child. Yet Henry interrupted him to say, "Pardon, but I don't want any of that. I am not in any way mentally disturbed. . . . My head does not need to be saved. I am not mad. I am perfectly aware of what I am doing." He argued that his act was intended to demonstrate that "those who suffer have finally had enough: they are showing their teeth and will strike even more brutally than they have been abused."[27] Responding to the notion that his *attentat* was uniquely heinous for its targeting of innocent people, Henry explained that anarchists would "not spare the women and

FIGURE 5. Mugshot of Émile Henry. Archives de la Préfecture de Police, Ba 1115, Émile Henry.

children of the bourgeois, for the women and children of those we love have not been spared. Must we not count among the innocent victims those children who die slowly of anemia in the slums because bread is scarce in their houses; those women who grow pale in your workshops . . . when poverty does not force them into prostitution . . . ?"[28] After all, in Henry's eyes "there are no innocent bourgeois."[29] And finally, in the hope of dissuading any considerations of leniency or pardons, Henry concluded with the following roll call of anarchist martyrdom:

> In the merciless war that we have declared on the bourgeoisie, we ask no mercy. We mete out death and we must face it. For that reason I await your verdict with indifference. I know that mine will not be the last head you will sever. . . . Hanged in Chicago, beheaded in Germany, garroted in Xerez, shot in Barcelona, guillotined in Montbrison and in Paris, our dead are many: but the bosom of a rotten society that is falling apart; [anarchism] is a violent backlash against the established order; it stands for the aspirations to equality and liberty which have entered the lists against the current authoritarianism. It is everywhere. That is what makes it indomitable, and it will end by defeating you and killing you.[30]

When the judge read the death sentence, Henry said, "Good," and shouted, "Courage, comrades! And *vive l'anarchie!*" as he was led out of the courtroom. Paul Brousse, former anarchist pioneer of propaganda by the deed turned reformist socialist, lamented that the execution would inevitably generate reprisals. As one who understood the dynamics of propaganda by the deed as well as anyone, he said Henry's execution "is the life of anarchism: to kill the doctrine, we must spare the indoctrinator."[31]

Whereas Henry's Parisian trial was open to the press and the public, the trial for the Spanish anarchists charged with involvement in the Gran Vía and Liceo bombings unfolded before a closed-door military tribunal at Montjuich Castle. The proceedings were carried out at a breakneck pace by Judge Enrique Marzo, lieutenant colonel of the infantry, skipping steps along the way. Several months earlier it seemed like this trial would be simple. The authorities were patting each other on the back for having rooted out a vast anarchist conspiracy that lurked behind the recent explosions. Thirty-two-year-old shoemaker Mariano Cerezuela and twenty-six-year-old locksmith Josep Codina confessed to their participation in the plots while Codina even revealed that he was the author of the Liceo *atentado* and the group's bomb maker. Although Pallás insisted that he acted alone, the Gran Vía case was left open after the Liceo bombing to connect both incidents. Civil governor Larroca basked in the media's adoration of his success.[32]

This neat narrative was scrambled, however, on the evening of January 1, 1894, when the police burst into Santiago Salvador's cousin's second-floor apartment near the Cathedral of the Savior in Zaragoza to find Salvador in bed, perhaps still hungover from New Year's Eve. The police shot him in the hip and prevented him from drinking a clear poison out of a flask he grabbed as they approached him. The civil guard had been tracking him for days after evidence started to mount back in Barcelona about his role in the Liceo bombing. When Salvador eagerly and fully confessed to sole responsibility for the Liceo bombing, allegations emerged that the confessions of Cerezuela and Codina had been coerced through torture.[33]

Cerezuela wrote a letter to El País (which was not published) recounting a week of sleep deprivation, beatings, and genital mutilation that eventually managed to break him so that "in a moment of frailty and cowardice I signed my declaration."[34] The head of the new anti-anarchist secret police force allegedly tortured other prisoners as well.[35] Rather than reassess the evidence given Salvador's confession, the case was simply expanded to focus on a broad alleged conspiracy revolving around the Benvenuto group so that as many anarchists as possible could all be guilty at the same time even if their stories contradicted each other. Although the federal republicans protested the treatment of anarchists and a few Madrid newspapers covered the allegations, momentum did not develop for a more thoroughgoing investigation into the treatment of prisoners as it would during el proceso de Montjuich.[36]

The Liberal Party did not engage with the accusations since they sought to fend off Conservative accusations of governmental laxity, and most republicans wanted to reaffirm their nationalistic credentials by distancing themselves as much as possible from the anarchists. When a paper in Nantes published the charge that confessions had been obtained through torture, the republican El País was thoroughly offended, arguing that the claim of "horrible treatment . . . does not seem to be true."[37] Since 1892, the paper's editor had been the fiery Alejandro Lerroux. Known for his aggressive, demagogic personality, Lerroux had established his power through a series of successful duels against rival journalists. Lerroux was focused on consolidating his hold over El País, honing his polemics against a myriad of republican microfactions, and projecting a masculine image of militaristic, nationalist populism. At this point, not only was there no room in his equation for the rights of anarchists, El País even suggested that anarchists be subjected to extrajudicial punishment.[38] As the historian José Álvarez Junco wrote, "There were already screams coming from Montjuich in 1894. But El País still didn't hear them." One of the most important causes of the reluctance of *El País* and the republicans to hear such screams was that their political center of gravity was Republican France, which had just passed harsh anti-anarchist laws, considered by *El País* to be "heroic remedies."[39]

As a result, very few raised an eyebrow when Manuel Ars, Mariano Cerezuela, Josep Bernat, Josep Sàbat, and Jaume Sogas were given death sentences, and Joan Carbonell and Rafael Miralles were sentenced to life, although they all affirmed that their confessions had been coerced with torture.[40] When the sentence was reviewed by the Supreme Council of War and the navy, Josep Codina was also set for execution, and Francesc Vilarrubias and Domingo Mir had their initial acquittals changed into life sentences.

On the gray evening of May 20, Judge Marzo read the sentences to each of the condemned. All but one prisoner refused to sign.[41] Shortly thereafter, their families came for one last heart-wrenching visit. Ars wrote a letter to his son clarifying that "the Barcelona bourgeoisie . . . has invented an unjust plot against me, using inquisitorial torture, to make unfortunate workers say what they want." Nevertheless, he assured his son that his father would "die happy, convinced that in life he has put his faculties to use in defense of a great and just idea; his death and that of his *compañeros* will serve to make obvious the crimes that the authorities commit behind the back of the law." Ars encouraged his son to vehemently refute any accusations that his father was crazy or a criminal, and urged him to study anarchism and give his life, just like his father, if circumstances should call for it. He signed off with "*¡Viva la humanidad libre! ¡Viva el Progreso! ¡Hurra por la Anarquía!*"[42]

Later the condemned prisoners were brought into the chapel where clergy tried to convince them to accept religious council, but only Sogas accepted. At 4:45 a.m. they were escorted out of the chapel by a platoon of soldiers along with the Brothers of Peace and Charity as the rain was letting up. In the castle's moat, they were put on their knees with blindfolds, faces to the castle, backs to the sea. They were shot in front of a crowd of two hundred who had hiked up the mountain during the night to witness the execution.[43] At about the same moment, the guillotine dropped down on Émile Henry in Paris. The date of Henry's execution was kept secret for days in advance to avoid a retaliatory *attentat*. There was so much anticipation and uncertainty that curious spectators had started showing up at the Place de Roquette every morning hoping to have arrived on the right day.[44] Historian José Álvarez Junco argued that the Spanish government decided to execute the six alleged anarchist conspirators on the same day as Henry "to protect itself from international criticism."[45]

Once word spread of Henry's impending execution, spectators started to gather in the plaza and on nearby rooftops as workmen assembled the guillotine. Guards woke Henry in his cell and offered him religious council and a drink of brandy, which he declined. After he was transported to the site of his execution, he was led, shackled and bound, up to the guillotine. He shouted, "Courage, comrades! *Vive l'anarchie!*" before he was shoved under the blade and his head landed in a basket.[46]

A little over a month after the executions of Émile Henry and the Barcelona anarchists, on June 24, 1894, French president Sadi Carnot was visiting the Universal Exposition in Lyon. Shortly past nine in the evening, his carriage was leaving the Palace of Commerce to head to the Grand Théâtre for a performance. The president told his guards to allow the lively crowd surrounding the carriage to come close. A young man rushed forward carrying a newspaper, which guards thought contained flowers but in fact concealed a knife.[47] The assassin lunged at the presidential carriage, thrusting his knife into Carnot and shouting, "Vive la Révolution! Vive l'Anarchie!" Carnot died three hours later.[48] The next day, Carnot's wife received a photograph of Ravachol in the mail. On the back was written, "He is well avenged."[49] Likewise, an anarchist poster put up the following day titled "To Carnot the Murderer" finished with the line: "You have had the head of Vaillant, we'll have yours, Président Carnot!"[50]

The assailant was Santo Jeronimo Caserio, a twenty-year-old anarchist baker from a poor family in Lombardy who had journeyed to Lyon from Cette to commit a "great feat" and avenge Vaillant and Henry. Caserio had embraced anarchism several years earlier before fleeing abroad after being convicted of distributing anti-militarist propaganda. After bouncing around between Switzerland, Lyon, and Vienne, he settled in Cette where he attended French anarchist meetings.[51] After Caserio read about the president's upcoming visit to Lyon, he bought a knife and planned a complicated route passing through Montpellier, Avignon, and other destinations to make it harder for the police to track him if he were under surveillance, walking the last leg of the journey.[52] Like his fellow anarchist practitioners of propaganda by the deed, Caserio claimed to have acted alone, and there is no evidence to suggest otherwise. Caserio was motivated not only by Carnot's execution of Vaillant but also by repression in Spain. In a May 1894 letter, Caserio concluded with "Long live Spain and her rifles that shot six comrades. One day we will avenge them."[53] Unsurprisingly, Caserio was quickly sentenced to death and brought before the guillotine on August 15, 1894.[54]

The assassination of Carnot spurred the proposal of a third anti-anarchist law on July 9, 1894, which passed several weeks later, outlawing anarchist propaganda.[55] The next day, across the Pyrenees, the Liberal Sagasta government finally passed their anti-explosives law in Spain. The Spanish law targeted not only those who fabricated explosives but also anyone who aided in the creation of explosives, provoked or apologized for their illegal use, or participated in any association that encouraged or facilitated such acts.[56] Some republicans complained, but in general Spanish republicanism was swept up in, or silenced by, the momentum behind anti-anarchist measures. Such measures by the French and Spanish governments were but the latest in a series of European anti-anarchist legislation. Previously, anti-anarchist/ anti-explosives legislation had been passed in the United Kingdom in 1883, Germany in 1884, Belgium in 1887, Portugal in 1892, Switzerland in April 1894, and Italy a month earlier in June 1894.[57]

Shortly after the third French anti-anarchist law, what became known as the "Trial of the Thirty" commenced in August 1894. Nineteen anarchist theoreticians and artists and eleven anarchist "criminals" were tried in a judicial attempt to target the perceived connection between ideas and actions in French anarchism. Although several notable figures fled the country, such as Émile Pouget, who would soon become a key figure in the revolutionary syndicalist CGT; Constant Martin, a former Communard turned anarchist who was Émile Henry's "mentor"; and Paul Reclus, physician and brother of famed anarchist Elisée Reclus, the trial featured some of the most prominent radical figures of the era.[58] The main targets of perennial anarchist nemesis prosecutor Bulot were Sébastien Faure, Jean Grave, Felix Fénéon, Charles Chatel, editor of *Revue anarchiste*, and Émile Henry's close friend Louis Matha. In the middle of the trial, Bulot had to ask for a recess to wash his hands because he had received a package in the mail containing feces. Throughout the trial, the agents of the state were unable to prove a connection between the thoughts of the defendants and illegal actions, but perhaps more importantly, they were consistently perceived to be outmatched by the wit of their interlocutors. What was originally intended as a showcase of the latent criminality residing in the writings of subversive dissidents quickly morphed into a spectacle of judicial absurdity as the defendants mocked the charges being leveled against them.

In the end, the intellectuals were acquitted (though Grave continued to serve his sentence until President Faure's 1895 amnesty) while three of the "criminals" were convicted to sentences of six months, eight years, and fifteen years.[59] The ability of the French system to stop short of spiraling into the kind of authoritarianism that socialist deputies feared helped end the cycle of *attentats*. The fact that France did not continue down the path of repression that Spain followed over the coming years had much to do with the relative power of socialists and radical republicans in Parliament, the higher level of respect for civil liberties in French governmental institutions, and the growing importance of notions of preventive policing. Although some of the defendants were convicted, their low profiles were insufficient to generate outrage, let alone retribution. The acquittals at the Trial of the Thirty and the presidential pardon a year later sapped some of the potential motivation for another *attentat*.[60] Over the next few years the popularity of revolutionary syndicalism would help seal the end of *l'ère des attentats* ("era of the attacks," 1892–94) in France.

Meanwhile, in late August 1894 word spread throughout the Spanish press that the Liceo bomber Santiago Salvador had renounced anarchism, had accepted communion, and even desired to become a Franciscan monk. "The grace of God has made this miracle," wrote *La Dinastía*, who blamed *atentados* on the "de-Christianization of the *pueblo*."[61] *La Protección Nacional* claimed that "we have inquired of people of undoubtable respect, who can't fool themselves or fool us, and we can assure the following: that Salvador persists in the retraction of his errors."[62] But most papers vacillated between the hopeful optimism of believing that "Salvador has opened his eyes to the true light" and the perspective that "Salvador converted doesn't convince anyone. These posthumous repentances of the great criminals always tend to be false."[63] While it is unclear based on the press coverage how many people believed him, many Catholics leaped at the supposed repentance of the anarchist. *El País* chided them by saying that in the Catholic press, "doubting the sincerity of Salvador is a worse sin than doubting Christ."[64] A group of aristocratic women organized a campaign for clemency, and the Association of Saint Vincent de Paul printed photographs of the newly Catholic Salvador to promote the conquest of their faith.[65] However, the civil governor banned the publication or sale of any portraits or biographies of Salvador fearing the potential ramifications of his glorification despite his supposed conversion.[66] In mid-October the police confiscated sixty-eight portraits of Salvador in one day.[67]

However, the sincerity of his conversion was called into question when Salvador lost his temper after the prosecutor ordered that all of the special treatment he had received after his conversion be revoked. For *La Época*, this showed that it was a "farce."[68] Once he was sentenced to death, the charade dissolved definitively and Salvador renounced the church. After refusing to sign his sentence, Salvador called out to the Jesuit father entering the prison

FIGURE 6. Santiago Salvador. *La Campana de Gracia*, July 14, 1894.

chapel saying, "I have been a phony! Don't stay with me!"[69] On learning the news, the bishop called off the Brothers of Peace and Charity who were collecting alms for Salvador, and, after a few hours, the Royal and Illustrious Archbrotherhood of the Purest Blood of Our Father Jesus Christ cancelled their collections after gathering 215 pesetas.[70]

Regardless of how many people believed Salvador's performance, the twists and turns of his final days captivated Barcelona where "no one speaks of anything but the attitude that the prisoner has suddenly assumed" and "the public grabs at the vendors of El Noticiero Universal to know the details of his time in the chapel."[71] They recounted minute details of the final hours of Salvador's life from his breakfast of fried eggs with bread and wine the day before his execution to the furniture of his room, to his pulse and temperature at different points in the day, reflecting the increasing interest in the relationship between physiology and criminality.[72] When the director of El Noticiero Universal came to visit the anarchist prisoner, Salvador wryly asked him if he could donate 200 pesetas to his daughter since his execution was generating such extraordinary profits for the paper.[73]

As with Pallás, clergy stayed at Salvador's bedside throughout a sleepless night leading into November 21, 1894, the day of his execution.[74] As he lay in bed, thousands of people gathered around 3:00 a.m. near the execution platform outside of the Reina Amalia prison in the Raval neighborhood of Barcelona, not far from the Liceo.[75] Shortly after 8:00 a.m., the prisoner was led out onto the patio surrounded by soldiers and spectators. Nearby terraces and balconies were packed with onlookers and police to prevent disturbances. As he emerged from the prison, Salvador's gait was "unsteady," no doubt owing to his lingering gunshot injury from his arrest as well as his nerves, but as he ascended the platform he straightened his posture on noticing the cameras pointing at him.[76] Looking out on the transfixed masses, Salvador shouted, "¡Viva la revolución social! ¡Viva la anarquía! Death to all religions!" and then sang the first stanza of the anarchist hymn "Hijos del pueblo":

Son of the *pueblo*, they oppress you with chains,
and this injustice cannot continue,
if your existence is a world of sorrows,
before being a slave I prefer to die.

"Get this over with quickly," Salvador asked. The executioner obliged. He was subjected to the "garrote vil," the death sentence reserved for the worst criminals in society. Salvador's last words were said to have been "Health, justice and love!"[77] His body was left on the platform until 4:00 p.m. to send a clear message to anyone who might consider following his example.

Santiago Salvador's public execution and the display of his corpse symbolized the predominant tendency in the Spanish state's response to its anarchist antagonists: if it was war they wanted, it was war they would get; if their bombs targeted the "bourgeoisie" as a whole, then the state's laws, prisons, and scaffolds would target anarchism as a whole. Yet elite sensitivity about the polyvalent spectacle of public executions and the "shameful and despicable curiosity" generated by the press outraged conservative senators, leading to a royal order several days later tightening the amount of information that could be printed about prisoners awaiting execution and ending public executions in Spain.[78]

Like its Spanish counterpart, the French state unleashed its own wave of repression during this era with its *lois scélérates*, mass arrests, and executions in response to the growing threat of propaganda by the deed and the aura surrounding the newly created (anti-)celebrity propagandist by the deed embodied in slightly different ways by Ravachol, Pallás, Salvador, Henry, Vaillant, Léauthier, Caserio, and others from 1892 to 1894. The anarchist targeting of "innocent" people and the multifaceted nature of popular fascination with this new personality heightened the urgency of silencing the bombs. It also served as a convenient excuse to link anarchist theorists to the bombers that they allegedly inspired and expand repression well beyond the practitioners and advocates of propaganda by the deed to attack the workers' movement as a whole. State officials and journalists in Spain and France legitimized the harshness of purportedly anti-anarchist measures by using the horrific nature of propaganda by the deed to craft an image of the anarchist as an atavistic creature existing outside and against humanity and therefore undeserving of the rights afforded to men in modern "civilization."

Little did they imagine that soon these very same ideas about brutality stifling the progress of "civilization" would be mobilized by anarchists and their allies to indict the inhumanity of their state tormentors. For although the Spanish and French narratives of dynamite and repression dovetailed each other with corresponding explosions, laws, mass arrests, and executions into 1894, their paths would fork over the remainder of the decade. The French Trial of the Thirty failed to extend repression to anarchist ideologues. In 1895 President Faure issued a broad amnesty to halt the cycle of reprisals that had characterized *l'ère des attentats*. Over the following years, the role of propaganda by the deed declined in French anarchism in favor of revolutionary syndicalism, educational initiatives, and other areas of focus.

The sensitivity to public opinion, civil liberties, and the interrelated dynamics of repression and reprisal that contributed to the French state's de-escalation mid-decade were largely foreign to Spanish officials. Although by the end of 1894 the fifth letter of protest from the Reina Amalia prisoners in Barcelona influenced the release of almost all of those allegedly involved in the recent *atentados*, this measure, and the lifting of the suspension of constitutional guarantees around the same time, did not represent a significant shift in the repressive logic of the Spanish state.[79] The royal order banning public executions and information on prisoners awaiting death certainly represented a greater sensitivity to the power of public opinion. Yet outrage on behalf of those erroneously incarcerated, tortured, and executed did not materialize beyond anarchist circles. It would take a much more dramatic sequence of events beginning a year and a half later for popular outrage on behalf of anarchist and other radical victims of the Spanish state to coalesce into a powerful international force for the rights of all.

PART II

El Proceso de Montjuich

CHAPTER 6

The Anarchist Inquisition

On the morning of June 16, 1896, a crowd of women and children gathered around the local jail in Reus, Catalonia, to see what had become of the director of the local lay school, Joan Montseny. When the civil guard came to his home at midnight a day earlier, Montseny refused to open the door, citing a long-standing policy that Spanish citizens were not obliged to open their doors to anyone at night. Locksmiths turned down the pleas of the aggravated civil guards to let them into the house, so they waited until morning to arrest Montseny as he walked out his front door. After threatening to arrest his entire family for disobeying authority, the civil guard threw Montseny into a small, windowless cell with a bucket. The next day he was informed that he would be escorted on foot over one hundred kilometers from Reus to Barcelona to face unspecified charges.[1]

As a curious crowd formed outside the jail, Montseny, handcuffed in the hallway, wondered why he had been arrested and ordered to march on foot to Barcelona. Reasons were not hard to come by. Was this an ultramontane effort to discredit his lay school? Was the thirty-one-year-old teacher being targeted for having written pamphlets that defended the Gran Vía bombing, exposed torture in Barcelona prisons, and raised money for the Pallás family?[2] For simply being an anarchist? Or was this revenge for adopting Paulino Pallás's daughter for five months until her mother could reclaim her? Undoubtedly Montseny's efforts to compile and disseminate the letters of tortured prisoners in the aftermath of recent *atentados* put him on the radar of local authorities even if his protests failed to generate a public outcry. These questions likely swirled through Montseny's mind as he was led out of the jail into the daylight and immediately pounced on by his Saint Bernard, who had been waiting for him outside all night. The guards walked him through rows of children from his school who burst into tears on seeing their teacher in cuffs. Montseny too sobbed. As he was led away from Reus, his dog followed along "as if he were another prisoner."[3]

That night, Montseny and his escorts reached the small village of Torredembarra. Throughout the evening, the intrigued townspeople flocked to his cell to bring him food and learn why Montseny had been detained. Farther along the journey, Montseny's mother caught up to her son to bring him some clothing from his *compañera* Teresa Mañé. Not long after, Montseny finally arrived at the prison of the Atarazanas barracks at the end of La Rambla in Barcelona. He was shoved into a cramped cell packed with thirty prisoners. After the cell door slammed shut, they told him about the recent sequence of events in Barcelona that had led to his incarceration.[4]

At 6:00 p.m. on June 7, 1896, Captain General Eulogio Despujol led one of Barcelona's nine Corpus Christi processions away from its starting point at the cathedral behind the *gegants*: giant street puppets characteristic of Catalan popular processions.[5] This Corpus Christi procession, the second most popular in the city, had marched from the cathedral to the Church of Santa María del Mar since the fourteenth century. This day, the clergy and representatives of Barcelona's historic guilds marched behind the *gegants*, followed by the military (which did not march in any of Barcelona's other Corpus processions) and then the common people. Several hours later, the procession was finally winding down as the host was entering the Santa María del Mar Church.[6] A light rain started to fall on the masses of people clogging up the entrance to the church as the tail of the procession continued down the small side street of Cambios Nuevos.

Around 9:00 in the evening, the sound of an explosion rang out, causing the priest in the church to faint.[7] Despujol hurriedly commanded the military band to play the royal march to stem the panic.[8] The crowd scattered as glass from streetlights and windows crashed down.[9] One witness claimed that just as the military contingent passed, he started to head home and came across a package the size of a melon wrapped in burning cloth. Thinking it might be a bomb, he immediately fled to safety right before it detonated. A second witness stated that around the same time he too saw a package wrapped in rags emitting smoke, but this man made the unfortunate choice of poking it with his foot, causing it to explode.[10] Although many historians claim that the bomb was thrown, overwhelming evidence suggests that the bomb was placed on the ground before its explosion, rather than thrown and detonated on impact like the more common Orsini bomb.[11] Not only did witnesses describe their encounters with smoking packages on the ground, but a member of the military drum core testified that he saw light coming from the ground immediately before the explosion.[12] The examination of the remnants of the bomb confirmed that it had been detonated by a burning wick.[13] Since the explosion occurred right after the military contingent had passed, thereby killing and maiming common people at the end of the procession rather than prominent authorities, it is plausible that the bomber intended to target the military but miscalculated the duration of time before the wick would finish burning or ignited it too late.

Immediately after the explosion, which killed twelve and injured forty to seventy more, the police arrested "suspicious" people near the scene and searched nearby homes.[14] By the following day, authorities had arrested thirty-eight suspects, canceled theatrical functions and other processions, and suspended constitutional guarantees in the province of Barcelona.[15] The *atentado* terrified and tantalized. While many fled to surrounding towns or hid indoors, so many curious visitors came to witness the site of the explosion that they clogged up transit.[16] Vendors even sold what they claimed were "little pieces of the shell of the bomb . . . for good prices."[17]

Unsurprisingly, the press was out for blood against the anarchists without proof that they were responsible. As in response to earlier *atentados*, journalists from across the political spectrum dehumanized anarchists as "wild beasts more ferocious than those raised in virgin jungles" or "fanatics of destruction and vengeance" without "ideas, but rather instincts" whose bombings aroused the "indignation of all of the civilized world" and therefore warranted the mass execution of anarchists "as if they were rabid dogs."[18] *La Época* pointed out that "few times have we seen such unanimity as shown by the press of the capital and the provinces regarding the absolute need to repress antisocial anarchist propaganda."[19] Although several years had gone by without explosions, and some may have come to assume that anarchist bombings had faded into history as they seemed to have done in France after the assassination of President Carnot, the Cambios Nuevos bombing of 1896 reignited the memories of the Gran Vía and the Liceo to make propaganda by the deed seem like a perpetual threat. *Las Noticias* asked, "When will this end? We don't want to blame anyone but if in Paris, the populous capital of the south, but if in London, the populous capital of the North, the panther has been shackled, why is it that in Barcelona there isn't even a break to control the wild beast? We are giving the world a show. Anarchism invades us. If firing squads aren't enough, find another way."[20]

Not only did anarchist bombs threaten physical destruction, they threatened the Spanish monarchy's international reputation by highlighting the impotence of the state to stop them. Nationalist tensions were already running high as the Spanish grip on Cuba and the Philippines was faltering while British and French imperial projects surged. *El Movimiento Católico* pointed toward deeper causes of anarchist violence by attacking the decay of traditional society through "industrialism without Christ and its unbridled pleasures."[21] Regardless of which anxieties it triggered, anarchism came to be seen by the press as "a tumor on the social body" that exacerbated the mounting perception of Spanish backwardness.[22] *El Heraldo* dubbed Spain the "Turkey of the Occident."[23]

To accomplish the urgent task of defusing anarchist bombs, it was generally agreed that exceptional measures were necessary to defeat "those who reject the human conscience."[24] This time, *La Dinastía* wrote, there was "unanimity of the Madrid papers in asking for measures of rare vigor, some asking for deportation, others for *lynchamiento*." *La Dinastía* also mentioned that while some suggested sending the anarchists to the penal colony of Fernando Po, others advocated "the system of the revolutionaries of Nantes in 1793" (i.e., the guillotine), sentiments expressed even by "those who profess the most advanced ideas."[25]

In the aftermath of the bombing, journalists argued that extreme repression was warranted against all anarchists regardless of their involvement in the bombing because "given that anarchist methods are murder, whoever continues to be affiliated with anarchism places themselves in solidarity with this crime. The distinction between theory and practice, between the ideal and action, has no place here given that the one is born from the other and that from the heat of anarchic propaganda emerge criminals like Caserio, Pallás, and Salvador."[26] Even the liberal *El Imparcial* was not at all concerned with guilt or innocence, writing that all anarchists "will be treated as wolves and exterminated as wolves are exterminated. No one asks if the wolf that is being pursued has done damage or not within a herd; it's a wolf, that's enough; if it still hasn't caused damage it could in the future."[27] Ultimately, it was necessary "that human justice not see anything more in any anarchist, whether peaceful or active, than a murderer; they deserve to be exterminated."[28] Even the republican *El País* argued that these anarchists were "inhuman criminals" who were "killing for the sake of killing . . . [without] any right to mercy or compassion. . . . We are not advocates of the death penalty; but in cases like this, in the presence of this devastating fever that aspires to social regeneration through extermination; before such repugnant brutality, reason fails and one can only hear the voice of indignation and ire."[29] *La Dinastía* argued that the new measures should target not only anarchists but "even socialists who walk very close" with them.[30] There was such disregard for due process that a former governor of Barcelona stated that, based on his experience, the best the authorities could do was simply arrest as many suspicious people as possible the night before big festivals and public events since the anarchist methods of operating in small groups and changing meeting places made actually uncovering a specific plot quite challenging.[31]

The only political factions opposed to harsh repression, apart from the anarchists themselves, were the federal republicans and the socialists. Francisco Pi y Arsuaga, son of the legendary former president of the First Republic, Francisco Pi y Margall, was aghast at the eagerness of supposedly liberal and democratic journalists and politicians to advocate for the most draconian measures. In *El Nuevo Régimen*, organ of the federal republicans, he wrote that "the press that calls itself liberal [is] surrendering, in an hour of fear, all of the conquests of a century. Calm, *señores*, calm."[32] Likewise, *El Socialista* warned liberals, democrats, and republicans against going down the path of punishing anarchists for their ideas: "can't they see that one day their [ideas] will be considered the same by the most retrograde elements of the bourgeoisie? . . . If today it starts with punishing anarchist ideas, tomorrow the same will be done with others that the exploiters dislike."[33] As *El Imparcial* noted, "For the first time since anarchist *atentados* have occurred in Spain, upon speaking of the need for preventative measures, no one has raised objections grounded in fears of governmental abuses."[34]

As opposed to the journalistic call for new anti-anarchist legislation following the Gran Vía and Liceo bombings, arguments about new laws were quite rare in the aftermath of the Cambios Nuevos *atentado*. For although the government's 1894 anti-anarchist legislation seemed to have been successful during the two-year lull in *atentados*, its failure to impede the recent explosion furthered a conception of the problem of propaganda by the deed as beyond the traditional liberal confines of jurisprudence. Laws were considered safeguards against the dangers of humanity, but if anarchists were not human, how could society rely solely on the law? Among the rare cases of appeals for new laws was an article titled "Vengeance!" from the satirical anti-clerical republican paper *El Motín*, run by the firebrand José Nakens, which argued that it was necessary "to annihilate, to exterminate" the anarchists and "if current laws weren't sufficient [to be able to do so], may they pass other laws. . . . The right to defense is primary, in society as with individuals."[35] Many believed that what was needed was a law justifying the extralegal persecution of anarchism, giving the authorities carte blanche to disregard legal safeguards in hunting down those whose actions had placed them beyond the law to begin with.

Such a law was presented to Congress a week after the explosion. Designed to augment the repressive powers of the 1894 law, this new piece of legislation, to be in effect for three years before being subject to renewal, authorized the arrest of anyone with anarchist sympathies and the closure of "all periodicals, centers, and places of anarchist recreation."[36] It also mandated a death sentence for anyone whose attacks with explosives or flammable materials killed anyone, and a life sentence if such an attack merely caused injuries or occurred in a public building (even if it caused no damage). Moreover, such cases were now to be adjudicated by military courts.[37] One of the only voices against the proposed law was the federalist El Nuevo Régimen, which cautioned that "if this law is approved, we will have put in the hands of governments a weapon, not against the anarchists . . . but rather against all those who for whatever reason arouse the displeasure of he who commands."[38] Federalist concerns would prove to be all too prescient over the coming months.

Yet this law should be understood not as the impetus behind the enormous wave of repression that struck the anarchist movement but rather as parliamentary window dressing for an escalation of brutal state methods that had been developing for several years, reaching especially intense levels after the recent atentado. After all, the mass arrests and censorship started well before the new legislation was signed into law in early September 1896. The police did not await the rubber stamp. After arresting thirty-eight people in less than twenty-four hours, the police raised their total to 224 by the end of June and 359 by early September 1896. About a year later, Despujol cited a figure of 424 total arrests in a letter to the minister of war, but historian Antoni Dalmau found the names of 558 people who were at one point arrested following the Cambios Nuevos bombing, and he estimates that the real total was between six and seven hundred.[39] The press recognized that the police were carrying out "innumerable arrests" and that "the majority [of those arrested] had already been prisoners after the Liceo [bombing]."[40]

Given the repression and torture that followed the Liceo bombing, the anarchists knew to expect the worst. Days after the Cambios Nuevos atentado, El Corsario ominously predicted that "they're going to repeat their inquisitorial acts."[41] Like most anarchists, El Corsario vehemently opposed the most recent bombing, since its "consequences tragically affect innocent beings," but they knew that, nevertheless, they would feel the repercussions as would "any political party in opposition to the government."[42]

Madrid socialists held a protest days after the announcement of the new anti-anarchist law.[43] They too saw the danger approaching.

The police arrested every "suspicious" dissident they could find. Beyond hauling in anarchist militants, editors, theorists, and especially those who had been detained for one of the earlier *atentados*, the police also arrested typesetters for anarchist periodicals, anyone who had ever subscribed to the anarchist paper *El Productor*, and those known to have visited an anarchist center or suspicious workers' center or café. The police were suspicious of working-class foreigners as well. In fact, a dispatch from the British consul to Barcelona stated that the police were keeping lists of them and questioning any known to "have frequented certain of the low class cabarets."[44] Police also arrested secular people who had not baptized their children or fasted during Lent, who had civil marriages, or who had given their relatives lay burials.[45] A sizable number of socialists and republicans were arrested as well, but, as we will see shortly, the number of republican arrests ballooned in August in a way that would dramatically affect responses to repression.

The inept and indiscriminate measures of the police were obvious to the French commissioner in Barcelona, who, days after the explosion, informed the French interior minister that the authorities had no idea who the bomber was and that their mass arrests had been fruitless. To compensate for their cluelessness, the commissioner wrote, alleged witnesses who would not cooperate would be "coerced."[46] Captain General Despujol admitted to the haphazard police strategy in an internal report, stating that since the authorities lacked "sufficient data to be able to skillfully conduct the investigation . . . it became necessary to arrest numerous individuals, who if they did not immediately offer sufficient reason for suspicion of participation in the act to fall upon them, were known as having anarchist ideas and were more or less secretly propagandists of their doctrine."[47] Little did police and military authorities suspect that their broad dragnet would soon prove counterproductive.

Finally, Joan Montseny knew why he had been taken on foot from Reus to Barcelona and thrown in a cell. He passed the time by listening to the tales of detention being recounted by workers from across Catalonia. Eventually a few were called out for interrogation. The first to return reported that the interrogations were being carried out by civil guard lieutenant Narciso Portas, director of the special section of the judicial police put in charge of the investigation. Montseny recalled that on hearing the name of the infamous Portas, "a tragic terror penetrated the cell." When Montseny was called out for interrogation, he was led to an infantry sergeant and Portas sitting behind a small table. Among other questions, Portas asked Montseny if he sang "anarchist hymns to his students." Montseny recalled replying, "No, *señor*. In my school hymns are not sung in any class." Later Portas took out copies of Montseny's *El Proceso de un gran crimen*, which reported the abuses suffered by those suspected of the "anarchist plot" behind the Gran Vía and Liceo bombings, and his *La ley de la vida*. When Montseny admitted to writing these pamphlets, Portas replied, "You will pay dearly."[48]

After the interrogations, Montseny and his fellow prisoners were bound and escorted by a civil guard squad to the prison of Reina Amalia in the Raval district, where Santiago Salvador spent his final days. After a few days he was moved into a cell with two of the most important Spanish anarchists of the era: Anselmo Lorenzo and Fernando Tarrida del Mármol. A veteran of the First International, Anselmo Lorenzo was known as "the grandfather" of Spanish anarchism for his longtime militancy and publishing in the anarchist press. Lorenzo had played a role in influencing Fernando Tarrida del Mármol's transition from federal republicanism to anarchism as a teenager in the late 1870s. Lorenzo and Tarrida remained friends and comrades over the following years, while Tarrida's stature in the anarchist movement grew as an editor of *Acracia*. Tarrida is perhaps best remembered for coining the term "anarchism without adjectives" in 1889 as a vision of anarchist unity in the context of the oft-debilitating conflicts between anarchist collectivists and communists.[49]

Professionally, Tarrida was an engineer. In 1896 he was the director of the Polytechnic Academy of Barcelona, where an agent of the "secret police" surprised him as he was walking up the stairs on July 21. The officer told Tarrida he had to come to answer a small question before the military judge, but he feared the worst given the suspension of constitutional guarantees. Tarrida was thrown into a filthy cell in Atarazanas with six workers, including the president and secretary of the train conductor and chauffeur society for which Tarrida had been a consulting engineer. The cell floor was "revolting," but they were not given even newspaper to sit on. Without a toilet they had to designate a corner of the cell for human waste. They spent the day in this cramped space awaiting a judge who never came before being chained and transferred to the national prison at midnight.[50]

At about 1:00 a.m., Tarrida was shoved into a cell packed with just under thirty prisoners at the national prison. It was dark, so Fernando could not really see the other men. There was only one small window and no furniture.[51] By the time Montseny was thrown in with Tarrida and Lorenzo, there were forty men in the cell. It was so cramped that the prisoners took turns moving. There was only one grimy toilet. Whereas the common prisoners spent all day in the outdoor patio, the political prisoners were never allowed outside.[52] Tarrida recounted that every day they were given a small piece of bread and two bowls of "a greasy soup that the dogs wouldn't want."[53]

The majority of the prisoners had no idea why they were imprisoned, and the authorities were not eager to explain. The judge only visited the prison once or twice a week to conduct interrogations with one or two prisoners. As a result, fifteen of Montseny's cellmates were there for seven weeks without seeing the judge. Tarrida, however, was interrogated on his third day in the national prison. As he sat before the judge, he heard the official reasons for his incarceration: he had attacked the army (in writing), he had "founded" anarchy in Spain, and he had written a supposedly incriminating letter to a prisoner in Valencia. Fernando could not hold back his laughter.[54]

Meanwhile, the police were also busy filling the women's section of the national prison. Fifteen women were arrested in the aftermath of the Cambios Nuevos bombing, including Teresa Claramunt, a textile worker and dynamic anarchist unionist, orator, and writer who came to be known as the "Spanish Louise Michel." Prison was certainly difficult for Claramunt, but it was nothing new. She had served four months in 1893 for her alleged instigation of a riot that broke out after a meeting that she was not even allowed to attend because she was a woman. Claramunt had been locked up again after the Liceo bombing.[55] Days after Cambios Nuevos, she was arrested with her husband, Antonio Gurri.[56]

Claramunt attempted to console incarcerated mothers wailing about the destitute state of their abandoned children. Although these women pleaded with the nuns who ran the prison to be allowed to see their children, they were denied because they had not been married in the Catholic Church.[57] Among the desperate mothers was thirty-five-year-old mother of three Teresa Maymí. Several days after the arrest of her *compañero*, police came to Maymí's home to inform her that the governor would like to "ask her a question." She spent a while in custody with her fifteen-month-old daughter before being asked anything, leaving her eight- and four-year-old daughters alone without supervision. After suffering through an interrogation filled with allegations of invented conspiracies, Maymí was thrown into a small cell without any light. The next day she was allowed to fraternize with the rest of the women in the prison, many of whom were sex workers. Although "some were lovely, the rest were rats," Maymí recounted.[58]

As the weeks turned into months, Maymí's daughters were housed at first in a military barracks and then in a Catholic "asylum" for orphans. Nightmares of her daughters' misery plagued Maymí, but at least she took some comfort in the solidarity she found with other political prisoners like

Asunción Vallvé, who was locked up with her two-month-old son. Her brother had been arrested a few hours after her, and her husband the next day. As soon as she walked into the prison, the "generous wives of *el Señor*" verbally attacked her when they learned that her son was not named after a saint.[59] They would have been especially horrified to learn that the baby's third name was "Anárquico."[60] Vallvé calmly responded that she did not believe in their religion: "to live in peace and love, Natural laws, are sufficient for me."[61]

Unsurprisingly, the political prisoners were treated worse than the rest of the prisoners. Teresa Maymí recalled that whereas the common prisoners were afforded hammocks, the political prisoners had only mats and small blankets with holes to use as they slept on the hard prison floor. Even worse for these anarchist and anti-clerical mothers was to witness the forced baptisms of their babies. Asunción Vallvé recounted that the spectacle "morally martyred me."[62] They were deprived of medical treatment and prevented from communicating with the outside world.[63] Once the mother superior walked up to Teresa Maymí to tell her that a letter had come from her husband before ripping it to pieces in front of her. Part of the motivation of the policy of prohibiting communication was the desire to wrench these "sinful" women away from their diabolical partners. A priest approached Maymí to get her to sign a document stating that she would leave her husband, and in exchange he offered her a job and her freedom. When she retorted that she'd rather stay locked up, the priest said, "Your protest is in vain; don't you know that they're going to kill you soon?"[64]

As it became clear that their imprisonment would continue for a while, the male prisoners started to carve out their collective life using the skills at their disposal. They organized a choir, which performed a concert every night with the permission of the prison officials. It was easy to organize the choir since many Catalan workers had participated in one of the sections of the Choral Federation established by the mid-nineteenth-century Catalan composer Anselmo Clavé. In addition, Tarrida, Montseny, and Lorenzo organized educational lessons and conferences. Tarrida taught chemistry and physics, Lorenzo spoke about politics and literature, and Montseny gave lessons on history and geography by sketching a world map on the prison floor.[65]

They stayed informed about the outside world by subscribing to *El Liberal*, *El Diluvio*, and *El Noticiero Universal*. Since there were few papers, low literacy, and only one window, every morning one reader sat by the window, and every evening by the candle, to read to their fellow prisoners. At visiting time, all visitors and prisoners squeezed together to communicate through a single door so that it was almost impossible to hear anything. Nevertheless, letters and papers were passed through the bars. On August 5 they received a letter that sapped their enthusiasm for the choirs and lessons and squashed hopes of eking out a tolerable existence in prison. The letter came from comrades imprisoned in Montjuich Castle, who wrote that "'the torture has already begun,' as if it were expected," Montseny recalled. "We looked at each other absentmindedly without knowing what to say or do."[66]

Around the same time, an old woman, "more dead than alive," was added to Teresa Claramunt's cell in the women's prison. The anarchist women tried to comfort her as she cried uncontrollably. After she calmed down, the old woman asked them why they were in prison. When they told her it was because of the *atentado*, she said, "What? Are you some of those who go up to Montjuich? Sacred Virgin! If you knew how they are martyred!" The woman went on to tell them that her daughter knew a Montjuich guard who had been traumatized by witnessing the torture of the prisoners by the civil guard. That night Claramunt had such a terrifying nightmare that her cellmates had to wake her to stop her crying.[67]

Among them was Francisca Saperas, whose *compañero* Tomás Ascheri was locked up in Montjuich Castle. Her fears about Ascheri potentially facing torture must have brought back memories of her husband of twenty-five years, Martín Borrás, who had committed suicide in prison after being incarcerated for the Gran Vía bombing. On his third attempt, the pioneering anarchist communist ingested dissolved phosphorous in a matchbox because he had grown "tired of living in a world of injustices where brother arms himself against brother." Tragically, a week later he would have been acquitted, but as he wrote to Francisca, even if he were acquitted his freedom would only be "another sentence given my impaired physical state."[68]

In the wake of her husband's suicide in 1894, Saperas continued her anarchist militancy by opening up her home in Gracia to comrades in need of refuge. She would come to be remembered as "the mother of the anarchists" who regularly "lodged, one, two, three Italian, Spanish, French *compañeros*."[69] Saperas took special interest in a young anarchist sailor, former seminarian, and military deserter born in Marseille of Italian parents named Tomás Ascheri. Although Ascheri was about twenty-six and Francisca was about forty-four, they developed a romantic relationship and he moved in permanently. All seemed to be going fine as Ascheri spent his days working for the paper *Ciencia Social*, but, unbeknownst to Saperas, her new lover was playing a dangerous game.[70]

Ascheri later recounted that in July 1895 he received an invitation to meet with the French consul general. The message surprised him, but he accepted out of curiosity. The consular official flattered Ascheri by telling him that, judging by the reports from his agents, he seemed to be highly intelligent. He then offered Ascheri a position as an informer for the French consul general, which Ascheri accepted, "thinking that it would be useful for my refugee comrades." After informing for ten months, his attitude toward the work soured and he quit. Before he could walk away, however, Ascheri accepted an offer from the governor of Barcelona to continue as an informant.[71]

According to Ascheri, in late March 1896 the governor told him that he had received reports of secret anarchist meetings and bomb plots. Ascheri vehemently denied the veracity of such reports, but the governor responded that police inspector Daniel Freixa had confirmed them. To discredit Freixa, Ascheri told the governor "something that wasn't a secret to anyone," that the police inspector had been partaking in illegal gambling and accepting bribes from gambling houses. Acting on this information, Freixa was caught red-handed but let off since he had been gambling with the governor's brother.[72] Ascheri had made some powerful enemies.

When a new governor came into office, Ascheri ended his collaboration with the Barcelona government until returning to the governor's office the day of the Cambios Nuevos explosion. Two days later he found himself behind bars.[73] The next day Ascheri's lover, Francisca Saperas, was also arrested, followed by her pregnant daughter, Salud Borrás.[74] Entire anarchist families were being locked up, as was evident when Borrás's partner, Luis Más, a twenty-five-year-old marble worker and member of the editorial staff of the anarchist *La Nueva Idea*, was arrested in August after having been detained in 1894 for the Liceo bombing.[75] When Borrás and Mas's child was born, Asunción Vallvé breastfed the baby along with her son since the new mother was unable. When the nuns learned about this, they put Vallvé in a special punishment cell for three days and sent her son to an orphanage.[76] Also incarcerated in the women's section of the national prison were the widows of Paulino Pallás and Santiago Salvador, Àngela Vallés and Antònia Colom i Vicens.[77]

As the days passed without any concrete evidence as to the identity of the bomber, the police seem to have started to see Ascheri as the perfect patsy. As *El Progreso* noted, he was "a foreigner, without family, his relationships were very few and no one complained on his behalf." He fit so well, *El Progreso* later noted, that "it was as if Marzo and Portas had fabricated him *ad hoc*."[78] Moreover, the French police considered him to be dangerous, he had links to the "suspicious" Centro de Carreteros, and the police likely realized that if his informant past were made public, it would dampen sympathy for his plight. Ascheri claimed that Inspector Freixa had it in for him from the moment of his arrest.[79] For weeks, the police leaned on Ascheri in his cell in Montjuich Castle to get him to confess to the crime, but he would not budge.

On August 4, 1896, the day of Santo Domingo de Guzmán (considered by many to be the founder of the Inquisition), the stakes were raised. That evening in Montjuich, soldiers came to escort several prisoners out of their cells. They were taken across the castle's central plaza and then down a set of stairs through a hall with five cells where each was locked up in isolation. Over the coming days, these prisoners faced a torturous ordeal. Each prisoner was tied up tightly and told to walk back and forth across their cell as a guard kept watch through a hole in the door. They were beaten when they faltered and given dried cod when they asked for water. If they revealed who threw the bomb, the guards said, they would be given rest, bread, water, and wine. Each prisoner pleaded that they had no idea who had committed the crime, but the walking only continued. The amount of time walking ranged between four and sixteen days. The republican Francisco Gana recounted that he walked until "the last night the walls seemed like houses in reverse, the doors seemed like men with guns, and the stones seemed like dead bodies."[80] After the walking, they asked Gana again what he knew, and when he again replied that he knew nothing, they grabbed and twisted his genitalia with such force that he fell unconscious. When he awoke, he could not walk because they had mutilated his toenails while he was asleep. After he made an unsuccessful attempt on his life, the prison authorities told him they had finally realized that he was not an anarchist, so they took off his cuffs, gave him some water and soup, and let him sleep on the floor. Despite this respite, the constant onslaught of flies around his open wounds plagued Gana, who was alarmed to notice that his right arm and leg had become paralyzed from the torture. Fortunately, the paralysis started to fade after five days. Nevertheless, for days he laid there on the cold, filthy prison floor listening to the screams of the other prisoners.[81]

Among them was Ascheri, who was in the middle of eight days and nights of continual walking back and forth in his cell without any water and only some bread and dried cod to eat. Ascheri later recounted that "when I had become delirious with fever and exhaustion . . . I fell to the ground screaming pleas for a sip of water, [and] my response was the lash; and although I still wanted to resist, I lied, and I said that I was the author of the explosion."[82] Despite his confession, this regimen of hot irons, beatings, sleep deprivation, and the twisting of genitalia continued for Ascheri and other prisoners.

Though initially stupefied by news of torture in Montjuich Castle, the men locked up in the national prison soon took action. They decided that it was their duty to make as many copies as possible of the letter they had received from the Montjuich prisoners to send to the newspapers and their families. One prisoner dictated the letter aloud from the center of the cell as the others transcribed the horrid accounts of brutality. Tarrida and Lorenzo wrote articles based on the letter, but initially Montseny was shell-shocked. While the others copied, he could not stop thinking about his tortured comrades. The torments of one of the prisoners named Sebastián Suñé were so haunting that "I saw him suffer and I heard him scream." Montseny's cellmates grew frustrated with his inaction, but "at that moment I heard nothing and saw nothing."[83]

Montseny eventually decided to channel the intensity of the images of Suñé's misery that were running through his mind into a letter to a sympathetic German paper. "I wrote as if I were Suñé. . . . I recounted to the world the torments that Suñé was suffering as if I were suffering them myself."[84] Montseny wiped the tears out of his eyes as he finished the letter and sent it to the German paper without telling anyone.[85] As the days passed, the prisoners kept writing and the frustrated whispers about Montseny's lack of participation grew louder. Yet, although some thought he was simply working for his own freedom, Montseny was chuckling to himself as he secretly wrote letters to the press under the pseudonym Federico Urales. "I have always been a little odd," he later explained. "I always preferred to work alone."[86]

Over the coming years, Montseny would use this invented persona to capitalize on the enhanced political importance of the newly coined term "intellectual." Though dating farther back in substance, the term would emerge from the heightened role of the intelligentsia, such as Émile Zola in the Dreyfus affair in France months later. As José Carlos Mainel demonstrates, the figure of the intellectual grew out of the literary genre of the essay, which had undergone a transformation from its earlier meaning as "proof" to become a work whose power stemmed from the authority of the voice behind it.[87] The "Je" in Zola's "J'accuse" and other essays written by intellectuals "established itself as a sufficient authority to announce itself and demand to be heard." "Federico Urales" was an intellectual persona who could command the "goodwill and collaboration" of his reader from the heights of his personal authority (he considered other mountain ranges before settling on the Urals for his pseudonym) and avoid state repression.[88] This role grew out of Montseny's relatively individualistic take on anarchism (though he dabbled in the workers' movement) and his belief that ideas and the intellectuals who spread them were the main agents of human "progress."[89]

On August 8, 1896, Montseny was among sixteen prisoners who were informed at 3:00 a.m. that they were to be relocated to Montjuich Castle. The civil guard cuffed one hand of each prisoner to a long cord that bound them together so they could use their free hand to hold onto their blankets, clothing, and personal items. The clip-clopping hooves of the civil guard horses pierced the early morning silence of the Raval neighborhood as the chain of prisoners was led away to Montjuich. Over the moat, across the drawbridge, and through the front gate they passed before filing into a single cell where "a single thought invaded all of our minds," Montseny recalled: "'to the torture, to the torture,' we said to ourselves."[90] Unfortunately, such fears were well founded. José Molas, Antonio Nogués, and other prisoners were tortured in the same gruesome fashion as Francisco Gana and others before them until they confessed to having been accomplices to Tomás Ascheri.

By mid-August, civil guard lieutenant Portas had completed the first stage of his project of constructing the vast anarchist conspiracy that he and others in the upper echelons of power envisioned. On the sixteenth, he reported that he had obtained confessions from Ascheri, the bomber, and accomplices Molas and Nogués by means of "continuous interrogation" (a phrase far more literal than officials might have guessed).[91] Interestingly, two days later, on August 18, the police arrested at least twenty prominent republicans, including lawyers Pere Coromines and Josep M. Vallès i Ribot, as well as several former deputies such as Nicolás Estévanez, Joan Martí i Torres, and the Federal Republican Baldomero Lostau, who had written a letter of protest to the minister of war about the torture of the Liceo prisoners.[92] While there had been a trickle of republican arrests since the bombing, the coordinated nature of these arrests on a single day could not have been a coincidence. Perhaps emboldened by Portas's success in extracting confessions from his prisoners, state authorities may have sought to use the repressive momentum to further quash opposition by attempting to lump republicanism in with anarchism.[93]

For Portas and his fellow torturers, the next stage of the plan was to use the men they had broken as tools to implicate other prisoners. They forced Nogués to wear a painful gag for a day until he agreed to implicate whoever they wanted. Prisoners who were brought before Portas and Judge Marzo remembered how Ascheri "seemed like a ghost, like he was hypnotized."[94] After Portas used Ascheri and Nogués to verify the preliminary allegations against the supposed accomplices in late August, Luis Mas, partner of Salud Borrás, was used in the same capacity in the pretrial hearings in late September. The torture Mas was subjected to not only destroyed his ability to defend his innocence; it seems to have destroyed his mental faculties. In large part this was due to the fact that by September, when Mas was tortured, the regular routine of walking and beatings gave way to insidious innovations. The Montjuich guards put an iron helmet on Mas's head that pulled his upper lip up over his nose and the lower lip down under his jaw, tearing the flesh from his face as the sides of the mask crushed his temples.[95] A shell of himself, Mas echoed the fabricated accusations leveled by Nogués and Ascheri against hapless Montjuich prisoners.

In August 1896 Teresa Claramunt was removed from the national prison and taken up the hill to Montjuich. Though the rumors of torture were terrifying, at least she "felt a certain comfort from having escaped the yoke of the sisters at the [national] prison." She heard "details of the crime against humanity [*crimen de lesa humanidad*]" that was being committed against the prisoners from torture victim Francisco Gana, who was in the neighboring cell.[96] According to Montseny, several different groups and individuals, including Gana and Claramunt, Montseny and his cellmates, and the lawyer Pere Coromines, all decided independently of each other to write letters exposing these atrocities around the same time.[97]

The challenge was getting the letters out of the prison. Some of the guards and military personnel were sympathetic to the plight of the prisoners. When Tarrida arrived in Montjuich, a guard stationed at his cell had been a student in Tarrida's math class. He was so saddened to see his former teacher in prison that he gave Tarrida his hand through the bars despite the potential backlash from his superiors. After that gesture, however, Tarrida never saw him again. An artillery sergeant even went so far as to deliver letters between cells. Nevertheless, the prisoners decided to entrust the dangerous task of transporting the letters out of Montjuich to Juan Talarn, the former owner of the pub where Paulino Pallás's supposed affinity group Benvenuto allegedly held their secret meetings.[98] Talarn still had the fever that had sent him to the infirmary in the national prison, so they decided to stitch the letters that Montseny, Lorenzo, Tarrida, and Oller had written to newspapers such as *El País*, *El Diluvio*, *El Socialista*, and others into the lining of his jacket and have him sent back to the national prison infirmary. The plan worked and the letters went out the next day.[99]

On August 27, Tarrida turned pale when prison authorities read his name aloud. Montseny turned and said, "Courage [*ánimo*]" as he left. Two hours later, Tarrida returned to tell his friends that he had been released. With a saddened and somewhat guilty heart, he begged his cellmates not to think poorly of him for his early release. As he left the prison, his comrades waved their handkerchiefs to say goodbye. Tarrida took his out to return the gesture, but before he could, he had to use it to dry his eyes.

Tarrida would later write that his freedom was the result of the pressure applied on his behalf by influential friends and relatives such as his cousin, a Barcelona senator.[100] While this may have been the sole reason for his release, Montseny wrote years later that in fact Tarrida had been released because he pretended to accept an offer to be an informant for Portas among international groups in Paris and London.[101] Tarrida would certainly spend quite a bit of time with international groups in Paris and London over the coming months, but not quite as Portas may have imagined.

CHAPTER 7

The Return of Torquemada

"From the very first day they clapped eyes on [the indigenous population of the Americas] the Spanish fell like ravening wolves upon the fold, or like tigers and savage lions who have not eaten meat for days," recalled the Dominican priest Bartolomé de Las Casas in his 1552 *A Short Account of the Destruction of the Indies.*[1] His attempts to challenge the brutality of the *encomienda* system of indigenous slavery through the courts having failed, Las Casas lifted his pen to denounce Spanish brutality. His actions had unintended consequences. In the sixteenth and seventeenth centuries, Spain's emergent colonial rivals in England and the Netherlands would pair Las Casas's critique of Spanish colonial atrocities with the horrors of the Spanish Inquisition to construct an image of innate Spanish Catholic "barbarity" in contrast to what they perceived as their Protestant righteousness. The trope of Spanish barbarity reemerged in the early nineteenth century in the context of the Spanish guerrilla war against the Napoleonic invasion and the wars of independence against Spain in Latin America.[2] During that era, a French diplomat claimed that "it is an error of geography to have assigned Spain to Europe. It belongs to Africa: blood, manners, language, the way of life and making war, in Spain everything is African."[3] It was not until 1912, however, that the term associated with this mythology of inherent Spanish cruelty and "backwardness" was coined: "the Black Legend."[4]

It is no coincidence that the term "Black Legend" emerged out of an era of increasingly globalized media that fostered the development of an international consciousness of what were perceived as national and "civilizational" hierarchies. As opposed to British or Russian officials who had developed a keen understanding of the importance of international public opinion decades earlier, Spanish elites were a bit slower to adjust to such developments. They learned about the international ramifications of unbridled repression the hard way: by having scrappy, incipient activist networks splash accounts of Spanish torture, mass arrests, and executions across the press of Europe and the Americas in the 1890s and early 1900s. The first campaigns in this series of international scandals were against Spanish atrocities in Cuba in the mid-1890s and opposition to *el proceso de Montjuich*, referring to the arrests, torture, and execution of those arrested for the Cambios Nuevos bombing of 1896. In fact, although the term was coined in 1912, the Spanish press used it sporadically starting in 1897 with an increased frequency from 1899 when the Montjuich campaign peaked and the colonial "desastre" was complete.[5]

Of course, the Spanish government was not unique in its brutality. Colonial atrocities committed by other European powers during this era matched or exceeded the death and suffering inflicted by their Iberian counterparts. Yet given Spain's low status among imperial powers (especially after the loss of Cuba, Puerto Rico, and the Philippines in 1898), activists could strategically leverage the historical image of "inquisitorial Spain"—the "land of Torquemada"—to paint the Spanish state as particularly insidious. The rhetorical power of lambasting Spain's "inquisitorial" nature rested on the prevalence of the ethics of modernity moving into the twentieth century. The centuries-old trope of Spanish cruelty fit perfectly into activist arguments that wielded the values of the ethics of modernity against peninsular torture in Montjuich Castle and colonial massacre in Cuba. These movements against the atrocities of the Spanish government (at home and abroad) and subsequent campaigns during the first decade of the twentieth century set the immediate historical context for the journalist Julián Juderías to coin the infamous term "Black Legend."

Against the "backwardness" of what was starting to be called the Black Legend, Montjuich activists across Europe, the Americas, and beyond counterposed the values of "modernity," "rationality," "progress," "science," and "humanity" culled from the era of the Enlightenment and the French Revolution. The confluence of these values formed a position from which socialists, republicans, freethinkers, anarchists, Freemasons, and anti-colonial nationalists could unite and constitute themselves as a nonsectarian antithesis to the image of the Black Legend. The campaign these activists formed against *el proceso de Montjuich* was waged "in the name of the rights of humanity," which were considered to be natural, universal rights that applied equally to everyone.[6] Though overlooked by historians, the foundational role of a universal notion of the "rights of humanity" in the Montjuich campaign's argument against torture and executions makes it one of the most significant international human rights campaigns of the turn of the twentieth century.

Ironically, perhaps, it was the Spanish government's lack of concern about the international impact of its repression that provided the spark that set off the Montjuich campaign. In August 1896 authorities released the anarchist engineer and professor at the University of Barcelona Fernando Tarrida del Mármol from Montjuich prison without concern about the possibility that he might flee abroad to tell his story—after all, dissidents and workers had been imprisoned and tortured in Spain for years without foreign outrage. This time, things would be different. Tarrida spared little time crossing the border to France. As soon as he could, he headed straight for Paris, where he met with the French anarchist Charles Malato in the office of *l'Intransigeant*. After Tarrida recounted the gruesome details of the torture in Montjuich, Malato introduced him to Henri Rochefort of *l'Intransigeant* and the Natanson brothers of *La Revue Blanche*.[7] Not long after, on October 15, Tarrida published the first article exposing the atrocities of Montjuich in *La Revue Blanche* under the title "One Month in the Prisons of Spain."[8] In this exposé, Tarrida recounted stories of unlawful imprisonment and mistreatment and included letters from some of those tortured and executed in 1894. The article produced a "profound sensation."[9] Over the following weeks excerpts of Tarrida's article were reprinted in *l'Intransigeant* and other sympathetic French papers.

Moreover, *L'Intransigeant* editor Henri Rochefort penned an article titled "Torquemada" that framed Spanish repression as a campaign against the irreligious that hearkened back "to the days of Philip II."[10] The paper argued that torture morally "banished [Spain] from humanity." Rochefort claimed to have inside knowledge that the real Cambios Nuevos bomber was still on the loose and was not even Spanish. Given the paper's support for "Cuba libre," it is unsurprising that Rochefort included Spanish atrocities in Cuba in his inquisitorial portrait. *L'Intransigeant* also published the first large-scale statement of an "official character" from the Montjuich prisoners. Signed by sixty-six prisoners including Teresa Claramunt and Pere Coromines, "belonging to diverse parties, many of whom have been quite far from politics," this letter was intended to "prove to the entire world the innocence of the men who have been involved in this *atentado*." The authors of this letter envisioned their audience as those with "a love of humanity and justice" rather than Spain or Europe specifically, and they sought to bring about "a movement that influences public opinion to rectify the action of justice" rather than appeal directly to the Spanish government to act.[11]

Not long after Fernando Tarrida del Mármol was released, his fellow anarchist prisoners Joan Montseny, Anselmo Lorenzo, and a number of their longtime cellmates who were not facing serious charges (in fact, many of them knew of no official charges at all) were transferred out of Montjuich to a different Barcelona prison.[12] The weary Montjuich prisoners were relieved to discover that they were provided with rice with seafood, meat, and potatoes at the new prison and allowed to communicate with prisoners in an open patio. Montseny, Lorenzo, and Francisco Cardenal continued to churn out protest letters to the press under assumed names.[13] In one such letter titled "For Humanity," Federico Urales (Joan Montseny) utilized the prevalent nationalist fear of sliding down the international hierarchy when he wrote that "[Spaniards] are deserving, very deserving of being the barbarians of the modern era. Years ago Turkey and Russia beat us; we have been outstanding students. Barcelona and the Philippines compete advantageously with Armenia and Siberia."[14] Their efforts did little to influence the situation, however. Montseny later recalled that "during the first months of our secret campaign, no element of the Catalan bourgeoisie stood at our side at all. . . . The Evil Castle, with its horrors, didn't exist for them."[15]

Yet, as a result of the traction that the campaign was developing in France and the high volume of leaked prison correspondence, the Madrid republican daily *El País* gradually started to pay attention, writing that "we are told from Barcelona that . . . the police are committing real abuses, imprisoning peaceful citizens that have never been, nor are, nor will be anarchists."[16] By the end of the month, *El País* published the collectively written prison letter, printed a summary of Rochefort's article, and started a column called "For the Love of Justice," which pointed out that "while public opinion was concerned with the wars in Cuba and the Philippines, little to no attention was given to the grave events that were developing in the interior . . . [but this is] very important, not only in terms of the honor and good name of Spain, [but also] the dignity and prestige of justice and the interests of humanity, which have a tight relationship with the so-called case of the anarchists."[17] Spanish national honor dictated that anarchists be treated humanely. After all, according to *El País*, Tarrida's article contained "very grave accusations that, if true, would put Spain well below the most savage African nations."[18] They would make Spain "more savage than Morocco and Turkey, and the Spanish people, if they consent to this great shame, are irresistibly lost for civilization."[19]

As months passed and the campaign started to take shape, Montseny, Lorenzo, and their comrades were transferred to yet another prison where a group of Filipino revolutionaries was being held.[20] When Spanish authorities in the Philippines discovered the nationalist conspiracy of Andrés Bonifacio and his revolutionary organization Katipunan in August 1896, they triggered a revolt that would become the Philippine Revolution. Filipino revolutionaries sought to capitalize on the Spanish government's entrenchment in the ongoing Cuban War of Independence, but their forces were ill prepared, poorly resourced, and outgunned against colonial forces.[21] The December 1896 execution of the nationalist icon José Rizal gave the movement an inspirational martyr while the imprisoned Filipino rebels who were shipped to Iberian prisons halfway around the world experienced their own personal martyrdom. They huddled together on the patio for warmth since they were still dressed for the tropical climate of their home country. Seeing their plight, Spanish prisoners tossed them shoes, pants, jackets, hats, and socks. After a while the political prisoners even opened a subscription for donations for the Filipino prisoners and asked their families to bring them old garments. Eventually, Montseny claimed, the government decided against incarcerating the Filipinos on the peninsula because of the potential intermixing of peninsular anarchists and nationalist rebels in the context of *el proceso de Montjuich* (a well-founded concern, as we will see shortly). Accordingly, a shipment of 269 Cuban and Filipino prisoners was sent to the African penal colony of Fernando Po in late February 1897.[22]

Though stretched thin by multiple anti-colonial insurrections abroad, back home authorities in Barcelona and Madrid seem to have been feeling confident about their response to the recent *atentado* after civil guard lieutenant Portas obtained confessions for the Cambios Nuevos bombing in August 1896. As more revelations of torture leaked to the press moving into November and December, however, official confidence started to waver right as the military trial of the supposed authors and accomplices of the bombing began.[23] Leading up to the trial, the governor of Montjuich had guards tear through the cells to confiscate any paper or ink. "Even in the prison cells there are echoes of their protests!" Montseny remembered the governor shouting. Unbeknownst to the governor, the paper and ink came from sympathetic guards, so by the evening the prisoners were restocked and writing.[24]

Meanwhile, as the first articles in support of the Montjuich prisoners were being published, the first public protest on their behalf was held at the Maison du Peuple in Paris on December 12, 1896. This protest meeting organized by the Franco-Spanish Revolutionary Committee was indicative of the composition, tone, and strategy of the emerging international Montjuich movement. With over five hundred in attendance, the protest featured speakers from across the Left, including anarchists like Charles Malato and Tortelier, who finished his speech with "Down with authority! Long live liberty!" to socialists like the Parisian deputy Marcel Sembat and the veteran of the Paris Commune Paule Mink. Charles Malato also read statements of solidarity from Louise Michel and Henri Rochefort.[25] Despite the fact that deputies of the Third Republic shared the stage with anarchists, there was a strong emphasis on unity in the name of "humanity." Malato argued that those in attendance were addressing a "question of humanity" and that although they may disagree about the shape of the future society, such atrocities aroused the contempt of anyone with a conscience and a heart.[26] A member of the Franco-Spanish Revolutionary Committee argued that such international unity was "an obligation of revolutionary solidarity and humanity." When the Parisian deputy Ernest Roche spoke, he described the Spanish victims as "the republicans," downplaying the role of revolutionary politics. In speaking about the need to unite this protest with outcries against Spanish abuses in Cuba, Roche proclaimed that "Paris is the head and the heart of the civilized universe; there isn't a human suffering or a social iniquity that does not have an immediate repercussion in its admirable brain."[27] Roche's comments point to the crucial role of nationalism in fueling not only the Spanish fear of being perceived as sub-European but also the French interest in highlighting the abuses of others to reaffirm their righteousness. This brand of nationalist humanitarianism provided a bridge to reach broader public opinion.

The Spanish government was far from oblivious to the rising tide of international public opinion. The day after the Paris protest meeting, Captain General Despujol wrote a telegram to the minister of war about the need to work with the Spanish embassy in Paris to combat the "truly grotesque views falsely attributed to the prosecutor of the anarchist trial by French periodicals."[28] Despujol feared that this case could spiral out of control: "What is to be done before radical France if every Spanish republican of every shade transcribes the atrocities of the Montjuich prisoners daily, copying them without doubt from anarchist pamphlets published after earlier analogous cases . . . ? What is to be done if some monarchist papers and even eminent conservative figures, without having examined the case, admit a priori that abuses and legal errors are possible and even probable and work in favor of one of the accused?"[29] Just as Spanish authorities were starting to feel confident about the outcomes of their offensive against anarchists, republicans, and dissidents, they suddenly found themselves on the defensive in the unfamiliar realm of international public opinion where dungeons, torture, and firing squads were useless.

The Spanish government was caught flat-footed by the start of the international campaign. For perhaps the first time Spanish elites were forced to consider how successful political repression required managing public opinion—especially *foreign* public opinion. *La Época* pinpointed the alien nature of this consideration by arguing that to a significant number of "public men," public opinion was nothing more than "a myth, a voice without substance."[30] Especially after debates over universal manhood suffrage in 1889–90, Spanish conservatives came to disdain public opinion as "a kind of God that certain people worship more than God the Creator" and characterize it as an "ephemeral" mob mentality. As opposed to liberals whose rhetoric revered "public opinion" as "the sovereign and absolute queen of the constitutional regime," conservatives had come to embrace what they called "national conscience" grounded in "Christian morality."[31]

Elite Spanish, and particularly conservative, disregard for international public opinion stood in sharp contrast with perspectives in Russia, the European state that had the most to fear from its exiled dissidents. In the years following the assassination of Czar Alexander II in 1881, czardom built a vast intelligence network to monitor and repress its dissidents that extended across the continent. In 1883 the Russian Foreign Agentura was founded to foil international conspiracies and counteract the perception that the Russian government was "barbaric." It manipulated the international press by hiring foreign journalists to write favorable articles in European periodicals, harassed émigré writers, and planted articles portraying Russia as the last bulwark against Jewish world dominance.[32] The Agentura even fabricated plots to demonstrate the imminence of the threat they were combating and the necessity of their repressive measures, such as an 1890 plot to assassinate Alexander III.[33] While the Russian government hounded its opponents across the continent, Spanish authorities deported as many "troublemakers" as possible without concern for what they did once they crossed the border. They never imagined that by releasing a prisoner like Tarrida they would unleash an international torrent of outrage that would threaten their ability to augment political repression.

From a media standpoint, it might have been prudent for military authorities in Catalonia to have delayed the Council of War trial against the alleged authors and accomplices of the Cambios Nuevos *atentado* until the outrage subsided. Sympathetic papers buzzed with the revelations of torture in late November and early December, and the trial provided a new outlet for the campaign to continue. If the trial had been put off a few months, the press might have run out of new material to sustain the momentum. But traditionalist army officers were not about to let the words of a few Parisian socialists or Madrid republicans influence their agenda.

The trial lasted from December 11 to 15, 1896. Despite the petitions of several newspapers and defendants, journalists were prohibited.[34] Along with the fact that the defendants often could not call their own witnesses, select their own lawyers, or represent themselves, the ban backfired by compounding the inquisitorial image of the proceedings. The most prominent defendant in the press was the young republican lawyer Pere Coromines. Although articles on the trial also mentioned supposed details of the main suspects, such as Ascheri or Mas, journalists were especially captivated by the travails of Coromines, whose education, social prestige, and supposedly moderate republicanism seemed to exemplify the injustice of the "clerical" reaction or demonstrate the insidious threat posed by "theorists of anarchy" depending on one's perspective.[35] Beyond the intrigue he generated, Coromines's status garnered some influential allies. Miguel de Unamuno and Joaquín Costa, prominent writers soon to be known as members of the "Generation of '98," organized a campaign for his release, as did former prime ministers of the First Republic Francisco Pi y Margall and Nicolás Salmerón and future liberal prime minister José Canalejas.[36] A number of professionals served as character witnesses at the trial, portraying Coromines as a centrist focused on sociological research rather than revolutionary politics. They included several doctors and a lawyer named Salvador Dalí, whose future son would take up painting. Dalí and fellow lawyer Amadeu Hurtado also advised Coromines's mandated military lawyer from the outside.[37]

Most of the other defendants lacked such influential supporters, and their personal plights received scant attention in the press. Despite minor leaks from the courtroom, the press published almost nothing of the most important development of the trial: the allegations of torture and widespread rejection of the confessions that it generated. On the last day of the trial the tortured defendants spoke openly about the abuse; some even removed articles of clothing to show their scars and bruises. Luis Mas was so mentally incapacitated from the cruelty he faced that he could not really testify at all.[38] However, very little of this information was reported. Initially there were twenty-eight death sentences and fifty-nine life sentences handed out, but a few days later the Council of War reduced it to eight death sentences (Ascheri, Nogués, Molas, Mas, Suñé, Jaume Vilella, Josep Vila, and Josep Pons) and more lenient prison terms.[39] The British anarchist paper *Freedom* claimed this reduction in executions as a victory, writing that it was "the result of a three month's agitation all over the world."[40] Yet despite the lack of press coverage on the courtroom torture allegations and the reduction of the sentences, the momentum against the "revival of the Inquisition" was only getting started.

The day after the announcement of the sentence in the Cambios Nuevos bombing case, Madrid socialists held the first protest meeting on Spanish soil, calling on "all those who have not had their sentiment of humanity completely crushed." The secretary of the Spanish Socialist Workers' Party (PSOE) emphasized that this issue "wasn't about the bourgeoisie and the proletariat, but rather to find out the accuracy of the allegations of torture in the French press . . . so that foreign newspapers can't say, as they have been saying, that Spain continues to be the country of Torquemada."[41] Even avowedly internationalist socialists were concerned about the national reputation.

Yet the Madrid protest was still an anomaly at this point since the campaign was spreading fastest in France and Belgium, where the echoes of the increasingly belligerent American press campaign against Spanish abuses in Cuba were being heard. Although the American press generally considered Captain General Arsenio Martínez Campos's initial response to the 1895 Cuban uprising to be humane and measured, this perspective shifted radically when he was replaced by the internationally notorious captain general of Catalonia, Valeriano Weyler.[42] Weyler's outlook was influenced by the time he spent as a military attaché in Washington during the American Civil War observing the vicious strategy of General Sherman, the "first to treat civilians as combatants in a modern war."[43] Whereas Martínez Campos merely organized a police response to the insurgency by guarding plantations and other strategic points from the rebels, Weyler launched an aggressive military strategy by pursuing the Cuban Liberation Army and confining the civilian population to "reconcentration camps" (sometimes referred to as "concentration camps") to prevent them from aiding the rebellion. Approximately 155,000–170,000 of the 400,000 reconcentrated Cubans died from disease and starvation.[44] Martínez Campos wrote to Cánovas that "as the representative of a civilized nation," he could not unleash cruelty on the Cuban people if they had not been vicious with the Spanish army. Weyler had no qualms about the ethics of warfare, famously quipping that "one does not make war with bonbons."[45]

In an effort to establish the moral legitimacy of an eventual American occupation of Cuba, the press in the United States attacked Spanish actions and increasingly alleged abuses against American citizens living in Cuba moving into the summer of 1896. The Spanish government simply responded to the American press campaign with censorship and the deportation of journalists.[46]

As would become evident with its response to the Montjuich campaign, the Spanish government did not fully understand the ramifications of international public opinion and the corresponding need for a proactive response to antagonistic press campaigns. Since journalists were prohibited from embedding themselves with the Spanish army, they followed the Cuban rebels who spoon-fed the American media their accounts of Spanish abuses.[47]

The American press campaign, fed by the bitter rivalry between Pulitzer's *World* and Hearst's *Journal*, reached new levels of intensity in the winter of 1896–97 at the same time that the Montjuich atrocities were receiving their first major international recognition with protests across France and Belgium.[48] Building on the momentum of the meetings in support of the Cuban insurrection that had been organized across France months earlier, this new wave of protest combined popular outrage against Spain's colonial and domestic atrocities.[49] The December 28 protest organized by the "Scientific International" featured a member of the French Committee of Cuba Libre,

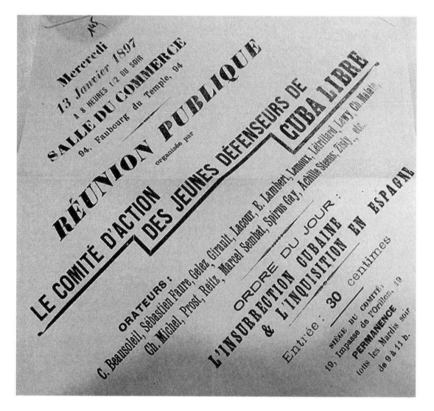

FIGURE 7. Flyer for Paris protest meeting against Spanish repression in Cuba and Barcelona. Archives de la Préfecture de Police, Ba 138, Explosions en Espagne de 1897–1898.

as well as anarchists Sébastien Faure, who spoke on the centrality of Jesuit-ism in the Spanish reaction, and Charles Malato, who lauded the interracial nature of the Cuban Liberation Army and argued that Spanish actions in Cuba "trampled all of their rights."[50] The meeting's announcement empha-sized the urgency of a nonsectarian approach in the face of such atrocities: "On this terrain, the differences of school disappear; sincere revolutionary socialists and anarchists should find themselves in accord to protest against the crimes of the Spanish government."[51]

Just as the critics of the monarchy were connecting Cuba and the Philip-pines with Montjuich, so too were its defenders. Since the start of the most recent Cuban conflict in 1895, the Spanish press had made a conscious effort to taint the insurrection by calling the Cuban rebels "anarchist dynamiters." In part this stemmed from the Cuban use of dynamite to destroy railroads, telegraphs, and other infrastructure in their guerrilla struggle, and from the collaboration of anarchists and Cuban nationalists in the failed assassina-tion attempt on Captain General Weyler in April 1896.[52] Nevertheless, the primary motive was to discredit the Cuban Liberation Army by associating it with anarchism. This was evident in La Época's description of a January 5, 1897, Parisian protest meeting as an "anarcho-filibuster demonstration."[53] This protest meeting organized by the anarchist Le Libertaire attracted two to three thousand people to hear the usual lineup of speakers, such as Faure and Malato, who compared Montjuich to the Haymarket martyrs ten years earlier.[54] But this time approximately two hundred rowdy protesters shout-ing, "Down with the executioners!" and "Death to Cánovas!" and singing the "Carmagnole" and "Ça ira" marched to the Spanish embassy. When they arrived, they shouted, "Vive Cuba libre!" and "Vive Maceo!" (honoring the recently deceased Afro-Cuban general) before the police charged, injuring some with their sabers and arresting others, including Ramón Sempau and Lorenzo Portet.[55] The conservative Spanish press was eager to emphasize that the embassy protest was given scant attention in France and condemned by "respectable" papers.[56] Over the course of the next week, Parisian anar-chists organized smaller neighborhood events against "Inquisitorial Spain," and Cuba Libre solidarity groups were increasingly incorporating peninsular oppression into their protests.[57] In January 1897 Dutch anarchist Ferdinand Domela Nieuwenhuis organized a protest in conjunction with the Socialiste-nbond in front of the Spanish embassy in The Hague.[58]

That month, Tarrida del Mármol fled to Portsmouth, England, "to thwart the infernal malice of the Spanish government, which sought to implicate me in a ridiculous history of bombs, to obtain my extradition." From the safety of liberal England, he published another article in La Revue Blanche called "To the Inquisitors of Spain." Apart from his attacks on the colonial and peninsular crimes of the monarchy, Tarrida aimed to persuade a moderate audience by presenting himself as neither unpatriotic nor radical. He clarified, "I do not intend to attack Spain, rather that which dishonors it." He emphasized that although the Cuban rebel was attacked as a "filibuster," the peninsular rebel as an "anarchist," and the Filipino rebel as a "Freemason," "I am Cuban, but not a filibuster; an autonomist, but not an anarchist; a freethinker, but not a Freemason." Rather than an anarchist, he took great care to present himself to the world as a non-ideological defender of "human liberty and dignity."[59]

Not long after Tarrida arrived in England, the campaign followed him. On January 28, 1897, at the Club and Institute Union Hall, "a humanitarian protest against the new Inquisition" was held that mirrored earlier French mobilizations in its range of speakers and universal outlook. The first orator was Joseph Perry, editor of *Freedom: A Journal of Anarchist Communism*, who argued, "All this is done in the name of law and order—the order which ruled at Warsaw after the people had been massacred, the order in the name of which John Brown and the Chicago Anarchists, Vaillant and Pallás were killed—the peace which we see in Madagascar, in Rhodesia, in Ireland." Perry's homage to anti-imperialist, anti-racist, and anarchist struggle framed the incipient Montjuich campaign within a much wider pantheon of resistance with which the British Left was largely familiar. J. C. Kenworthy, a Tolstoyan pastor active with the Land Colonisation Society, which sought to relocate people from the cities to rural cooperatives, also compared the torture in Montjuich to the suffering of Irish prisoners before echoing Perry's anarchist critique of the state: "This is done by persons who in ordinary life need not be monsters but who are under a fascination perpetrated for centuries, the superstition of government by force." Other prominent anarchists spoke, such as Louise Michel, Sam Mainwaring, and Pyotr Kropotkin, who pointed out that the Spanish government had been torturing prisoners for years since the aftermath of the Gran Vía and Liceo bombings and argued that "everywhere, where there is a prison there is torture."[60] The explosive dynamic between excessive repression and international backlash was taking shape.

Apart from the anarchists, Herbert Burrows of the Social Democratic Federation and former Russian populist leader Nikolai Tchaikovsky spoke, and Joseph Perry read letters of support from the socialists Tom Mann, Robert Blatchford, Rev. Steward Headlam, the artist and illustrator Walter Crane, Edward Carpenter, who called the torture a "violation at once of justice, good sense and humanity," and Humanitarian League founder and animal rights pioneer Henry S. Salt, who argued that "if *Cruelty* is international, that is all the more reason why *Humanity* should be international also, and why a protest of this sort should be made as worldwide as possible." Reflecting the interest that *Freedom* had in Turkish oppression of Armenians, Perry also read a letter of solidarity from Avetis Nazarbek, editor of the Armenian paper *Hentchak*. The nonsectarian outlook of the meeting was reflected in words from the exiled Russian socialist Felix Volkhovsky, who wrote, "I am no Anarchist myself, but it is indifferent to me what is the platform or the doings of any victim of such a mockery of justice."[61]

Taking a nonsectarian stance against extreme injustice in far-off places, a hallmark of humanitarian and modern human rights politics, was central to Volkhovsky's political outlook since he was a member of the Society of Friends of Russian Freedom and onetime editor of its newspaper, *Free Russia*.[62] Founded in 1890 by Russian émigrés and sympathetic British progressives, the Society of Friends of Russian Freedom (SFRF) sought "to aid, to the extent of its powers, the Russian patriots who are trying to obtain for their country that Political Freedom and Self-government which Western nations have enjoyed for generations."[63] During this era invectives against injustice often rested on nationalist reaffirmations of advanced righteousness. Although the society's founders included Kropotkin and Sergei Kravchinskii (known as Stepniak, the former assassin and author of *Underground Russia*), *Free Russia*, which Stepniak edited for a while, distanced itself as much as possible from anything that smacked of political violence, anarchism, or socialist revolution.[64] The paper limited itself to highlighting abuses and presenting a sympathetic portrayal of liberal Russian democrats yearning for political freedoms. When William Morris proposed that the establishment of socialism in Britain was an important prerequisite for Russian liberation at a society meeting in 1891, SFRF members critiqued him for bringing British politics into the conversation. For many progressive campaigners, domestic neutrality was important to unite public opinion against foreign "savagery." Stepniak understood this dynamic perfectly, and so he clarified in his writings in the British press that there was no need to alter the political system of the United Kingdom.[65] The society expanded to have chapters in six British cities, *Free Russia* was distributed across western and central Europe and translated into Russian for clandestine delivery to Saint Petersburg, a German edition of *Free Russia* was founded in Switzerland, and Stepniak even founded an American Society of the Friends of Russian Freedom in Boston in 1891 with Mark Twain, William Lloyd Garrison, and explorer George Kennan. Despite an up-and-down existence and a small membership of predominantly affluent liberals, groups were established in several major cities, including a New York branch cofounded by Emma Goldman.[66]

The influence of the SFRF on the direction of the Montjuich campaign in Britain was evident in the participation of not only Volkhovsky but also fellow SFRF member Herbert Burrows and *Free Russia* collaborator Walter Crane in the late January protest. The next month, Burrows and Crane joined a number of the other speakers at the protest, including Perry, Carpenter, Headlam, and Salt, in forming a commission that went to deliver a letter of protest to the Spanish ambassador. When their request to meet with the ambassador was rejected, they returned the next morning with Cunninghame Graham of the Scottish Labour Party and Gertrude L. Mallet of the SFRF. They delivered their protest letter against abuses occurring "under a civilised government" and called for the end of acts "opposed to all human feeling and principles." Despite three follow-up letters, there was no response from the Spanish embassy. Perry also sent letters to officials in the Foreign Office and the Royal Courts of Justice, who said that unless British subjects were injured, the matter could not be raised in the House of Commons (although atrocities against Armenians and Cretans were being similarly discussed in the House at the time). On February 22, however, MP Patrick O'Brien raised the accusations of torture in the House of Commons where it was agreed to make an inquiry of the Spanish government on the matter.[67]

Building off of "the politics of pressure groups" developed by earlier humanitarian campaigns, these Montjuich protest actions in Britain coalesced into the Spanish Atrocities Committee (SAC).[68] Although the first officially constituted British group in this campaign was the Anglo-Spanish Anti-Inquisitorial Club, which included Herbert Spencer, William Gladstone, Jaime Brossa, and Joseph Perry, it was really the SAC that spearheaded the campaign in the United Kingdom. The SAC included a range of leftist figures, including Edward Carpenter, SFRF collaborator Walter Crane, Gertrude L. Mallet of the SFRF, J. Frederick Green of the SFRF and the Fabian Society, Henry S. Salt of the Humanitarian League, Paul Campbell of the Independent Labour Party, Cunninghame Graham of the Scottish Labour Party, James McDonald from the London Trades Council, W. G. Barwick of the Social Democratic Federation (SDF), Herbert Burrows of the SFRF and the SDF, and Joseph Perry and Nannie Florence Dryhurst of the Freedom Anarchist-Communist Group. The guiding light of the campaign in England was always Joseph Perry, whose real name was Joseph Presburg. He was an insurance agent who had been a part of the Socialist League before joining the Freedom Group in 1895. Quickly, he became extremely active in the group and was the driving force of the SAC.

Perry's comrade Nannie Florence Dryhurst was also committed to exposing atrocities around the globe. Born in Dublin in 1856, Dryhurst was devoted to the Irish freedom struggle before identifying with anarchism and joining the Freedom Group around 1890. For a brief time in 1894, she edited *Freedom*, and she participated with Louise Michel in the anarchist women's group *L'Union internationale des femmes*.[69] A gifted linguist, Dryhurst translated her close friend Kropotkin's *The Great French Revolution 1789–1793* into English from the original French, and she learned Georgian from former Georgian aristocrat turned anarchist communist Varlaam Cherkesov (or Tcherkesoff) before traveling to Georgia in 1903 to learn about Russian oppression of the Georgian people.[70] During the first decade of the twentieth century, Dryhurst met with activists from Persia, Poland, Georgia, Finland, and Egypt as well as Sinn Feiners, and she became the secretary of the Nationalities and Subject Races Committee.[71] Yet her formal advocacy for oppressed peoples around the world started with the Montjuich prisoners and the Spanish Atrocities Committee in 1897.

After the first wave of international protests, the momentum of the Montjuich campaign declined without ceasing altogether. In part this was because there were no shocking new revelations during this period, but perhaps as importantly it owed to the shift of European interest in atrocities from Spain to Turkey. Ever since the Greek uprisings of the early 1820s that would culminate in Greek independence from the Ottoman Empire in 1830, Europe had been flooded with tales of Turkish atrocities. In 1823 a London Greek Committee was formed to publicize Turkish abuses such as the infamous Scio massacre of 1822, while ignoring or downplaying Greek atrocities, and to pressure the British government to support Greek independence. A clear precedent for both the SFRF and SAC, the London Greek Committee included a number of MPs and famous intellectuals such as Lord Byron, Jeremy Bentham, and David Ricardo.[72] Western European attention was captivated again in the 1870s by Ottoman abuses in Bulgaria as William Gladstone organized a speaking campaign across Britain. Most recently, in 1897 a conflict emerged over the Ottoman island of Crete, culminating in a war between Greece and its former imperial rulers. European opinion was enraptured with this "east versus west" conflict and took every opportunity to portray the Turks as brutal oppressors in the context of the Hamidian massacres of Armenians. The oppression of the Armenians had been so well known internationally since the start of the 1890s that it had become a standard for "inhumanity." Massacres of Armenians in 1894 and 1895 led to the creation of a number of foreign advocacy groups such as the Anglo-Armenian Association, the British Armenia Committee, the Scottish Armenian Association, and the Comité Franco-Arménien (the older Eastern Question Association had been publicizing abuses against Armenians for decades).[73] The international notoriety of the Armenian plight was evident in American newspaper coverage of Weyler's abuses in Cuba with the *San Francisco Examiner* arguing that "Cuba is our Armenia" and the *New York Journal* cautioning, "The American people will not tolerate in the Western Hemisphere the methods of the Turkish savages in Armenia."[74] For several months starting in early February 1897, *L'Intransigeant* put the Montjuich campaign on the back burner to attack Turkish "barbarity" against Greeks in Crete with a significant though lesser focus on Turkish massacres of Armenians. Daily front-page articles on the developing Greco-Turkish War overshadowed Charles Malato's occasional updates on the plight of the Barcelona prisoners.[75] By the 1890s, a thirst for new tales of exotic atrocities had developed among the Western European public, but campaigners had to struggle to get their cause into the headlines.

L'Intransigeant also took great care to document the groundswell of protests that emerged in support of Crete and Greece, including large demonstrations organized mainly by Greek émigrés and students in cities such as Milan, Chicago, Cairo, London, Manchester, Vienna, and Brussels.[76] There were also protest meetings throughout France, such as a Parisian event organized in February by "students of the antisemitic circle of boulevard Saint-Michel" that culminated in a crowd of three hundred demonstrators cheering Henri Rochefort outside of *L'Intransigeant*'s editorial office.[77] Demonstrators at another anti-Turkish demonstration in France chanted, "Long live Greece! Down with the Jews!"[78] This was the same month that the royalist Jules Guérin reestablished the Ligue nationale antisémitique.[79]

Populist antisemitism was simmering in the months leading up to the start of the campaign for the revision of the sentence of Captain Alfred Dreyfus, and Rochefort was at its center. While references to Dreyfus's alleged treason had largely disappeared from the French press as he languished on Devil's Island, Rochefort continued to write articles with titles such as "The Traitor Dreyfus" alongside pieces about "inquisitorial" Spain.[80] Although Rochefort's coverage of the Montjuich campaign rarely hinted at his antisemitism, his no doubt contradictory relation to campaigns for justice was not as strange or as uncommon as it might at first appear, especially given long-standing antisemitism among the French Left. Discourses of human rights and humanitarianism have always accommodated themselves within conflictual political contexts and served the complex purposes of those who have wielded them. Rochefort was no different, nor was Alejandro Lerroux, editor of the Spanish republican paper *El País*.

Lerroux's coverage of the Montjuich campaign was more consistent than Rochefort's, since *El País* was a Spanish paper, but it was still overshadowed by coverage of the colonial wars in Cuba and the Philippines. Yet *El País* had invested too much support in the Spanish war effort in Cuba to acknowledge General Weyler's extreme brutality despite its ongoing campaign against the monarchy's "inquisitorial" practices. *"El País* is prepared to raise its voice for all human causes," Lerroux's paper wrote of itself, including the "horrors in Crete" perpetrated by "Muslim barbarism," the torture of anarchists, the Spanish execution of Filipino nationalist figure José Rizal, and even the mistreatment of Cuban POWs brought to Spain, but not the Cuban war effort itself.[81] When describing the crimes of the monarchy, *El País* would write "the same in Montjuich as in the Philippines" without a mention of Cuba.[82] Rochefort's antisemitism and Lerroux's imperialism marked the limits of their interest in "human causes."

Nevertheless, the Barcelona prisoners had few allies in Spain apart from *El País, El Diluvio*, and a few other minor papers. In early March 1897 *El País* published a letter from sixty Montjuich prisoners protesting the fact that they had only been permitted one visit from their families over the past nine months.[83] Later that month, mothers and wives of the prisoners took matters into their own hands by visiting the captain general en masse and successfully demanding that he allow them to visit their loved ones.[84] Around the same time, a correspondent from *El País* visited Barcelona's national prison to report on conditions firsthand. His investigation confirmed allegations of overcrowded cells and prisoner mistreatment.[85] *El País* may have gotten the idea of sending a correspondent to visit a Barcelona prison from *Frankfürter Zeitung*, which had sent its own reporter to Barcelona a month earlier. The German reporter spoke with lawyers, former prisoners, friends, relatives, and even military officials who attested to the ghostly appearance of the main suspects at their trial. He concluded, "I am sorry to have to confess that I have acquired the strongest conviction that the published details of the Barcelona horrors are quite correctly reported—perhaps, even, they understate what has happened."[86] Interest in the "revival of the Spanish inquisition" had spread to Germany by the start of 1897 with demonstrations and reports in a number of newspapers including the anarchist *Der Sozialist* and SPD organ *Vorwärts* in addition to "several capitalist papers."[87] A key figure in the collective behind *Der Sozialist* was Gustav Landauer, who penned the widely distributed pamphlet *Die Justizgreuel von Barcelona*.[88] A debate over the plight of two German prisoners in Barcelona developed in the Reichstag. In response to defenses of the legitimacy of torture for anarchists, the novelist Friedrich Spielhagen wrote an article titled "Thou Shalt Not Torture" in a Vienna paper that argued that this commandment was not included in the Ten Commandments because they were intended for men and torture was not fit for rational human beings. Protest meetings were also organized in Switzerland and Norway, and a New York City group called Jovenes Anarquistas (Anarchist Youth) published the pamphlet *Savage Spain*. In the spring of 1897 Emma Goldman spearheaded a New York City group that organized a multiethnic protest outside of the Spanish consulate. Likewise, in Philadelphia Voltairine de Cleyre kicked off a Montjuich campaign by writing letters to Congress and disseminating fifty thousand copies of a pamphlet called *The Modern Inquisition in Spain*.[89] Protests, subscriptions to raise money for the prisoners, and supportive propaganda were also organized in Argentina, Uruguay, Cuba, Brazil, and elsewhere in Latin America.[90]

As the final trial for the primary suspects in the Cambios Nuevos bombing approached in late April 1897, supporters of the Spanish prisoners attempted to maintain public interest in the case, "although currently the attention of Europe is turned to the Helladic peninsula," as Charles Malato pointed out.[91] Although Captain General Despujol pushed for twenty executions, rather than the initial ruling of eight, domestic and international pressure seems to have been influential not only in convincing the tribunal to allow the press to witness the proceedings, but ultimately in reducing, rather than raising, the number of death sentences from eight to five.[92] The men condemned to death were the supposed bomber, Ascheri, and his alleged accomplices, Mas, Molas, and Nogués, as well as Joan Alsina, who had not been given the death sentence in the earlier ruling. Thirteen were sentenced to eighteen to twenty years as accomplices, and another seven were given ten years for conspiracy.[93] The republican lawyer Pere Coromines was fortunate enough to have been among the sixty-two prisoners who were acquitted along with anarchist unionist Teresa Claramunt.

On May 3, 1897, the day before the execution, the captain general mobilized squads of police and military to guard the castle while down in Barcelona the police were tearing down anonymous posters that said, "Murder them, you killers. Soon the anarchists will be avenged!"[94] All functions at the Liceo were suspended for the day of the execution and the day after out of concern about a sequel to the *atentado* of 1894.[95] That day Francisca Saperas and her daughter Salud Borrás were transported from the women's prison up to Montjuich to participate in compulsory weddings with their *compañeros* Tomás Ascheri and Luis Mas before their executions. Antonio Nogués was also forced to marry his *compañera*. If they did not comply, their children would be taken away. Mas seems to have agreed to the wedding in order to see Borrás once more before he died.[96] Teresa Claramunt was deeply saddened to see the coach bearing the *compañeras* of the soon-to-be-executed prisoners enter the castle. To her, the marriages were merely "an act to give pleasure to several frocked Jesuits and the tiger, [Judge] Marzo." She was aghast at the "weakness" of the women who consented to the ceremonies, but she was relieved to see that at least Nogués refused at the last minute.[97] Nogués, Molas, and Alsina had been singing anarchist hymns all day in the chapel to the aggravation of Ascheri who was trying to pray.[98]

But there was no more singing the next morning, May 4, 1897, when the Montjuich Castle door swung open at the break of dawn. Instead, the band of bugles marched out in front of the soldiers of the firing squad. Behind them followed clergy holding a cross in front of the five prisoners. Teresa Claramunt witnessed the slow march of the condemned through her cell window. To her, Ascheri moved "like a robot."[99] Francisco Gana also peered out of his cell window to see Alsina walking upright shouting, "Assassins! Assassins! We are innocent; it is murder!"[100] Lurking behind the prisoners were the forensic doctors who would give the final word on their imminent demise. *El País* described the prisoners as "serene" as they looked out at the crowd of onlookers, mostly women, which was so massive that the police and military struggled to contain it. As they were put on their knees in the castle moat, they shouted, "We are innocent!" "This is an inquisition!" and "¡Viva la anarquía!" Only Ascheri remained silent and kissed the cross. A wave of the commander's handkerchief cut short the cries of anguish with a volley of bullets.[101]

CHAPTER 8

Germinal

On May 30, 1897, weeks after the execution of the Montjuich prisoners, a multinational crowd of 2,500 supporters gathered in London's Trafalgar Square to attend a protest organized by the Spanish Atrocities Committee against the Spanish monarchy's "outrages on humanity and civilisation" and to demand respect for "the rights of humanity."[1] Though the execution of the alleged conspirators behind the Cambios Nuevos *atentado* had drained momentum from the campaign, and papers like the Spanish *El País* had fallen silent moving into the summer (apart from occasional prison letters and articles from Joan Montseny), the transnational network of anarchists at the heart of the campaign pressed onward.[2] In front of a large red flag wafting in the breeze, Fernando Tarrida del Mármol recounted the atrocities committed by General Weyler in Cuba, General Polavieja in the Philippines, and Narciso Portas in Montjuich from his new book *Les Inquisiteurs d'Espagne: Montjuich, Cuba, Philippines*.[3] That day organizers distributed a similar text published by the SAC titled *Revival of the Inquisition*. In addition to Tarrida del Mármol, who spoke on behalf of the Parisian *Revue Blanche*, Charles Malato lambasted Turkish massacres of Armenians with his diatribe against Spanish crimes on behalf of the Parisian *L'Intransigeant*. Other speakers including Joseph Perry of SAC and *Freedom*, Keir Hardie of the Independent Labour Party, and J. F. Green of the SFRF critiqued prison conditions in England and Ireland and referenced Oscar Wilde's letter on Reading Prison in addition to highlighting Spanish abuses.[4]

In the crowd that day was the well-known American anarchist Voltairine de Cleyre, who had journeyed to the United Kingdom for a speaking tour, and the not-so-well-known Italian anarchist Michele Angiolillo. Or rather, Angiolillo was unfamiliar to the thousands who flocked to Trafalgar Square that day, but he was quite well known to French authorities as a dangerous "anarchist of action," and his name would soon be well known among the crowd and far beyond. Born June 5, 1871, in Foggia, Angiolillo joined the Italian army in 1892 but was imprisoned for subversive propaganda. It was likely during his incarceration that he shifted from his early republicanism to anarchism in 1894. The next year, he fled to Marseille after being sentenced to eighteen months' imprisonment for protesting Prime Minister Crispi and writing a seditious letter attacking the prosecutor.[5] Having worked in a print shop back in Foggia, he found similar work for a few months while hiding out in southern France before traveling in late 1895 to Barcelona, where he assumed the identity of Giuseppe Santo.[6] He soon joined the workshop of the anarchist sociological journal *La Ciencia Social*, recently founded by Anselmo Lorenzo, where he worked alongside Tomás Ascheri (who would be accused of masterminding the Cambios Nuevos bombing about a year later) and fellow Montjuich prisoner Cayetano Oller.[7] Reports from the French consul in Barcelona in April 1896 include Angiolillo among anarchists in attendance at alleged bomb-making meetings, some of which were held at the Centro de Carreteros where the Cambios Nuevos bombing was allegedly hatched.[8]

After the bombing of Cambios Nuevos, *La Ciencia Social* was shut down; Ascheri, Oller, and Lorenzo were imprisoned; and Angiolillo escaped from Barcelona, never to return.[9] For a short time he returned to Marseille where he allegedly planned an attack against Kaiser Wilhelm II and Italian king Umberto I on Wilhelm's visit to Italy. In the course of his plotting, Angiolillo was arrested for adopting a false identity and deported to Belgium in November 1896. There he worked in the print shop of the president of the Belgian Socialist Party and met Ramón Sempau, a lawyer, coeditor of the republican *El Diluvio*, and member of the Catalan intellectual circle Colla del Foc Nou who had fled Barcelona after the bombing like Angiolillo.[10]

And like Angiolillo, Sempau dreamed of avenging the Montjuich martyrs. In Paris he was arrested at the rowdy demonstration in front of the Spanish embassy in January before crossing into Belgium. Undoubtedly the two men had a number of friends in common from the tightly knit world

FIGURE 8.   Michele Angiolillo. *Blanco y Negro*, August 21, 1897.

of the Barcelona radical press, and quite possibly they discussed ideas about fighting back against the wave of repression that had forced them both out of Barcelona.[11] After all, according to Elisée Reclus, Angiolillo developed the idea of assassinating the Spanish king Alfonso XIII and his mother, the queen regent, during his time in Belgium.[12] Angiolillo's coworkers at the print shop remembered how often he voiced his outrage at the Montjuich torture and defended propaganda by the deed.[13] Soon Sempau and Angiolillo would part ways. They would never see each other again, but they would both see Spain again quite soon.

In March 1897 Angiolillo traveled to London where he got another typography job at a print shop alongside Catalan anarchist Jaime Vidal. Vidal introduced Angiolillo to the prominent German anarchist unionist Rudolf Rocker, and the three of them socialized on occasion in Vidal's apartment. In his memoirs, Rocker remembered Angiolillo as an intelligent man who "always carried with him in his bag one or another of the cheap editions of the classics of the Bibliothèque Universelle, whose margins were full of marks and annotations that probably only he could read."[14] To Rocker, Angiolillo had a "thin, pale face framed by a short beard and thoughtful eyes that looked out through his glasses, giving the impression of a well-educated man with moderate manners so that he could have been taken for a doctor. He was always serious in his manner of being and spontaneously inspired respect. . . . [When he ate] I admired the long, thin fingers of his well-cared-for hands, which had something aristocratic about them." Although he was serious, Angiolillo always carried candies for the local children he had befriended, who called him "Uncle Noni."[15] During his brief stay in London, Angiolillo attended the SAC rally in Trafalgar Square in late May and participated in a small private meeting of eight or nine comrades, including former Montjuich prisoners Juan Bautista Oller, Francisco Gana, and Tarrida del Mármol as well as Rudolf Rocker.[16] At the request of an English comrade, Gana told of his torment and showed his scars. Rocker recounted the scene as follows:

> That night when [Gana] showed us his crippled limbs and the scars that the cruel torturers had left on his body, we understood that it was one thing to read about the facts in the papers and another to hear them from the very lips of one of the victims. Gana had recounted his story without excitation; exactly because of this the impression was stronger. We were all left petrified and several minutes went by before anyone could find any words of indignation. Only Angiolillo didn't say anything. But shortly after he stood up all of a sudden, said goodbye to us tersely, and left.[17]

That was the last time Rocker saw Angiolillo. Little else is known about his time in London, but when he left for France he carried a newly acquired 38 mm revolver with him.

In Paris Angiolillo got in touch with a group of Spanish and French anarchists and their allies, including Anselmo Lorenzo, Charles Malato, Francisco Ferrer, and Henri Rochefort, who told Angiolillo that the man to see was the Puerto Rican nationalist icon and Parisian delegate of the Cuban Revolutionary Party, Dr. Ramón Emeterio Betances.[18] The radical journalist Luis Bonafoux claimed that Betances dissuaded Angiolillo from targeting the young king and his mother, who were not making policy decisions, and encouraged him to assassinate Prime Minister Cánovas.[19] Angiolillo allegedly agreed. According to a police informant, the assassination was planned in a Parisian restaurant by Sébastien Faure, *Les Temps nouveaux* editor Jean Grave, the German Jewish anarchist Siegfried Nacht, and Fernando Tarrida del Mármol, who had recently returned to France from England. The plan, according to the informant, also included assassinating French president Faure to avenge Angiolillo after taking out Cánovas.[20] There is no other corroborating evidence for these conspiracies, but it is possible that Angiolillo had some help. Contemporary accounts vary about whether Angiolillo's return to Spain was financed by Betances, Rochefort, Malato, or some combination thereof.[21] Yet historian Francesco Tamburini highly doubts that Angiolillo was given any significant financial support beyond minor donations since he was described as carrying a thin suitcase containing nothing more than a copy of Tarrida's *Les Inquisiteurs*, "the book that he read and reread," when he stayed with the French anarchist Antoine Antignac in Bordeaux on his way south. Shortly before Angiolillo was scheduled to leave, Antignac said, "'Au revoir, comrade.' 'No, we shall not meet again. Farewell.' At this moment [Angiolillo's] eyes blazed behind his glasses. We were stupefied."[22]

As Angiolillo plotted to avenge the Montjuich martyrs, the prisoners who were fortunate enough to be acquitted at the Cambios Nuevos trial found themselves in legal limbo. They were informed that they had fifteen days to leave the country or they would be shipped to the African penal colony Río de Oro, tantamount to a death sentence given its high mortality rate.[23] Prime Minister Cánovas explained that since France, Italy, and Germany refused to take the prisoners, the government was left with little choice. The deep effect the international campaign against the "revival of the Inquisition" had made on Spanish elites was evident in the protest that the proposed deportation of innocent people to Río de Oro sparked in mainstream circles. For example, the liberal *El Imparcial*, which months earlier had demanded that all anarchists be "treated as wolves and exterminated as wolves are exterminated," criticized the deportation of anarchists to Africa, asking, "Where can they go in that country of savages?"[24] For *El Imparcial*, anarchists had returned to humanity at a level just above the "savages." It was no longer proper to exterminate them, but, like wolves, they were still thought to be dangerous. Therefore, *El Imparcial* opposed Cánovas's suggestion that they could be sent to Fernando Po since "there are many deported *ñáñigos* [Afro-Cubans] and there is a risk that they will unite with the anarchists." Anarchist bombings and anti-colonial risings haunted the withering Spanish Empire, but the specter of their unity was too much to stomach. *El Imparcial* proposed sending the anarchists to a deserted island in Oceania or the Carolinas where they could put their ideas into practice for themselves without harming anyone else. "This," *El Imparcial* argued, "would be the most human."[25]

Opposition to the deportation of anarchists to Africa forced Spanish authorities to creatively rethink their options. The easiest outlet for anarchist deportation was always France, yet the French were not fond of unexpected anarchist deliveries. In early April the French consul in Barcelona got wind of plans to expel 150 to 160 anarchists to France, which led the French government to warn Spain not to send anyone who was not a French national.[26] Nevertheless, on June 12, 1897, fifty-two prisoners including Anselmo Lorenzo, Francisco Gana, Francisca Saperas and her daughter Salud Borrás, Teresa Maymí, Asunción Vallvé, and Juan Esteve were "literally abandoned" just across the border in Cerbère without any documentation. Although the fear of foreign anarchists was exacerbated by the failed assassination attempt on President Félix Faure the following day, the French government reluctantly accepted the Spanish exiles to avoid an incident with the firm understanding that such episodes would not be repeated.[27]

Since the Spanish government had exhausted the good graces of neighboring France, they decided to send their next shipment of former Montjuich prisoners to Britain. On July 15, 1897, Spanish authorities loaded twenty-eight anarchists including Joan Montseny and Teresa Claramunt onto the ship *Isla de Luzón* bound for Liverpool. The prisoners had to pay the cost of their own deportation. Earlier that month, the Barcelona civil government casually asked a British government representative about their immigration policy, and when they heard that Britain had open borders, the plan to deport the prisoners was put in motion without informing the United Kingdom.[28]

As the days passed, word spread in England of the impending arrival of a shipload of unannounced anarchists. On July 22, the British secretary of state announced that "the British Government are not disposed to receive more anarchists in the United Kingdom."[29] The British government could not have been very surprised at the news since the press had been speculating about it for months.[30] On July 23 a deal was arranged where the British would allow the ship to arrive in Liverpool in exchange for a Spanish promise not to send any more anarchists without approval.[31] The *Isla de Luzón* pulled into Liverpool harbor on the evening of July 28.

Shortly thereafter, a group of English workers took the weary anarchists to a festive reception at a local hall. They were given a warm welcome, but the language barrier was difficult to overcome. "The men and women looked at us, caressed us with care, they kissed us fraternally. What a shame they couldn't understand us!" The only person who spoke some Spanish was a police officer who helped out as much as he could. The best way to transcend the difficulties in communication was through song. The Catalans sang "¡Arre, Moreu!" and "Les flors de Maig" to warm applause. Then, to finish the festivities, the English workers sang "God Save the Queen." "How strange that seemed to us!" Montseny remarked. It was immediately evident to the exiled anarchists that they were in a very different country, one "where the police are more attentive and helpful than a duke's servant and where the men of advanced ideas . . . seriously sing a song that calls for God to save the [queen]."[32]

The day after their arrival, Prime Minister Cánovas persisted in his story that the anarchists were not sent to Liverpool officially but instead traveled voluntarily.[33] By the next day, however, he shifted toward emphasizing that there was no official protest on the part of the United Kingdom against the Spanish deportation.[34] With a shipment of anarchists sent to England, another group deposited across the border in France, and a decline in the European coverage of the torture allegations, the Spanish authorities may have started to feel confident that they were moving on from Montjuich. Their efforts to counteract the international campaign were buoyed by a letter written by a Swedish diplomat about his experience visiting Montjuich that was published in the *Times* on July 26. This diplomat, "free from any bias on the subject" according to the *Times*, spent "nearly four hours" touring the prison. He found that "all the cells are excellent, healthy, and light," certainly "better than most basements in London houses." He recounted that the general of the castle was exceptionally warm with the prisoners, and that the guards "do their duty humanely and as kindly as the circumstances will allow."[35]

Yet it quickly became apparent that such articles only reignited interest in the issue and gave opponents of the Spanish monarchy an opportunity to voice their protest. In a response published in the *Times* two weeks later, a group of Montjuich prisoners made this very point, writing that "if [the diplomat's] object in publishing his letter in the *Times* was to deny indirectly the insults and arbitrary acts perpetrated in Montjuich, he has only succeeded in giving us an opportunity to place them once more in relief for the opprobrium and shame of the inquisitors of a new stamp."[36] The prisoners refuted the findings of the diplomat's choreographed prison tour, stating that none of them had seen him when he visited. According to the French ambassador, Cánovas had invited the diplomat to visit Montjuich, where he was only shown prisoners who were about to be freed and were therefore happy and compliant.[37]

The *Times*, which had largely ignored the issue in the spring, also published a reply from Joseph Perry of the Spanish Atrocities Committee. Perry called the diplomat's claim that the prisoners were happy "an impertinent piece of cynicism only worthy of callousness."[38] He described the evidence of torture carved into the unfortunate flesh of Francisco Gana, who had made a declaration before the commissioner for oaths at the *Daily Chronicle* the day the diplomat's article was published.[39] Characteristic of the campaign's tendency to depoliticize the atrocities and portray the victims as moderates, the anarchist-communist Perry described the prisoners as "Freemasons, Republicans, trade unionists, and Radicals."[40] Unless Spain acknowledged its crimes, Perry cautioned, "the black cloud that now overhangs her will surely burst with terrible havoc." The campaign had broken into the mainstream press of Britain to the point where the *Times* acknowledged, "It is possible that some of [the prisoners] may at first, before the appointment of the present Governor of Montjuich prison, have been treated with a severity from which prison discipline is, in modern times, commonly free; we express no opinion on this doubtful point."[41] *Freedom* rejoiced at the shift in coverage, writing that "at last the work that *Freedom* first began in London is now being taken up by the whole of the English press."[42]

British interest in the "revival of the Inquisition" in Spain was compounded by the arrival of the refugees the day after the publication of the diplomat's letter. Spanish authorities clearly did not understand how deported anarchist prisoners would take their campaign with them in a way that made the torture immediate and tangible for the British and French people. The curiosity and fascination generated by the arrival of the anarchist exiles propelled the campaign immeasurably. From the start the exiles were swarmed with interview requests that allowed them to describe their torture and torment firsthand.[43] This was especially true for Montseny since Tarrida del Mármol had told the press that he was a teacher. Shortly after their arrival, Joseph Perry arrived to accompany the exiles to London. According to Montseny, a very large crowd gathered at the train station to say goodbye. As the train pulled out of the station the crowd waved their handkerchiefs shouting, "Long live the victims of Spanish atrocities!"[44]

On arriving in London, Montseny and his comrades were welcomed by the legendary French anarchist Louise Michel, Fernando Tarrida del Mármol, and members of the Spanish Atrocities Committee who took them to eat lunch at a German anarchist club on Tottenham Court Road. Turn-of-the-century London had become the preeminent European haven for anarchists fleeing repression on the continent. German, French, Italian, Russian, and Jewish anarchists from eastern Europe, among others, established a vibrant, multinational community through a network of clubs and newspapers in the English capital that provided fertile ground for the transnational campaign against the "revival of the Inquisition."[45]

One morning in July 1897 a visitor came looking for José Nakens in the editorial office of *El Motín* in Madrid. Founded in 1881, Nakens's *El Motín* was the preeminent vehicle for a bitingly satirical brand of anti-clerical republicanism that was paving the way for a historic transition from the elitist, old guard of First Republic–era republicanism to a new mass, working-class republicanism heading into the twentieth century.[46] As Nakens was working on the latest issue of the paper, he was handed the business card of a visitor in the other room. The card said, "Emilio Rinaldini, Book-keeper, Correspondent for 'Il Popolo.'" Nakens came out to meet "a young man of 26 to 28 years old, of medium stature, with an expressive face and fine manners, dressed in a light American suit." According to Nakens, Rinaldini explained to him that he wanted to interview him about the war in Cuba. Although Nakens replied that he was not important enough to merit such an interview, Rinaldini insisted, explaining how familiar he was with Nakens's work. After Nakens finally agreed, Rinaldini said he would return soon for the interview.[47]

Days later, Rinaldini returned with a copy of Fernando Tarrida del Mármol's *Les Inquisiteurs d'Espagne* in his hand. Rinaldini grew extremely animated as he lifted the book up and spoke about torture in Montjuich castle. Soon the conversation shifted to the topic of propaganda by the deed with Nakens attacking the idea and Rinaldini fervently defending it. Nakens argued that anarchist bombs would bring reaction to all of Europe, while Rinaldini saw it as a step toward a future without "exploiters nor exploited, neither hunger nor misery." Irritated by the conversation, the two men parted ways again. Two days later Nakens saw Rinaldini again, but this time the Italian's "expressive face and fine manners" had darkened. Rinaldini reluctantly explained that he had been two days without food and had gone sleepless the night before since he was kicked out of where he was staying. Sympathizing with the journalist's plight, Nakens took him in and fed him. When Rinaldini finally left, he turned to Nakens and remarked, "Since you have been so good to me, I'm going to tell you a secret: I have come to Madrid to kill Cánovas, the king, or the queen regent." Nakens thought nothing of the comment and simply smiled since he had "heard such things said many times before."[48] But unbeknownst to Nakens, Rinaldini was really Michele Angiolillo, a man far more serious than those who had casually uttered similar proclamations in the past. Or maybe this was all made up and Nakens knew exactly who he was hosting. After all, Nakens had every interest in distancing himself from a very dangerous man. We know that on July 10, 1897, Angiolillo went into a Madrid print shop and ordered the set of the business cards that Nakens described, but little else can be definitively documented about his time in Madrid. We will return to Nakens and his story shortly, but for now let us follow Angiolillo as he left Madrid.

After parting ways with Nakens, Angiolillo traveled north to the spa of Santa Águeda in the Basque Country where Prime Minister Antonio Cánovas del Castillo was a scheduled guest. Since his first wedding in 1861, Cánovas had the tradition of taking a July vacation in San Sebastián, spending much of August in nearby locales such as Biarritz, Bagnères, and Santa Águeda.[49] This year was no different. Days before Cánovas arrived, Angiolillo checked into a room at the spa as *Il Popolo* correspondent Rinaldini.[50] Presumably Angiolillo decided to arrive early in order to familiarize himself with his surroundings, but he also ran the risk of raising suspicion as an unknown Italian in a small, tightly knit world of elites and aristocrats. Yet, for whatever reason, it seems like no one was sufficiently alarmed by his presence to do anything about it. For example, days later the Marquis de Lema recalled noticing Rinaldini walk into the cafeteria as he was eating with his mother and aunt. Although Rinaldini was well dressed, there was something that alarmed Lema's aristocratic palate. The Italian reminded him of a "servant." "Who is that? We all asked ourselves since he was the only unknown person in the establishment; but after a few comments we changed topics of conversation and I didn't think of him again."[51] In retrospect a number of guests commented on their observation that although this unknown guest claimed to be a journalist, no one ever saw him send any telegraphs or write anything down. He just kept to himself and spoke no more than was necessary to order food.[52]

Days later, Cánovas arrived at the spa. On the morning of August 8, 1897, he attended Sunday Mass and sent a telegram before returning to his room to change for lunch. He left with his wife to go to the cafeteria a little after 12:30 p.m. On the way down the stairs they bumped into an acquaintance.[53] Cánovas's wife stopped to chat while he continued down the stairs and sat on a bench in a large open gallery next to the cafeteria to read *La Época* while he waited for his wife.[54] Monitoring his actions from afar, Angiolillo walked into the room "without awaking the most minor suspicion," pulled out his revolver, and blasted Cánovas three times at point-blank range.[55] Newspapers of the era claimed that the last words of the fallen "colossus" were "¡Viva España!" but since the first bullet went through his temples he could not have said anything at all.[56]

Newspaper accounts stated a journalist and an engineer who were nearby charged at Angiolillo who fired several shots, missing them both, but historian José Piqueras claims that Angiolillo was actually pushed by an official of the civil guard as he fired his third shot.[57] Cánovas's wife came running down the stairs when she heard the shots to find her husband lying in a pool of his own blood. Angiolillo is reported to have said to her, "I respect you because you are an honorable woman, but I have completed a responsibility, and I am tranquil: I have avenged my brothers of Montjuich."[58] Yet if he was in the process of being physically apprehended and addressing a panic-stricken woman coming to terms with the death of her husband, then it is unlikely that such dialogue would have transpired. Nevertheless, Cánovas died shortly thereafter and Angiolillo was apprehended.

How was Angiolillo allowed such an easy opportunity to assassinate the most important politician in the country? Where was his security? Spanish authorities had every reason to fear for Cánovas's safety given the enemies he was making through his intransigent oversight of the colonial wars and the repression of domestic opposition. More specifically, the French consul in Barcelona claimed that back in November 1896 French authorities had sent a photograph of Angiolillo to Portas, and as recently as June 30, 1897, the Spanish embassy in London informed Cánovas of a plot being organized against him from London.[59] In mid-July Spanish authorities received word of a conversation about avenging the Montjuich prisoners overheard at the Charing Cross telegraph office in London, which supposedly stimulated enhanced security measures for the prime minister.[60] The French embassy in Madrid was aware of Angiolillo's trip from Paris to Madrid and had provided Spanish authorities with regular warnings about him, but to no avail.[61] The day after the assassination, the French consul expressed frustration, writing that "last year the local authorities were warned by the consul general of France of the presence in Barcelona of Miguel Angiolillo. It is unfortunately demonstrated today that our information was accurate. The photograph of the criminal was sent to the director of police, and despite all of these elements of surveillance that we had provided for the Spanish authorities since January 1896, Angiolillo has been able to commit his crime without being the least disturbed."[62] In recognition of the incompetence of the Barcelona police, later that month the Spanish foreign minister asked the Italian government to station a police agent in Barcelona to monitor Italian anarchists in the city.[63]

Despite the mismanagement of the information they had received from the French, Spanish authorities did at least provide Cánovas with a not insignificant retinue of nine police officers and twenty-five civil guards. Yet none of them were remotely close enough to the man they were supposedly protecting to be able to intervene at the key moment, let alone conscientious enough to vet every guest at the spa. It would be some time until modern tactics of body guarding were widely incorporated to protect heads of state.[64]

El proceso de Montjuich hovered over the assassination. *El Imparcial* speculated that "the Montjuich prisoners filled certain disturbed spirits with terror with the story of made-up cruelties and supposed humiliations; perhaps they prepared the crime of Santa Águeda."[65] The paper also used Angiolillo's culpability to reinforce its argument about the guilt of Montjuich prisoners by claiming that Angiolillo had "very direct participation in the crime of Cambios Nuevos."[66] It appeared more subtly when *La Época* went out of its way to assure readers that thus far Angiolillo "has not been the object of bad treatment," a clear reference to the treatment of the Montjuich prisoners.[67] Yet despite the supposedly universal grief of the Spanish nation, an early biographer of Cánovas lamented that the "general mass of the country . . . welcomed [Cánovas's death] with mortal indifference."[68] Puerto Rican revolutionary and alleged Angiolillo collaborator Betances took the diplomatic route by limiting his remarks to the comment, "We don't applaud but we don't cry either."[69] Many anarchists and revolutionaries were not interested in restrained rhetorical diplomacy. *Les Temps nouveaux* sarcastically wrote, "May the God of Saint-Dominique and Torquemada rest [Cánovas's] soul in his protection."[70] Montseny recounted that the day of the assassination "was a day of jubilation in London, particularly in the popular centers and clubs. In the German Club there was a party where only Spanish music was played and where we returned to sing our songs of Clavé. The party lasted until dawn, and the Germans drank so much beer that they used chamber pots—new ones, of course—to drink it."[71]

In prison Angiolillo asked to read newspaper coverage of his assassination but was denied.[72] The government was so concerned about the ramifications of the publicity his act generated that it banned the press from providing details on Angiolillo's trial or execution as part of its extension of the anti-anarchist law of 1896 to cover the entire country.[73] While *El Imparcial* adhered to the law so fully that it stopped printing Angiolillo's name entirely,

instead referring to him as "the murderer of Cánovas" or simply "the prisoner," *El País* argued that such draconian measures were counterproductive:
"Freedom and the law at the mercy of fear and official cowardice, is a fact
that, consented to without protest, humiliates us and lowers our national
level to the level of such unfortunate nations . . . as Portugal."[74] Nevertheless,
the press managed to learn that Angiolillo decided to use a pistol rather than
dynamite in order to prevent any collateral damage.[75] In fact, he is said to
have waited until Cánovas was alone before striking in order to ensure that
no innocents would be harmed.[76]

Although Angiolillo claimed to have acted alone and José Nakens denied
knowingly assisting the future assassin, the degree of collaboration behind
the *atentado* is unclear. In his later account Nakens argued that the death
of the "distinguished" Cánovas was a tragedy. His public opposition to
the assassination lends credence to the notion that he was not knowingly
involved in a conspiracy, but Nakens also argued that if he had to do it over
again he still would not have alerted the police because "the political crime
does not dishonor. The denunciation of this crime does. More than any
other human act."[77]

At Angiolillo's trial the artillery lieutenant acting as his defense attorney argued that he was insane and irrational. When the defendant tried to
explain his actions and link them to Montjuich and the colonial wars, he was
kicked out of the courtroom.[78] On August 20, a mere twelve days after he
pulled the trigger, Angiolillo was brought out onto a platform in the patio
of the Vergara jail and subjected to the *garrote vil*. Right before the garrote
crushed his windpipe Angiolillo shouted, "Germinal!"[79] Perhaps he thought
of the last line of Zola's work: "Men were springing forth, a black army of
vengeance, germinating slowly in the furrows, growing toward the harvests
of the next century, whose germination would soon overturn the earth."[80]

Two days after Angiolillo's execution, the Spanish Atrocities Committee held a large demonstration against the Spanish monarchy in Trafalgar
Square. The shocking assassination of Cánovas only fueled the popular interest in lurid details of Spanish "barbarism" that had developed in response to
the landing of the twenty-eight anarchists in Liverpool. As opposed to the
May 30 SAC public meeting, which was completely ignored, this time the
Times even ran stories on the planning meetings at the German Club leading
up to the demonstration.[81] When the day arrived, a "vast crowd" showed
up to hear a wide variety of speakers including the recently exiled Teresa
Claramunt. The organizers framed the event as a "protest against these
detestable outrages on the common humanity of the civilized world" and

showed "a certain degree of resentment . . . at the gathering being called an anarchist demonstration." Meeting chairman Pete Curran of the Gas Workers' Union emphasized that this was not an anarchist event and that none of the speakers endorsed violence or political crime. Although they disagreed with anarchism, he claimed, they supported anarchists' rights to free speech. This was certainly not entirely accurate, especially given the presence of anarchists such as Joseph Perry and John Turner, who received a hearty applause when he self-identified as an anarchist during his speech, but it is indicative of the nonsectarian emphasis of the campaign.[82] This emphasis was useful in gaining the support of organizations such as the National Secular Society, which appointed three delegates to the SAC but threatened to withdraw them if "they found that the protest was not humanitarian but political."[83] G. W. Foote of the National Secular Society injected some nationalist humanitarianism into the proceedings by arguing that England was the only European country that could have such a protest meeting (despite examples to the contrary).[84]

The main argument of the speakers was that when it came to abuses as severe as those alleged in Spain, politics did not matter. Such abuses transcended sectarianism to strike at humanity itself. This was clear in a letter Malato read on behalf of *L'Intransigeant* editor Henri Rochefort, which explained that the campaign was being waged "not in the name of party, but of humanity." Likewise, in a letter that Perry read from Walter Crane, Crane stated, "I am not an Anarchist, but I detest all forms of violence, coercion, and cruelty, under whatever name perpetrated. The revolting tortures practised upon Spanish citizens, according to the published statements, ought to move every humane person to protest."[85] Montseny recalled that there were platforms in all the different corners of the square with orators speaking French, German, Russian, and Italian in addition to the main English-language podium. Some of the Spanish exiles spoke, including Fernando Tarrida del Mármol, who received the loudest applause. Tarrida had been deported from France shortly after the death of Cánovas because of a vitriolic speech he gave about the prime minister at approximately the same time as his death, which many considered to be more than a coincidence.[86] Teresa Claramunt also spoke, saying, "We must protest against torture in Spain, in the Philippine Islands and in Cuba until Spain is free and the torturers are no more."[87]

The SAC distributed a pamphlet titled "Spanish Tortures! Official Tortures!" boasting "absolute proof of the tortures."[88] It included Gana's affidavit before the *Daily Chronicle* and reports from Dr. Betances in Paris and Dr. William McDonald in Glasgow verifying the truth of Gana's allegations based on their examinations of his scars, abrasions, and other signs of abuse. This initiative stemmed from one of Tarrida's articles published in the spring called "To the Witness Stand" where he proposed the formation of "a new trial, logical and genuine, where the former victims appear as the accusers, the former accusers as the accused," prefiguring elements of the Russell Tribunals of the 1970s, which addressed American atrocities in Vietnam and dictatorship in Latin America.[89] Alongside *Daily Chronicle* editor Henry William Massingham, Tarrida proposed to create a "jury of honor" composed of prominent men to put the torturers and executioners on trial before the world. After all, Tarrida remarked, "one cannot resuscitate the dead, but one can rehabilitate their memory." Massingham was tasked with creating a jury of eminent figures in London, including William Gladstone; Tarrida was to create one in Madrid, and the proposed lineup in Paris was to include Henri Rochefort of *L'Intransigeant*, Paul de Cassagnac of *L'Autorité*, Édouard Drumont of *La Libre parole*, Georges Clemenceau of *La Justice*, and Alexandre Natanson of *La Revue blanche*. Tarrida made a point of emphasizing the impartiality of this jury, writing that it included "a socialist, a monarchist, a Catholic, a radical, and an independent."[90] Having "impartial" doctors inspect Gana provided these juries with evidence on which to base their decision. Needless to say, the Spanish government was found guilty.

There was no mass roundup of anarchists and other radicals following the assassination of Cánovas, although this *atentado* was far more threatening to the government than the bombing of Cambios Nuevos. In part this was because most of those who would have been arrested were already in jail or abroad, but it also seems to stem from a reluctance on the part of state authorities to stir up more international protest (which always had the potential of spawning more propaganda by the deed). While there were scattered arrests of "suspicious" foreigners across the country, such as a German on his way to Bilbao who was a little too proficient in Italian,[91] the mass roundup that likely would have occurred had Cánovas been assassinated before *el proceso de Montjuich* did not materialize. But simply refraining from unleashing a wave of mass repression following the assassination of Cánovas was not sufficient to stem the tide of transnational protest against "the revival of the inquisition." Before long Joan Montseny would sneak back across the border under an assumed name and help trigger broad support for the revision of *el proceso de Montjuich* within Spain for the first time in the context of the Dreyfus affair and the monarchy's loss of its overseas colonies to the United States.

CHAPTER 9

Montjuich, Dreyfus, and *el Desastre*

Turn-of-the-century London was boring. Or
at least that is what many exiled continental European anarchists thought.
True, the United Kingdom's relatively broad civil liberties and open asylum
policy provided anarchists on the run with a safe haven in troubled times
(though the degree to which anarchists took advantage of this policy would
contribute to a tightening of the British border). But for revolutionary anarchists who lived for the smoldering tension of latent class war, safety could
be stultifying. In the 1880s Kropotkin was so frustrated with Britain's lack of
popular struggle that he returned to France to risk incarceration rather than
remain. After all, "better a French prison than this grave," he quipped. Similarly, Charles Malato wrote of "the monotony of this exilic life" of "inaction . . .
[that] is both lethal and depressing."[1] Joan Montseny, Teresa Mañé, and many
of their Spanish and Catalan comrades agreed.

Yet the challenges of life in exile in Britain extended beyond boredom.
Many exiles struggled to survive, although some found work, like Teresa
Mañé who was hired at a needlework shop, and the Spanish Atrocities Com-
mittee and the anarchist German Club provided material support and food.
Apart from linguistic and cultural challenges, they faced a powerful anti-
Spanish prejudice. This was evident with one exile who simply could not
convince anyone that someone from Spain could be a qualified electrician.
Therefore, many emigrated to continental Europe or the Americas. Even

this was not so simple, however. Some of those who journeyed across the ocean were turned away at every port, such as one of Joan Montseny's former cellmates who returned to Europe after being denied entry at Montevideo and Buenos Aires.[2]

Mañé and Montseny followed their comrade Teresa Claramunt to France where she had obtained work in a cloth factory. By tapping into Western European anarchist networks, they rented a room in Paris from a German woman named Delbeck and her French husband. They soon learned that the couple had a clandestine printing press in their basement operated by the Italian husband of Angiolillo's former lover. According to Montseny, Angiolillo's former lover intended to avenge him by traveling to San Sebastián to assassinate the queen regent. Montseny explained in his memoir that Delbeck, Tarrida del Mármol, Joseph Perry, and others in the SAC had organized the plot. To finance her journey, Montseny claimed that the SAC asked some of the Spanish exiles to sign for sums far higher than what they were actually given in support so that the difference could be laundered to Angiolillo's former lover for her act of vengeance.[3] The Foreign Office caught wind of this plot, alerting the Spanish embassy in London that she left London for Bordeaux with two men on her way to Spain. British sources described her "as 33 years of age, short, dark hair, and complexion, and full bust," matching Montseny's description.[4] According to Montseny, she made it to San Sebastián, but the royal family had ended their vacation early to return to Madrid for Cánovas's funeral, foiling her plot. "I met her and greeted her as she returned from Spain," Montseny recounted. In his judgment, had she been successful the queen regent "would have been, like Cánovas, a victim of the inquisitors of Montjuich who had flagellated the flesh of the innocent."[5]

Since Tarrida del Mármol no longer lived in Paris after being deported following the assassination of Cánovas, Montseny and Mañé sought out Tarrida's close collaborator, the "elegant and gallant" Charles Malato. They dined with Malato on occasion, and he introduced them to the Parisian anarchist scene. Not long after, a comrade from *Les Temps nouveaux* brought them to meet the paper's legendary founder, Jean Grave, at his home/office on rue Mouffetard. Yet they were horrified to see him living "dreadfully" as compared to the living conditions of Catalan workers. Instead they were much more comfortable spending time with their longtime comrade Anselmo Lorenzo who had found work as a printer through his Masonic connections. One evening Lorenzo invited them to eat dinner with him at the Café Terminus so they could see the site of Émile Henry's infamous bombing three years earlier. To their dismay they "left as hungry as when they arrived" since the restaurant served such small portions.[6]

Throughout all of the traveling, however, Montseny's mind remained fixed on those still imprisoned in Montjuich. He spoke with Mañé about launching a press campaign to free the remaining prisoners. Perhaps as importantly, they longed to return to Spain. They hatched a plan to clandestinely sneak back across the border and head toward Madrid where Montseny would attempt to convince a newspaper to provide him with space to propagandize on behalf of the prisoners. Montseny wrote to friends in his native Reus to acquire a fake ID in the name of Federico Urales. Fortunately, a municipal guard whose son had studied at Montseny's school came through for him with the ID. He shaved his beard, put on new clothing, and bought a ticket to Madrid, where he arrived on November 28, 1897.[7] Montseny's decision to return to Spain would have a profound effect on the reinvigoration of the Montjuich campaign, but its revival owed as much to two monumental developments that were well out of his control: the Dreyfus affair in France and the Spanish-American War.

A lot had changed since Joan Montseny was deported in July 1897. With the death of Cánovas, the Liberal Party and their historic icon Práxedes Mateo Sagasta assumed power in early October. After the destruction of the First Republic and the restoration of the Bourbon monarchy in 1874, Sagasta, the republic's final prime minister, and his followers were granted liberal concessions and guaranteed a significant parliamentary minority by the Conservatives to bring them into the fold so they could marginalize intransigent republican elements.[8] By the middle of the next decade the two parties established an agreement to alternate power through an anti-democratic parliamentary mechanism known as the *turno pacífico*. Over the last quarter of the century the Janus faces of the *turno* were the Conservative Cánovas, who died during his sixth term, and the Liberal Sagasta, who in 1897 was about to start the sixth of what would be a total of seven terms as prime minister (five of the seven under the Restoration). Although Spain incorporated universal manhood suffrage relatively early in 1890, it was widely known that elections were rigged by local landowning political bosses known as *caciques* who coerced, concocted, or otherwise fabricated electoral outcomes favorable to their party.

It would not be until the first decade of the twentieth century that the two-party system would face its first serious electoral challenges, but fissures in the restoration facade with far-reaching consequences started to develop in the mid-1890s as a result of the Cuban War of Independence. Shifts in Liberal foreign policy were evident with the slogan "Not a man or a peseta more" developed in response to Cánovas's sharp vow to fight "to the last peseta and the last drop of blood."[9] In the spring of 1897 Liberal critiques of Cánovas's policy intensified to the point where Liberal leader Segismundo Moret promised to pursue a proposal for Cuban autonomy the next time his party held power. After the death of Cánovas, the Liberals made good on their promise by drafting a new Cuban constitution granting the island limited autonomy. They also replaced Captain General Weyler in mid-November 1897, thereby ending his brutal policy of reconcentration. An extra incentive for these policy shifts was the enhanced pressure put on the Sagasta government by McKinley, who promised to encourage the Cuban rebels to disarm if Spain would implement reforms. Unlike the intractable Cánovas, Sagasta made every effort to appease the United States, and his new captain general implemented a more passive strategy toward the rebels in the hope that military de-escalation could provide space for a diplomatic solution.[10]

A domestic corollary to Sagasta's foreign policy was his effort to get rid of the Montjuich prisoners and the negative press and retaliatory *atentados* that followed them. Days after taking office, the 112 remaining Barcelona prisoners published a letter in several papers affirming their innocence and demanding their freedom.[11] More prison letters were published over the coming days.[12] The colonial wars and the potential of American intervention were already enough for the new Sagasta government to deal with on their own without the lingering headache of Montjuich. As a result, less than a month later, on November 1, 1897, fifty-four prisoners were released from the Reina Amalia prison, and another fifty-eight were released from Montjuich on November 3. Although eleven of them were too "dangerous" to reside in Catalonia, the rest were unconditionally free. The liberation of the remaining Barcelona prisoners (there were still prisoners in North Africa) stood in stark contrast with the exile of those released earlier, leading to a royal order on December 16, 1897, allowing the deported anarchists to come home as long as they reported their domiciles to the authorities. The next day the suspension of constitutional guarantees in the province of Barcelona, in effect for a year and a half, was lifted.[13] Sagasta had presided over the mass arrests and torture of 1893–94, but the political landscape had shifted since then. The havoc wrought by the colonial wars created a context in which the international campaign enhanced the political cost of repression to the point where leniency became the most expedient option. Given the profound reversals in policy regarding both Cuba and Montjuich that followed from the assassination of Cánovas del Castillo, one could argue that Angiolillo's assassination was the most effective act of propaganda by the deed carried out by an anarchist during the era.

The new government tried to brush the Montjuich scandal under the rug, but until there was an official acknowledgment of the innocence of those arrested, the reality of the torture, and the falsified confessions behind the executions, Montseny and his comrades would not rest. Days after his arrival in Madrid, Montseny went to find Alejandro Lerroux at the editorial office of his new paper, *El Progreso*, down the street from Puerta del Sol. For years Lerroux had been at the helm of Spain's most prominent republican paper, *El País*, but recently had fallen out with the paper's owner. In large part the conflict developed over the succession of the leadership of the Partido Republicano Progresista after the death of Manuel Ruiz Zorrilla, a former president of the First Republic and the prototypical late nineteenth-century revolutionary republican conspirator.

General Prim once described Spanish republicans as "generals without soldiers." Apart from certain federalist factions that produced their fair share of anarchists over the years, the landscape of Spanish republicanism was littered with tiny factions and micro-factions of middle- and upper-class professionals each revolving around their chosen figurehead without any connection to the working class and peasant populations around them. The fate of a faction rested in the hands of its leader, and when he died or was discredited a serious shakeup was to be expected. In this case the owner of *El País* was critical of José María Esquerdo, the successor to Ruiz Zorrilla, while Lerroux came to his defense. When the conflict got heated, Lerroux brought up his boss's underground casinos to tarnish his reputation. Reconciliation was out of the question, and Lerroux left with most of the editorial staff to found *El Progreso* in October 1897.[14]

Montseny had not been especially impressed with Lerroux's actions in defense of the Montjuich prisoners, writing that "he didn't behave poorly, but not as well as one would have hoped for." Nevertheless, Montseny "had the impression that of all of the directors of Madrid dailies, he was the only one who would allow such a campaign in his paper." When Montseny asked Lerroux if he would be interested in bringing him on as a contributor to jump-start the campaign, "Lerroux, not seeing more than the economic and popular part of the question answered: 'I tried that in the columns of *El País*, which I also directed, and sales in Barcelona didn't exceed 150 copies.'" Montseny pleaded with him, saying, "But you don't have the documents that I have nor were you as well informed or as qualified as I am." A week later Lerroux acquiesced and notified Montseny that he would become an editor at *El Progreso* in charge of the Montjuich campaign starting January 1, 1898.[15]

Over the coming months, Lerroux and Montseny printed numerous letters from prisoners and their relatives, and Montseny wrote a daily column called "Revision of the Case: The Infamies of Montjuich." To Lerroux's delight, the campaign immediately tripled sales of the fledgling republican paper.[16] The newfound success of the campaign owed in part to the emergence of the Dreyfus affair, which established a powerful international example of campaigning for the rights of the downtrodden. Although Captain Alfred Dreyfus, a Jewish artillery officer in the French army, was wrongfully arrested for allegedly selling military secrets to the Germans in 1894 and banished to Devil's Island in 1895, it was not until the fall of 1897 that the campaign for his exoneration took shape in the French press. The first significant development occurred when an honorary senator named Scheurer-Kestner publicly supported Dreyfus in October 1897. Immediately, Henri Rochefort and *L'Intransigeant*—important French allies in the Montjuich campaign— went on the attack, calling Scheurer-Kestner an "abominable old scoundrel" and insinuating that he was related to a prominent German Jewish banker.[17] The opening of this public conflict between Scheurer-Kestner and the antisemitic press created a strong pro-Dreyfus camp for the first time.

Although most histories of the Dreyfus affair limit their accounts to writings and orations of prominent politicians and journalists, anarchists played a significant and overlooked role in the campaign to defend Alfred Dreyfus. For example, in February 1895 Alfred Dreyfus's brother Mathieu reached out to the Jewish anarchist writer Bernard Lazare, "the first Dreyfusard," after learning of his recent book on the history of antisemitism.[18] As an anarchist and a Jew, Lazare argued for the cultural assimilation of French Jews through collective social revolution. The rabid antisemitism he experienced as the affair exploded across French society would shake his hope in assimilation and lead him to craft a form of anarchist Zionism grounded in a federalist vision of Jewish autonomy.[19] Lazare heartily embraced the cause of the imprisoned captain and crafted his brand of Zionism into a foundation for arguments on behalf of Dreyfus in his 1896 *Une Erreur judiciare*. This highly influential text expounded on the facts of the case and personally influenced the support of some of the most significant Dreyfusards, including Jean Jaurès, Léon Blum, Georges Clemenceau, and Aristide Briand.[20] Lazare also managed to convince the prominent anarchist Sébastien Faure to devote his newspaper *Le Libertaire* to defending Dreyfus.[21] Initially, most socialists and anarchists were reluctant to get caught up in a "bourgeois civil war" by supporting an imprisoned army captain, but once the case started to generate mainstream debate and provide opportunities to attack the army or the church, most became Dreyfusards.[22]

In December 1897 Sébastien Faure and the famous veteran of the Paris Commune, Louise Michel, organized the first of three hundred anarchist events in the course of the Dreyfus affair.[23] In fact, Faure organized approximately two Dreyfusard meetings a week throughout the peak of the campaign.[24] The anarchists also worked closely with the Ligue des droits de l'homme et du citoyen, which was created in February 1898 to defend Alfred Dreyfus and anyone else whose rights were threatened. Its founders included a wide range of journalists, lawyers, artists, and professors. The Ligue opened itself to "all those who, without distinction of religious belief or political opinion . . . are convinced that all forms of arbitrariness and intolerance threaten to tear the county apart and menace civilization and Progress."[25] Faure was among the invited speakers at the Ligue's constitutive assembly, the anarchist Paul Reclus was on its central committee, and joint meetings were organized between the Ligue and the Coalition révolutionnaire (a group of anarchists and anti-parliamentary socialists).[26] Although the Ligue was initially wary of mass politics and public meetings, which the first Ligue president considered to be "occasions for troubles," the failures of their early high-level petitions convinced the central committee to issue an "Appeal to the Public" and start an impressive campaign of public events that was essentially a "traveling road show of Dreyfusard celebrities."[27]

As many have noted, the Dreyfus campaign was propelled by the support of the newly coined "intellectuals," such as Anatole France, Émile Durkheim, Stéphane Mallarmé, and Claude Monet. But excessive focus on the orations and writings of elite professionals has obscured the impact of grassroots mobilizing and the role of anarchists in counteracting antisemitic mob violence. In January 1898 Émile Zola published his famous "J'accuse" (I accuse) denouncing the recent acquittal of Major Esterhazy, the real traitor to the French government, and accusing the officers behind the affair "in the name of humanity."[28] The publication of "J'accuse" triggered antisemitic riots in dozens of French cities. Mobs of antisemites sacked Jewish shops and synagogues and even killed several people in Algeria.[29] Days after the looting and rioting, anarchists and their socialist allies started to organize Dreyfus supporters to forcibly interrupt and disperse meetings of the Ligue antisémitique and other anti-Dreyfusard groups. Over the coming months, anarchists and their allies formed the Coalition révolutionnaire inviting people to "fight the reactionary gangs in the glorious street, the street of energetic protests, the street of barricades." The coalition followed through on its mission by confronting the violence of the antisemitic ligues and organizing protection for Dreyfusard orators at meetings and pro-Dreyfus witnesses outside of courthouses. "If 'J'accuse' mobilized the intelligentsia," Jean-Marc Izrine argued, "the anarchists and [nonparliamentary socialists] mobilized the streets." In addition to their newspapers, pamphlets, and public meetings, anarchists and their allies made a significant contribution as the shock troops of the movement. As the Catholic socialist poet Charles Péguy remarked in February 1898, "The anarchists are the only ones to respond to the war cry of Zola."[30] The mounting threat of a right-wing coup heightened the urgency of the campaign and even caused many anarchists to form a bloc at the massive march in defense of the republic in June 1899. Yet the revolutionary Dreyfusard faction ruptured over the tension inherent in the fact that fighting the antisemitic, monarchist right could mean implicitly defending the very republic that the anarchists lived to destroy. It was much easier to maintain coalitions between revolutionaries and reformists in the Montjuich campaign in Spain, where all parties could agree on the need to eliminate, or at least significantly restructure, the Spanish government, than in France, where the Dreyfus campaign revolved around the defense of the institutional status quo through appeals for the republic to live up to its egalitarian values. Nevertheless, many anarchists made significant, though often overlooked, contributions to the campaign for the liberation of Alfred Dreyfus.

Although the Dreyfus affair redirected the focus of French allies away from the Montjuich campaign, its international prominence inspired the movement in Spain. "Like France regenerated itself," *El País* asserted, "we will regenerate ourselves. . . . We will imitate France. . . . In France one man [Dreyfus] is accused and they rise up for justice. In Spain many are accused. . . . What will we do?"[31] Hopes for the revision of *el proceso de Montjuich* were buoyed by the January 1898 announcement that the Spanish judiciary was opening an official investigation into the allegations of torture citing evidence published in *El País*, *El Progreso*, and *El Nuevo Régimen*.[32] On the heels of this unprecedented announcement, the first major demonstration in Barcelona against "methods of torture that humanity hates and civilization stigmatizes" was organized on February 13, 1898, by a predominantly republican executive committee with the support of a wide range of groups including republican, Masonic, socialist, anarchist, Catalanist, student, spiritist, freethinking, and educational groups, in addition to sympathetic newspapers, choral societies, intellectual and literary groups, women's societies, and workers' organizations and labor unions.[33] The massive march of thirty to fifty thousand that set off from the Tivoli Theater to city hall to protest this "crime against humanity" demonstrated not only the power of the Montjuich campaign to unite broad sectors of society across class and cultural divides but also how it provided a potent forum for dissent that had been suppressed for years while constitutional guarantees were suspended.[34] In late February 1898 Alejandro Lerroux launched an ambitious Montjuich speaking tour with at least fifteen engagements through La Mancha and

Andalusia. Despite the ferocity of his pen, Lerroux had been hesitant about public speaking. Yet, as he would later recall, these rousing speeches about the revision of *el proceso de Montjuich* and obligatory military service, flavored by an increasingly anti-electoral revolutionary posture, reinforced his confidence. These speeches, along with another hundred talks over the next two years, "made me an orator," he later recalled.[35]

In appreciation of Montseny's role in sparking this lucrative campaign, Lerroux increased his salary to 100 pesetas, which allowed him to send for his wife, Teresa Mañé. Meanwhile, Montseny was working to convince Nicolás Salmerón and Francisco Pi y Margall, heads of some of the various factions of Spanish republicanism, to join Esquerdo and Lerroux on a Madrid commission for the revision of *el proceso de Montjuich* that *El Progreso* had created following the initiative of the Catalan organizers of the large February 1898 march. The Barcelona republicans had proposed that every city create its own local commission that would send a representative to a central committee in Barcelona.[36] At that time Pi y Margall was working with Pere Coromines and other leftist republicans on a local electoral project in Barcelona called Candidatura de Justicia to promote the revision of *el proceso de Montjuich*, but this initiative ended in failure.[37] Nevertheless, Pi y Margall and Salmerón agreed to join the committee and endorse a march that *El Progreso* had organized with the Socialist Party. Montseny remembered the April 3 march that made its way from the Atocha Basilica past the botanical gardens and the Prado as having been rather successful, but newspaper accounts portray it as somewhere between a minor success and a frustrating disappointment with between fifteen hundred and five thousand in attendance.[38] Later that month, *El Progreso* published the findings of a professor of clinical surgery and a professor of legal medicine and toxicology who verified Francisco Gana's accusations of abuse after a physical inspection.[39]

A week after the medical report, the campaign was overshadowed by the outbreak of war with the United States. Tensions had been building since the explosion of the USS *Maine* in February 1898. Although a number of contemporary experts reported that coal fire problems had caused the explosion, a claim verified by subsequent historical investigation, the American secretary of the navy marginalized such reports while President McKinley was handed a report attributing the blast to a Spanish submarine mine. The American army was relatively unprepared for the war, but it did not take long to dispatch with the desperate, starving, and diseased Spanish soldiers after Admiral Dewey destroyed the Spanish Asiatic Squadron in Manila Bay on May 1, 1898.[40] Spain surrendered in mid-July and eventually ceded Cuba,

Puerto Rico, the Philippines, and Guam to the United States, which, despite its earlier rhetoric, did not grant independence to its newly acquired colonies.

Predictably the ruling Liberal Party was blamed for the country's loss of overseas colonies, often referred to as *el Desastre*. Protests against Sagasta's decision to recall Weyler had erupted since the end of 1897, and events such as an attack on the office of the Cuban *El Reconcentrado* by Weyler supporters in January 1898 had precipitated the arrival of the *Maine* in Havana.[41] Alejandro Lerroux shared this antagonism toward Cuban autonomy and support for General Weyler in the pages of *El Progreso*.[42] Yet Montseny recalled that since the paper had attracted a large number of anarchist and leftist readers as a result of its advocacy for the Montjuich campaign, the paper received a lot of backlash for its support of Weyler and the suggestion that he could be the forward-thinking military strongman to lead the long-imagined republican coup. Such articles aggravated underlying political tensions that the campaign had often managed to gloss over and eventually contributed to the end of *El Progreso*.[43]

A more significant blow to the fortunes of the paper was the eight-month imprisonment of its editor, Alejandro Lerroux, for an article he published on *caciques* in the first issue of Montseny's new venture, *La Revista Blanca*, inspired by the French *Revue blanche*.[44] Montseny could tell that the end was near with *El Progreso*, and he yearned to publish on a wide range of topics, from the arts and sciences to sociology and political commentary, in addition to the Montjuich campaign. The new journal, *La Revista Blanca*, could not refer to itself as an anarchist periodical given the prevailing anti-anarchist laws, but it explicitly addressed anarchism quite a bit in articles from mainly anarchist contributors. The journal spurned narrow anarchist sectarianism in favor of a wider intellectual scope that gave space to the ideas of socialists and republicans. Teresa Mañé wrote a significant number of articles, often under her pseudonym Soledad Gustavo, and she and her sister carried out important logistical tasks for the journal, though Montseny clarified in his memoirs that "all initiatives were my own."[45] As relations with Lerroux soured, the fortunes of Montseny and Mañé's future campaigning rested on their newfound publishing autonomy.

Months after the Spanish government lost the war to the United States, it suffered another embarrassing loss in a Barcelona courtroom when a seemingly open-and-shut case against the would-be assassin of Montjuich torturer civil guard lieutenant Portas went awry. A year before, in the early morning hours of September 4, 1897, Portas, who had come to be known as "the Spanish

Trepov" after the brutal Saint Petersburg police chief that Vera Zasulich shot in 1878, was walking home with other police officials from a performance they had attended at the Circo Encuestre on the Plaza de Cataluña. Amid a large Friday night crowd pulsing through the heart of the Catalan capital, the officers paused between two lampposts as they reached the start of La Rambla. Suddenly, someone opened fire on Portas and his fellow officers. The first bullet missed Portas, but the second grazed his chest before striking his arm. Undaunted, Portas ran at the gunman, who shot again but missed. Portas pulled out his revolver and returned fire, but his target fled into a nearby pub. The police pursued the attacker, finding him hiding under a table inside.[46] It was the radical journalist Ramón Sempau, who had fled abroad after the Cambios Nuevos bombing.

Weeks before, Sempau had returned clandestinely to Barcelona under an assumed name. For days he kept a low profile as he plotted his attack, which, according to Montseny, had been planned in Paris.[47] Unfortunately for Sempau, his plan to avenge the Montjuich martyrs by striking down the man most directly responsible for the torture had failed. Sempau was imprisoned in Montjuich Castle in a cell with the Filipino anthropologist and journalist Isabelo de los Reyes, who had been chained and shipped halfway around the world for his opposition to Spanish rule.[48] Although a secret council of war initially sentenced Sempau to death, the captain general disagreed with the military judge about the sentence, so the case was transferred to civil jurisdiction.[49] This shift from a secret military death sentence to a public jury trial was influenced by pressure from the liberal press. More deeply, however, it reflected the political toll that the international campaign against Spanish judicial irregularities was taking on state officials.[50]

More than a year passed between Sempau's *atentado* and the start of his trial. In the interim, he grew quite close to his Filipino cellmate Isabelo de los Reyes, who was impressed with Sempau's knowledge, selflessness, and "absolute lack of fear." Sempau introduced him to anarchist and radical ideas through smuggled books and newspapers. For de los Reyes it "really opened my eyes" to learn that anarchism "espoused the abolition of boundaries; that is, love without any boundaries, whether geographic or of class distinction."[51] After his release, de los Reyes participated in the Montjuich protests and wrote articles on the situation in the Philippines for Lerroux. When he returned to the Philippines, he brought back European books, including what were perhaps the first anarchist and Marxist texts ever disseminated on the islands. He also "took advantage of the occasion to put into practice the good ideas I had learned from the anarchists of Barcelona" by helping organize the first Filipino labor union, the Unión Obrera Democrática, which triggered a massive strike wave in Manila.[52]

Sempau remained in prison for many months after de los Reyes's release. According to Montseny, Charles Malato, who had helped plan the attack on Portas, traveled to Barcelona to break Sempau out of prison. Apparently, he rented the top floor of a house that was right next to Sempau's cell with the plan of somehow breaking through the wall to free him.[53] The plausibility of the existence of such a plot is enhanced by a report from the French consul in Barcelona in the spring of 1898 that an international anarchist network spanning Barcelona, Paris, and London was planning a jailbreak for Sempau.[54] The scheme went awry, however, when a prisoner informed the authorities. A few days later the other prisoners murdered the prisoner who revealed the plot, and Malato went on the run to Cartagena before arriving in Madrid, where he supposedly recounted the entire fiasco to Montseny.[55]

With escape out of the question, Sempau's fate was in the hands of the jury. Perhaps to his surprise, the jury agreed with the defense's argument that, given the reputation for extreme and often unprovoked brutality that Portas and his associates had developed, Sempau had every reason to fear for his safety and had therefore acted in legitimate self-defense. Outraged, the prosecutor called for a second trial that was held two months later. To his dismay, however, the second jury returned with essentially the same opinion, only sentencing Sempau to two months and a day in prison. The civil jurisdiction of the tribunal provided space for mounting popular outrage to put the "Inquisitors" on trial instead of Sempau. His acquittal was their conviction. As the former prime minister of the First Republic, Nicolás Salmerón, wrote in *La Revista Blanca*, "The second absolution of Sempau demonstrates anew the desire that the Spanish people feel to bring light to the sinister *proceso de Montjuich*. The jury . . . declares that it also condemns the torture applied in the famous Catalan castle."[56] The verdict was also an opportunity for the influential novelist Vicente Blasco Ibáñez to lament Spain's place in the world:

> And it's that all of Spain is embarrassed by the vile spectacles of ferocity that we have given the world in these recent years. We even dreamed that Europe would be at our side in the conflict we sustained with the United States! Why? Paris is the mind of Europe: there, continental opinion is formed, there, the floodgates of sympathy and antipathy for the nations open. And in Paris, a sensational drama has been performed throughout this entire past year. *Les mauvais bergères* by Octave Mirbeau. In this drama, the Parisian public cried hearing accounts of

their protagonist, an enlightened and revolutionary worker who spoke of the torments suffered in the cells of Barcelona, like an explorer in Morocco would speak about the prisons of Fez, or Stanley of the sacrifices of the tribes of central Africa.[57]

As Ibáñez's remarks demonstrate, the loss to the United States played a critical role in alerting the Spanish population to its government's isolation in the international arena and the Montjuich campaign compounded this popular shame by indicting Spanish identity before a European stage. For many there was no greater disgrace than being put on a moral par with African "savages." The embarrassment that the torture and executions generated in the wake of the devastating loss of the last remnants of Spain's once expansive empire renewed governmental interest in coordinating with other countries to combat the international anarchist menace.

Therefore, Spain sent a representative to the International Conference for the Social Defense against Anarchists held in Rome from November 24 to December 21, 1898, which was organized in response to the Italian anarchist Luigi Lucheni's assassination of Austro-Hungarian empress Elisabeth in Geneva earlier that year. The debates of the conference attendees hinged on differences over civil liberties and the legitimate frontiers of dissent. Ultimately, the conference voted on Monaco's proposal that an anarchist be defined as one who commits an "anarchical act," understood as any act aimed at the "destruction by violent means of any social organization."[58] Countries like France and the United Kingdom bristled at such a broad, vague definition. Ultimately the United Kingdom did not even sign the final conference protocol, which was nonbinding and almost entirely ineffectual.[59]

Yet while European officials were attempting to craft broad measures to repress anarchism, the efforts of the Spanish government to use the Cambios Nuevos *atentado* of 1896 as a pretext for repressing the movement were faltering. Once the dust settled after the momentous loss of Spain's overseas colonies, the Montjuich campaign exploded across the country as a pivotal outlet for a collective expression of nationalist insecurity and humanitarian rejuvenation.

CHAPTER 10

"All of Spain Is Montjuich"

Though the Montjuich campaign went into forced hibernation during the war with the United States and remained in a state of inactivity during the winter of 1898–99 as the country came to terms with *el Desastre*, once the dust settled the anger and frustration generated by the loss of Spain's overseas colonies catapulted the Montjuich campaign to the forefront of national politics. The military defeat and forfeiture of the last vestiges of the once "glorious" Spanish Empire in the Americas heightened the urgency of remedying the political and social ills responsible for Spain's plummeting position in the global order. This widespread yearning for societal rebirth would produce the literary "Generation of '98" over the coming years, and it found an ideal outlet in the renewed agitation for the revision of *el proceso de Montjuich* that blossomed anew moving into the spring of 1899 under the Liberal politician José Canalejas's slogan "All of Spain Is Montjuich." Given the centrality of ethical norms in Western conceptions of modernity and progress, the allegations of torture in Barcelona vividly demonstrated the rotten core of the "degenerated" Spanish monarchy to many sectors of society. How could Spain be expected to move into the twentieth century at the forefront of innovation when it remained mired in the brutality of centuries past? If something were not done, Spain would be left behind. In this spirit Nicolás Salmerón referred to a large Montjuich meeting in June 1899 as "the first step in the regeneration of Spain."[1] Of course, such considerations were far more pressing for middle- and upper-class journalists and politicians than they were for workers and peasants who were forced to focus on feeding their families and avoiding incarceration. For that reason, the Montjuich campaign developed into a powerful cross-class force that united lower-class outrage at abuses with more elite insecurity about the diminutive stature of Spain among the concert of powers.

Throughout this period the Dreyfus affair beaconed from across the Pyrenees as a model of dissident unity in the face of a retrograde injustice. As a group of Spanish republicans based in Cette, France noted, "To make justice a fact, to demolish militarism, in the Dreyfus affair the moderates like Pressensé, the radicals like Clemenceau, and the socialists like Jaurés have no objection to uniting with the anarchist Sébastien Faure, and with those who are at the forefront of the Universities, the *intelectuales*."[2] Not long after the Dreyfus affair cemented the importance of the newly coined *intellectuel* in the first "battle of opinion where the press played the crucial role,"[3] Montjuich campaigners attempted to bridge the gap between the lower classes and their own *intelectuales*. Shortly after Émile Zola's trial for insulting the French military unfolded on the world stage, liberal prime minister Práxedes Mateo Sagasta was replaced with the conservative Francisco Silvela.[4] The return of a conservative administration dimmed hopes that the government would rectify the situation on its own, which in turn accentuated the need for popular action and outrage.

Into this fertile context emerged the radical journalist Alejandro Lerroux after his eight-month stint in prison for his subversive article in *La Revista Blanca*. Undaunted by the collapse of *El Progreso* during his imprisonment, Lerroux created the similarly named *Progreso* in March 1899 to continue the campaign. Joan Montseny and his journal supported the new venture. As opposed to its predecessor, *Progreso* was a weekly rather than a daily, and it lacked a fixed staff after a number of its early collaborators abandoned the project, leaving the bulk of the writing and production work to Lerroux. The majority of the collaborators who stuck with *Progreso* were anarchists invested in the campaign.[5] In fact, over time Montseny noticed that Lerroux and his paper were drawing closer and closer to a revolutionary anarchist position, but he always doubted Lerroux's sincerity. As Montseny recalled years later, on his speaking tour Lerroux "acquired the conviction that in Spain there were many anarchists in the working class that, for their good faith, could be easily tricked. . . . [Lerroux] knew how to be an anarchist wherever he understood that the majority of his audience [was anarchist]." But to Montseny Lerroux "couldn't be an anarchist; he didn't have a soul that was sufficiently self-abnegating to be one." Montseny was upset with what he considered to be opportunistic politicking, and his feelings toward Lerroux soured further after *Progreso* published an article that was critical of him at the instigation of the famous writer Azorín. Azorín was angry that he had been passed over in favor of Montseny when Lerroux was selecting the paper's anarchist editor. Embittered, Azorín had his revenge, souring the relationship between Montseny and Lerroux.[6]

Yet the campaign was growing and expanding well beyond the purview of their relationship. On May 15, 1899, the Barcelona committee organized a large protest meeting that demanded the revision of *el proceso de Montjuich*, the immediate dismissal of those responsible for the torture, and the demolition of Montjuich Castle. The tone, if not necessarily the actual intentions, of the republican orators shifted in a noticeably revolutionary direction as speaker after speaker asserted that if their demands were not granted, they would have to be taken by force. One speaker even predicted a rejuvenating sequel to the French Reign of Terror of 1893, to which the ecstatic crowd responded, "Let's begin! Let's begin!" The meeting ended with shouts of "Death to the executioner Portas!"[7] At the same time the campaign received a boost from the announcement that a civil guard corporal who was held responsible for some of the torture in Montjuich and a civil guard sergeant recently returned from Cuba were being charged with torturing a worker to get him to confess to a robbery.[8] The brutality that the corporal unleashed on this unfortunate worker seemed to demonstrate the legitimacy of the Montjuich torture accusations.

A monumental shift occurred in late May when the recently established newspaper *Vida Nueva* convened a broad press committee to coordinate the growing Montjuich campaign. This impressive committee included five liberal papers, *El Imparcial*, *El Correo*, *El Liberal*, *El Globo*, and *El Heraldo de Madrid*; three conservative papers, the Canovite *La Época*, *El Nacional*, and *El Español*; and even the Carlist *El Correo Español*, in addition to the republican *El País*. Newspapers that had called for the indiscriminate slaughter of anarchists regardless of their culpability months earlier had been won over to the side of revision. Even more surprising, perhaps, was the announcement by *El Heraldo de la Guardia Civil* that it would dissociate itself from any members of the military who had participated in torture.[9] The near unanimity of the Spanish press about the need to revise *el proceso de Montjuich* shocked Captain General Despujol, who wrote that "every day, not only in more or less radical papers, but in the press of temperate opinions, they call Lieutenant Portas and his guards murderers and executioners; and even in military periodicals (God forgive it!)."[10]

The complete transformation of the outlooks of many of the country's major periodicals certainly owed a great deal to the perspective that the bad press generated by the campaign had contributed to Spain's isolation when confronted with the United States and the looming specter of Montjuich becoming "our 'affaire,'" as *La Época* phrased it. This conservative paper, which had recently made an abrupt about-face to support the campaign, derided how Spain was continually "swept up in imitation of our neighbors" and cautioned against imitating the example of the Dreyfus affair too closely because of its social division and "street conflicts."[11] The republican *El Nuevo régimen* seized on these comments to argue that *La Época* changed sides because it "fear[ed] the social unrest that was born in France during the Dreyfus affair."[12] In addition to the fear of popular upheaval if a revision of *el proceso de Montjuich* were not undertaken, another immediate impetus for support of the campaign was the publication of drawings of the torture implements. For although the Spanish public had read a great deal about the Barcelona atrocities over the past few years, it was not until the spring of 1899 that they saw them. The first images were published in *Vida Nueva* two weeks before it

FIGURE 9. Images of torture in *La Campana de Gracia*, May 20, 1899.

formed the press commission, and *La Campana de Gracia* and the *Suplemento a la Revista Blanca* published more over the coming weeks.[13]

In a culture that was far less visual than our own, where realistic images of pain and suffering were far less common, the sight of genital mutilation, beatings, and other forms of torment was exceptionally startling. For many,

FIGURE 10. Images of torture from *El Suplemento a La Revista Blanca*, June 24, 1899.

the images likely endowed the arguments of the campaign with an immediacy, directness, and emotional impact that written or oral descriptions could not quite muster especially for the illiterate.[14]

The power of such images was evident in La Vanguardia's explanation of its shift in favor of the campaign the day after the publication of Vida Nueva's images: "While the accusations weren't concrete, the nature of the affair could oblige the authorities and public opinion to take them with reserve . . . but when concrete cases are cited, and the papers even publish, without any correction, images of the denounced instruments of torture, it is an elemental duty of those who govern, and a necessity of the good name of the nation, to provide satisfaction to the public sentiment of justice and humanity."[15] The images of torture didn't bring about this dramatic about-face on their own, but they proved powerful enough to overcome the lingering reluctance of many papers to join the movement.

Among those moved by the images of torture was an American woman named Katherine Lee Bates who was writing a travelogue of her journeys across Spain. While living in Madrid, Bates subscribed to the "daring Madrid weekly" Vida Nueva. One day in late June 1899 she noticed that her copy of Vida Nueva contained two tickets to a "most unusual occurrence, a Madrid mass meeting" for the revision of el proceso de Montjuich at the Frontón Central. She and her friend decided to undertake "so harebrained an expedition" as to attend the meeting. As they approached the venue, they found themselves swamped in a sea of thousands of people spilling into the Plaza del Carmen trying to get into the building. Their cabman was reluctant to leave them in such "tempestuous surroundings" but they were determined to attend. As they grew closer they "saw men fighting fiercely about the door, we heard the loud bandying of angry words, we were warned again and again that we could never get through the jam, we were told that, tickets or no tickets, ladies would not, could not, and should not be admitted; it was darkly hinted that, before the evening was out, there would be wild and bloody work within those walls." There were quite a few women in attendance, however, and seeing some of them made the Americans more confident about pressing forward.[16] Once inside, an usher helped them navigate a massive crowd of ten thousand, many of whom were standing, to comfortable gallery seats. After settling in, they listened to fourteen "representatives of all political ideas, of all social classes" call for the revision of el proceso de Montjuich weeks after the French Supreme Court of Appeal gave Dreyfus a second chance by annulling his court-martial.[17] Among the speakers were many of the most prominent journalists and politicians in the country, including liberals like José Canalejas, Segismundo Moret, and

El Imparcial editor Rafael Gasset; republicans such as Alejandro Lerroux, Pere Coromines, Blasco Ibáñez, and Nicolás Salmerón; socialist leader Pablo Iglesias; and even the conservative Count of Almenas, who announced that although he was conservative and Catholic, he was in favor of "reason and justice" above all else. Speakers also represented groups from other locations, such as a representative of seventy-four Catalan workers' societies, and Menéndez Pallarés, who, on behalf of workers from Almería, stated that "he did not come to carry out an act that was political, nor patriotic, nor of protest against affronts to nationality. We have come to carry out— he said—an act in the name of the rights of humanity."[18] Similarly, Bates wrote, "*Montjuich* has become a Liberal rallying cry, although the movement is not bound in by party lines. It is the Dreyfus *affaire* in a Spanish edition."[19] Canalejas closed out the meeting by thanking Doña López de Ayala for coming to represent the orphans and widows of Montjuich and lamenting that she could not address the audience because the time had passed for new orators to be added to the program. After he finished, however, López de Ayala, the secretary of the Barcelona committee, shouted out, "I solemnly protest this abuse" of being denied the right to speak.[20] The faux pas of excluding the woman representing those most affected by the topic of the meeting apparently did not greatly concern organizers.

The night before, an "immense bonfire" was constructed in Barcelona to burn symbols of Montjuich, including torture implements, dried cod, riding boots, an image of the castle, and a woman in mourning.[21] A little over a week later, Barcelona hosted another large meeting of ten thousand in the Nuevo Retiro Theater with thousands more outside. The meeting resolved to rescind the anti-anarchist law, fire and punish those responsible for torture, and support a legislative proposal that it be made easier to reopen cases based on faulty or coerced evidence. Although the government had recently announced that Montjuich Castle would henceforth only be used for military purposes rather than a prison, the meeting nevertheless demanded its demolition. The resolutions were endorsed by seventy-three societies and fourteen periodicals.[22]

The audience was very excited to hear the speakers but was especially ecstatic about Lerroux. As he stepped up to speak, the audience showered him with several minutes of lively applause before he uttered a word.[23] Having honed his oratory skills during his 1898 speaking tour, Lerroux had the room enraptured with his reflections on the campaign, his "evil obsession." Once he managed to whip the room into a lively applause, he "modestly" scolded his listeners for directing their admiration toward him when they should have been directing their respect toward the Montjuich victims. When one person shouted, "¡Viva Lerroux!" he replied, "No! ¡Viva la justicia!" This tragedy, Lerroux argued, was "the stamp that Spain wears on its forehead and makes it the mockery of the other nations."²⁴ In conclusion he shouted, "To arms, to arms, sons of the people!" which triggered ten minutes of applause.²⁵

At the conclusion of the meeting, the speakers left the theater only to be engulfed in an eager and energetic crowd of supporters that pleaded with Lerroux and Iglesias to accompany them to their local club. They were scheduled to speak at another meeting in nearby Sabadell that afternoon with the director of *Vida Nueva*, but they had no choice but to follow what was rapidly becoming an impromptu march down the Rambla de Cataluña.²⁶ Before long, they were confronted by the chief of police who ordered them to disperse. When the crowd simply whistled derisively and called him "an inquisitor," he lifted his baton, which many interpreted as a threat, causing the crowd to fall on him, striking him several times and relieving him of his baton and hat as he fled into a nearby house. Undeterred, the crowd pursued the chief up to the fourth floor, where they "argued about whether they should kill him" as he pleaded for his life. For whatever reason he was spared. Mounted civil guards arrived on the Rambla de Cataluña, threatening to charge into the crowd. The protesters defiantly called them accomplices of Portas, but the march seems to have dispersed with one group smashing all of the windows of a Jesuit college and another cheering outside of the French consulate because of the annulment of the Dreyfus verdict.²⁷ According to *La Dinastía*, one group chased Lerroux as he was getting on a tram in the Plaza de Cataluña, stoning the windows of the tram to get him to join the crowd. Leaving him no choice, Lerroux apparently rejoined the crowd, which set out for the Paseo de Gracia where they stoned a house thought to belong to a conservative deputy who recently argued that protesting the Montjuich verdict empowered anarchist bombers.²⁸

That same day Montjuich meetings were held across Catalonia and in cities like Zaragoza, Valencia, La Línea, and Palma de Mallorca. During the summer of 1899 the campaign spread across the country and beyond to Tangier, Morocco, where the city's Spanish Commission organized an event in July.²⁹ Although the Montjuich campaign was born in Paris and thrived abroad because of the inhospitably repressive political climate in Spain, once the Liberal government restored civil liberties in Spain the movement surged into the public spotlight at home. With the shift back to a Conservative government in 1899, authorities may have hoped to clamp down on the popular agitation that the campaign had unleashed, but it had already attained such substantial proportions that censorship and arrests would only have inflamed the situation.

A more subtle governmental response was necessary to end the campaign. The first part of this response was articulated on January 4, 1900, when the prosecutor in charge of the governmental inquiry into the allegations of torture finally released his report fourteen months after the start of an intentionally lethargic process. The report found that it was impossible "to admit that in the Civil Guard, in this Institute of honorable men, of anonymous heroes, of dark martyrs of duty . . . there could be brought together a half dozen of the cruelest wild beasts in the same Command." Rather than orchestrated brutality, the accusations were found to be the inventions of Pere Coromines and Fernando Tarrida del Mármol. The report affirmed the explanation of "the military doctors that the very same supposed victims of torture inflicted certain lesions upon themselves to be able to create a scandal, to interest the press that doesn't reason or doesn't want to reason . . . and manage through this method to obtain the revision of their case." This line of argumentation was taken to its extreme regarding the severe torture suffered by Sebastián Suñé. The report stated that since he worked as a cane cutter he would receive "injuries and show scars on his arm and hand and left side, on his thigh and even on his scrotum for working with a sharp knife. . . . Moreover, such workers work on high ceilings on provisional scaffolding so they frequently experience falls that, naturally, produce lesions and the consequent scars."[30] Apart from the absurdity of blaming such extreme abuse on workplace accidents, Suñé had actually left his cane-cutting job to become a doorman before he was arrested.[31] Although the campaign pushed the crimes of Montjuich to the forefront of the national agenda, it was simply inconceivable for the government to explicitly admit such grave abuses.

Since the report denied any evidence of malfeasance, the only way for the government to squelch the Montjuich campaign was to issue a royal pardon, which is exactly what happened on January 25, 1900. Thanks to Alfonso XIII's "sentiments of forgiveness and forgetting," those still languishing in African prisons were to have their sentences commuted to banishment from Spain.[32] The Spanish foreign minister explained to the British ambassador that the decision was intended to "calm the passions a little."[33] The pardon was an effective means of alleviating the mounting pressure for revision that risked boiling over after the governmental report denying wrongdoing without fully alienating the army or the upper classes. It also succeeded in splitting the Montjuich movement between those who were satisfied with the pardon and those who saw it as an arbitrary palliative designed to torpedo the campaign without admitting any wrongdoing. Yet, with the judicial avenue closed and the remaining prisoners liberated, hopes of continuing the pressure dissipated. The campaign drew to a close.

On the evening of April 16, 1900, Montseny stood on a Barcelona dock with relatives of the dozen prisoners on board the ship *Hernán Cortés* as it slowly approached land. The former prisoners hoped to be brought to the French border the next night, but they spent a week in jail before they even had the opportunity to inform authorities that they wanted to go to Marseille.[34] When France declined their request, the prisoners left for Cuba, Mexico, and Algeria.[35] On April 27 Barcelona authorities once again loaded eleven prisoners onto a ship bound for Liverpool.[36] Although the identical act had caused an international incident three years earlier, the government was eager to rid itself of the last remnants of Montjuich. During an era when other European governments were struggling to implement accords and measures to facilitate extradition so they could prevent their dissidents from operating abroad, Spain was simply trying to get rid of them.

On May 1, 1900, the British ambassador asked for an explanation of this blatant violation of the agreements of 1897. A day later, the Spanish Ministry of State clarified that they were not sending dangerous criminals but simply men who had been imprisoned for propaganda (thereby tacitly confirming the accusations of the protests), and that they would take them back if they caused problems in the United Kingdom.[37] After their arrival, the newly liberated prisoners were taken to London, where Tarrida del Mármol, Kropotkin, and other comrades and allies organized a warm reception at the German Club.[38] British authorities were utterly shocked to catch word of yet another shipment of anarchists heading their way on May 10, only days after the recent arrival in Liverpool. When confronted, the Spanish replied that the ship was stopping in La Coruña rather than continuing to the United Kingdom. With the plan to banish more anarchists to England foiled, the ship stopped in Santander where the six prisoners were initially freed before being thrown back in jail thirty-six hours later. These prisoners had asked to go to Mexico but were denied. Now the government did not know what to do with them. After another letter of protest from the Santander prisoners, in mid-July the government decided to solve the matter by simply rescinding the order of expulsion as long as the former prisoners did not reside in Catalonia.[39] Yet it was not until the middle of September that the Santander prisoners were released. The next month some of them returned to Catalonia anyway, defying the royal decree, and although they were initially arrested, they were released shortly thereafter, essentially nullifying the final limitations on their freedom.

Although the prisoners were freed, the government did not mete out any punishment for those responsible for the torture. To some extent the public did, however. One day in early 1900, one of the alleged torturers from Montjuich Castle went to the Sans market to sell handkerchiefs to supplement his income (reflecting the poor wages paid to guards and police in general). As he laid out his wares, "a transient" recognized him and started to berate him. Before long the crowd started to harass him and he was forced to flee "to save his skin." The market vendors were advised not to allow him to return.[40] The press campaign succeeded most strikingly in making Lieutenant Portas, the main torturer who had come to be known as "the Spanish Trepov," a household name. Writing months after Sempau's failed *atentado*, Azorín described Portas as living in a constant state of terror: "Portas is haggard, his physiognomy reveals the torture of fear; he is always escorted by six or eight officers. . . . He goes out very little at night, and when he does he is disguised; he never walks on the sidewalk, but rather in the middle of the streets, and when it is dark he carries a revolver in his hand, as if he fears that from behind each door or each corner an avenger is about to strike."[41] According to Kropotkin, who undoubtedly spent hours speaking with the exiled Montjuich martyrs in London, Portas had become a societal outcast in Catalonia: "The cafés are left empty when he enters, the owners of hotels beg him to leave, because of the fear of losing clientele, since they have been appropriately warned, and the same happens to other vendors: if they sell to Portas, no one will enter their establishment. He will end up as a rabid dog; because he can't be pardoned for his crimes, humanity cries for vengeance against him."[42]

Sometime around 1900 the Catalan anarchist pedagogue Francisco Ferrer was at a train station in Barcelona with two small children he was transporting to Paris when he noticed Portas across the platform. In an exaggerated, loud voice he started to explain to the children how Portas had tortured many people. His explanation started to generate a spectacle, causing the infuriated civil guard lieutenant to confront Ferrer and ask for his identification.[43] This perpetual insecurity and harassment eventually led Portas to resign his post with the judicial police and accept a transfer to Madrid, where there was less popular outrage around Montjuich. Even in Madrid, however, there were still those who remembered his crimes, as we will soon see.

If the Montjuich prisoners were innocent, then who bombed the Corpus Christi procession in June 1896? Many anarchists blamed the police since the bomb exploded at the rear of the procession where the common people marched rather than at the front where it would have injured elites.[44] Some anarchists may simply have expressed this speculation publicly in order to resist the negative association between the bombing and anarchism. For example, the *Suplemento a la Revista Blanca* argued that the bomb had been detonated by current and former police as part of "a Jesuit-bourgeois plot," but in his memoirs years later Montseny clarified that he did not actually believe this interpretation.[45] Instead it seems that a French anarchist named Girault (or Giraul) was responsible.[46] In November 1896 Henri Rochefort published a controversial article in support of the Montjuich prisoners claiming that the real author of the bombing was not Spanish and had fled overseas. While this was certainly a convenient story to deflect guilt from Spanish prisoners, it seems that this may have been based on accurate information from Malato. In April 1899 Tarrida del Mármol claimed that he could finally reveal the identity of the bomber since he had died. According to Tarrida, the bomber had been a thirty-year-old French tailor named Giraul who had fled to London days after the bombing and laid low for a few months in a place near Fitzroy Square. Rudolf Rocker recounted years later how Girault soon realized how his actions had affected the hundreds who had been arrested, and he sought out Tarrida and Malato to confess and ask for guidance. They beseeched him to turn himself in to save the many who were in jeopardy, but he did not like the advice he received so he fled to Argentina instead.[47] According to Luis Bonafoux, in London Girault was hiding with an Italian anarchist named Mataini. To help him escape, Mataini shared Girault's story with his comrades at the local anarchist club and they raised the money for his voyage to Buenos Aires.[48] Years later the prominent anarchist Diego Abad de Santillán recounted a conversation in 1925 with Jean Grave, where Grave claimed that Girault had just passed away in Argentina after spending years there without any contact with the anarchist movement.[49] Although there's no definitive evidence to verify this claim, a number of well-connected anarchists affirmed it and historians generally consider it to be fairly plausible.[50]

For Alejandro Lerroux, the Montjuich campaign was a "clear, concrete . . . grand and noble" cause that could unite "all the radicals."[51] And unite them it did. The campaign's broad, apolitical focus on affronts to humanity allowed for the collaboration of republican factions that barely spoke with each other in conjunction with dynastic Liberals whom many republicans considered to be traitors to the First Republic, along with the anti-bourgeois Socialist Party and working-class unions and labor organizations, and anarchists who until recently were the universal pariahs. "Intellectuals" were also stirred into this mix in a significant way for the first time. As historian José Álvarez Junco wrote, "It was the first time they used their mobilizing capacity to influence the media."[52] Like the Dreyfus affair, the Montjuich campaign was the ideal venue for intellectual participation since it oriented itself around expressing an argument to influence public opinion. As opposed to the labor movement, where the average worker had a more direct connection to the struggle than any journalist or writer, the press campaign developed a very clear division of labor wherein the intellectual, journalist, or politician would articulate the maliciousness of the atrocity (sometimes giving space in their text to the direct testimony of the victim) while the workers and peasants would endure the majority of the suffering and provide the bulk of the demonstrators to cheer the speeches of formally educated orators. Certainly, the fact that a number of middle-class, educated figures were incarcerated blurred this dynamic slightly and lent more credibility to the public testimony of men such as Pere Coromines and Fernando Tarrida del Mármol. Nevertheless, it was clear that the prisoners who languished in Barcelona and Africa moving into 1898, 1899, and 1900 were those who lacked the money to pay for their exile and the political connections to push for their release.

Alejandro Lerroux capitalized on the opening that the campaign provided to parlay his extensive network of journalistic, literary, and political contacts into serious working-class credibility for editing the first Spanish paper to seriously take up the cause. His flirtation with anarchism to appeal to the popular classes was indicative of a growing frustration within republican ranks over their failure to fully appreciate the economic demands of the lower classes. This rhetorical shift toward insurrection and working-class issues allowed him to use his recently acquired revolutionary prestige to make *Progreso* the organ for the short-lived Unión Socialista, which united Marxists, anarchists, and revolutionary republicans in the same organization around the principles of collectivized property and anti-electoralism. One of the organizers of the initiative credited the Montjuich campaign with creating the climate necessary for such broad collaboration. Moreover, *Progreso* became the unofficial organ of the new anarchist Federación de Sociedades Obreras de la Región Española (FSORE) formed in October 1900, and Lerroux was even entrusted with the honor of reading the final manifesto of the federation before its first assembly.[53] Moving into the next decade, Lerroux would funnel the popular support he generated into a series of controversial electoral campaigns in Barcelona that ultimately reconfigured the region's political landscape. While Lerroux was busy refining his anti-authoritarian appeal, Montseny and his allies organized more "campaign[s] of liberation" oriented around what I refer to in chapter 11 as the "Montjuich template of resistance."[54] Over the next decade Montseny, Mañé, and new and old allies would take the lessons learned in the Montjuich campaign and apply them to new transnational struggles against "Spanish atrocities."

PART III

The Shadow of Montjuich

CHAPTER 11

The General Strike and the Montjuich Template of Resistance

Armed with shotguns, sickles, knives, and pistols, five to six hundred peasants streamed into the Andalusian town of Jerez de la Frontera shouting, "Death to the bourgeoisie" and "Viva la anarquía" shortly before midnight on January 8, 1892. Some of them headed to the jail to liberate comrades, mostly anarchists, who had been arrested days earlier for allegedly plotting an insurrection. Others set fire to the town hall and courthouse. Similar uprisings burst forth that evening in three nearby towns. The insurrectionaries sought to spur local populations to join the revolt, as they had in similar instances in Cádiz in 1868, Jerez in 1869, and Sanlúcar de Barrameda in 1873, but they were sorely disappointed. Rain and fear kept away what organizers expected would be thousands of rebels, the garrison of soldiers resisted rebel attempts to win them over to insurrection, the civil guard thwarted the siege of the jail, and ultimately the only spontaneous acts of resistance that the rebellion inspired were the random murders of a clerk and a traveling salesman for their bourgeois appearance.[1]

The ferocity with which the townspeople tore apart their victims attests to the vitriolic legacy of class war in Andalusia. The intense toil of agricultural workers on the large estates of local caciques in the production of sherry and other products yielded great wealth that did not trickle down to the impoverished rural population. In an exceptionally repressive political climate, even by Spanish standards, the centuries-old tradition of communal insurrection periodically burst forth in Andalusia when tensions erupted over the course of the nineteenth century. Ultimately dreams of social revolution fell flat. When efforts to storm the jail stalled, rebel peasants fled the town. Army reinforcements scattered those who remained.[2]

Though the Jerez insurrection of 1892 may have been the "last great spontaneous insurrectionary action of the Andalusian peasantry," out of its suppression "were born the first Spanish anarchist martyrs, the Martyrs of Jerez."[3] Of the 315 arrested for the insurrection, twelve were sentenced to life and twenty-three to long prison sentences, and four were executed by *garrote vil*. Another died mysteriously in his cell on February 10, 1892, the day of the executions. Testimony was coerced through torture.[4]

At the time, the international anarchist movement responded with demonstrations in New York, Milan, and Paris. It also responded with bombs that exploded at the Spanish consulate in Lisbon and Barcelona's Plaza Real, in addition to one that failed to go off at the consulate in Messina.[5] Not much of anyone else paid attention, however. Mass arrests. Torture. Executions. Lack of due process. In 1892, four years before *el proceso de Montjuich*, this cocktail of repression unleashed against impoverished Andalusian peasants failed to raise an eyebrow outside of anarchist circles. Eight years later, however, the Montjuich campaign had awakened public outrage at the "revival of the Inquisition"—outrage that the Spanish state now took seriously.

"Part III: The Shadow of Montjuich" analyzes the dramatic unfolding of five transnational Spanish prisoner campaigns over the next decade modeled on the precedent set by the Montjuich campaign. The successful template that the campaign established included the looming specter of retaliatory *atentados*. Though the mere threat of such attacks contributed to the urgency of acceding to the demands of campaigners, the attempts on the life of Alfonso XIII in 1905 and 1906 ought to be included within this broader movement of resistance against the "revival of the Inquisition." Yet the increasingly counterproductive nature of propaganda by the deed helped inspire a shift back to revolutionary syndicalism among the anti-authoritarian milieu shortly before the Tragic Week of 1909 when the general strike, human rights campaigning, and insurrection collided.

The Jerez de la Frontera prisoners of 1892 and the remaining prisoners from the Mano Negra affair of 1882—when Andalusian anarchists were accused of belonging to a murderous secret organization—took note of this unprecedented outrage over the treatment of anarchist prisoners in Montjuich Castle. As the Montjuich campaign gained momentum, they wrote to the editors of *La Revista Blanca* for help. Joan Montseny was already very familiar with their plight. Back in 1892 he had been imprisoned for more than three months for his coauthorship with a group of anarchists in Reus of a protest leaflet against the abuse of the "Jerez martyrs." This time, in 1900, Montseny agreed to organize campaigns on their behalf, but only once the Montjuich campaign ended, "fearing that if we ask for everything at once we'd get nothing." With state repression loosened in the wake of *el proceso de Montjuich*, they would first work for the liberation of the prisoners of 1892, then those of 1882 in order to narrow the focus of the public.[6]

Ironically, however, public sympathies were still tied up in efforts to obtain the legal revision of *el proceso de Montjuich* in order to definitively prove governmental malfeasance. *La Revista Blanca* kicked off its campaign for the Jerez prisoners in early February 1900 by calling on its readers and allies to "do for the Jerez martyrs what up until now we have done for those of Montjuich." Yet, in order to move on to the next campaign, the paper argued against the Barcelona commission's effort to push for a legal revision of the Montjuich case. "The revision of *el proceso de Cambios Nuevos* was for us nothing more than a pretext," the paper's editors argued. "In reality we pursued the freedom of the prisoners. . . . Revision, then, at this time is legal sensationalism that does not lead to any practical goal."[7] While liberal and republican Montjuich campaigners pursued their interpretation of justice through the framework of the legal system, the anarchists of *La Revista Blanca* rejected the notion that any justice could be found through the state beyond the release of their comrades.

To do for "the victims of the Andalusian bourgeoisie" what had been "done in favor of the victims of the Catalan bourgeoisie," the editors of *La Revista Blanca* attempted to capitalize on the momentum of the Montjuich campaign: the first "campaign of liberation," as Montseny later termed it. In his mind, it had created "in the popular consciousness a consideration that it never had previously" and demonstrated "that there was an idea and a social being with sufficient power to battle and win."[8] To reawaken this "social being," Montseny, Mañé, and their comrades turned to what I call the Montjuich template of resistance.

This template had four main components. The first was an aggressive press campaign that aroused passions through emotional appeals to empathy with victims of torture and execution grounded in the threat that "premodern barbarism" posed to national/civilizational status in accord with the ethics of modernity. Week after week *La Revista Blanca* published letters from current and former Jerez prisoners describing in graphic detail how the civil guard hung them from the ceiling with chains and whipped them until they signed false confessions or implicated others. Later, *Revista Blanca* editors published a letter from the mother of one of the prisoners and another from a daughter who was eight years old when her father was incarcerated. The paper's editors encouraged readers to copy and mail to newspapers and politicians a letter they had received from a prisoner who described having his genitals mutilated.[9]

The Jerez prisoners believed they could influence "liberal opinion" through these letters since readers would "understand our travails because [they] know how to feel."[10] By reaching out "to men of goodwill," the prisoners and their allies hoped to transcend political divides to tap into a broader sentiment of justice. For many readers, however, this sentiment was inextricably bound to their sense of national pride within an imagined civilizational hierarchy. *La Revista Blanca* included a flyer in one of their issues, which they encouraged their readers to insert into every copy of their local papers. In this flyer Urales argued that "without the colonies, we will lose our own nationality if we do not know how to embrace the conquests of the moral universe that constitute the political life of modern peoples."[11] The colonial loss of 1898 triggered a public debate on how to "regenerate" the nation moving into the twentieth century. *La Revista Blanca* sought to inject their interpretation of moral regeneration into the debate to free the Jerez prisoners.

As the months of 1900 passed, a handful of small newspapers, like Alejandro Lerroux's *Progreso*, supported the campaign, but the momentum of the Montjuich campaign did not automatically shift in favor of the Jerez prisoners.[12] Former Montjuich prisoner Teresa Claramunt lamented, "In Spain no one finds out about hidden infamies unless four distinguished periodicals recount them." Therefore, the way to combat "this crime against humanity" was to organize "an energetic and continuous campaign . . . that manages to interest opinion to the point where the dogcatcher papers see in the Jerez case a way to sell more papers."[13] *La Revista Blanca* "trust[ed] that if the foreign press [took] up the story of Andalusian torture with enough persistence and strength," then Spain would catch on, but that never happened.[14]

Part of the reason that the Jerez campaign struggled to develop was its lack of notable heroes and villains. Whereas the Montjuich campaign benefited from the high profile of the imprisoned lawyer Pere Coromines and the infamy of civil guard lieutenant Portas and Judge Marzo, the Jerez prisoners were "humble campesinos," and the brutal civil guard remained faceless eight years later. Jerez prisoner José Crespo Sánchez understood this dynamic when he argued that "it is necessary that Spain and the world realize that in Jerez we had a Marzo and a Portas."[15] Four months into the campaign, Teresa Mañé lamented popular disinterest. Writing as Soledad Gustavo, she concluded that "it was reserved uniquely and exclusively for the anarchists to find justice," but "it is said that a continual drop of water drills a hole in marble; we will be this drop." Though Mañé collaborated with her husband on the Montjuich campaign, she never wrote "even a single line in favor of those imprisoned in the evil castle out of the belief that [she] was not needed."[16] But given the lack of support for the Jerez prisoners, she took the lead in the press and in person by aiming to replicate the second main component of the Montjuich template: large public demonstrations and meetings.

Sporadic demonstrations for the Jerez prisoners had been organized around the country starting in the summer of 1900, but popular engagement with the campaign escalated when Mañé organized a speaking tour of Andalusia and Morocco with the radical journalist Alejandro Lerroux starting in September.[17] After a successful event in Seville, a planned demonstration at the Plaza de Toros in Jerez de la Frontera was canceled when local authorities pressured the venue owner to hold a bullfight instead of the demonstration. The comrades housing the speakers were threatened with arrest if their guests did not leave. Undaunted, Mañé was determined to stay one step ahead of the police as she spread word of the plight of the "Jerez martyrs." A planned meeting in Cádiz was canceled by the governor. Days later, the demonstration in Málaga was shut down in the middle of Mañé's speech. She fled before authorities could lock her up. Though Mañé had witnessed her share of wrongful arrests and police violence in Barcelona and Madrid, she was baffled by the level of repression in Andalusia. "In the Jerez countryside you need a character of iron to sustain the struggle. . . . Nothing less is possible to be an anarchist in this region."[18] When Lerroux canceled his role in the tour, he was replaced by the feminist director of La Conciencia Libre, Belén Sárraga. Having Mañé and Sárraga at the top of the bill attracted a lot of women out to the Jerez demonstrations. Recognizing the nature of her audience, Mañé "dedicated poetic and moving phrases to the Andalusian woman, inviting her to think of the future and join the cause of justice."[19]

One of the goals of the speaking tour was to promote the development of the third component of the Montjuich template: broad coalitions composed of groups and prominent individuals across the political spectrum. Initially this occurred on the local level where a coalition of republican, freethinking, and Masonic groups organized Mañé's meeting in Seville in September. By November, Emilio Junoy, the republican journalist and president of the Barcelona Revisionist Committee for el proceso de Montjuich, agreed to dissolve the Montjuich committee and create a Jerez committee.[20] That same month allies in Paris created an international solidarity group called "The Liberty of Opinion and Solidarity Group." Writing on behalf the group, the anarchist Charles Albert argued that "every individual who fights for their right of opinion, whatever that opinion may be, serves the cause of all humanity." The anarchist initiators of this group managed to attract many notable figures across the left spectrum, including Émile Zola, Georges Clemenceau, Séverine, and the soon-to-be president of the Ligue des droits de l'homme, Francis de Pressensé, in addition to anarchists like Kropotkin, Elisée Reclus, Paraf-Javal, and Charles Malato. *La Revista Blanca* and *Progreso* signed on to the organization, and sister groups were formed in Barcelona and Madrid.[21] The group donated over 300 francs to the Montjuich exiles and likely would have contributed more to the Jerez campaign had it not ended abruptly, though successfully, with a general pardon issued signed on February 7, 1901, on the occasion of the marriage of the princess of Asturias.[22]

One might be tempted to conclude that the ominous potential of a sequel to the Montjuich campaign terrified authorities enough for them to relent before the Jerez campaign could gain momentum. Yet the Jerez prisoners were among many who were pardoned along with journalists who had been sentenced for press crimes, military deserters, and others. According to *La Época*, this was the thirteenth general pardon issued by the Restoration regime. Given the campaign's lack of journalistic and popular support, the government was by no means compelled to release the Jerez prisoners. Without the campaign, however, it is unlikely that their plight would have gained the attention of the government officials who decided who to pardon for the princess. After all, several general pardons had been issued since their conviction in 1892, but it was only once the campaign began that they were included.[23]

While the liberation of the remaining Jerez prisoners may have had as much or more to do with the fortunate timing of the royal wedding as the actual strength of the campaign, when assessing the dynamics of anarchist prisoner campaigns, it is important to bear in mind the fourth component of the Montjuich template: the explicit and implicit threat of reprisals. Much of the success of the Montjuich campaign was owed to the conciliatory policies of the Liberal prime minister, Sagasta, who replaced Cánovas after he was assassinated by Angiolillo. Anarchist campaigners were well aware of the looming threat posed to intransigent government officials. Days after the assassination of Italian king Umberto in the summer of 1900, and a month before her speaking tour began, Teresa Mañé explained that the goal of her tour was "to remedy an injustice, to protest against a juridical outrage, and to form as a result a public opinion powerful enough for the government to see that it is absolutely necessary that these men who were snatched from their families at night are returned to them if it does not wish to run the risk of daring reprisals from below born of the injustice of those of above." It is unclear whether such calculations played into the state's decision to include the Jerez prisoners in the general pardon. Clearer is the fact that anarchist campaigners recognized, and to varying degrees lauded, the menacing specter of retaliatory *atentados*. In response to the assassination of Umberto, the editors of *La Revista Blanca* addressed the "powerful of the earth," asking, "If you have made a god of force, why do you condemn this same god when it comes for you?"[24]

Though the threat of the retaliatory *atentado* may have terrified elites, by the end of the century more and more anarchists bemoaned its counterproductive effects. Labor-oriented anarchists Ricardo Mella and José Prat asked their comrades for "a moment of cold reflection" because *atentados* had "alienated the sympathies of the masses." The time had come, they argued, for "a politics of attraction that will return to us what has been lost."[25] Over the coming decade, the revived role of anarchists and antiauthoritarians in the labor movement in Spain and France would infuse a greater focus on proletarian struggle into the rhetoric of Spanish prisoner campaigns and make labor struggles a more significant aspect of campaign strategy. After the repression of *el proceso de Montjuich* had subsided, that "politics of attraction" started to manifest itself when 157 labor groups from across the country representing approximately 52,000 workers formed the Federación de Sociedades Obreras de la Región Española (FSORE) in Madrid in October 1900. Although the inaugural congress announced that the FSORE was apolitical and open to workers of all tendencies, its federal structure, hostility to electoral politics, and rejection of a potential "government of the proletariat" were indicative of its thoroughly anarchist character. The FSORE was the first libertarian labor federation in Spain since the Pacto de Unión y Solidaridad de los Trabajadores de la Región Española, which replaced the FTRE in 1888 and formally dissolved in 1896, though its power peaked in the early 1890s. Spanish socialists created their own Unión General de Trabajadores (UGT) in 1888 to compete with their anarchist counterparts, but in 1900 its 14,737 members were less than a third of the new FSORE.[26]

While Teresa Mañé was touring Andalusia in support of the Jerez prisoners, Joan Montseny was among the delegates in Madrid who signed the FSORE platform calling for an eight-hour day, a living wage, maternity leave, an end to child labor, and other demands.[27] By its second congress in October 1901, the 73,000 members of the new federation fully embraced the newly reinvented strategic weapon that most definitively distanced them from their socialist counterparts: the general strike.[28]

Emerging out of English Chartism and Owenite "utopian socialism" in the early nineteenth century, the theory of the general strike of all workers started to develop concretely in the debates of the First International. Though Engels considered the notion to be unrealistic, the third congress of the IWMA in 1868 declared that the general strike could be a useful anti-war weapon. Though many anarchists continued to agitate in workers' circles moving into the 1880s, the movement's general estrangement from organized labor in much of Europe opened space for the rise of propaganda by the deed. The exception was Spain, where anarchist influence on labor continued after the destruction of the FRE with the anarchist FTRE (1881–88). Like the FRE before it, the FTRE prohibited its member unions from striking for higher wages or to protest work conditions, and it required member unions to obtain federation approval for any strike—a lengthy bureaucratic process in the context of a heated labor grievance. Only defensive strikes against slashed wages or increased hours and large coordinated general strikes were allowed in an effort to prevent a slide into reformist bread-and-butter unionism. In practice, however, the moderate FTRE sought to rein in frequent, unregulated wildcat strikes and push back against anarcho-communist insurrectionism among its rural Andalusian base.[29]

The general strike had been "forgotten since the end of the 1870s" in Spain before it was reinvigorated by the successor to the FTRE, the Pacto de Unión y Solidaridad, for May 1, 1890. Seeds of change were evident when a dissident faction of the FTRE led by Anselmo Lorenzo launched a solidarity campaign with the upcoming general strike for the eight-hour day in the United States that culminated with the police bombing that produced the Haymarket Martyrs in 1886. Though the FTRE rejected the struggle for the eight-hour day in 1887, the new Pacto embraced it and vowed "unconditional support for every strike." The crippling state repression triggered by the Pacto's failed May 1 general strikes of 1890 and 1891 and the waves of mass arrests following the *atentados* of the mid-1890s pushed the prospect of a coordinated general strike to the margins.[30]

The general strike's return to prominence in Spain with the FSORE owed a great deal to the influence of French revolutionary syndicalism. Though the influence of the general strike started to return with its inclusion in the Bordeaux-le-Bouscat congress of 1888, its full reemergence in France came about after the end of *l'ère des attentats* with the creation of the Confédération générale du travail (CGT) in 1895 and the rebirth of the libertarian labor politics of the First International in the form of revolutionary syndicalism. The revolutionary syndicalists of the turn of the century sought to create "one big union" of all workers that would serve as a "laboratory of economic struggles," of "revolutionary gymnastics," which would simultaneously train the working class to seize power through a revolutionary general strike that would "abolish all political power" and form the embryo of the new economic order wherein the union would became "the owner of the instruments of production" after the defeat of the capitalist class.[31] The Second International was increasingly divided between syndicalists and reformist socialists who considered the strike to be a purely defensive tactic. Though important factions of the Belgian, German, and Italian socialist parties were beginning to theorize the revolutionary general strike, Spanish socialists were among the most recalcitrant. Pablo Iglesias, founder of the PSOE and UGT, considered the general strike to be a "thoughtless movement without a determined objective that lacked the revolutionary potential that some have attempted to endow it with."[32]

Anarchist unionists could not have disagreed more. In Spain the arrests, torture, executions, and forced exile suffered by many labor leaders in the 1890s opened space for a new generation of young anarchists to champion libertarian politics in the workers' movement. Alienated by the backlash from propaganda by the deed, but also thoroughly distanced from the cautious unionism of the FTRE of the 1880s, this cohort of early twentieth-century organizers was increasingly enthralled with the promise of the general strike. Its prestige radiated from pamphlets and newspapers disseminated from across the border and articles from longtime anarchist labor militants like Anselmo Lorenzo and José López Montenegro, who provided generational continuity from the era of the FRE. Through their writings, older terms like *societarismo* and *sociedad obrera* were replaced with *sindicalismo* and *sindicato* of French derivation. Historian Joaquín Romero Maura points out, however, that most Barcelona organizers were interested in the general strike "as an insurrectionary act" rather than as a component of the full theory of revolutionary syndicalism, which valued painstaking agitation for incremental victories on the way to the eventual seizure of the means of production.[33] That broader theoretical appreciation would not come in Spain until the formation of Solidaridad Obrera in 1907. As Eduardo González Calleja phrased it, "Step by step the old conceptions of insurrection and the individual *atentado* were dissolving or integrating into the vaguest idea of 'direct action,' as the principle of the general strike became a modernized expression of the insurrectionary and subversive component of Bakuninist anarcho-collectivism."[34] The first few years of the new century presented

Catalan anarchists with auspicious conditions for the fomentation of the insurrectionary general strike. With the legalization of unions in 1897, "implicit" state recognition of the right to strike in 1901 followed by a memo from the Supreme Court permitting strikes in 1902, and the end of *el proceso de Montjuich*, "for the first time in a long while Barcelona anarchists enjoyed an almost complete freedom to organize."[35]

They exercised that freedom as the shockwaves of *el Desastre* of 1898 began to ripple through the Catalan economy. Prior to its military defeat by the United States, Spain sent a third of its exports to Cuba alone in 1897. The importance of colonial markets compensated for, and in turn perpetuated, Spain's inability to export goods outside of the empire. Despite imperial protectionism, the only legitimate export industry the country could boast at the end of the century was textiles, and even the textile industry had been experiencing an artificial demand for material to clothe soldiers fighting colonial wars in the 1890s. The disappearance of colonial markets in 1898 did not immediately crash the Catalan economy because of elevated exchange rates, a significant repatriation of capital, and good harvests. In 1899 budget stabilization policies passed by the minister of finance to stem the coming tide of economic destruction triggered the *tancament de caixes*—a merchant and small business taxpayer strike that escalated into bloody conflicts in Zaragoza, Valencia, and Barcelona—which witnessed the construction of barricades, exchanges of gunfire with the police, and the declaration of a state of war.[36]

In 1900 crisis finally struck an unstable economy that had already been weathering significant inflation since the mid-1890s and a 70 percent increase in the cost of living since the early 1870s.[37] Over the coming years, anarchist unionists led the fight to resist wage reductions and extended hours because they had come to "dominate the most conflict-ridden trades on the back of aggressive union demands and strike action."[38] Among the most militant laborers in Barcelona were the tram workers, of which about 1,300 belonged to the anti-authoritarian FSORE when they went on strike in May 1901. Barcelona's tram network, recently electrified in 1899, stood still. The ability of transportation workers to grind a city's economy to a halt gave them a central role in any plans for a general strike. Days later they decided to wield that power by calling for a general strike after their demands for wage increases and exclusively union labor in the industry were rejected. When threats from union delegates to smash up factories that remained open led to numerous closures, authorities declared a state of war and sent in the military, quashing the strike.[39] Other major strikes broke out in Gijón, Zaragoza, Seville, and La Coruña, where a general strike was called after the civil guard gunned down a striker. Soldiers killed seven more and arrested 104 when a state of war was declared in the Galician port city.[40]

Teresa Mañé and Joan Montseny had planned to launch a campaign in support of the Mano Negra prisoners after freeing the "Jerez martyrs," but labor conflicts in Barcelona and La Coruña grabbed their focus. The columns of the *Suplemento a la Revista Blanca*, which had a print run of ten thousand by this point, recycled the rhetorical themes of earlier campaigns by appealing to "workers' societies, to the honorable press and to all men of goodwill in general" for a "campaign of . . . meetings of resonance, meetings of truth, that make opinion, that create an atmosphere to impede new crimes." If this were not accomplished, they argued, Spain could "disappear from the world of independent nations."[41] Solidarity with Catalan and Galician workers extended to demonstrations across Spain and abroad in London, Paris, Berlin, Montevideo, New York, Chicago, and Tampa, in addition to an event in Havana organized by the "Grupo Montjuich." Certainly, the Montjuich campaign had succeeded in creating a new Black Legend of Spanish cruelty that could be mobilized against new atrocities. This was evident when *La Protesta Humana* of Buenos Aires wrote, "A new Montjuich as odious as that of Barcelona rises on the heads of workers in La Coruña. In La Coruña, as in Barcelona, as in Jerez . . ."[42] Yet the centrality of labor in these protests infused *La Revista Blanca*'s defense of abstract humanity with an explicit focus on "international workers' solidarity."[43]

As workers mobilized to protect their interests, so too did industrialists organize to improve their standing. In the wake of *el Desastre*, the patriarchs of the twenty to thirty households that controlled the textile industry pressured the government in Madrid to grant them fiscal exemptions to offset their financial hardships. When the Catalan textile industrialists were rebuffed, they shifted their political loyalties to the Catalan nationalist movement, which had been percolating in literary and middle-class federal republican circles since the 1880s. In 1901 cotton magnate Alberto Rusiñol was named the president of the Lliga Regionalista de Catalunya, the first Catalan nationalist political party and the first serious challenge to the stranglehold over Catalonia that the dynastic parties had maintained for decades.[44]

In addition to their political machinations, Catalan textile magnates responded to the economic crisis by slashing wages, introducing new electric automatic spinners, lengthening the workday to thirteen hours, replacing men with women workers who were paid half as much, and illegally employing children, some under twelve years old.[45] Shortly after a meeting of Barcelona workers' societies on January 1, 1902, where one worker argued that "each workshop is a Montjuich and every boss a Portas," the textile workers and cartwrights joined metallurgical workers who had been striking since mid-December 1901 for increased wages and a nine-hour day.[46]

Employer intransigence opened space for anarchists such as Teresa Claramunt, Mariano Castellote, Leopoldo Bonafulla, and José López Montenegro to push workers' resistance further. Affiliated with the recently relaunched *El Productor*, these four had been locked up months earlier for their instigation of the previous general strike. Claramunt took to the podium at a workers' meeting on February 16, 1902. In an appeal to workers who had not yet walked off the job, Claramunt, then pregnant, clutched her womb and screamed, "This child of mine will not be a coward like you all!"[47] The next day began the largest general strike for labor demands (as opposed to the 1893 Belgian general strike for universal suffrage) that Europe had ever witnessed. A day-long general strike in Trieste had brought out twelve thousand workers, but the Barcelona general strike of 1902 included eighty thousand. Though anarchist attempts to coordinate the strike nationally in Madrid and Bilbao failed, the strike wave managed to spread across Catalonia.[48]

Strikers and other insurgents in Barcelona erected barricades in the working-class neighborhoods of Poble Sech and Pueblo Nuevo. Women armed with sticks marched from the Boqueria market through the streets, shutting down buses and trolleys and smashing the windows of businesses that refused to close. Markets and bakeries were sacked and an attempt was made to burn down a convent. With Barcelona effectively ground to a halt, strikers sang and danced in the streets. Authorities declared a state of war outlawing public congregations of more than three people and sent in the military, who were booed and hissed at every turn. A squadron of cavalry charged strikers blocking a train, killing one man and seriously wounding another. The message from the most militant strikers was scrawled on posters around Barcelona: "Think about it, Bourgeoisie!" They warned that the rifles of the military would be answered with dynamite.[49] The British consul general in Barcelona wrote, "The appearance of the city is that of a place in a state of anarchy and revolution. Everything is closed, no vehicles (not even the carriages of doctors nor hearses) infantry and cavalry everywhere, mails and food carts escorted by troops; firing heard first in one part then in another of the town, and the red cross society about with their ambulances."[50] The Barcelona upper classes were not content to trust that their security would be ensured by the rifles of the military, however. In addition to the government's military and police, local industrialists created an urban version of the *somatén*: a largely rural, bourgeois militia that was created in 1855 based on a medieval precedent. Among the creators of this new force was the Marquis de Comillas, who decades earlier had helped form counterrevolutionary defense units during the Ten Years' War in Cuba. *Somatenistas*, police, and military unleashed machine guns on insurgent barricades and charged into massive crowds. At times the sheer number of lower-class militants could overwhelm the official and unofficial agents of the state and de-arrest strikers as snipers took shots at soldiers from balconies above.

The modernist painter Ramón Casas i Carbó immortalized dramatic scenes such as these in *La Carga*, a landscape of urban class war inspired by Goya's depiction of urban guerrilla resistance to the Napoleonic invasion a century earlier in *El dos de Mayo*. Foreign diplomats and newspapers condemned daily scenes of urban warfare that took the lives of about a hundred and produced five hundred arrests. Newly attuned to the importance of international public opinion, Spanish authorities were "mortified" at foreign outrage, with one official lamenting that "they speak about us as if we were Poland."[51]

Elite fears abated when the strike ended in failure after a week on February 24, 1902. About fifteen hundred of the most militant workers were fired and labor leaders like Teresa Claramunt and Leopoldo Bonafulla were locked up. According to Anselmo Lorenzo, Catalan anarchism hit a period of "sad stagnation" after the strike. Though anarchists would continue to pursue labor action through 1903, the prestige of revolutionary syndicalism within anarchist circles declined. It would not recover until the creation of Solidaridad Obrera in 1907. The void left by the failure of the strike was filled by the creation of new alternative projects (i.e., cultural centers, mutual aid societies, cooperatives, educational ventures, etc.), a return to clandestine affinity groups inclined toward propaganda by the deed, and the flourishing of *lerrouxismo*: Alejandro Lerroux's innovative brand of fiery, populist demagoguery that swept the Barcelona working class mid-decade.[52]

Lerroux made a name for himself in the late 1890s as the journalistic voice of the Montjuich campaign after bringing Joan Montseny on board at *El Progreso*. In an era when republicanism was fragmented into marginal factions orbiting aging leaders of the First Republic, Lerroux debuted his unique gift for incendiary oratory on his 1898 Montjuich speaking tour when he sculpted an image of himself as a vigorous man of action. He wooed the Barcelona masses by denouncing electoral politics as a "waste of time and energy," accentuating his anti-clericalism, and calling for revolution: "a monster that needs new, young, virile, intelligent, selfless men that are audacious to the point of recklessness . . . faith and heroism."[53] Since the destruction of the First Republic in 1874, revolutionary republicans had searched high and low for a military strongman, like General Villacampa, to lead a republican revolution from above. Though the last relevant gasp of this conspiratorial militarism had expired in the 1880s, Lerroux and many other republicans held out hope that Valeriano Weyler or another general could take advantage of *el Desastre* to proclaim the republic.[54] As this dream faded and Lerroux attracted a popular following, he moved from Madrid to Barcelona to pioneer a new brand of populist republicanism from below.

Lerroux had already fallen out with Montseny, but many Barcelona anarchists considered Lerroux to be a fellow traveler when he arrived in 1901 to run for Congress despite his about-face on electoral politics. Montseny claimed that "the majority of Barcelona anarchists supported Lerroux," including some former Montjuich prisoners. The conflict between the former allies grew so bitter that Barcelona *lerrouxistas* organized protest meetings against *La Revista Blanca* calling for a boycott of the paper.[55] Despite portraying himself as the "flesh of the *pueblo*," Lerroux "avoided implicating himself" in the 1901 tram workers' strike. Similarly, he was advised to stay in Madrid for the duration of the 1902 general strike. His cautious flirtation with the working class won him regular seats in Congress on vote tallies that reached 35,000 in 1903.[56] As we will see, however, his electoral success did not entirely dispel his extraparliamentary aspirations.

Despite fallout within the ranks of Spanish prisoner activism, in October 1902 began the full thrust of the international campaign to liberate the eight remaining prisoners of the Mano Negra affair—when authorities claimed to have discovered a shadowy group of murderous anarchist campesinos in Jerez de la Frontera in 1882. Although Teresa Mañé had single-handedly maintained a regular Mano Negra column in *Tierra y Libertad* (the new name for the *Suplemento a la Revista Blanca*) since January 1902 that included prisoner letters and condemnations of "barbarism in the midst of civilization . . . like in the times of Attila," her appeals were entirely ignored. In part this owed to the fact that the wave of protests organized across Europe and Latin America in solidarity with Barcelona workers who had been arrested, fired, and assaulted during the general strike monopolized international outrage. In August Mañé gave up her campaign of one.[57]

The fortunes of the Mano Negra prisoners shifted when the Parisian anarchist newspaper *Les Temps nouveaux* published all of Mañé's articles and letters in late 1902. In turn, Mañé's campaign in *Tierra y Libertad* gained new life by translating articles from her new Parisian ally. The French translations of Mañé's articles and letters were then retranslated, allowing the campaign to spread to the United Kingdom, Belgium, the Netherlands, Morocco, Germany, Switzerland, Italy, Brazil, Austria, Algeria, and Argentina.[58] Protests included a large demonstration in Trafalgar Square supported by trade unions and a conference in Amsterdam on Spanish atrocities. In Spain unions and other allies (with the notable absence of the socialists) organized a coordinated day of protest on January 1, 1903. Outside of Spain, the flame of the Mano Negra campaign burned most brightly in France in the afterglow of the Dreyfus affair.[59] The campaign emerged as an outlet for the energy that had been diffused with the end of the affair's "heroic era" after Dreyfus's 1899 presidential pardon and the 1900 amnesty for all Dreyfus-related charges.[60] For months, *Les Temps nouveaux* and their allies called on prominent Dreyfusards to support the Andalusian prisoners, asking ironically, "Could a millionaire captain be more interesting than our Spanish brothers?"[61] The paper's editors argued that "saving them will save others" and "it is necessary to make governments see that not for nothing will they turn the most elemental principles of humanity into a dead letter."[62]

Appeals to the legacy of the Dreyfus affair worked. Many of the leading Dreyfusards rallied to support the Mano Negra prisoners, including Anatole France, Georges Clemenceau, and Jean Jaurès, while the Ligue des droits de l'homme and the syndicalist labor confederation CGT officially endorsed the campaign.[63] In their eyes, "the drama of the Dreyfus affair [had] prepared them to understand other dramas."[64] Soon-to-be *ligue* president Francis de Pressensé made an impassioned appeal to transfer the momentum of the Dreyfus affair to the Mano Negra campaign.[65] After beginning his article in *L'Aurore* by pointing out that "up until now the Montjuich affair is known" and establishing the bloody history of Spanish torture and repression, Pressensé concluded by arguing that "public opinion was moved in the past by the iniquitous suffering of Captain Dreyfus; it did well. If unfortunately, it is not moved before the tortures of these unfortunates; if the good and sensible bourgeoisie that left their shells of egoism and impassivity for *l'Affaire* shake their heads saying that they don't care about this *affaire* . . . we will have more proof that in our capitalist society not only is there no justice, there isn't even humanity."[66] The power of the campaign caused the Spanish government to "worry about this matter," according to the foreign minister. He attempted to pressure the French government to influence press coverage and shut down the "tumultuous agitation" across the border, but without success.[67] With the campaign in full swing across Western Europe, the Spanish government pardoned one of the prisoners in January and the remaining seven Mano Negra prisoners in early March 1903.[68] On declaring victory for the third time in three years, the editors of *Tierra y Libertad* reveled in the success of "the idea of international solidarity among good men" in the Montjuich, Jerez, and Mano Negra campaigns in addition to the Dreyfus affair, but they added that "it is necessary that our work continue in Spain, France, Italy, Russia, Macedonia, and wherever there is an attack on human individuality."[69]

That spring, Mañé, Montseny, and much of the Spanish Left broadened their focus beyond specific campaigns toward building a movement to liberate all imprisoned in Spain for "social questions." This initiative dovetailed with the continued allure of the general strike. Despite the failure of the 1902 Barcelona general strike, anarchists made several more unsuccessful attempts to foment general strikes throughout 1903. Meanwhile, their competitors, the socialist UGT, organized a campaign against the strategy of the general strike. Though thirty of the seventy-four strikes launched in 1903 became general within their trade, only six ended victoriously. Failed strike campaigns paired with aggressive solidarity striking resulted in widespread job loss and a 30 percent decline in union membership by the end of the year as employers created yellow unions.[70] Every strike put more workers behind bars and fueled turnout for regular protest meetings organized across the country with the support of the FSORE in the spring and summer of 1903 for the release of all political prisoners. In contrast, El Socialista argued that the way to free the prisoners was by focusing on the next municipal elections. These meetings culminated in a coordinated general strike across the country for August 1, 1903. In Barcelona soldiers took up positions at key locations around the city, including the tram depot, and the police raided radical editorial offices and workers' locals. Repression and incomplete adherence to the strike on the part of the tram drivers damaged the strike's ability to shut down the city.[71]

Unfortunately for its organizers, the strike wave did not gain steam in most regions. In the Andalusian town of Alcalá del Valle the civil guard opened fire on strikers, killing fifteen-year-old Sebastián Aguilera and seriously injuring several others. Several civil guardsmen were "seriously injured" in the ensuing clash as striking workers fought back with "firearms, sticks, and rocks." Tensions had been brewing in Alcalá del Valle since authorities shut down the workers' center in July and banned demonstrations in favor of the general strike. On the day of the strike, groups of strikers led by campesina women created "three large bonfires fueled by gasoline," into which they hurled furniture and official documents from government buildings, and set fire to the municipal archive and the local courthouse. In total, 118 strikers were arrested and charged.[72]

Within a week of the general strike, Mañé and Montseny started to report on rumors of torture that presaged a "new Montjuich in Alcalá del Valle." Over the following weeks their newly daily Tierra y Libertad published letters from Andalusian prisoners documenting how the civil guard committed "crimes against humanity" such as beating strikers unconscious, driving spikes under their nails, twisting their genitalia, and even allegedly causing a pregnant prisoner to miscarry by beating her womb in order "to kill the anarchist cub inside" of her.[73]

Spanish authorities responded to growing unrest and outrage by issuing an amnesty for two hundred prisoners in mid-August and escalating repression. *Tierra y Libertad* was confiscated and fined while Joan Montseny went into hiding in a cave after barely escaping from the police.[74] Over the coming months the government attempted to quash the new campaign against "legendary Spanish cruelty . . . in defense of humanity and civilization" that was developing across the country by suspending protest meetings, threatening venue owners, or shutting them down midway by prohibiting any mention of "Alcalá del Valle."[75] Despite such measures, and an official denial of allegations of torture by the interior minister, the Alcalá del Valle campaign grew across Spain on the strength of the same basic coalition of anarchist, republican, and labor groups that propelled its recent predecessors.[76] "I fear that

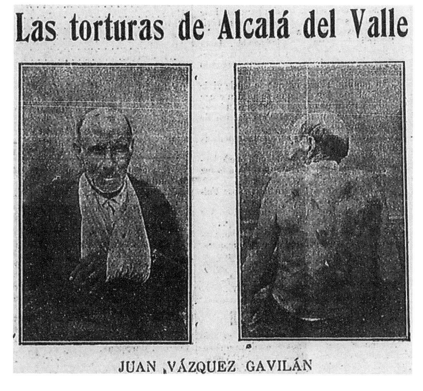

FIGURE 11. Photos of the injuries suffered by Alcalá del Valle prisoner Juan Vázquez Gavilán. *El Rebelde*, August 18, 1904.

this could be the start of a new campaign like they organized for the events of the Mano Negra years ago," the Spanish foreign minister worried.[77] The campaign in the Spanish press made the most of the latest publishing technology by printing photographs of the tortured workers and their injuries.

Although the half-tone process of reprinting photos in newspapers became economically viable in the United States and United Kingdom in the 1890s, it was only after 1900 that most Spanish papers started to implement the method.[78] By printing photographs rather than drawings, papers like El Gráfico and El Rebelde gave their readers a much more visceral connection to the plight of the prisoners and lent claims of torture a seemingly more factual basis. State officials also lamented the sensational impression given by El Gráfico's use of "colors rarely used in the printing of daily papers." El Rebelde also printed photographs of the handwritten prison letters, which also enhanced the immediacy of the reader's connection to the Alcalá del Valle prisoners.[79]

From late 1903 into early 1904 the Alcalá del Valle campaign in defense of the "rights of humanity" spread internationally by tapping into transnational networks that had been established through earlier campaigns and utilizing connections with exiled Spanish anarchists like the former Montjuich prisoners Baldomero Oller and Fernando Tarrida del Mármol in London, Fermín Salvochea in Tangier, and Pedro Vallina in Paris.[80] According to an informant in the pay of the Spanish embassy in Paris, the campaign also benefited from "an absolutely secret meeting" held at the 1904 Amsterdam congress of the International Antimilitarist Association where the delegates decided to organize "a large agitation . . . in favor of the Alcalá del Valle prisoners." Vallina attended that meeting and played a central role in spearheading the creation of a network of "International Committees" in Paris, Barcelona, Madrid, Valencia, Lisbon, London, Amsterdam, and Tangier that would agitate in their own regions against "Spanish atrocities" and edit a French-language periodical called L'Espagne inquisitorial: Organe de l'indignation internationale contre la tyrannie espagnole whose print run hit six thousand copies.[81] The campaign peaked in March and April 1904 with newspaper articles and protest meetings in Spain, France, Portugal, Belgium, the Netherlands, England, Austria, Croatia, Uruguay, Brazil, Argentina, Cuba, Germany, Italy, Switzerland, Morocco, Sweden, Russia, and the United States.[82] The Spanish embassy in Buenos Aires managed to plant an article in El Diario refuting the allegations, but attempts by Spanish embassies to influence foreign governments accomplished little.[83] The Parisian International Committee called for a boycott of Spanish ships and goods that was supported by the revolutionary syndicalist CGT. Apparently, dockworkers in the French Mediterranean cities of Cette and Marseille carried out the boycott so successfully that Spanish merchants pleaded with the Spanish government to release the Alcalá del Valle prisoners.[84] Pressure also came from the French government, which urged Spanish authorities to release the prisoners before the royal visit of Alfonso XIII to Paris a year later.[85] As chapter 12 demonstrates, the French fear of retaliation was well founded.

Other strategies for liberating the Alcalá del Valle prisoners were on the table as well, however. In late March 1904 the anarchist *El Rebelde*, which had a print run of eight thousand, wrote that it "considers necessary all methods, as violent or extreme as they may be, to arrive at the goal of the Humanitarian Campaign [i.e., the Alcalá del Valle campaign]." Days earlier, the secretary of the Federation of Metallurgical Workers in Madrid chastised the crowd by saying that "if everyone here had the same conviction as that brave anarchist [Angiolillo], everything would be sorted out already." An orator at a meeting in Paris was even more specific when he argued that Maura, the current prime minister, "is the successor of Cánovas. We propose him as such to all advocates of individual action." To which the crowd replied, "Death to Maura, the successor of Cánovas!"[86]

Exactly one month later, on April 12, 1904, a nineteen-year-old anarchist sculptor named Joaquín Miguel Artal answered the call. During Prime Minister Antonio Maura's visit to Barcelona, Artal jumped up onto the edge of his carriage and stabbed him with a knife. Maura received only a minor wound, however, and Artal was immediately arrested.[87] In prison, Artal wrote that he did not attack Maura as a person but rather as one who "personified the highest representation of the principle of authority" to avenge "the tormented of Alcalá del Valle." Rather new to anarchist theory, Artal claimed to have never met an anarchist. "Before entering prison, I knew the idea," he explained, "but I did not know the selfless men who defended it."[88] Although Artal attempted to assassinate the prime minister, he was not executed. Rather, he was given seventeen years and four months, though he died in prison in 1909.[89] After the cycle of reprisals that developed in the 1890s, the Spanish government was still loath to create more martyrs. According to the French inspector stationed in Barcelona, the government was even reluctant to pursue the possibility of a wider conspiracy, writing that "it was as if the government wanted Artal not to have had accomplices."[90] Another French source explained that the Spanish government was so "worried in August 1904 about the fantastic legends echoed in the European press" that Spanish judges were ordered to "immediately clarify the facts" of "any denunciation of so-called poor treatment" in order to "correct even the smallest abuse."[91] Months later, the mayor of Barcelona pleaded with Maura to discontinue his plan for a new anti-anarchist law because it would produce "terrible reprisals." Anarchists noticed this broad shift. According to an informant, Spanish anarchists in Paris "remarked that the Spanish government would not dare— as they had during the era of *el proceso de Montjuich*—to commit mass arrests. They say that the government fears that the time is ripe for demands."[92]

Over the summer of 1904 authorities released most of the Alcalá del Valle prisoners, but, according to *Tierra y Libertad*, thirty-nine remained incarcerated. An infiltrator reporting to the Spanish consulate in Lisbon claimed that the anarchists involved in the campaign "consider this a triumph," but they continued agitating through the end of the year to free those remaining behind bars. International attention evaporated, however. Moreover, the Spanish government published a report in late 1904 "considering it in the national interest . . . that it be known in Spain and abroad" that allegations of torture were untrue.[93] Meanwhile, conflicts emerged between different factions within the campaign. For example, *Tierra y Libertad* denounced Alcalá del Valle meetings organized by Alejandro Lerroux, calling his Revolutionary Federation a "revolutionary farce." In an open letter to his "ex-*compañero*" Lerroux, Montseny wrote that "we have become adversaries, almost enemies" because Lerroux allegedly capitalized on the fame he gained from the Montjuich campaign to "trick workers" and Lerroux accused the anarchists of having accepted money from the Catalanistas for their anti-electoral meeting, a charge Montseny vehemently denied.[94]

Relations were no better within the anarchist camp. Conflicts developed with other anarchist papers *El Productor*, *Natura*, and *El Rebelde* that caused Montseny a "very great moral depression." Police repression, anarchist infighting, and ongoing polemics with various republican and socialist factions caused Montseny to always walk the streets with his revolver cocked. On top of everything else, Teresa Mañé was pregnant. The final issue of the first era of *La Revista Blanca* published the birth notice for Federica Montseny, who would go on to become one of the most important leaders of the anarcho-syndicalist Confederación Nacional del Trabajo during the Spanish Civil War and the first woman to serve as a cabinet minister in Spain under the Second Republic.[95]

The strategy of the nonsectarian "campaign of liberation" that Montseny and Mañé had helped pioneer crystalized organizationally with the creation of the Liga de Defensa de los Derechos del Hombre in Barcelona in July 1905. Created by Lerrouxist republicans, labor unions, freethinkers, and anarchists in the image of the French *ligue* to give free legal support to the persecuted, the new *liga* split the anarchist movement between advocates of strategic collaboration with politicians, like Tomás Herreros, who sat on the *liga*'s board, and critics like Leopoldo Bonafulla and former Montjuich prisoner Teresa Claramunt, who argued that "we all know that the hungry wolf and the sheep cannot live together, and that politicians have always been the hungry wolves when they have tried to lend support to workers' causes."[96] Despite the success of the campaigns in support of the Jerez de la Frontera prisoners of 1892, the Mano Negra prisoners of 1882, and the Alcalá del Valle prisoners of 1903 over the short span of four years (1900–1904), some anarchists were incredibly uneasy about forming broad alliances to liberate incarcerated comrades. Others were increasingly impatient with the primarily defensive tactic of international solidarity campaigning. As the fourth element of the Montjuich template suggests, the specter of the retaliatory *atentado* heightened the urgency of state capitulation, while the public sympathy for those *atentados* that were actually carried out was significantly augmented by the negative press about the Spanish government. As we will soon see, over the next few years key anarchists and republicans at the center of earlier prisoner campaigns against Spanish atrocities would seek to funnel the international outrage they had helped generate into plots against the monarchy that aimed to end the revived "inquisition" once and for all.

CHAPTER 12

The Iron Pineapple

The young King Alfonso XIII quietly chuckled after whispering into the ear of French president Émile Loubet during intermission at the Paris Opera House on the evening of May 31, 1905. His first royal visit to the City of Light was going quite well. Thus far *Le Figaro* seemed to be right that "Alfonso XIII can expect a respectful and cordial welcome." That day a "warm spontaneity of the masses" accompanied Alfonso as he joined French dignitaries on a tour of landmarks like Notre-Dame, the Panthéon, and Les Invalides before enjoying a lavish lunch at the Spanish embassy. Later he attended a performance of Camille Saint-Saëns's *Samson and Delilah* before an "extremely elegant" audience surrounded by arrangements of roses in the two national color schemes.[1]

After the performance, Alfonso's cavalcade started down the avenue de l'Opéra on its way to the palace on the quai d'Orsay. Ebullient onlookers lined the avenue beside gilded lampposts bearing special arrangements of hydrangeas, roses, and palms for the royal visit. Yet the Duke of Sotomayor and the foreign minister who rode in the car behind the king became increasingly unnerved as they heard coordinated whistles every time the procession passed a side street. Shortly after midnight, they turned down the short rue de Rohan in front of the Louvre, which was dark compared to the "dazzling light" of the avenue de l'Opéra. As the lead car turned right on rue de Rivoli, a small bomb exploded near the car carrying Alfonso XIII and President

Loubet. About twenty members of the procession and spectators were injured and a horse died, but the intended targets were unharmed. A second bomb failed to explode.[2]

Much of the Spanish press blamed the campaign building up to the arrival of Alfonso XIII "that has been exciting the passions by appealing to the memory of the history of Montjuich and the alleged martyrs of Alcalá del Valle"—and with good reason.[3] The bomb that exploded beside the royal carriage was but the latest salvo in a nearly decade-long symbiotic cycle of campaigns of indignation and retaliatory *atentados* targeting the Spanish government. While the specter of dynamite heightened the urgency of acceding to the demands of campaigners, the seething context of popular indignation at the "revival of the Inquisition" in Spain lent an air of approval to well-targeted attacks on the "inquisitors" themselves. But the relationship between the two sides of the "anti-inquisitorial" coin—protests and dynamite—seems to have extended beyond an implicit (or sometimes explicit) strategic synergy. By delving into the shadowy world of turn-of-the-century Parisian revolutionism, and the transnational networks that overlapped in its cafés,

FIGURE 12.   Aftermath of the rue de Rohan *attentat*. Upper "x" in the image indicates the site of the explosion. Lower "x" in the image indicates location of second unexploded bomb. Archives Nationales, F7 12513, Attentat de la rue de Rohan.

bars, and union halls, this chapter explores how some of the main organizers against Spanish atrocities seemed to have considered propaganda by the deed to be an additional way to pursue the campaign. Amid the exuberant international context of the ongoing Russian Revolution of 1905 a regicidal plot was hatched that allegedly involved British, Cuban, French, Spanish, Argentine, and Italian anarchists and revolutionary republicans. When the smoke cleared on the rue de Rohan, everyone agreed that years of agitation against the "revival of the Inquisition" had lit the fuse.

It all started in late October 1902 when the Andalusian anarchist medical student Pedro Vallina arrived in Paris with fantasies of "the heroic times from Ravachol to Caserio." After fleeing repression following arrest for his alleged involvement in a plot to assassinate Alfonso XIII at his coronation in Madrid, Vallina wasted little time integrating himself into the vibrant world of revolutionary Paris. Within hours of his arrival, the young Andalusian medical student presented a letter of introduction from his mentor, the legendary Andalusian anarchist Fermín Salvochea, to the republican revolutionary Nicolás Estévanez, who would "make me a participant in his conspiratorial restlessness," Vallina recalled cryptically years later. The destruction of the First Republic forced into exile revolutionary republicans who refused to accommodate themselves to the Bourbon Restoration. Manuel Ruiz Zorrilla and many others made their way across the mountains to France. In 1901 Estévanez followed this familiar route to exile in France after being prosecuted for an inflammatory article about *el proceso de Montjuich*. What had already been established as a familiar route of Spanish republican emigration was relatively new for their anarchist counterparts, however. Prior to the 1890s, Spanish anarchists usually fled to the Americas. An 1893 registry of foreign anarchists in France, for example, does not include any Spanish names. The Pyrenees only became a familiar path of anarchist exile with the mass exodus of *el proceso de Montjuich* in the late 1890s. Whether they were marched across the border in irons or fled prior to incarceration, Spanish anarchists established themselves in the transnational milieu of French revolutionism amid the Montjuich campaign and the Dreyfus affair.[4]

Vallina was already well versed in the dynamics of anarchist-republican collaboration from his time in Madrid frequenting the Casino Federal, a space for local anarchists, unionists, federal republicans, and other workers who did not subscribe to the "authoritarian socialism" of Pablo Iglesias. There, Vallina had gained the trust of seasoned republican revolutionaries who welcomed him into their world of conspiratorial insurrectionism. For example, in 1901 Vallina participated in a famous anti-clerical scheme with the federalist "man of action" Rosendo Castell. At the time anti-clerical passions surged in the context of the Ubao Supreme Court case of 1901 when an aristocratic mother sued her daughter's Jesuit confessor for committing a "moral kidnapping" by allegedly coercing her to become a nun without parental consent. Initially Vallina and his comrades ordered dynamite to blow up a church, but after rigging it, the dynamite failed to detonate. Instead, Vallina and Castell devised a more creative anti-clerical action. The Casino Federal was celebrating the opening of a lay school the night of an early performance of Benito Pérez Galdós's *Electra*, the tale of a young girl who is torn between a Jesuit who wants her to become a nun and her anti-clerical stepbrother who resists her "enslavement."[5] Vallina and Castell brought their comrades down to the theater on the false premise that Jesuits had disrupted the production. As the workers arrived, they heard shouts of "Down with Liberty!" and "Death to Galdós" off in the distance. Little did they know that these "Jesuits" were actually paperboys put up to the provocation by Castell. When the police approached, Castell set off a legendary anti-clerical riot by hitting the police inspector with his cane. Thousands of anti-clericals showed up to protect the theater over the following nights and *Electra* became a massive success.[6]

These and other experiences prepared Vallina for the Parisian nexus of anarchism and radical republicanism grounded in overlapping personal relationships dating back decades and shared opposition to the Crown and the cross. Vallina met Charles Malato, one of his most significant collaborators, through their shared friendship with the republican journalist Nicolás Salmerón y García. Born in 1858 of a Sicilian revolutionary father and a French mother, Malato had grown up with Louise Michel and other radicals who had been banished to the penal colony of New Caledonia in the South Pacific for their role in the Paris Commune. Malato was an "eclectic internationalist" who bounced around Europe in the 1880s and 1890s participating in a general strike in Belgium, planning an insurrection in Italy, languishing in prison in France for inciting "murder, pillage, and arson," and surviving the boredom of exile in Britain by making wine and enmeshing himself in London's transnational revolutionary community—all the while publishing anarchist theory and journalism.[7] The cosmopolitan and dapper Malato knew just about everyone who mattered in turn-of-the-century Western European anarchism, from unionists like the German Rudolf Rocker to bombers like the French Émile Henry to theorists and journalists like the Russian Pyotr Kropotkin, but his contacts extended beyond anarchism to include a wide range of republicans and socialists. After all, it was Malato who first triggered the Montjuich campaign by introducing the former Montjuich prisoner Tarrida del Mármol to his employer, Henri Rochefort of *L'Intransigeant*, and the

Natanson brothers of *La Revue blanche* in 1896. Like many struggling anarchist journalists of the era, economic hardships forced Malato to work for the republican Rochefort. Eventually Rochefort's antisemitism led Malato to sever ties and work for the Dreyfusard *L'Aurore* managed by the future prime minister Georges Clemenceau. Under Malato's influence, *L'Aurore* became a significant supporter of the Mano Negra and Alcalá del Valle campaigns, which were spearheaded in France by Jean Grave's anarchist *Les Temps nouveaux*. Pedro Vallina met Grave through the Spanish republican journalist Luis Bonafoux. Vallina often strolled around the corner from his place behind the Panthéon to Grave's house on rue Mouffetard. Though Montseny and Mañé were appalled at how "dreadfully" Grave lived when they visited in the late 1890s, Vallina fondly recalled Grave's large editorial table covered with newspapers and a closet with a long crocodile hide hanging in front of it bearing a sign saying "Skin of a capitalist."[8]

French authorities were well aware of the inroads Vallina was making in the Parisian revolutionary milieu. One morning in June 1903, police burst into his room, arresting him and confiscating all of his books, letters, and writings. Since they were never returned to Vallina, they are available for examination at the French National Archives as a snapshot of the intellectual world of a transnational anarchist. Vallina had twenty-six French-language pamphlets on anarchism from figures like Kropotkin, Reclus, and Malatesta, on anarchist education from Jean Grave and Domela Nieuwenhuis, on Christian anarchism from *L'Ère nouvelle*, on the Dreyfus affair and the Mano Negra campaigns and other topics. The police carried away three books, Max Stirner's *The Ego and Its Own*, a signed copy of Estévanez's memoirs, and *De Ravachol à Caserio* by Varennes; seventy-one issues of Spanish, French, and Italian periodicals including *Tierra y Libertad*, *Le Libertaire*, and *La Protesta Umana*; and eighty-three letters and postcards from comrades like Jaime Vidal in London and his mentor Fermín Salvochea in Madrid who advised Vallina to exercise, avoid alcohol, study, and "have good judgment." Vallina also lost dozens of his poems with titles like "Liberty," "May 1st," and "When I Die." At the police station Vallina was told that he would be deported, but they would release him so that he could make his own plans to leave.[9]

On his release, Vallina was approached by the English anarchist Bernard Harvey who lived nearby and had noticed Vallina being arrested. Harvey took Vallina to the Place de Vichy to meet the legendary Garibaldian and Communard Amilcare Cipriani, who worked for the socialist daily *L'Humanité*. Cipriani embraced Vallina and vowed to prevent his deportation. Cipriani took Harvey and Vallina to see Francis de Pressensé, the president of the Ligue des droits de l'homme, who then convinced the radical socialist prime minister Émile Combes to annul the expulsion. By navigating overlapping radical networks and social circles stretching from unknown exiled Spanish anarchists up through to the prime minister of France, Vallina managed to remain in the country. Over the following months he ate lunch once a week with Harvey and Cipriani. Cipriani, who had written a defense of Gaetano Bresci's assassination of the Italian king Umberto, complained to Vallina about the indifference of Spanish republican leaders in Paris to his plans to overthrow the monarchy. The same could not be said of Vallina.[10]

Though by now he was fully aware of being under the microscope of French authorities, Vallina only enhanced his revolutionary activities. He played a key role in stimulating the international dynamic of the Alcalá del Valle campaign in early 1904. Not only did he organize a tour of presentations around France about being framed in the Coronation Plot and fleeing into exile, thereby exacerbating the new Black Legend of Spanish cruelty, as well as writing a regular column for *El Rebelde* on the international movement, he seems to have been the main figure behind the creation of the International Committee in Paris. This committee, which initiated the creation of equivalent groups across Western Europe, was formed in Paris by the federation of the Spanish republican Junta de Acción y Unión Republicana (Junta of Republican Action and Union) with the anarchist Grupo de Acción Revolucionaria (Revolutionary Action Group), which included the French Charles Malato and Albert Libertad, the German Siegfried Nacht, and Spaniards like Vallina, Jesús Navarro, and the group's treasurer, José Prat. Vallina recalled years later that most of the approximately fifty anarchists from Spain active in Paris were Catalan, and many of the rest came from Valencia. According to reports from an informant, they also collaborated with Russians and Polish Jews who were especially knowledgeable in "the fabrication of bombs."[11] The International Committee in Paris published *L'Espagne inquisitoriale*, a newspaper that supported the popular campaign to free the Alcalá del Valle prisoners and glorified retaliatory *atentados* as part of the campaign. The paper's third edition featured a photograph of the would-be anarchist assassin Artal on the front page surrounded by his prison letter explaining his stabbing of Prime Minister Maura. The same issue included an open letter from Charles Malato to King Alfonso XIII in anticipation of his royal visit a year later. In an ironic tone, Malato explained to Alfonso that in Paris "there are many interesting things that can make you reflect, if you are capable. This is where they chopped the neck of Louis XVI, toppled Charles X [and] Louis-Philippe and finished off Napoleon III. These men practiced the same profession as you so it is very interesting to learn the history of past and present colleagues."[12] Malato and other anarchists often engaged with the satirical genre of playful insurrectionism that emerged when they navigated the gray area between freely expressing their desire for bloody vengeance and avoiding governmental censure. This did not always work, however, since the French government still prosecuted *L'Espagne inquisitoriale* for promoting "the assassination of the Leaders of the Spanish Government."[13]

Yet sometimes Vallina and his comrades were more direct. The Grupo de acción revolucionaria published a Spanish-language manifesto called "To the Spanish revolutionaries" that lamented how the coordinated weekend of international protest against "Spanish atrocities" in March 1904 turned out to be "useless," how "an intellectual plague has come to blind the simple minds of many of the exploited . . . trusting everything to the efficacy of their empty and ridiculous phrases." Instead the manifesto, likely written by Vallina, acclaimed "the heroic sacrifice of Angiolillo and Artal." Printed in the thousands to be smuggled across the border, the leaflet ended with the following appeal: "Forward! May the explosion of the bomb shout your hatred; may the poisoned blade shine in the sun, bringing vengeance for our brothers in Montjuich, for our brothers in Alcalá del Valle." Yet "To the Spanish revolutionaries" distinguished itself from most anarchist appeals to dynamite by emphasizing that since "European opinion is prepared, it will applaud our emancipatory struggle and justify our vengeance." Rather than the standard formulation of positing the deed as the spark to shift the political tide, the leaflet's author cites the importance of the transnational preparation of "European opinion" in paving the way for the deed. Indeed, the relative popularity of Angiolillo's assassination of Antonio Cánovas del Castillo in European radical spaces owed a great deal to the Montjuich campaign that preceded it. As the Dutch anarchist Domela Nieuwenhuis wrote in *L'Espagne inquisitoriale*, "When Cánovas was executed by Angiolillo, the entire civilized world sighed and said: one less tyrant."[14]

As the months passed, the Spanish government came to learn that these were not idle words. In May 1904 the Spanish embassy in Paris enlisted the services of Aristide Jalaber de Fontenay, a staunch royalist deputy and the former director of the reactionary *Revue royaliste* during the Dreyfus affair. Under the pseudonym Sannois, over the coming years he would provide the Spanish embassy with regular updates on anarchist activity from an informant who had established himself within the inner circles of the transnational milieu and possibly also from a police commissioner he was paying.[15] In late 1904 Sannois reported that Vallina was in the process of acquiring dynamite "so that when we need it we will have it." Although early reports from Sannois suggested that Vallina's group intended that dynamite for Prime Minister Maura, by early 1905 it was clear that they had settled on King Alfonso XIII.[16]

In early January 1905 Vallina and his Spanish anarchist comrades met with their Italian counterparts in the eleventh arrondissement for the purpose of merging to form a "groupe hispano-italien" that would meet every Saturday in preparation for the royal visit in May. The dynamite-wary "moderates" of the Spanish milieu were not invited to this meeting, which seems to have been instigated in large part by Charles Malato, "the most dangerous man in France for the Spanish government," in conversation with Tarrida del Mármol, Baldomero Oller, and other Spanish comrades in London. According to Sannois, "Malato seeks to influence the others without compromising himself personally." Malato argued that the attempt on the life of the king should be carried out by the Italians or the French rather than the Spaniards.[17] One of the first actions of the joint Spanish-Italian anarchist group was to march together with tens of thousands of mourners in the funeral procession for the legendary communard and anarchist Louise Michel on January 22, 1905.[18]

That same day the czar's soldiers gunned down petitioners outside the Winter Palace, triggering the 1905 Russian Revolution. The general strikes and waves of popular resistance on the other side of the continent emboldened anarchists and revolutionaries around the world. It may have been particularly inspirational for Spanish anarchists, however, given their belief that the situation in Spain was "only comparable to that which is done to Russian workers under the despotic government of the czar."[19] If revolution was possible in Russia, then why not in Spain? Sannois had been monitoring Vallina's relations with a doctor named Roubanovitch, the director of the socialist revolutionary organ *Tribune russe*, since the summer of 1904 when— much to the delight of many Western European anarchists—a member of the Socialist Revolutionary Party assassinated the Russian minister of the interior. Sannois believed that Roubanovitch was at the center of this plot and that plans to assassinate Alfonso XIII were being supported by "Russian terrorists."[20]

Or at least that is what Sannois believed when Pedro Vallina disappeared from Paris for about a month in February 1905 after receiving 4,000 francs in foreign currency. In a desperate effort to figure out where he had gone, Sannois's sources guessed that he had traveled to Poland to gain support amid the tumult of the Russian Revolution. After all, "he had purchased a lot of winter clothing." Meanwhile, sources indicated that dynamite had been sent to Paris from Río Tinto along with bomb-making instructions translated from an article in the *New York Herald*. Confusion mounted when the

Spaniards stopped meeting as an entire group in favor of small encounters of two or three at a time to avoid police detection.[21]

In fact, Vallina had traveled south, not east. After subtly hinting to the police officer who "visited [him] every day like a friend" that he was journeying to Madrid, Vallina took the last train to Barcelona. Wearing a disguise, carrying a concealed pistol, and bearing fake Latin American papers, Vallina crossed the border to meet with seven delegates of the new Catalan anarchist federation about an "imminent anti-monarchical revolution" that was likely planned to coincide with the anticipated regicide in Paris. Though this new federation had twenty-one groups, repression prevented its entire membership from ever meeting together. Instead, a delegate was named to communicate on behalf of every three groups in what were by outward appearances casual chats at cafés, "never in the same location." In his memoirs Vallina claims to have provided his comrades with chemicals and instructions for the fabrication of explosives and rented a large house to store rifles purchased on the black market. French authorities, always disdainful of the "Catalan police, always poorly informed," claimed that the plan to assassinate the king entailed plans for "a simultaneous rising in Madrid, Barcelona, Valencia, and Cadiz" in conjunction with republican leaders, including Lerroux and Junoy, and "certain high-ranking military officers."[22]

Such a conspiracy was confirmed years later by Barcelona governor Ángel Ossorio, who wrote that a meeting in the border town of Figueras in 1905 solidified the "union of Lerroux's revolutionary republicans with the anarchists" (who did not completely despise him) and formalized the bonds between Lerroux and Francisco Ferrer, both of whom "supported the initiatives of Malato and the League of the Rights of Man" in Paris. According to a French informant, Lerroux preferred to work with anarchists because they were "readier than the republicans to sacrifice themselves." If the anarchists could pull off an assassination, Lerroux allegedly promised to take the opportunity to start a revolt against the Crown in Spain. Around the same time, republicans in Argentina sent 10,000 pesos for the "republican treasury," and Lerroux's followers organized revolutionary nuclei around Catalonia. Sources indicate that the chemical supplies Vallina delivered were used to create two hundred small bombs that would be unleashed when the moment arrived. The entire operation was allegedly financed by Francisco Ferrer, who frequently visited Paris but "never left without visiting" Pedro Vallina. One source indicated that Vallina stayed at Ferrer's house during his time in Barcelona. Ferrer was even closer with Malato, who may have been his most trusted lifelong comrade. An anarchist informant told Governor Ossorio that "Lerroux was the leader of the movement, Ferrer the capitalist, Vallina the chemist."[23] Years later Lerroux acknowledged preparing for a revolutionary situation should something happen to the king, but he denied involvement in the conspiracy (though this denial was made in the early 1940s in an effort to return to Franco's Spain). Lerroux also added in his memoirs that when he asked Fermín Salvochea about Vallina's plans for the royal visit, Salvochea spoke about how "these days no king had their life assured though they are very protected. . . . The Italians have really perfected the technique of the *atentado*." Other sources with intimate knowledge of the world of Barcelona revolutionism affirmed that Lerroux was in fact a key player.[24]

Vallina claimed that when rumors of his presence in Barcelona started to spread, comrades encouraged him to return to Paris, which he did on March 18, 1905. Days later, he made a quick trip to London, where he explained his plan to spark a Spanish revolution with the "terrorist elimination of Alfonso XIII" to the legendary Italian anarchist Errico Malatesta.[25] With about two months remaining before the royal visit, authorities (and possibly the conspirators themselves) were still unsure whether the *atentado* would take place in Madrid or Paris. Either way, Sannois reported that "currently in Spain the quantity of hidden dynamite is *enormous*" and that "Vallina always talks about an *attentat* against the king as a sure thing." Yet he was also convinced that "it will not be known anarchists—like Vallina, for example—who will carry out the *attentat*, but rather those unknown to the police. . . . It is indispensable to closely surveil well-dressed foreigners."[26]

Such precautionary surveillance included monitoring correspondence between Spain and France. In early April 1905 Sannois reported that the Spanish anarchists in Paris had sent a large quantity of the "Manual of the Perfect Anarchist," a bomb-making guide from the 1890s, to Spain.[27] Around the same time, French police noticed that letters about the royal visit were being sent from Barcelona to a Parisian shoemaker named Eugène Caussanel, who would then pass them on to Charles Malato. Malato seems to have directed his more sensitive correspondence to Caussanel, whose wife worked for him as a domestic servant, because Caussanel was unknown to the police. On April 14 he received a letter from Francisco Ferrer clarifying that "the official date has been set for May 30," the day Alfonso XIII was scheduled to arrive in Paris, along with a check for 150 francs for Malato. A week later, Caussanel received another letter alerting him to the imminent arrival of a package. Indeed, on April 19 a tall, slender man in his mid-twenties with a dark brown mustache, prominent cheekbones, and curved beard listing what turned out to be a fake name and a fake address walked into a Barcelona post office to mail Caussanel what he claimed was "machinery." When French customs agents opened the package, they were surprised by what they found: an iron pineapple with a hole in it.[28] Weeks earlier authorities learned that Vallina was "very up to date on the manipulation of dangerous materials. In Barcelona he constructed an enormous quantity of small bombs in a new system. These bombs look like eggs and have the same dimensions. Their surface is absolutely smooth; they only explode when thrown forcefully."[29] Sannois described these "new" bombs as "'grenades' that one throws by hand similar to those used by the Japanese at Port Arthur."[30] Although variants of the hand grenade had been used in earlier conflicts, the siege of Port Arthur in the Russo-Japanese War demonstrated the strategic importance and technological viability of the grenade, inspiring further experimentation with handheld explosives.[31]

Without proof of illegal intentions, authorities allowed delivery of the package. The iron pineapple made its way from Caussanel to Malato to Vallina, but it was too big to be easily concealed and thrown, so Vallina allegedly requested smaller pineapples. On May 12 the same mustachioed man in Barcelona mailed four smaller iron pineapples that were delivered to Caussanel. The next day, Vallina came to collect them at Malato's house alongside a comrade, whom authorities identified as a member of the Hispano-Italian anarchist group, named Alejandro Farrás. Unbeknownst to them, the real Farrás had died a year earlier. Nevertheless, according to authorities Vallina and "Farrás" left on bicycle (Vallina had just learned how to ride weeks earlier) with the iron pineapples and hid them in two separate locations in the forest outside of the city.[32]

Sannois explained to the Spanish embassy that his infiltrator could provide the address of the house in question, but since he was in "great danger" he "requested a large sum in exchange for this information." After the Spanish embassy authorized payment of 200 francs to the informant, he got "to work," as he phrased it to Sannois, gaining the confidence of Vallina to find out where the explosives were being constructed. Days later the infiltrator learned that the bombs were not being constructed in Paris but rather in a remote suburb—which explained Vallina's "long and remote excursions to the countryside." The conspirators were feeling the heat as well. Sannois reported in mid-May that "the Spanish comrades in Paris are intimidated by the surveillance, Farrás especially who is stunned and dares not move." Vallina told the infiltrator that if they chose to assassinate the king in Paris he would leave town in advance, suggesting that he was not planning on throwing the bombs himself.[33]

Meanwhile, the protest campaign against the royal visit was slowly gaining momentum. Though attendance failed to crack two hundred at events in April, a protest meeting on May 10 against repression in Russia and Spain

FIGURE 13.   Iron pineapples. Archives Nationales, F7 12513.

drew five hundred, while another on May 24 exceeded a thousand participants. The latter meeting protested Alfonso not only for Montjuich, Alcalá del Valle, and Mano Negra but also because organizers claimed he sought "the conquest of Morocco," which would "unleash a new Franco-German war." "We hope that a workplace accident prevents [Alfonso] from finishing his voyage," CGT leader Georges Yvetot announced. Yet the CGT did not attempt to organize such an accident. Rather, the union bought whistles so that workers could audibly harass the king as their Italian counterparts had done when the czar visited Italy. Though the French Left sought to unite against the king, the socialist president of the city council, Paul Brousse, was attacked by many for his decision to participate in the delegation that welcomed the Spanish monarch. Much had changed for Brousse since his anarchist days when he coined the term "propaganda by the deed" in 1877. Though French authorities had confiscated five thousand copies of *L'Espagne inquisitoriale* earlier that month, another thousand were distributed at the May 24 protest meeting. A large banner draped from the Bourse du travail read "Down with the assassin of Montjuich, Barcelona, Alcalá del Valle."[34]

   A week before the royal visit, an informant accompanied Vallina to the woods to dig up two bombs (the informant did not know where the other three were hidden). Allegedly, the plan was for Vallina to head to the border, where the king would be attacked on his way to Paris.[35] Perhaps fearing that the principal conspirators might disappear, the police moved in. According to his memoirs, on the evening of May 25 Vallina was eating dinner at a friend's home in Paris. After sitting down to eat, the doorman informed them that there were two bicycle police outside waiting for Vallina. "I ate hurriedly," Vallina recounted, "and I figured this could be about some explosives that I had deposited that night at a *compañero*'s house in my neighborhood" (presumably the two bombs he had disinterred days earlier). When he left, the two police officers followed. Vallina turned up a steep embankment and discarded his reflector. Fifteen minutes later Vallina had managed to lose the police, warn his comrade to move the bombs, and make it back home. Two hours later police arrested him in bed. They also arrested Eugène Caussanel, the English anarchist Bernard Harvey, and Spanish anarchists Jesús Navarro and Fermín Palacios (who had been implicated with Vallina in the Coronation Plot of 1902).[36]

The next day, Sannois lamented that "unfortunately these partial arrests aren't very important since the bombs were not found." Moreover, "Farrás, Vallina's Spanish anarchist accomplice, has not been arrested. . . . This is regrettable because Farrás is the only one besides Vallina who knows where the three bombs are hidden." The day before Alfonso's arrival, small leaflets were scattered around the city warning of "danger" near the royal carriage. Nevertheless, when the king finally arrived Sannois felt fairly confident that the "Spanish and Italian anarchists who have not been arrested won't try anything during the royal visit to Paris; if there were a danger, it would come from the French anarchists."

That confidence snapped a day later when Sannois sent an urgent telegram to the Spanish embassy three hours before the bombing warning them that it was "necessary in particular to monitor the King's return, *tonight*," from the opera.[37] Indeed, Sannois had been tipped off but it made no difference. Despite the surveillance, infiltration, and preemptive arrests, the bombs still exploded beside the royal carriage.

The bombing's connection to years of international campaigning against the "revival of the Inquisition" in Spain was lost on no one. *La Época* confidently argued that "this crime carried out in Paris germinated out of the seed planted by those who have slandered their country with fantastic stories of abuses and outrages that have only existed in their extravagant imagination."[38] The bombing was simply an extension of the recent prisoner campaigns by other means according to the Spanish government, the conservative press, and many anarchists as well. After the dust settled, the Parisian police

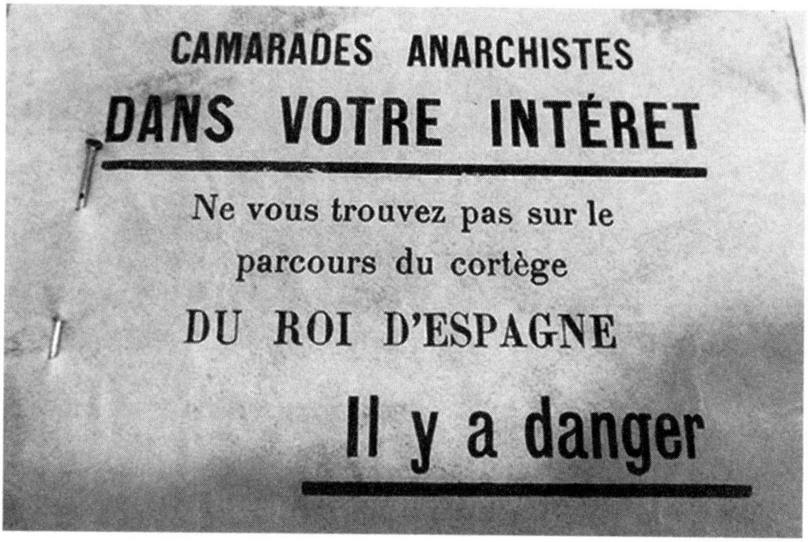

FIGURE 14.   Leaflet warning of danger near the royal carriage. "Anarchist comrades: It is in your interest to avoid the route of the King of Spain. There is Danger." Archives de la Préfecture de Police, Ba 1317, Voyage en France du roi d'Espagne.

determined "with absolute certainty" that "Farrás" had thrown the bomb, but he had disappeared.[39] In his absence, the prosecution of the bombing of the rue de Rohan became the "trial of the four" alleged accomplices: Vallina, Harvey, Caussanel, and Malato, who had been arrested at his home hours after the bombing.

Proceedings began on November 27, 1905. Léon Bulot, who had prosecuted Ravachol and Émile Henry, and presided over the Trial of the Thirty in the 1890s, had a very strong case against the alleged conspirators. Bernard Harvey admitted having dabbled in creating fulminate of mercury, having written instructions for constructing a bomb identical to that used by the bomber(s) in his agenda, which also included writings on the "legitimacy of revolutionary *attentats*," and having met with Farrás about twice a week in recent months, although he denied involvement in the *attentat*. Malato also denied any participation in the plot but admitted that Caussanel had received mail on his behalf, including the two packages of bombshells. Yet Malato claimed to not have opened the packages before discarding them. Moreover, in Vallina's residence, the police found a mortar and pestle, a test tube, and mercury nitrate alongside photographs of Ravachol, Vaillant, Émile Henry, Bresci, and the Russian socialist revolutionary who had recently assassinated the Russian minister of the interior. Though Vallina claimed that the mercury nitrate was for photography, he admitted having ordered bombshells

from Spain, having received them, and having asked for more. He acknowledged that the bomb used on the rue de Rohan was identical to those that he
had constructed and suggested that maybe the illusive "Farrás" had thrown
them without his knowledge. Vallina admitted nearly everything, but, his
lawyer clarified, he did not intend to throw bombs in France but instead save
them for when a revolutionary moment akin to 1789 erupted in Spain.[40]

The French tradition of revolutionary republicanism factored into the
defense strategy. Defense witness Séverine portrayed Vallina as "a Spanish
republican" whose role in the struggle was similar to that of Orsini, who
tried to blow up Napoleon III. Similarly, Lerroux argued that Vallina was
simply a "radical" and that anyone who resisted was labeled an "anarchist" in
Spain. One of the defense attorneys described the accused as "rebels against
Spanish tyranny." The defense simultaneously denied and legitimated the
culpability of the defendants by putting the Spanish Crown on trial. A parade
of prominent French and Spanish leftists, such as Jean Jaurès, Aristide Briand,
Francisco Ferrer, and Fernando Tarrida del Mármol, recounted the abuses of
Montjuich, Mano Negra, and Alcalá del Valle following months of articles on
"Spanish atrocities" in the French press. Séverine described in detail the torture of Francisco Gana in Montjuich Castle, and Francis de Pressensé of the
Ligue des droits de l'homme argued that Malato was being charged because
of his advocacy for the Montjuich prisoners years earlier. The Spanish
embassy in Paris sent strict instructions to the French court to forbid "declarations that could be offensive to Spain," but such requests did little to ease
growing official concerns about testimony regarding "the supposed martyrdom and maltreatment of the Montjuich and Alcalá del Valle prisoners."
Especially influential was Alejandro Lerroux, who spent two hours painting
a vivid portrait of police malfeasance in Spain in order to argue that the rue
de Rohan bombing had been orchestrated by the police. The left-wing press
in France had been pushing the angle of police conspiracy for months, with
papers like *L'Action* even calling the bombing a "pseudo-*attentat*."[41]

The defense strategy was so successful that the prosecutor spent much
of the last day of the trial clarifying that he too would "protest in the name
of humanity if there were infamies in Spanish prisons" and attempting to
refute the suggestion that the bombing had been carried out by the Spanish
police. The defendants had variously admitted to having received bomb-
making materials, writing down bomb-making instructions, and even fabricating bombs of the very same kind as were thrown at the royal procession,
yet the prosecution found itself on the defensive. Years and years of international press campaigns and protest movements against Spanish atrocities
simultaneously made the prospect of assassinating the king more reasonable

FIGURE 15. Mugshots of Vallina, Harvey, Palacios, and Navarro. Archivo General de la Administración, Asuntos Exteriores, Embajada en Paris, 5858.

Figure 16. Mugshot of Charles Malato. Archivo General de la Administración, Asuntos Exteriores, Embajada en Paris, 5858.

and the prospect of the Spanish police having orchestrated a nefarious plot more plausible. After two hours of deliberation, on December 1, 1905, the courtroom burst into applause as all four defendants were found not guilty. Despite their acquittal, Vallina and Harvey were deported to England.[42]

"I know perfectly well," Sannois wrote on the day of the acquittal, "that the infamies that were recounted about the treatment inflicted on the anarchists by the Spanish government influenced the jury enormously." He also noted "the role played by Freemasonry, which sought to save Malato at any price." Sources told Sannois that if Malato had not been among the accused, Vallina and his accomplices would have been convicted. Malato had certainly established himself among elite Masonic and socialist circles. Because he was such a prominent figure, when Pedro Vallina readily admitted having fabricated bombs, many anarchists concluded that he was a police provocateur sent to torpedo Malato. Jean Grave made a similar accusation against Harvey, which Malato emphatically denied. Vallina was so appreciative of the role of Masonry in their acquittal that he joined a Parisian lodge.[43]

There is no evidence to corroborate suspicions that Vallina or Harvey were provocateurs, but historians agree that there is plenty to suggest that these four men participated in the plot behind the bombing of the rue de Rohan in conjunction with collaborators who may have included Alejandro Lerroux, Francisco Ferrer, Nicolás Estévanez, and countless others on both sides of the border.[44] Vallina, Malato, and Harvey all denied any support for "the individual act" in general, but we know from his memoirs and worship of Ravachol and other propagandists by the deed that this was untrue of Vallina, that Harvey had writings to the contrary in his agenda, and years later Malato explained that "as long as it follows from a high motive, the individual act seems to me to be as admissible as the collective insurrection, though I do not have a blind admiration for the use of explosives." He lauded Bresci and Angiolillo (whom some claimed he funded) because they did not "escape from the police." For Malato the propagandist of the deed "must sacrifice their life," something that the rue de Rohan bomber did not do.[45]

So what about the bomber? Since the real Farrás died about a year before the bombing, who threw the bombs? Though the Parisian police initially concluded that "Farrás" was the bomber, over the coming months they detained, and then released, several suspects who could have used the Farrás alias to commit the *attentat*.[46] Police suspicion also fell on a twenty-three-year-old anarchist named Eduardo Aviño who had been implicated in a 1903 bombing of the home of Barcelona chief of police Antonio Tressols, who was associated with the Montjuich persecution of the 1890s.[47] Allegedly Aviño had fled Barcelona after the bombing and moved in with Fermín Palacios in Paris.

Some historians conclude that Aviño was "Farrás." Others point the finger in the direction of the young administrator of Francisco Ferrer's Modern School publishing house, Mateo Morral, whom we will follow in the next chapter. There is evidence to suggest, though not to prove definitively, that Morral was both the enigmatic mustachioed man who mailed bombshells from Barcelona to Paris and the real "Farrás."[48]

The argument that Morral mailed the bombshells is supported by the match between his appearance and the police description, the fact that the owner of the establishment where they were mailed and three of his workers testified that a photograph of Morral matched the man who had mailed the iron pineapples, and a report to that effect from an informant close to Vallina. The plausibility of Morral's involvement is enhanced by the fact that he shared many of the same friends and worked on many of the same projects as Vallina and Malato. According to historian Eduard Masjuan, Malato knew Morral through his work translating the CGT organ *La voix du peuple* into Spanish in support of the burgeoning revolutionary syndicalist movement in Spain. Prior to leaving Spain, Vallina was active in Madrid in the creation of the FSORE and agitation for the 1902 general strike while Morral was similarly involved in Sabadell. Morral and Malato both collaborated with Francisco Ferrer's paper *La Huelga General*. In fact, Ferrer seems to have been the main figure at the center of this transnational revolutionary milieu. Ferrer worked with Morral, was very close to Malato, and frequently visited Vallina in Paris. Ferrer, Morral, and Vallina all passionately championed the transnational neo-Malthusian movement, which advocated reproductive autonomy for working-class women, and the growing anti-militarist movement. In 1906 Morral published a series of interviews with the insurrectionary republican Nicolás Estévanez, who was a partner in "conspiratorial restlessness" with Vallina and penned the lyrics to a song for Ferrer's Modern School. As discussed above, there is evidence to implicate Ferrer and his collaborator Alejandro Lerroux in the rue de Rohan bombing. In his memoirs, Lerroux claimed that Estévanez, Ferrer, and Malato were all involved and Morral mailed the bombs from Barcelona. If there was an anarcho-republican conspiracy behind the bombing, it is likely that Ferrer played a key role connecting the dots, one of which may have been Mateo Morral.[49]

But the argument for Morral's involvement runs deeper than guilt by association. According to witness testimony, in October 1904 (the same month Sannois reported the arrival of Farrás in Paris and Harvey claimed to have first met him) Morral recruited two Spanish workers in Marseille to assist him in his plot to assassinate Alfonso XIII. Morral, whose father was a wealthy industrialist, had the resources to bring his conspirators to Paris and lodge them in an expensive hotel while plans were developed. Morral then allegedly threw the bombs at the king with one of these workers, Alfredo de la Prada, and then fled the country by joining the French Foreign Legion in Algeria (a different witness claimed that Aviño had fled to Algeria in the summer of 1905). This element of the story is based solely on the testimony of a member of the Foreign Legion in Algeria who claims to have met Morral there, though Morral's involvement was also affirmed by the republican journalist Luis Bonafoux and Morral's childhood friend Albà Rosell.[50]

In his memoirs Malato wrote that although he had "never met, let alone seen Farrás," a claim contested by police accounts of Farrás picking up bombshells at Malato's house, years later he saw a photograph that reminded him "of a Spanish anarchist with whom I had exchanged ten words for a few minutes without knowing his name." The man in that photograph was Mateo Morral. "I asked myself," Malato recounted, "if Morral could have been that enigmatic Farrás." Vallina's memoirs are full of detailed accounts of relatively trivial political conversations, but they are very curt about the rue de Rohan bombing. This brevity is surprising given the fact that Vallina went to great lengths to explain his innocence in the Coronation Plot, for example. In 1961 Vallina wrote quite cryptically that he had "dealt with Morral intimately."[51] This seems to imply more than distant correspondence, but prior to leaving Spain in 1902 Vallina and Morral never lived in the same city. It is possible this could refer to collaboration in Barcelona when Vallina secretly crossed the border in 1905, but he was there for only about a month. Ultimately, we are left with nothing more than fragments of clues. All we can be certain of when it comes to the tale of Mateo Morral is that its climax was yet to come.

CHAPTER 13

Tossing the Bouquet at the Royal Wedding

It was an "open secret" that the true objective of the young Spanish king Alfonso XIII's diplomatic voyage of 1905 was to find a bride. In part, the urgency of finding the next queen of Spain hinged on the need for a royal heir. Alfonso XIII's birth on May 17, 1886, a half year after the death of his father Alfonso XII, had relieved state officials given the lingering threat of a Carlist insurgency. Though Alfonso XIII was born a king, his mother, María Cristina, ruled on his behalf until his official coronation at the age of sixteen in 1902. The coronation instilled the monarchy with a much-needed dose of optimism after el Desastre of 1898, but the question of succession loomed given the Crown's bevy of enemies on the Left and Right. After the 1904 death of Alfonso's eldest sister, the prime minister named her three-year-old son the official heir to the throne. A parliamentary commission urged the king to find a bride as soon as possible.[1]

Finding a bride was not just about royal succession, however. After the loss to the United States in 1898, Spain could no longer afford to remain aloof to international relations. Transnational campaigns behind the revival of the Black Legend had left the Crown's reputation in tatters, and the US Navy had sent Spain's outdated gunships plummeting to the bottom of Manila Bay. The once-massive Spanish Empire had shrunk with the loss of Cuba, Puerto Rico, and the Philippines while imperial competition was heating up and the alliance system that would culminate in the carnage of the First World War was falling into place. A royal wedding seemed like a quick fix for diplomatic isolation, but which bloc to marry into? Unsurprisingly, Alfonso's Austrian mother joined many conservative politicians in arguing for a rapprochement with central European powers through marriage to an Austrian or German bride. Liberal and reform-minded conservative politicians favored union with a British princess so that the formidable British navy could support Spain while it rebuilt its decimated fleet.[2]

With these considerations in mind, Alfonso XIII crossed the English Channel in early June 1905, days after surviving the bombing of the rue de Rohan in Paris. To prevent another attempt on his life, British authorities guarded his carriage with a squadron of the royal guard and shut down the road on the way to Buckingham Palace. The next night, King Edward VII organized a lavish dinner where Alfonso mingled with a variety of eligible British princesses. Alfonso was seated beside Victoria Patricia, the leading candidate according to both the Spanish and British press. Yet when Alfonso attempted to charm her, she rebuffed his advances. Later he greeted one of Queen Victoria's granddaughters, Victoria Eugenia of Battenberg, in English, even though he had vowed to never utter the language of his country's adversary after the defeat by the United States in 1898. To his delight she replied in French. Though initially she was not attracted to the Spanish king, she agreed to exchange postcards. To appease his mother, Alfonso continued his tour of European princesses with trips to Berlin and Vienna, but his heart (and/or geostrategic calculus) was set on Victoria Eugenia, known to her family as Ena, who accepted his proposal in December 1905.[3]

That same month, the trial of the rue de Rohan bombing ended in an acquittal for the accused accomplices of the bomber, who was never definitively identified, let alone apprehended. That illusive bomber may have been the Catalan anarchist Mateo Morral Roca. After (possibly) crossing paths with King Alfonso XIII in Paris in the spring of 1905, Morral had allegedly deserted his post in the French Foreign Legion to return to his native Sabadell, while Alfonso had returned home to Madrid after visiting the princesses of Europe.[4] Worlds apart, the journeys of these two men would soon intersect—possibly for the second time—with deadly consequences.

On his return to Madrid, Alfonso XIII busied himself planning a spring wedding that would bring two royal families together. On his return to Sabadell, Mateo Morral was disowned by his father, a progressive textile factory owner, after years of family turmoil. Those who remembered Morral as a shy, frail boy recounted how his deeply religious mother despised him growing up. In 1892 thirteen-year-old Morral was sent to apprentice with a wool merchant in Reims, France. Several years later he supported himself working in a wool textile factory in Leipzig, Germany. There, he organized with the metallurgical workers' federation and joined an anti-militarist anarchist group. In 1899 Mateo Morral was summoned home to run his father's factory after his mother died and his older brother became gravely ill. On his return, Morral eagerly and adeptly applied the innovative technical knowledge he had gained abroad to the modernization of his father's antiquated factory. Yet he had also gained political knowledge during his years abroad in France and Germany. An ardent anti-clerical, Mateo removed Corpus decorations from his family's balcony and closed the doors that opened out onto Sabadell's Rambla so his siblings could not see religious processions. At the factory, Morral started to encourage his father's workers to demand higher pay and better working conditions. He only agreed to continue operating his father's factory on the condition that his younger brother be allowed to study in Germany and his younger sister be allowed to attend Francisco Ferrer's controversial new Modern School.[5]

Indeed, Morral's story is inextricably linked to the chain of events that would generate unimaginable notoriety for the Catalan anarchist pedagogue Francisco Ferrer and his groundbreaking school. Ferrer was an autodidact from a large rural family who began his political career as a courier for the exiled revolutionary republican leader Manuel Ruiz Zorrilla in the early 1880s. Ferrer's faith in republicanism suffered, however, when he moved to Paris in 1885. His firsthand experience of the French Third Republic, the ultimate incarnation of justice for Spanish republicans, soured him on his political creed. He concluded that "God was replaced by the state, Christian virtue by civic duty, religion by patriotism, submission to the king, the aristocracy, and the clergy by subservience to the official, the proprietor, and the employer." After a brief flirtation with the socialism of Jules Guesde's Parti ouvrier français in the mid-1890s, Ferrer drifted toward anarchism.[6]

As the legacy of *l'ère des attentats* of the early 1890s faded, Ferrer was influenced by two developments in the French anarchist milieu that would also impact Morral: anti-authoritarian pedagogy and revolutionary syndicalism. Strongly influenced by the educational writings of Paul Robin and Jean Grave, France experienced a "golden age" of anarchist education at the turn of the century that included an initiative on the part of the League of Libertarian Education to create *l'école libertaire*. Though *l'école libertaire* never materialized for a lack of funds, Ferrer came into a great deal of wealth that allowed his vision for a scientific, rationalist school to come to fruition. After running a wine shop that became a restaurant, Ferrer supported himself by teaching Spanish while living in Paris. Over time, he

FIGURE 17. Mateo Morral. Ateneu Enciclopèdic Popular.

managed to radicalize one of his wealthy students named Ernestine Meunié away from her conservative Catholic beliefs in the heat of the Dreyfus affair. She was so taken with Ferrer's pedagogical vision that she left him part of her fortune in her will less than three months before she died in 1901. That fall, Ferrer opened the Modern School in the Ensanche neighborhood of Barcelona. Though it would take a few years for some of the more egalitarian principles of the Modern School to be put into practice, Ferrer's educational vision emphasized a rationalist and positivist engagement with the natural world, an active rejection of religious "superstition," a disavowal of rewards, punishments, and exams, and coeducation of the sexes. In his private correspondence, Ferrer explained that the school would be "internally libertarian . . . without broadcasting it externally."[7] In fact, in order to maintain an image of scientific objectivity Ferrer never *publicly* embraced anarchism. But whether he and his school used the label or not, the ideals of the Modern School presented a grave threat to the hegemony of Catholic education in Spain.

Though Ferrer cultivated an image of pacifistic rationalism in public, *privately* he penned bombastic screeds in favor of anarchism and the revolutionary general strike under the pseudonym Cero in the pages of *La Huelga General*, the revolutionary syndicalist paper that he created in late 1901. Strongly influenced by the role of anarchists and anti-authoritarians in infusing the Confédération générale du travail (CGT), founded in 1895, with an updated version of the libertarian labor politics of the First International, Ferrer was part of a new generation of Spanish anarchists that sought to reignite anarchist unionism after the wave of repression unleashed by *el proceso de Montjuich*. These anarchists organized the Federación de Sociedades Obreras de la Región Española (FSORE) in 1900. Shortly thereafter *La Huelga General* became the official organ of the new federation and a key spark for the massive Barcelona general strike of 1902.[8]

Mateo Morral also supported the development of the FSORE through his work with a Sabadell affinity group called Gente Joven (Young People), which took active part in the leadership of the union. Using the time made available by his elevated class position, Morral took on a significant amount of the local union's administrative tasks. Never content to merely push papers, however, when the 1902 general strike began, Morral and other anarchist unionists in Sabadell hatched a plot to kidnap reactionary bosses to be executed whenever authorities killed a striking worker. When the time came to put the plot into action, however, Morral was frustrated to see that he was one of only four anarchists to show up. Ferrer and Morral, who allegedly edited a pamphlet commemorating Angiolillo's assassination of Prime Minister Cánovas del Castillo, were among many anarchists of the era with sympathies for a wide variety of revolutionary strategies, from unionism to insurrection to propaganda by the deed, defying the one-dimensional categories that some later historians have attempted to impose on this epoch of resistance.[9]

Morral also put his French and German connections and language skills to use by translating articles from the CGT organ *La Voix du peuple* and other papers as well as writing an international news section for *La Protesta*. Through his translations he gained the amity of Charles Malato (with whom he may have collaborated in the rue de Rohan bombing) and his efforts disseminating anarchist propaganda brought him into the orbit of Francisco Ferrer. Beyond support for anarchism and the revolutionary general strike, the two had a lot in common politically. For example, Morral shared Ferrer's passion for working-class education. Shortly after they met, Morral started distributing copies of an anarchist children's book that he had received from Ferrer to students at the local lay school. Before long, Morral had convinced his father to enroll his younger sister in the Modern School, and he took on the position of administrator of the Modern School publishing house. Over the summer of 1903, Morral led the students of the Modern School on a tour of his father's factory, where they were said to have marveled at "the beauty and utility of labor!"[10]

Morral and Ferrer also advocated neo-Malthusianism. As opposed to Thomas Malthus's paternalistic arguments for moral restraint, neo-Malthusians emphasized the reproductive autonomy of working-class women. In the 1890s the French anarchist educator Paul Robin played a key role in promoting the doctrine after learning about the first neo-Malthusian group, which had been founded in 1877, during his time in London. Robin then helped found the French Neo-Malthusian League in 1896 in Paris where Morral was living at the time. Morral's interest in neo-Malthusianism seems to have grown in Germany, where he became acquainted with the director of the organ of a German group that had been founded in 1889. When he returned to Spain, Morral became a correspondent for *Régénera-tion*, the periodical of the Neo-Malthusian International, and he received the first shipment of condoms from the league to distribute to Spanish workers. Along with Pedro Vallina, who ran the foreign section of *Régéneration* from Paris, Morral and Ferrer were among the most influential promoters of birth control and sexual education in Spain early in the twentieth century. Morral helped organize a neo-Malthusian theatrical production in Sabadell accompanied by a presentation on venereal diseases from a Barcelona medical specialist—the first public presentation of sexual medical information in the city's history. In 1904 a Spanish section of the International Neo-Malthusian League was formed with many adhering groups. During this era, neo-Malthusianism came to be associated with anarchism throughout

southern Europe. Anarchists such as Luigi Fabbri were among the first promoters of the doctrine in Italy and Portugal.[11]

Not all anarchists were so enthusiastic about neo-Malthusianism, however. Joan Montseny and Teresa Mañé made a natalist argument in *La Revista
Blanca* that workers should have a lot of kids "with good genitals" to push the
population balance farther in favor of the proletariat. Leopoldo Bonafulla
argued that the issue was not population or reproduction but rather the dis-
tribution of resources under capitalism. The neo-Malthusian argument was
even more disturbing for the church and the state. In 1908 the government
announced a prize of 500 pesetas for families with twelve or more children
and a ban on all contraception in Barcelona. Ferrer tried to incorporate
sexual education into the Modern School curriculum, but parental outrage
quickly ended the experiment.[12] Revolutionary syndicalism, anarchist pedagogy, neo-Malthusianism, radical theater and literature, insurrection, anti-
militarism, asceticism, labor journalism, propaganda by the deed—Mateo
Morral's political activities and attitudes represent the astounding breadth
of forms of resistance in motion among anarchist movements in Catalonia
and beyond at the turn of the twentieth century, though he is remembered
almost exclusively for the latter.

While Alfonso XIII was busy planning a marital union between two of
Europe's most legendary royal families—the first Anglo-Spanish royal wedding since Felipe II and Mary Tudor in the sixteenth century—Mateo Morral was beginning a whirlwind romance that linked two of Europe's most
insurrectionary anarchist movements. In December 1905 Morral moved to
a boardinghouse on Plaza de Cataluña in Barcelona after falling out with his
industrialist father. There he met a short, blonde woman in her mid-twenties
whom the owners of the boardinghouse knew as the "señorita francesa"
despite her odd French accent. Yes, she had come to Barcelona from Paris,
but she was not the French daughter of a musician that she claimed to be.
Her name (or at least her revolutionary pseudonym) was Nora Falk, and she
was a recently exiled member of one of the "battle detachments" of Chernoe Znamia (Black Flag)—an infamous insurrectionary anarcho-communist
organization that had made a name for itself by launching a relentless series
of attacks against the upper class and the state amid the Russian Revolution
of 1905.[13]

Originally formed in 1903, the year that "a lasting anarchist movement"
developed in the Russian Empire, Chernoe Znamia was "the first anarchist
group to inaugurate a deliberate policy of terror against the established
order." The overwhelmingly young factory workers, students, artisans, and
peasants from the empire's southern and western provinces that composed

Chernoe Znamia organized themselves into affinity groups of ten to twelve that met clandestinely in factories, in the homes of members, in the remote woods of Bialystok or Odessa, or sometimes even in graveyards under the guise of mourning. Most anarchists in the Russian Empire were Jewish, and the membership of Chernoe Znamia was no exception. Legally disenfranchised and terrorized for generations by Cossack pogroms throughout the Pale of Settlement, Jews were disproportionately represented among the ranks of revolutionaries. When the Revolution erupted in January 1905, Chernoe Znamia detachments looted gun stores and military arsenals to wage social revolutionary warfare amid a chaotic landscape of revolutionary violence unleashed by a wide range of leftist formations, including other anarchist groups like Beznachalie (Without Authority) and the Socialist Revolutionary Party. They threw dynamite into police stations, assassinated employers, and carried out expropriations or "exes" against merchants and businessmen. "Down with the bourgeoisie and the tyrants! Long live terror against bourgeois society! Long live the anarchist commune!" a Vilna group declared. The scale of violence produced by these waves of propaganda by the deed dwarfed equivalent attacks elsewhere in Europe because it unfolded in conditions of civil war. Some estimate that anarchists killed approximately one thousand people during this brief but tumultuous period. Of course, czarist forces killed far more, including gunning down more than a hundred outside of the Winter Palace on "Bloody Sunday."[14]

The Charnoznamentsy were especially active in the southern regions of the Russian Empire. On December 17, 1905, they detonated a bomb in Odessa's Libman Café in an attack reminiscent of Émile Henry's 1894 bombing of the Café Terminus in Paris.[15] Backlash generated by the Libman bombing may have driven Nora Falk into exile since she arrived in Barcelona via Paris about two weeks later, in early January 1906, where she received correspondence from Odessa, but there is no concrete evidence of the exact chain of events that caused her to take flight. A French neo-Malthusian connected to the world of Parisian émigré anarchism suggested that Falk get in touch with Francisco Ferrer in Barcelona. From the moment Ferrer set her up in the same boardinghouse as Morral, she and Morral became inseparable companions. They attended anarchist meetings and soirees together, they were lovers according to later testimony from the proprietor of the boardinghouse, and weeks after meeting each other Falk accompanied Morral to Sabadell when he definitively broke off relations with his father.[16]

Those who knew Falk in Barcelona claimed that she had a doctorate in philosophy, which likely appealed to Morral, who preferred to spend his free time attending lectures on physics, chemistry, and the natural sciences at the University of Barcelona rather than indulging in vices like alcohol and tobacco. Morral had a "character that did not lend itself to jokes," according to Joan Montseny, who briefly met him at a Modern School picnic to celebrate the anniversary of the liberation of the Montjuich prisoners. When they raced to the top of a nearby mountain Morral came in first, Montseny second. Morral was so enthralled with nature that he almost moved to California to join an anarchist commune in 1903. He was dissuaded by the outbreak of an epidemic among the inhabitants and by words he read from his favorite anarchist theorist, Élisée Reclus: "it is necessary that we [anarchists] never close ourselves off. We must remain in the world to receive all of its impulses, to take part in all of its vicissitudes and receive its teachings."[17] Morral took these words to heart by vowing to take the struggle out into society rather than retreating to a commune.

In February 1906 Morral claimed to have traveled to Paris with a letter of introduction from Ferrer to meet Nicolás Estévanez, the veteran anarcho-republican conspirator distantly implicated in the rue de Rohan bombing. If Morral was the bomber of the rue de Rohan, they may have already crossed paths. Either way, with funding from Ferrer, Morral printed four thousand copies of the interview/dialogue he organized with Estévanez in Paris under the title *Pensamientos Revolucionarios* (Revolutionary Thoughts) in April 1906. Morral was intrigued by Estévanez's arguments about the need to transition away from the outdated urban insurrectionism of stationary "barricades that have become useless" that he experienced in his youth toward a kind of modern urban guerrilla resistance oriented around the strategic use of electricity and explosives. Estévanez urged Morral and all revolutionaries to study physics and chemistry but clarified that such "useful formulas and principles can be learned without any scientific background. Perhaps the most difficult part is the execution, which requires very personal conditions of serenity, abnegation, and moral energy"—qualities that Morral likely saw in himself.[18]

Days later, Morral said goodbye to his closest friends, telling them he was bound for the royal wedding. Though he did not spell out his intended activities, they could surely read between the lines. On May 20, 1906, Morral boarded a train bound for Madrid carrying a fancy new English suitcase filled with clothing, business cards in the name of an alias (Manuel Martínez, Valencian wool merchant), and ingredients for the fabrication of explosives. When he arrived, Morral checked into the Hotel Iberia on the recommendation of Francisco Ferrer, though he did not have many choices.[19] At the time Madrid had only a single luxury hotel, Hotel París, which was still quite mediocre compared to the grandeur of Barcelona's Hotel Colón. Madrid had been the national capital since the reign of Felipe II in the sixteenth century, but it remained an administrative city that lagged behind Barcelona and other European capitals in urban development and industrialization. Madrid was not a destination. That much was reflected in the absolute paucity of accommodations for the royal wedding. As the continent's aristocrats, politicians, and other dignitaries descended on Madrid—a national capital in provincial clothing—Alfonso XIII was embarrassed that they had to stay with local nobility or even in their national embassies for lack of hotels. This disgrace spurred the construction (with significant royal investment) of several regal hotels over the following years, including the iconic Hotel Ritz and Hotel Palace.[20]

Mateo Morral rented a room on the fourth floor of calle Mayor 88 from which he would be assured to have an excellent view of the royal procession returning from the wedding to the palace around the corner. On the 23rd and 24th of May, he purchased more bomb-making supplies: bottles of permanganate capsules, a crystal syringe, and two small safes to pack the bomb for greater effect. Witnesses later recounted seeing Morral dining with two men who "spoke with a markedly Catalan accent." We do not know who they were or whether they were assisting Morral, but they knew why he had come to town. They were seen accompanying Morral to Retiro Park, where he carved an ominous note into a tree: "Alfonso XIII will be executed on the day of his wedding," signed by "An unrepentant." On the side was written "dynamite." A passerby reported the threatening carving to park staff, but nothing came of it.[21]

Such a brazen declaration of intent suggests that Morral was not at all concerned about state surveillance. Generation of '98 luminaries Pío Baroja, Azorín, and Valle-Inclán remembered seeing a man they would later recognize as Mateo Morral threaten to "break the head" of a painter who had disparaged anarchists at a literary café they were attending in late May. Despite the tree carving, despite getting into public altercations, despite practicing his bomb-throwing skills by launching oranges out of his window at night, he did not arouse the slightest suspicion. He came across as an even-keeled, responsible lodger who had requested that his hosts bring him fresh flowers in the days preceding the wedding. Morral, who did not hide his identity when he checked into the boardinghouse on calle Mayor, even left the door to his room open all day, only closing it when he returned at night. Even so, had the owner of Morral's boardinghouse complied with a police mandate requiring logs of all visitors, authorities would have known of his presence. But most boardinghouse owners failed to comply, and the owner of Morral's boardinghouse was no exception, although the police requested his log the day before the royal wedding.[22]

Given the hundreds of death threats against Alfonso XIII and the precedent of the rue de Rohan bombing a year before, authorities were very concerned about a sequel. The state's entire diplomatic infrastructure was devoted to monitoring the activities and journeys of suspicious anarchists in Paris, Rome, Lisbon, Buenos Aires, Tangier, and beyond. But intense monitoring of train stations only began a week before the wedding. Morral arrived in Madrid ten days in advance. Around the same time, the Italian, French, and British governments each sent police agents to help coordinate security given "the deficiency of our police," as a government minister put it. Royal decrees in 1905 and 1906 attempted to address the woeful state of the country's police by announcing the creation of new police schools, an augmentation of police ranks, and an increased focus on knowledge of foreign languages. The infamous Policía Judicial or anarchist police were restructured under a new authority two months before the royal wedding.[23] Despite these reforms, however, Spanish authorities were uneasy in advance of the wedding. The presence of foreign police agents was largely symbolic with the exception of Jules Bonnecarrère, the special *commissaire* of the French police in Barcelona. Bonnecarrère, who oversaw a network of informants deeply embedded in the anarchist movement, was "almost sure that the anarchists will attempt something against the king during the festivities in Madrid." He exclaimed, "What an occasion this royal wedding offers someone who is disgusted with this world and imbued with subversive ideas! All the crown princes of the reigning houses, all the representatives of the bourgeois republics, gathered in the same capital and, at times, in the same place!"[24]

Spanish officials agreed with Bonnecarrère about the importance of protecting the wedding service at San Jerónimo el Real diagonally across from the Prado. At 10:30 on the morning of May 31, 1906, Alfonso XIII anxiously awaited the arrival of his bride, Victoria Eugenia of Battenberg, before a regal audience that included future British monarch George V and the Austrian archduke Franz Ferdinand. Unbeknownst to Alfonso, his bride was running late because her escort, Prime Minister Moret, had overslept. While everyone waited, Mateo Morral attempted to gain entry to the church by presenting himself as a journalist, but the police turned him away without questioning him.[25] Had he managed to smuggle the bomb he was carrying in his satchel into the church, the course of European history would have unfolded very differently. At the very least, the assassination of Franz Ferdinand (which sparked the First World War in 1914) might have occurred eight years earlier.

Instead, the royal wedding concluded without incident and the newlyweds set off for the royal palace amid popular jubilation. As the royal carriage carrying Alfonso and Queen Ena passed in front of calle Mayor 88, Morral peered down on them with a bouquet of flowers in his hand. An instant after an onlooker exclaimed, "What a beautiful bouquet!" he lobbed the flowers at the royal couple. When the bomb that the flowers concealed hit the ground, it unleashed "an explosion like the discharge of a large cannon, a nauseating odor, a flash." The bomb killed between twenty-six and thirty-three people and injured about another hundred but left the royal couple unharmed. Nine of the dead and twenty of the injured were soldiers in Alfonso's retinue. Among the injured were one of the bride's brothers and the son of the infamous general Valeriano Weyler. The moment of the explosion was captured for posterity by an unlikely spectator. That morning a seventeen-year-old medical student named Eugenio Mesonero Romanos decided to buy a camera to photograph the royal wedding. Perched on a balcony opposite Morral, he happened to snap the shutter at the very instant the bomb exploded. The definitive image of the *atentado* in the Spanish press, Mesonero's photo launched graphic journalism in Spain.[26]

Had the authorities not banned throwing objects at the royal procession, Morral's bouquet would have blended into a shower of flowers. But the ban made evident the source of the lethal bouquet to all onlookers. Royal security sealed the entrance to calle Mayor 88 as a growing mob of the outraged attempted to push through to unleash their vengeance on the bomber. But Morral had already slipped out of the building amid the chaos. About an hour later, he sought out José Nakens, the firebrand editor of the anti-clerical paper *El Motín*, at the paper's office near Plaza Dos de Mayo. "I just threw a bomb at the king on calle Mayor," Morral immediately confessed to Nakens, according to his later testimony. "I don't think I got him, but there were casualties. I read what you wrote about Angiolillo. . . . Are you going to turn me in?" Morral asked. Fortunately for the flustered bomber, Nakens would help him escape just as he had aided the anarchist assassin of Prime Minister Cánovas nine years earlier. That night Nakens brought Morral to stay with his friend on the pretext that Morral was a journalist who had escaped from prison. As Nakens left, Morral allegedly said, "Thank you. How great it is that you know Ferrer!"[27]

If this is true, Nakens must have reflected on a strange correspondence he had conducted with Francisco Ferrer over the past week. In late 1905 Nakens wrote to Ferrer, whom he had known for years, to ask whether he could sell him some books from his personal library to raise funds for the publication of his newspaper, *El Motín*. Ferrer turned him down. Then out of the blue Ferrer sent Nakens a check for 1,000 pesetas on May 26, 1906— five days before the royal wedding—accompanied by a letter explaining that

Ferrer wanted to publish some of Nakens's manuscripts with the Modern School. "It could seem strange that I am asking an enemy of the anarchists for two manuscripts for my library, whose purpose is, I confess, to make committed anarchists," Ferrer wrote Nakens, "but leaving aside the fact that you are an enemy of the anarchists, you know how to write things that they would sign off on." Surprised and confused by this seemingly random offer, Nakens declined, saying that his style did not fit children's books. Nakens did not cash the check, but neither did he return it because, he claimed, he was "inexperienced in bank operations." The day after leaving Morral at the home of his friend, Bernardo Mata, Nakens received a reply from Ferrer dated May 31, the day of the bombing. Ferrer urged Nakens to "do me a favor and cash the check" even if there were no children's books to publish, suggesting perhaps that the check was compensation for helping Morral. He continued to write that "if we want a revolution and if we want someone to personify it, that someone is Lerroux. . . . Naturally I don't agree with Lerroux about many things, but I consider him to be the most important figure today. I follow him."[28]

Ferrer's political relationship with the republican leader stretched back to 1892 when he first met Lerroux at a "Universal Freethinkers Congress" in Madrid. Lerroux was among the few, or perhaps the only, adherent to Ferrer's hastily composed appeal to create a kind of revolutionary vanguard among the congress participants.[29] Over the coming decade, Ferrer would move toward anarchism while retaining traces of his early republicanism, and Lerroux would reinvent radical republicanism by infusing it with populist rhetoric—earning him the moniker of "Emperor of the Paralelo," a lower-class district of Barcelona—that was inspired in large part by the anarchist movement. At the juncture of Ferrer's heterodox anarchism and Lerroux's incendiary republicanism emerged a small anarcho-republican nucleus that may have orchestrated both the rue de Rohan bombing of 1905 and the calle Mayor bombing a year later.

The aged conspirator Nicolás Estévanez epitomized this blurring of political tendencies in the interest of immediate action. In March 1906, shortly after meeting Morral in Paris, Estévanez wrote to Ferrer with the following request: "do me a favor and tell Roca [Morral] from me that only in the last few days have I gone out since I had the flu but that I will send him books on electricity. . . . The decisive acts can be hoped for from the youth."[30] The supposition that this letter referred to the construction and utilization of explosives is bolstered by Estévanez's presence at a lunch atop Mount Tibidabo overlooking Barcelona with Lerroux, Ferrer, and Morral days before the latter left for Madrid. Lerroux claimed to have been ignorant of Morral's identity at the time. Only later did Ferrer allegedly suggest to Lerroux that they should prepare for the likely scenario that "some kind of nonsense" would occur at the royal wedding. Lerroux believed that Ferrer knew about the conspiracy but claimed in his memoirs to have abstained from asking too many questions.[31]

Whether Lerroux was fully knowledgeable about the plot or not (most likely he was), he admitted to stationing groups of armed supporters at strategic locations around Barcelona and the surrounding provinces. After the assassination they were to capture Montjuich Castle and other key points and declare the republic. According to Lerroux's memoir and a police witness, on the day of the wedding Lerroux and Ferrer waited at separate tables in a café on Plaza de Cataluña for word from Madrid. Around the time of the explosion, Lerroux tried to call Madrid, but authorities had shut down telephone communications. Morral's failure to kill the king squelched any potential rising.[32] The French police came to believe that Estévanez provided the explosives to Morral, who utilized them with funding from Ferrer in order to launch a revolution led by Lerroux.[33] In the months leading up to the *atentado*, informants working for the Spanish embassy in Paris reported that Lerroux was laying the groundwork for a military rising in collaboration with Estévanez, who may have been receiving funds from Cuban revolutionaries.[34]

The notion that Ferrer would have supported a revolution that put Lerroux in power is supported by a comment from one of Ferrer's closest friends, Charles Malato, that Ferrer "would have welcomed a simply republican revolution like the one in Portugal as a first step while continuing to advance from the governmental and capitalist republic toward the ideal social and libertarian res publica."[35] The prospect of a republican transition period between monarchy and anarchy was anathema to anarchists, most of whom loathed Alejandro Lerroux by 1906, but Francisco Ferrer's politics never fit cleanly into any category.

While Ferrer and Lerroux anxiously awaited word from Madrid, the police wasted no time in rounding up anyone suspicious in the vicinity of the explosion, including an Englishman who was forced to run the gauntlet of public abuse by his civil guard captors, causing a minor diplomatic scandal once his innocence was established.[36] They also arrested prominent Madrid anarchists like Joan Montseny and Antonio Apolo.[37] After a few hours, however, the police discovered the true identity of the bomber because Morral checked into the boardinghouse on calle Mayor under his real name and left behind shirts and handkerchiefs with the initials "M. M." It is unclear why Morral did not simply use an alias like Manuel Martínez, the name on his fake business cards. Perhaps he was so confident in his plan and the revolution that it was supposed to spark that he did not worry about the future. His decision to seek out José Nakens appears premeditated, but everything that followed seems purely improvisational. One of Morral's friends later claimed that the Chernoe Znamia insurrectionary Nora Falk was in charge of planning her companion's escape, but there does not seem to have been much of a plan. Police searched for Falk after the bombing, but she escaped the police dragnet (and the curiosity of historians) without leaving a trace.[38]

Mateo Morral found it much more difficult to disappear. The morning after the bombing, he changed clothes and set off on foot into the Castilian countryside. Morral found work pulling weeds on a farm, but this bourgeois son of an industrialist was promptly fired for his agricultural ineptitude. That night he slept out in the open. The next day, June 2, Morral wandered around the countryside in search of food and a train to Barcelona. Everywhere he went locals could not help but notice that this strange wanderer resembled published descriptions of the infamous bomber. Around six in the evening he stopped at an inn somewhere between Ajalvir and Torrejón de Ardoz where the suspicious innkeeper served him tortilla with a slice of bacalao, bread, and wine. Moments later, a police officer and two of his friends came in for a drink. Noticing that Morral spoke Catalan, they struck up a conversation about Catalonia that led to chatter about the recent *atentado*. They mentioned how the bomber had cut his finger and then noticed that Morral had a small bandage on his right hand. The cop asked Morral to accompany him to the nearby town of Torrejón. Morral politely complied. He followed behind the officer for about fifty meters before quickly pulling out a pistol and fatally shooting him in the face. Then he turned the gun on himself, ending the saga of Mateo Morral.[39]

On his death, Mateo Morral's legacy branched off in several directions. Though official public opinion severely repudiated the *atentado*, supporters and sympathizers came to imagine Morral as a "tragic hero," as the Generation of '98 novelist Ramón del Valle-Inclán phrased it. He and Pío Baroja, whose 1908 novel *La dama errante* was inspired by Morral, visited the would-be assassin's body as it lay cold on the examining table in the hospital. The working-class and poor street kids of Madrid relived the drama of Morral's *atentado* by playing the "bomb game." Kids would collect coins to buy some calcium carbide. The player chosen to play the role of Mateo Morral would then place the calcium carbide in a hole filled with water and covered with dirt beneath a tin can. The other kids simulated the royal procession and the soldiers lining the route. When the gas exploded, the can would fly up in the air, the soldiers would collapse to the ground in agony, and the young Mateo

Morral would run away throwing stones at the police officers chasing him until he gave up and shot himself.[40]

The fear of the polyvalence of anarchist *atentados* in Spain dated back to the police confiscation of lithographic portraits of Paulino Pallás in 1893. Authorities took a definitive step toward entrenching their interpretation of events in 1908 with the construction of a monument to the victims at the site of the calle Mayor bombing. It featured a large statue of the Virgin Mary supported by three columns representing the aristocracy, the army, and the *pueblo*.[41] In 1910 an Italian anarchist named José Corengia Tabocelli exploded a bomb near the monument before committing suicide.[42] With the advent of the Second Republic the monument was destroyed and calle Mayor was renamed calle Mateo Morral. In his hometown of Sabadell the name of the main street was changed from Alfonso XIII to Mateo Morral, and his father's factory was collectivized.[43] Predictably, Franco returned the streets to their original names, and a new monument to the victims that was dedicated in 1963 stands opposite calle Mayor 88 to this day.

Though Mateo Morral had committed suicide, his alleged conspirator Francisco Ferrer sat in prison awaiting his sentence.

Despite being associated with a bloody attempt on the life of the royal couple on their wedding day, Ferrer's supporters would manage to generate a vigorous campaign of support in countries across Europe, with the notable exception of Spain itself, by making use of the popular tropes

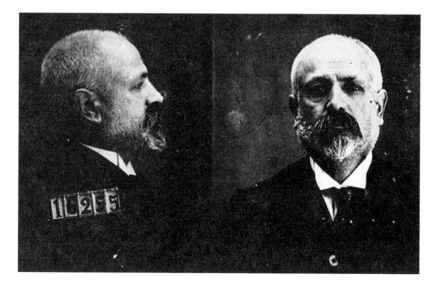

FIGURE 18. Mugshot of Francisco Ferrer in 1906. University of California San Diego, Special Collections, Francisco Ferrer Collection, box 17, folder 7.

of Spanish "barbarity" and tapping into the formidable networks that had been established in earlier Spanish prisoner campaigns and the Dreyfus affair. While the pro-Ferrer campaign of 1906–7 continued on the path pioneered by the Montjuich campaign of 1896–1900, Morral's failed *atentado* of 1906 marked the end of a brief era of mid-decade anarcho-republican insurrectionary scheming. Over the next few years the effects of propaganda by the deed would continue to make themselves felt, above all in Barcelona, which came to be known as the "City of Bombs," but these explosions seemed random compared to the obvious political calculus of targeting a king. Meanwhile, the reemergence of revolutionary syndicalism in the form of the Solidaridad Obrera federation in 1907 shifted the trajectory of libertarian politics in Spain.

Yet one cannot help but wonder what course history might have taken had Morral's explosive bouquet landed a few feet closer to its intended targets. Despite the relatively modest preparations that Lerroux and his allies made for any potential "nonsense" at the wedding, there is no reason to believe that revolution would have been imminent. Nevertheless, the tumult generated by a successful *atentado* that would have left Alfonso XIII's five-year-old nephew on the throne could have shaken up the course of history, perhaps in ways we would never imagine.

CHAPTER 14

"Truth on the March" for Francisco Ferrer

Sitting alone in Madrid's Cárcel Modelo (Model prison), Francisco Ferrer could only express his agony by putting pen to paper. "My friend," he wrote Charles Malato, "I have been suffering two martyrdoms: the moral martyrdom of being surveilled at my door by the guard, and the material martyrdom of suffering an electric light over my head all night."[1] After months of uncertainty, on that day, September 23, 1906, the prison director Millán Astray finally informed Ferrer that he would face the death penalty for his alleged complicity in Mateo Morral's failed attempt on the life of King Alfonso XIII nearly four months earlier. "I responded," Ferrer recounted to Malato, "that I was indifferent to [facing the death penalty] but I asked him to remove the light." Millán Astray, whose son of the same name would become Francisco Franco's "military mentor" years later, refused Ferrer's request.[2] Feeling the effects of sleep deprivation induced by constant light and guard visits every five minutes, Ferrer asked Malato, "Is this how it started in Montjuich?"[3]

Fortunately for Ferrer, and the workers' movement as a whole, the aftermath of the calle Mayor bombing did not resemble *el proceso de Montjuich*. True, authorities shut down Ferrer's Modern School in Barcelona. Initially they explained the school's closure in terms of missing documentation before changing their justification to "a question of morality," as Ferrer phrased it.[4] But more broadly, rather than concoct an inchoate conspiracy as a pretense for arresting hundreds of dissidents, a blunt strategy of repression whose limitations had manifested themselves over the previous decade, authorities brought charges against only seven alleged accomplices. They included Ferrer, the editor of the anti-clerical *El Motín*, José Nakens, and his six friends who had abetted Mateo Morral's escape. Each defendant faced nine years except Ferrer, who faced sixteen years after the minister of justice, the Count of Romanones, interceded on his behalf to eliminate a potential death sentence.[5]

The year 1906 had been a tough one for the Liberal politician and future three-time prime minister of Spain, Álvaro Figueroa y Torres, the Count of Romanones. As the minister of the interior, his department had been in charge of security for the royal wedding. Though he had offered 25,000 pesetas of his own money for the capture of the bomber before Morral's suicide, he could not shake public criticism of his ministry's ineptitude or his connection to the anarchist Joan Montseny, who had been arrested briefly after the bombing while serving as the evening editor of Romanones's newspaper, *Diario Universal*. This constellation of public condemnation led Romanones to resign his post in the Ministry of the Interior, only to take over the Ministry of Justice later in the year in the continuing game of musical chairs that was high politics in Spain. The former editor of *La Revista Blanca* faced equivalent backlash from the anarchist movement for his critical article "Mateo Morral the Mystic" published in *Diario Universal* shortly after the failed assassination attempt. Montseny sought to marginalize the neo-Malthusianism of Morral, whom he described as having "hostility toward the passions and women, [and] physical degeneration."[6]

Romanones's efforts to reduce Ferrer's sentence may have been a pragmatic effort to avoid retaliatory *atentados* or an indication of his relationship with Montseny, who encouraged Romanones to support Ferrer.[7] Montseny campaigned for Ferrer from the pages of *Diario Universal* despite the pedagogue's ardent neo-Malthusianism. "Francisco Ferrer," Montseny wrote, "has never professed an anarchist faith. . . . A longtime republican and freethinker, his work as director of the Modern School can be reduced to scientific teaching, without preference for any philosophical or social school." In his memoirs, Montseny admitted to actively working to remove "the anarchist stigma" from Ferrer, but "in reality the founder of the Modern School was not an anarchist" in Montseny's opinion, although his ideas "were very close." Far from his Barcelona community, Ferrer paid Montseny and his sister-in-law to bring him food and clothing every day while his compañera Teresa Mañé stayed home with their little daughter, Federica. Learning that his support had gotten Montseny fired from *Diario Universal*, Ferrer offered him the same salary to direct the campaign for his exoneration. Montseny claimed to have accepted on the condition that he ghostwrite all of Ferrer's articles in the press.[8]

Montseny had an intense fondness for writing in disguise. In part, this owed to the need to avoid repression, but it went further than that. Apart from the many essays he wrote under the nom de plume Federico Urales, Montseny invented a wide variety of identities in La Revista Blanca, from medical doctors to women, to give himself artificial authority to expound on a given topic, like when he wrote his first Montjuich article from the perspective of the tortured prisoner Sebastián Suñé. Under the pseudonym Angel Cunillera, Montseny even attacked the coalition politics promoted by "the organizers of the Montjuich campaign" for producing a kind of "parliamentary anarchism" that paved the way for Lerrouxism.[9] Despite his fondness for writing behind the scenes, throughout his life Montseny carried a serious chip on his shoulder about not receiving credit for his writing and intellect. Several years earlier, Ferrer wanted to publish stories from La Revista Blanca written by "a Vagabond." When Montseny instead offered to write something himself for publication by the Modern School, Ferrer turned him down. Outraged, Montseny triumphantly revealed that he was the true "Vagabond." Out of that conversation came the Modern School publication of Federico Urales's Sembrando Flores.[10] Despite the prickly aspects of Montseny's personality and his litany of political feuds, most notably with his former Montjuich collaborator and Ferrer's intimate comrade Alejandro Lerroux, he and Ferrer set out to mount an international press campaign to free the founder of the Modern School from prison.

The Ferrer campaign of 1906–7 achieved immediate international scope by tapping into the networks forged by the Montjuich campaign and those that followed in its wake. Ferrer's close comrade Charles Malato directed the French campaign from the pages of the Parisian republican daily L'Action, which had hired him shortly after his acquittal in the trial for the rue de Rohan bombing. Malato successfully gathered the support of a wide range of traditional allies by coordinating the collaboration of two "Comités Ferrer": a more moderate committee composed of socialist deputies and representatives of freethinkers' associations and another "composed exclusively of anarchists." According to the informant Sannois, the two committees occasionally met jointly at the Grand Orient Masonic lodge, "but it is evident that they each work separately."[11] As their meeting location suggests, many Ferrer supporters across the political spectrum were Freemasons like

Ferrer who had risen to rank 31 out of 33, called "Grand Inspector Inquisitor," since becoming a Mason in 1883.[12]

At the end of the nineteenth century, Freemasonry had developed a broad network for radicals and freethinkers in Europe and around the world. Although Freemasonry originated in London in 1717 to promote spirituality beyond religious and political sectarianism, by the turn of the twentieth century it had shifted toward rationalism and liberalism, constituting a "secular cult of reason." Masonry became far more political and anti-clerical when lodges in France and Belgium eliminated the requirement that members believe in God. Masonry became the "Church of the Republic" as republican politicians and leftists networked through its archaic rituals and rites. A similar shift occurred in Spanish Masonry, which became a forum for collaboration between republicans, anarchists, anti-clericals, and others after it returned to legality with the advent of the First Republic in 1873. Pope Pius IX called Masonry the "synagogue of Satan."[13]

Despite Ferrer's having lived in Paris for sixteen years where he climbed the heights of Freemasonry, Malato recounted how Ferrer was "unknown to nine-tenths of our comrades" when the campaign began.[14] Nevertheless, Malato, Sébastien Faure, and their collaborators managed to promote the cause of the founder of the Modern School by tapping into the networks forged by the Dreyfus affair and Spanish solidarity campaigns. The most prominent face of the French campaign for the "Spanish Zola" was the Ligue des droits de l'homme led by its president, Francis de Pressensé, who insisted that Ferrer be disassociated completely with anarchism. In the interest of practical expediency Malato agreed, but many Parisian anarchists felt marginalized within the campaign. Moreover, others asked why so many resources were being devoted to saving a single "bourgeois" figure while lesser-known comrades were languishing in French prisons.[15]

Such concerns were only aggravated with the absence of anarchist orators at the first major Parisian meeting organized by the *ligue* before a crowd of one to two thousand in early January 1907 at the Grand Orient Masonic lodge.[16] Instead, irritated anarchists listened to the prominent Dreyfusard and president of the Rennes section of the *ligue*, Victor Basch, claim that Ferrer was "not an anarchist but a reformer."[17] As Pressensé advocated, the adamant denial of any embrace of anarchism on the part of Ferrer became a hallmark of the international press campaign. *Le XIXe siècle* claimed that "Francisco Ferrer is not an anarchist; not a deed, not a word shows him to be a propagandist of violence and direct action. . . . He has chosen education—the school—as his means of propaganda by the deed."[18]

Though this was true of Ferrer's comments as the founder of the Modern School, when writing under his Masonic pseudonym Cero in his revolutionary syndicalist newspaper *La Huelga General* he argued that "it would be better not to organize a general strike if it had to be peaceful" and that "the new era of peace and justice" would come "with the last baptism of human blood."[19] The vast majority of Ferrer's supporters had no knowledge of his secret insurrectionary inclinations. Rather, they believed his self-presentation as a strictly objective, rationalist, scientific educator. Writing in *España Nueva*, Ferrer (or possibly Montseny writing as Ferrer) explained, "I should be an Anarchist insofar as Anarchism adopts my ideas of education, of peace, and love, but not to the extent that I would have adopted any of its particular proceedings."[20] The tone of the campaign was captured by the words of the prominent Dreyfusard and novelist Anatole France, who asked, "What is his crime? His crime is being a republican, socialist, freethinker. His crime is having promoted lay education in Barcelona, instructing thousands of children in independent morality; his crime is having founded a school and a library."[21] Ferrer committees organized protest meetings in cities and towns across France.[22] Yet the nonsectarian unity of the anti-clerical left that had undergirded Spanish solidarity campaigns for a decade foundered in the spring of 1907. Months after the Dreyfusard politician Georges Clemenceau became prime minister, his government unleashed an "odious campaign . . . against the CGT and syndicalism in general," according to *Le Libertaire*.[23] The class struggle that erupted between the moderate and radical factions of the solidarity campaign derailed momentum for Ferrer and his codefendants in France.

In London the former Montjuich prisoner Fernando Tarrida del Mármol organized the "Defense of Freedom of Conscience in Spain" committee to defend Ferrer in collaboration with William Heaford, secretary general of the English Freethinkers' League, the anarchist Pedro Vallina who had been deported from France shortly before Alfonso's wedding, and Vallina's German comrade Siegfried Nacht. According to the informant Sannois, this committee was composed of "militant anarchist refugees, notably many Italians."[24] Similar Ferrer committees organized demonstrations, protest meetings, and combative press campaigns in Italy, Portugal, Belgium, and the Netherlands. Few events were organized in Latin America, but press coverage set the stage for major pro-Ferrer protests in 1909.[25]

In the fall of 1906, the Ferrer support network organized a plan to bring delegates from each international committee to Barcelona for a joint demonstration on the occasion of the inauguration of a new Casa del Pueblo social center. Sannois reported that the Barcelona committee sent funds to Malato in Paris to pay the expenses of the French delegation, which included radical French deputies, newspaper editors, and two former deputies of the short-lived Russian Duma. Initially the Parisian Russian Committee was going to send four delegates, but "they thought it too dangerous to jeopardize four comrades." Their concerns were well founded. In London Tarrida del Mármol organized a Barcelona delegation in collaboration with the legendary Russian revolutionary and founder of the influential "Tchaikovsky circle," Nikolai Tchaikovsky. Like his Russian counterparts in Paris, Tchaikovsky was reticent to risk traveling to Spain. But the English anarchist journalist Guy Bowman, who would go on to cofound the Industrial Syndicalist Education League in 1910, was willing to brave "the country of the Inquisition" to conduct an investigation into the Ferrer case. Shortly after arriving in Madrid, however, Bowman was arrested and deported to France. The Spanish government unintentionally handed Bowman the sensational story he desired as he toured Western Europe recounting the harrowing tale of his time south of the Pyrenees.[26]

Despite the uproar that Ferrer's prosecution generated abroad, at home he found few defenders. "In Spain," historian Joan Connelly Ullman wrote, "there was no pro-Ferrer campaign" apart from the support generated by Alejandro Lerroux and a handful of small newspapers.[27] But even Lerroux's support "was not from sympathy, but rather because of the money he has received from Ferrer for his newspaper," according to Sannois.[28] Indeed, Lerroux had been backed into a corner by the rise of his political rivals in Solidaritat Catalana and his loss of La Publicidad, the paper he had directed for five years. Desperate for financial support to revive his political fortunes, he threw his lot in with Ferrer, who helped him fund the creation of four new papers: the dailies El Progreso and El Intransigente and the weeklies Los Descamisados and La Rebeldía. In an effort to channel the prestige of the Dreyfus affair, Lerroux launched his Ferrer campaign under the Dreyfusard slogan "Truth on the March." Beyond Lerroux and his most loyal supporters, most Spanish republicans kept their distance from Ferrer, who was a little too much of an anarchist and a little too guilty to be worth the trouble. While some professors and educators supported him in France, their Spanish counterparts remained silent. The master of the Spanish Grand Orient publicly signed onto republican calls for Ferrer's exoneration, but behind the scenes he encouraged Italian lodges to withhold their support. Pablo Iglesias's socialists had no interest.[29]

At least Ferrer's cell in the Cárcel Modelo finally went dark at night. In November 1906 Romanones transferred prison director Millán Astray to the position of Madrid chief of police and replaced him with the progressive criminologist Rafael Salillas. Ferrer was elated with Astray's replacement who immediately turned off the lights at night and removed the guards from his cell. Salillas later published an article analyzing Ferrer's prison behavior, from the poems he scrawled on the walls to the disdain he showed to the prison chaplains.[30]

Ferrer certainly had a lot of time to decorate his walls with press clippings and poems as months passed without a trial. Organizers had intended to launch the start of their campaign about two to three months before the start of the trial so that international momentum would peak at the key moment, but Spanish authorities delayed the trial multiple times with "the goal of tiring public opinion and erasing the impression caused by the campaign on the spirit of the popular masses," according to Sannois. By March 1907 reports indicated that "these delays dishearten the organizers of the pro-Ferrer movement." Sannois explained, "Malato claims that this delay will probably make the anarchists adopt a new tactic."[31] Though this cryptic claim could mean many things, in the midst of lingering reports of plots against the royal family it certainly conjured nightmares of explosions. As with earlier prisoner solidarity campaigns, pro-Ferrer anarchists occasionally hinted at repercussions that might follow a conviction. Malato concluded an article in Le Libertaire by "sharply advising" Spanish authorities that it was "in their own interest" to release Ferrer—a tongue-in-cheek understatement whose meaning was evident to any reader.[32]

When the trial began on June 3, 1907, tensions had been eased by the reduction of Ferrer's potential sentence from death to sixteen years—an outcome Romanones certainly had in mind when he reduced it—but the possible repercussions of a conviction were clear. Efforts by Ferrer's lawyer to transfer the trial from military jurisdiction to a trial by jury were rejected, but Ferrer wrote, "I prefer to find myself faced with the servants of the government, throne, or Jesuits, but all men who could be supposed to be my enemies" rather than "before a jury of imbeciles."[33] Montseny, Lerroux, and Ferrer's compañera Soledad Villafranca testified on his behalf. Villafranca argued that Morral had committed the atentado because she rejected his romantic advances. She supported her claim by showing three postcards he had sent her from Madrid professing his affection. Yet those closest to Morral denied that he had any real interest in Villafranca. The anarchist Albà Rosell claimed that the ascetic Morral "felt a strong aversion to the woman that he was supposedly in love with, as much for the artificiality of her appearance as for her lack of a consciousness of a free woman." Years later Pedro Vallina affirmed in no uncertain terms that Morral threw the bomb "to unleash the revolution in Spain . . . not because of disillusionment from his love for Soledad Villafranca."[34] Regardless of the nature of Morral's feelings for Villafranca, Ferrer's lawyer certainly intended to portray his actions as those of a lovesick young man rather than efforts to promote a broader political conspiracy with Ferrer at the center.

Yet Ferrer's relations with Morral, his bizarre correspondence with José Nakens, and other fragments of evidence suggested that the founder of the Modern School played a role in the attempt on the royal wedding. The likelihood of his participation increases when the insurrectionary tracts he wrote under the pseudonym Cero in *La Huelga General* are taken into account. Many historians believe that he was involved and they are probably correct, but no definitive proof of his guilt has ever been uncovered. Surprisingly, especially in light of later events, the court agreed and acquitted Ferrer of all charges. The other defendants were acquitted as well except José Nakens and two of his friends, who were sentenced to nine years for housing Morral after his escape. They were pardoned a year later.[35] "Judicial decisions had undergone an important transformation with the turn of the century," historian Ángel Herrerín López writes, "and the state, with good reason, preferred to avoid any decision that would entail national and international disgrace for a regime that was already quite vilified."[36]

The Spanish state had allowed Francisco Ferrer to walk free, but they would never allow the reopening of his precious Modern School. After being mobbed by two thousand jubilant supporters packed onto the train platform to greet him on his return to Barcelona, Ferrer and Soledad Villafranca were eager to leave Spain to tour the cities that had supported him in his bleakest hour. Ferrer had won this battle, but this would not be the last time he would struggle against "Jesuitism and religious fanaticism in Spain."[37]

CHAPTER 15

The Birth of the "City of Bombs"

When writing about bombings and street-fighting, the two forms of non-state political violence that came to define Barcelona politics from 1907–1909, one could do worse than begin with the events of Sunday January 20, 1907. That morning, approximately 15,000 Catholics representing "every kind of reactionary fauna," as the republican *El País* derisively phrased it, from Carlists to *integristas* to members of the Conservative Party and *Soldaritat Catalana* packed the Arenas bullfighting ring to protest a civil marriage law and a new *Ley de Asociaciones* that would enhance state supervision of religious orders.[1] Surrounded by Carlist banners, a speaker read a letter sent from a Cardinal who lambasted the *Ley de Asociaciones* as "inspired by cowardice, hypocrisy, and surrounded by an inquisitorial halo."[2] Even ultramontane clergy who reminisced about the era of the inquisition sought to harness the rhetorical power of the term to slander their enemies. Among those listening on was the shipping magnate Claudio López Bru, better known as the second Marquess of Comillas, who was orchestrating his own campaign against the law at the head of the lay political organization, *Acción Católica*.[3] A shift within the Liberal Party toward the anti-clerical radicalism of José Canalejas that threatened "to convert Spain into a moral colony of French Jacobinism," as the right saw it, helped to promote "an active, militant form of Catholicism" as the bonds that had united the dynastic left and right since the Restoration continued to fray.[4]

Not long after the Liberal and Conservative parties started to drift away from each other, their collective hegemony over Catalan politics ended with the emergence of the struggle between the political Catalanism of the *Lliga Regionalista* (founded in 1901), which united with other parties to form *Solidaritat Catalana* in 1906, and Alejandro Lerroux's populist radical republicanism. After winning city elections in November 1905, Lerroux's electoral fortunes declined as those of his Catalanist adversaries soared. In January 1907, Lerroux and his followers sought to bounce back from various political failures by throwing themselves into the campaign to liberate Francisco Ferrer who was imprisoned for his alleged role in Mateo Morral's attempted regicide in Madrid in May of 1906.[5] That day, January 20, 1907, Lerrouxistas and their allies were holding a protest meeting in support of Ferrer at Barcelona's Frontón Central at the same time as the right-wing Catholic meeting against the *Ley de Asociaciones*. Midway through the republican meeting, the idea emerged to go confront the clericals at the bullring. As the Catholic demonstrators filed out of Las Arenas cheering for "Catholic Catalonia," they were confronted by the shouts and whistles of the republicans. Jeers led to volleys of rocks and the crackle of revolvers. Sabers aloft, mounted civil guard charged into the fray. Roving bands of clerical and anti-clerical militants exchanged gunfire all the way down the Gran Vía to the Plaza de la Universidad.[6]

Blocks away from the Plaza de la Universidad, Arturo Vives Pla and his wife Pilar were descending the staircase of their building on the Rambla de Canaletas near the Plaza de Cataluña early that afternoon when they noticed a package wrapped in paper. Despite his wife's admonition to leave it alone, the package exploded in Arturo's hands when he inspected it.[7] Just as the "pitched battle on the Gran Vía" was not the first confrontation between the *"solidaris"* of *Solidaritat Catalana* and Lerroux's *"antisolidaris,"* the explosion on the Rambla de Canaletas was far from the first *atentado* Barcelona had experienced.[8] Yet, the violence of January 20, 1907 existed at the intersection of a variety of overlapping developments that would come to shape Barcelona politics over the coming years. The "indignation among the popular masses" aroused by this bombing and another down the street on the Rambla de las Flores a week later led city officials to take the unorthodox and sensational step of recruiting a Scotland Yard detective named Charles Arrow to lead a new anti-terror investigative unit in Barcelona.[9] More importantly, it doomed the liberal government of Antonio Aguilar, thereby ushering in the "long government" of conservative Antonio Maura.

By essentially attempting to revive the infamous anti-anarchist law of 1896 that had set the stage for *el proceso de Montjuich* in an effort to silence the explosives, Maura would inadvertently trigger a massively popular campaign against his law's infringement upon rights and liberties that helped to "give birth to the modern Spanish left."[10] While some of the many bombs planted around the city during this era were likely planted by anarchists, others, including those that exploded on January 20 and 27, 1907, were not. They had been planted by an ex-anarchist turned police informer named Joan Rull who had secretly turned *dinamiterismo* into a lucrative enterprise. In so doing, the spectacle of explosions became a political football for struggles between radical republicans, Catalanists, anarchists, and others. Many anarchists were turning away from propaganda by the deed, however, as the profile of revolutionary syndicalism within anarchist ranks grew with the establishment of the Solidaridad Obrera labor federation later that year. Nevertheless, despite a shift away from explosives in the Catalan anarchist movement, despite the creation of a new police force, despite the proposal of new laws, and despite a myriad of political resignations, the terrifying roar of dynamite continued in what was coming to be known as the "city of bombs."

Though Barcelona seems to have been dubbed the "city of bombs" for the first time in the Spanish press in a late 1906 issue of the satirical magazine *Gedeón*, dynamite was nothing new to the city.[11] Between 1886–1900, fifty-five bombs had exploded, including those thrown by Paulino Pallás on the Gran Vía in 1893, Santiago Salvador in the Liceo Theater weeks later, and an unknown bomber outside Santa María del Mar in 1896. Another thirty-five had been discovered without exploding over the same period. But the explosions and *atentados* slowed down in the city during and after *el proceso de Montjuich*. This is not to say that tranquility reigned in the absence of dynamite. After a tram workers' strike paralyzed the city in 1901, an insurrectionary general strike brought 80,000 workers off the job a year later. But after the average number of explosions had declined from 4.6 a year over the eleven years between 1886–1896 to one a year between 1897–1900 to zero between 1901–1902, the recrudescence of urban explosives in the new century stood in sharper contrast.[12] Six explosions occurred in 1903, but they were of "little importance." They were easily surpassed by eight public explosions the next year, such as a bombing near city hall that left fourteen injured months after Joaquín Artal's failed attempt on the life of Prime Minister Antonio Maura during the royal visit to the city.[13]

As this destructive trend continued into 1905, it became evident that not only were the explosions increasingly numerous, they also seemed to be increasingly indiscriminate in their targets. Apart from an explosion at a Jesuit College in May of 1904 whose potential anti-authoritarian motivations were evident, bombs were exploding on public thoroughfares like the Gran Vía Diagonal (today Avinguda Diagonal).[14] On September 3, 1905 an explosion at the Rambla de las Flores killed two and injured another twenty-five.[15] Many anarchists publicly denounced this seemingly indiscriminate carnage. In response to the Rambla de las Flores bombing, *El Porvenir del Obrero* argued that the bomb "could not have been thrown by anarchists" because although they supported those who have "responded to force against force, injuring governors and the powerful . . . throwing bombs at the people cannot be the object of revolutionaries."[16] "Everyone with humanitarian sentiments" could agree that someone who "throws a bomb in the middle of the street . . . is a savage" according to a collective statement titled *"nuestra protesta"* issued by Catalan anarchist groups during this period. They also emphasized that recent *atentados* were uncharacteristic of anarchists because bombs placed at intelligible targets, like the Jesuit college, "did nothing more than break windows" while "such dreadful bombs that exploded in public streets covered innocent workers in blood."[17] Since "recent *atentados* have caused the revolutionary idea great damage without any benefit," anarchists blamed the usual cast of reactionary characters in whose interest it was to discredit anarchism: the capitalist elite, state institutions, "the Jesuits" and the "bourgeoisie."[18] Anarchists printed 2,000 copies of another protest leaflet called "Enough of the Farce" that blamed "the celebrated bomber, Civil Guard lieutenant Morales" who would, in fact, be fired and sent to prison for planting explosives.[19]

The press generally assumed that "the anarchists—or whoever they are" were responsible for the bombs.[20] While the authorship of the vast majority of the bombings during this era remains unknown, and popular opinion was actually favorable at times to the notion that the police or other elite actors were truly responsible, there were at least some Barcelona anarchists who were planning *atentados* during the first decade of the twentieth century. Among them seem to have been some of the organizers of the *Centro Obrero de Estudios Sociales* (Workers' Social Studies Center) which served as "the principal headquarters of Barcelona anarchism from 1904–1908" according to historian Antoni Dalmau, and was linked to the newly formed International Antimilitarist Association. After attending a protest meeting in support of the Alcalá del Valle prisoners in Perpignan in August of 1904, a group of anarchists affiliated with the *Centro* planned *atentados* against the mayor of Alcalá del Valle and Prime Minister Maura to avenge their Andalusian comrades, but their plans were thwarted and recriminations of police collaboration among anarchist ranks spread. In late 1904 the main organizers of the Barcelona Antimilitarist Committee affiliated with the *Centro* were charged with the September 1904 bombing of the Rambla de las Flores. Among them were Maurice Bernardon, "the indisputable teacher of the construction of bombs," in Barcelona after he brought the technology behind the inversion bomb to the city starting in 1902, and his first roommate in the city, Joan Rull.[21]

By early 1906 Joan Rull and his comrades had all been exonerated thanks to their lawyers' ability to convince the jury that the charges were a police plot and possibly as a result of jury intimidation generated by "anarcho-lerrouxista" forces.[22] But after his acquittal something had changed for the twenty-four-year-old Rull while spending more than a year in jail. Years later he would explain that he had been "a committed and ardent novice" to the anarchist creed and "a principal element of the antimilitarist committee which planned anarchist *atentados*, but I was appalled." Therefore, Rull recounted, "as penitence for my thoughtlessness I changed course to dedicate myself to pursuing men of this sort."[23] While the course of events that followed would cast doubt upon the sincerity and accuracy of important elements of this statement, what is certain is that Rull promptly switched sides.

In the early evening of February 13, 1906 witnesses noticed a well-dressed man in his thirties with a black mustache leave a suspicious package that contained "a kind of iron saucepan with five bolts" packed with explosives at the Boquería market.[24] This first bomb discovered in the new year of 1906 did not explode, but it prompted the arrests of some of Rull's former *Centro* comrades. That same day Antoni Andrés Roig (aka Navarro) of the municipal brigades visited Rull to propose that he use his familiarity with the anarchist milieu to become a paid informant. Rull agreed and Navarro introduced him to his former employer, the textile heir and director of insurance and railroad companies, Eusebi Güell, best remembered as patron of the modernist architect Antoni Gaudí.[25] Influenced by the early nineteenth century English tradition of top-down socialistic industrial experimentation, in 1890 Güell had created an industrial colony with new houses, schools, and other facilities outside of Barcelona to foment class harmony. Apart from the imperatives of his elite class position, Güell's hatred for class struggle likely stemmed from an incident in his youth when an anarchist killed the manager of one of his family's bread factories.[26] Güell, who had established himself as an important power-broker not only as a result of his family's wealth but by having married the sister of the second Marquess of Comillas, arranged a meeting for Rull with the Civil Governor of Barcelona, the Duke of Bivona.[27]

Bivona agreed to pay Rull for information about "when, how, and where the next *atentado* would be committed." The Governor also funded trips to Mallorca and Marseille where Rull requested additional money after allegedly being robbed at a bordello. Though Rull failed to present any productive information (despite his expensive journeys), at least no bombs had exploded in Barcelona thus far in 1906 while the country's attention was turned toward Mateo Morral's failed attack on the royal couple in Madrid. Rull's gravy train dried up, however, as the carousel of Spanish governmental bureaucracy continued to spin with the end of Bivona's six-month tenure as Governor in late June, 1906. Although Bivona's successor, Francisco Manzano Alfaro, advanced Rull about 150–200 pesetas, the new governor refused to pay a cent more without results. Growing increasingly desperate to justify payment, Rull informed Güell that a British police officer in Barcelona was being tracked by two dangerous anarchists. The veracity of Rull's allegations evaporated when the Commissioner of Metropolitan Police replied that none of their officers had been sent to Barcelona.[28] In late 1906, Rull escalated his pursuit of government funds by sending a message to the mayor of Barcelona through a friend, warning that bombs would explode in the city between Christmas 1906 and Candlemas in early February 1907, and that he would share information on the details—for a price. After the mayor declined the offer, Rull told his friend "then there will be bombs."[29]

On Christmas Eve 1906, a large iron shell weighing 17 kilograms was discovered in the doorway of a building on the Rambla de las Flores. When the police tested it in an open space, the suspicious object detonated metal shards as far as 400 meters in distance. This was another inversion bomb of the style introduced to Barcelona by Rull's former comrade, Maurice Bernardon. Though harmless while sitting horizontally, turning it triggered a massive explosion. Though this was the fourteenth bomb discovered in and around Barcelona that year, including an incident in May when children came across a stash of eight bombs in the countryside, none had yet exploded. This changed on the afternoon of December 26, 1906 when a bomb exploded inside a public bathroom on Rambla de las Flores after a tourist from a small town in the province of Zaragoza stepped in to relieve himself. Though he survived, the bomb "completely destroyed" the tourist's leg. Public bathrooms had been first installed in the city for the Universal Exposition of 1888.[30] City planners had not taken into account how they provided opportunities for the discreet placement of explosives in highly trafficked areas. Broken was the silence that had reigned in Barcelona for more than thirteen months. But Joan Rull was just getting started.

This brings us to January 20, 1907, where we began this chapter with the street fight between radical republicans and militant Catholics on the Gran Vía and the explosion on the Rambla de Canaletas. That day, Rull was seen leaving the Arenas bullfighting ring, the location of the Catholic protest meeting, carrying an object wrapped in a scarf. Possibly aiming to take advantage of the commotion stirred up by Catholic meeting, Rull took a tram to La Rambla and planted the third bomb in his profit-seeking campaign of destruction. Though tensions had been simmering since the December explosion, they boiled over in the wake of the bombing of January 20, 1907. *La Publicidad* denounced "the repugnant and tragic spectacle of the bombs . . . that separate us from Europe as we approach uncultured and uncivilized Africa . . . we are worse off than in Russia." "If the authorities cannot manage to deal with the criminals," *El País* warned, "terror will be the absolute master of this capital." It did not take long for heads to roll. Days later, the Vega de Armijo national government fell, the Civil Governor of Barcelona who had refused to put Rull on the payroll resigned, and the police chief stepped down, all owing in large part to backlash from Rull's recent *atentados*.[31]

But for many a simple change of leadership was not enough. *La Publicidad* argued that it was necessary "to copy the methods used by governments of nations like France and England." In fact, the same argument had been put forward weeks earlier in the Barcelona city council in the aftermath of the bombing of late December. In its session of December 27, 1906, the Catalanist members of the town council approved a resolution petitioning the central government for "an immediate reorganization of the police in this city" with specifications that their police force be composed of Catalan officers. If the government were unresponsive, however, and "if these brutal acts repeat themselves regularly," one member argued that it would be necessary to seek help from a "foreign consulate."[32]

The importance of regional control for political Catalanism had been accentuated by *"el desastre"* of 1898 when Catalan industrialists demanded protective tariffs to offset the loss of colonial markets from the war. That the Spanish military remained incredibly bitter over the defeat to the United States was evident in the 1905 "fets de *Cu-Cut!*," a defining moment in the history of the Catalanist movement. In November of that year a group of 300 soldiers attacked the offices of *La Veu de Catalunya* and *Cu-Cut!*, papers affiliated with *Lliga Regionalista*, the first Catalanist party, in response to the attempted publication of an anti-military cartoon on the part of the latter satirical periodical. Though *Cu-Cut!* had been publishing anti-military content since its inception in 1902, and the military and various political factions had protested and attacked editorial offices in the past, the confluence of events that broke out in November 1905 had profound ramifications. The "fets de *Cu-Cut!*" sparked both a resurgence of the role of the military in Spanish politics, evident in the new *Ley de Jurisdicciones* which placed before military jurisdiction offenses against the military or the country, and the (tenuous) unity of the Catalanist movement in the new *Solidaritat Catalana*, formed in February 1906.[33]

Though the radical republican leader Alejandro Lerroux opposed the *Ley de Jurisdicciones*, he and his followers eagerly embraced the eruption of Spanish nationalist fervor in the wake of the "fets de *Cu-Cut!*" to continue the ongoing struggle they had been waging for predominance over the ballot boxes and streets of Barcelona. It was, in fact, a clash in which stones were thrown and bullets fired between radical republicans and jubilant supporters of the *Lliga* after a "victory banquet" held by the Catalanist party in celebration of improvement in their electoral fortunes in November 1905 that set the stage for *Cu-Cut!* to create the legendary political cartoon that would ignite so many passions. As his electoral fortunes waned, Lerroux's followers launched assaults on *Solidaritat Catalana* meetings throughout 1906 into 1907 leading to the aforementioned "pitched battle on the Gran Vía" on January 20. Notable among them were Lerroux's paramilitary youth wing, the *Juventud Escolar Republicana de Barcelona*, known as the "young barbarians." That same month, Lerrouxists attacked the editorial office of the Catalanist paper *La Tralla* to avenge its publication of a comic that depicted Castillian women as licentious. As Lerroux "lost moral stature" with these attacks, his Catalanist adversaries blamed him for the new *atentados* and sought to present themselves as representatives of "modernizing morality."[34]

Rull provided the leadership of *Solidaritat Catalana* with an opportunity to put these principles into practice a week after his bombing of the Rambla de Canaletas. On January 27, 1907 he placed two bombs in the doorway of a candy shop on the Rambla de las Flores. One exploded on the spot, slightly injuring a passerby, while the second exploded days later in police custody injuring several soldiers. The next day, *Solidaritat Catalana* convened a meeting at city hall featuring representation from 382 public entities to "end terrorism" in Barcelona. With mounted Civil Guard patrolling the streets and the Plaza de la Constitución "occupied militarily" to prevent any disturbances, the leadership of *Solidaritat Catalana* pushed the agenda beyond petitioning the central government for assistance. "Barcelona is dying," Francesc Cambó began, "we are defenseless, and the State, failing in all of its fundamental responsibilities, does not care to guarantee lives nor property, as if it took treacherous satisfaction in the downfall of Barcelona." Instead of turning to a state that allegedly seemed to delight in Catalan chaos, the meeting proposed creating a commission to "step in for the State in regard to all of the functions that it is too impotent to fulfill."[35]

Over the coming days the commission allocated 50,000 pesetas to bring foreign police methods to Barcelona. Not long after, a representative of the Lliga Regionalista traveled to London to contract the services of Charles Arrow, a 26-year veteran of Scotland Yard, to head the new *Oficina de Investigación Criminal* (OIC) starting in July of 1907.[36] Though the mystique of the English detective, popularized by the Arthur Conan Doyle's Sherlock Holmes series, may have elicited some enthusiasm for Arrow's arrival, "the progressive entities of Barcelona" wasted little time organizing against this new "bourgeois police." That summer anti-Arrow protesters marched through the streets of Barcelona shouting "Down with Arrow!" and "Death to the foreign police!"[37]

At least the Spanish government would support his efforts to end the "bomb outrages," Arrow must have imagined. After all, he had been under the reasonable impression that the Lliga representative "was acting with the authority of the Spanish Government," when he recruited Arrow. He would soon learn otherwise. Although his force was officially created by Barcelona officials in August 1907, the skeptical central government withheld recognition until about a half year later in early 1908. In the interim, his force lacked the legal authority to carry out police functions. Or it would have if there had been a force for Arrow to command. Though it was agreed that he would have thirty-six agents, as late as January 1908 he only had three municipal police officers.[38]

Though Arrow did not speak Spanish or Catalan, it did not take long for him to discern the political machinations behind his appointment that explained the hostility of the central government and the lack of local support. From its inception, early Catalanism was a politics of pressure applied on Madrid in the interest of enhanced autonomy and financial concessions. Catalanist politicians had focused on the creation of an autonomous Catalan police force as far back as the drafting of the Bases de Manresa, the founding document of political Catalanism, in 1892. Yet, the decision to put such a proposal into practice in 1907 caught the attention of Antonio Maura, the new Conservative Prime Minister, far more urgently than another series of proclamations.

This was not the first time that Catalan politicians had threatened to create their own police force in response to ongoing *atentados* nor the first time Maura had received such an ultimatum. After an explosion on calle Fernando on November 17, 1904, Catalan politicians protested Barcelona's "almost non-existent" police force, threatening to create their own if the central government did not respond. Heeding their call, Maura enhanced the ranks of local law enforcement as calls for a new independent force faded.[39] About two years after the end of his first term, Maura found himself back in office confronting a similar array of challenges. Maura had established himself as one of Spain's most ambitious reformers during his first term as Prime Minister. Calling for a "revolution from above" to restore the rule of law, reanimate the democratic participation of the "neutral mass" of the middle class, and engage the lower classes through Catholic popular politics, Maura's advocacy of reformism was the culmination of a profound shift in the nature of liberalism that was affecting Spain, Europe, and beyond moving into the twentieth century. After faith in classical liberalism peaked in Spain mid-century, the emergence of a powerful labor movement and the perceived inability of the market to solve poverty in the 1870s and 1880s led politicians of both dynastic parties to begin questioning classical liberal orthodoxy by the 1890s in line with ideas associated with "new liberalism" elsewhere in Europe. As the historian Miguel Ángel Cabrera notes, this process took hold more rapidly among Conservatives whose distrust of individualism and more corporate interpretation of society paved the way for state intervention into the economy in a way that was harder among Liberals (with the exception of José Canalejas) who had a greater investment in the classical liberal principles of the free market and unfettered individualism.[40]

During Maura's second term, this former Liberal would enact an array of interventionist legislation—the "only concrete and significant reforms of the decade"—including protectionist legislation for industry and railroad construction, measures to restrict emigration, the creation of the *Instituto Nacional de Previsión* (an antecedent of social security), and laws legalizing (and regulating) strikes, limiting labor for women and children, and restricting work on Sundays.[41] Moreover, Maura differed from Cánovas and most other dynastic leaders of both parties in his sympathy for decentralization and regionalism. As the Minister for Colonial Affairs in 1893 he had advocated decentralization as a solution to the Cuban Question.[42] Years later as Prime Minister, this native of Palma de Mallorca sought to pacify Catalanist leaders by acceding to their demands and granting them enhanced regional autonomy—thereby wooing Catalan industrialists to his party.

Over the course of the year or so after the proposed creation of Arrow's force, Maura, his Interior Minister Juan de la Cierva, and Barcelona's new civil governor Ángel Ossorio drastically enhanced police funding for Catalonia, augmented the ranks of Barcelona's various police divisions, increased police salaries and enhanced job security, ordered the Civil Guard to patrol the city center, sent police agents abroad to Paris, London, and Rome to learn foreign police methods, and implemented the Parisian method of criminal record organization.[43] Years later, Eusebi Güell informed Arrow that, in the words of Arrow,

> even before I took up my appointment, a change had come over the situation. Certain promises were made by Maura to Cambó [leader of the Lliga Regionalista] ... in fact the Police was placed on an entire new footing and really vastly improved. The condition was that I should be allowed to do nothing to demonstrate the weakness of the Government Police.[44]

Perhaps as important to the pacification of Catalanist politicians was Maura's presentation of the *Ley de Administración Local* in June 1907. Designed to uproot the longstanding control of rural caciques, the law sought to enhance local governmental control in line with Catalanist demands for greater autonomy. Though the proposed law would eventually fail, by the summer of 1907 Maura had already promised Catalanist politicians everything they wanted—before Arrow had even arrived.

Meanwhile, word of Joan Rull's prescient anticipation of recent *atentados* reached the new civil governor Ossorio, who agreed to bring the former anarchist back on to the governmental payroll. Rull's gambit had succeeded: by taking up dynamite himself, he had fabricated evidence of his own usefulness. Not only was Rull granted a salary that eventually reached 42 pesetas a week (almost twice the cost of living for a family of four), he managed to convince Ossorio that he needed a headquarters for his operation and funds to pay his own task force. The headquarters became a hangout spot for smoking and playing cards while his task force consisted of his friends and family. Despite a significant investment of funds on the part of Ossorio, Rull failed to provide any accurate information over the following weeks. Suddenly in early April, Rull informed Ossorio that he needed 500 pesetas to avoid an imminent explosion. The incredulous Ossorio declined, and so one of Rull's co-conspirators placed a bomb at the Boquería market on April 8, 1907 that exploded inflicting fatal wounds on a young girl and injuring six others. Later that evening, Rull's crew set off another bomb near the Palace of Justice that did not harm anyone. According to governor Ossorio, Rull claimed that "since he lacked the money to gather sufficient information, the bombs exploded."[45]

Miraculously, perhaps, Rull managed to convince Ossorio to continue funding his operation in the wake of the Boquería bombing. Nevertheless, Rull could not maintain his charade indefinitely. Over the summer of 1907 Tomás Herreros, the long-time revolutionary syndicalist, anarchist, and organizer of the Barcelona League of the Rights of Man, informed Ossorio that his informant was playing a double game. Around the same time, some of Rull's collaborators shared details of their machinations to the press. Rull's scheme ended on the evening of July 5, 1907 when he and sixteen of his friends and family (including his parents and three siblings) were arrested for their part in the explosions.[46]

Rull's arrest was a media bombshell that seemed to inflame the accusations and suspicions of every political faction. Alejandro Lerroux and his supporters seized upon the arrest to press their unfounded allegation that the Catalanists were responsible for the bombs and that Rull was actually an agent of *Solidartitat Catalana*. In part the Lerrouxistas fixated on the Rull Affair to deflect from their attempted assassination of the *Lliga Regionalista* leader Francesc Cambó in April of that year to avenge the death of a radical republican worker whose death they blamed on the *solidaris*. Vindicated after years of denying responsibility for the Barcelona bombs, the anarchists emphasized Rull's alleged links to influential figures like Eusebi Güell, with whom "there existed more than friendship." Such suspicions were echoed by the notorious Barcelona Inspector Tressols who claimed that "behind Rull there are other more important people; I don't know who they are." Governor Ossorio interpreted Tressols's comments as pointing the finger at the Catalan "separatist campaign." Rull threatened to implicate important people if he were convicted, but failed to do so when he and his accomplices were found guilty. No concrete evidence exists of any high-level intrigue. On August 8, 1908 Joan Rull became the first person executed in Barcelona's new Model Prison.[47]

As the months passed, Rull's arrest seemed to presage an end of explosions in Barcelona. Although a bomb went off at a Barcelona chalet that seemed to be a case of "personal vengeance" in September of 1907 and two Orsini bombs were discovered in a canal in November, about eight months without an explosive *atentado* passed after Rull's bombings on April 8, 1907. The silence was shattered, and the ability to blame everything on Rull and his accomplices was dashed, when dynamite returned to the city in December. On December 23, 1907, a bomb exploded injuring a soldier and a rosary vendor on calle del Hospital and a second bomb that was discovered on calle de la Boquería exploded in police custody injuring two officers. Eight days later, on December 31, a bomb killed two and injured several more on calle de San Pablo.[48] Ten bombs exploded in Barcelona in 1907 while another seven bombs were discovered without detonating. Popular panic spread farther, however, given the frequency of false alarms, rumors, "joke[s] in bad taste," braggadocios threats from teenagers, and threatening graffiti such as a warning scrawled on a wall about an imminent explosion allegedly written by "a woman dressed in black."[49]

On January 1, 1908, constitutional guarantees were suspended in the provinces of Barcelona and Gerona for five months. Years earlier, Maura had lambasted the decision of a Liberal government to suspend guarantees following the 1905 military attack on Catalanist editorial offices arguing that it was "a regression in the political progress of our country, and moreover, far from curing social ills it aggravates them." An ardent defender of the rule of law, Maura had written on the importance of not "turning the actions of the authorities to extirpate [terrorism] into a battle against political liberties and the rights of the human personality." In 1907, Barcelona Civil Governor Ángel Ossorio had agreed with Maura that suspending constitutional guarantees would have been "very dangerous," but the persistence of explosions convinced both Conservative leaders of the necessity of the measure despite a strong public backlash. Ossorio had also been pushing Maura to discard his reservations about "another law for the repression of anarchism" despite his own belief that such a measure "would be a dangerous complication." For although Ossorio found it difficult to determine who the bombers were, he "saw clearly that these mercenaries or delusional people are inspired by a group of very well-known opportunists of anarchism." Therefore by "reviving the Law of '96 (although without military jurisdiction) and closing a few circles and a dozen schools; shutting down three or four periodicals" the government could conceivably break the influence of "the aristocrats of anarchy and the impassioned Lerrouxistas."[50] Moving into 1908, Maura came around to Ossorio's position.

On January 24, 1908 Maura's Minister of Justice proposed adding a new article to the 1894 anti-explosives law that had been passed by a Liberal government in the wake of the *atentados* of Paulino Pallás and Santiago Salvador. The 1894 law served as a foundation for the more repressive anti-anarchist legislation of 1896, whose three-year term was not renewed owing in large part to the pressure applied by the Montjuich campaign. Like the law of 1896, Interior Minister La Cierva's proposal, popularly as the "Terrorism Law," allowed for the closure of "anarchist periodicals and centers" and the deportation of "people who by word, writing, printing, or engraving... propagate anarchist ideas," but unlike the 1896 law this measure would not require renewal. A similar proposal from the future Prime Minister Joaquín Sánchez de Toca to the Senate in 1905 had failed, but the bombs had continued unabated in the interim.[51] After a quiet January, where only two bombs were discovered without exploding, one bomb exploded on February 15 and two more detonated, killing one woman and injuring another five, two days later. A total of seven bombs exploded in public in February and March of 1908, including another at the Boquería market that injured seven.[52]

Barcelona anarchists continued to deny authorship of "crimes that only favor reaction," as the "4 de Mayo" group behind the newspaper *Tierra y Libertad* phrased it, as they waged a campaign against the suspension of guarantees, the arrests of comrades, and subsequently the proposed "Terrorism Law." A day after the law was proposed, one thousand people, including "many women," filled a Barcelona hall to listen to Teresa Claramunt and other anarchist speakers proclaim that "the more repressive laws that are introduced, the more anarchists there will be."[53] The campaign against Maura's law and other repressive measures was also supported by Solidaridad Obrera, Barcelona's new anti-authoritarian labor federation whose name was a jab at Solidaritat Catalana.

After the failure of the 1902 Barcelona general strike, the anti-authoritarian labor federation FSORE dissolved and Barcelona trade societies who were hostile to the socialist UGT formed their own municipal federation in 1904 called *Unión Local* or *Federación Local de Sociedades Obreras*. Nevertheless, the downward trend in the power of the labor movement continued over the following years until the Catalan economy began to rebound in 1907 in part thanks to Maura's protectionist policies. Increasingly influenced by the development of French revolutionary syndicalism in the form of the neighboring CGT, anarchist and syndicalist unionists gained the support of fifty-seven of the city's seventy workers' societies for the new Solidaridad Obrera by the end of its first month of existence in August 1907. By September of 1908, Solidaridad Obrera would become a regional federation throughout Catalonia before expanding nationally in 1910 to become the *Confederación Nacional del Trabajo* (CNT), the most significant anarcho-syndicalist union in history and a major player in the Spanish Civil War decades later.[54]

In early 1908, however, Solidaridad Obrera joined the Barcelona anarchist movement in its "campaign against the two terrorisms: that of the iron bombs that dynamiters explode in the streets and that of the legal bombs that the government throws to kill" the lower classes. The anarchist campaign consisted of meetings around the country and theatrical fundraisers including performances of Ibsen's "An Enemy of the People" and Mirbeau's "The Bad Shepherds." It was not until early May, however, that opposition to Maura's law expanded beyond the anti-authoritarian movement. One of the main figures behind this shift was Miguel Moya, the president of the Press Association and the creator in 1906 of the Editorial Society of Spain, the first Spanish media conglomerate, better known as "el Trust," which grouped *El Liberal*, *El Heraldo de Madrid*, and *El Imparcial* with four provincial papers. On May 4, 1908, Moya convened a meeting with representatives of seven of Madrid's major newspapers including some of the Trust's main competitors to form a press defense committee to fight back against this "true attack on the Press and individual liberty" that "evokes the sinister shadow of Montjuich and presents us [to the world] as a people who have fallen into the most extreme cruelties of power."[55]

"Although a little late," the editors of the anarchist *Tierra y Libertad* explained, it was "beautiful to see the liberal press wake up" to the dangers of the terrorism law. Yet, the rhetoric deployed by the anarchist and liberal wings of the campaign evidenced their deep ideological differences despite facing off against a shared opponent. While liberal papers like *El Heraldo de Madrid* stood up for the "fundamental rights of citizenship" guaranteed by the Constitution, the anarchist campaign claimed to defend "the rights and liberty of all" without turning to the state for protection. In fact, *Tierra y Libertad* clarified that in the campaign "the anarchists have not protested against this law exclusively, but against all laws because all are tyrannical and inquisitorial."[56] After the Senate approved the law in early May, mass meetings featuring speakers from across the left political spectrum, from anarchists to republicans to Liberal politicians, were held around the country in late May 1908. The campaign's backbone was the labor movement, however, and calls for a general strike if the law were passed were likely given increased credence given labor's recent resurgence. Nevertheless, Solidaridad Obrera (or at least the anarchist editors of the labor federation's newspaper of the same name) were very uneasy cooperating with the Liberal campaign against the law. They rejected the Liberal focus on the proposed law's legality because union tactics "will always seem illegal" to Liberal politicians. Instead, *Solidaridad Obrera* argued for defending "our dignity as free men...without accepting or asking for pernicious relations with carpetbaggers and lawyers."[57]

The socialists of the PSOE were no more enthusiastic about uniting with capitalist politicians. As Liberal and republican forces united against Maura in what some were starting to think of as a "left bloc," *El Socialista* dismissed such an idea as a "bloc of bourgeois politics." Although the socialists remained disdainful of the capitalist parties and considered the anarchists to be "our enemies," they vowed to fight the terror law. In late May 1908 PSOE and UGT founder Pablo Iglesias took the floor of the Congress to explain that "We, socialists, aspire to transform property, to conquer political power, and we understand that this conquest and this transformation will not be done through evolution but rather revolution...which is to say with violence." Therefore, Iglesias argued, socialists who had thus far limited their struggle to the bounds of legality would be targeted by the proposed law and therefore, given no other choice, "we will be terrorists."[58]

Pressure to abandon the Terrorism Law cascaded down on Antonio Maura from nearly every direction. Allegedly, the uproar generated by the campaign had started to outweigh the potential benefits of the law to such a degree that Alfonso XIII planned to veto. Governor Ossorio, who had pushed Maura on the law in the first place, also started to get cold feet in the face of the backlash against his reputation. Of course, the looming potential of a retaliatory *atentado* must have informed the reluctance of Alfonso and Ossorio months after the Portuguese king was assassinated. Ultimately, Maura was willing to negotiate. Miguel Moya, head of *"el Trust,"* offered to allow the passage of the municipal section of Maura's prized *Ley de Administración Local* in exchange for the withdrawal of the Terrorism Law. Similarly, republican leaders were said to have offered to support Maura's Naval Law in exchange for an end to the Terrorism Law. On June 1, 1908 Maura reinstated constitutional guarantees for Barcelona and Gerona and on June 5 he withdrew the controversial Terrorism Law.[59] Yet, this compromise did not end popular outrage at Maura's repressive measures. The next year a far more dramatic eruption of violence in the Catalan capital would leave more than a hundred dead, thousands arrested and exiled, and Antonio Maura without a job.

CHAPTER 16

Francisco Ferrer and the Tragic Week

Tucked into the French Pyrenees on a mountain neighboring the seventeenth-century Fort-les-Bains stood the luxurious Hotel Pujade. There, Francisco Ferrer partook in hot mineral baths and strolled through "groves of fig, cherry, cork, and chestnut trees" with his ailing *compañera*, Soledad Villafranca, during the summer of 1908. After a Western European victory tour to celebrate his 1907 acquittal, the fifty-year-old Ferrer could have paused his political activities to simply enjoy winding paths of "ferns, brambles, [and] honeysuckle."[1] But anyone familiar with the former director of the Modern School knew that this restless revolutionary could not "conceive life without propaganda."[2]

And so, over the summer of 1908, Ferrer got to work promoting the three main avenues of social transformation that animated his radical spirit: education, the general strike, and insurrection. Since the Spanish government prohibited the reopening of his cherished school, he explicated his "rationalist" pedagogical vision in *The Modern School*. Although the book would not see publication during the brief remainder of his life, his passionate appeals for the elimination of rewards and punishments and the coeducation of the sexes inspired translations into dozens of languages and fueled the eruption of a global educational movement after his death. In addition to writing the book, Ferrer journeyed around Western Europe after his exoneration promoting the creation of his new International League for the Rational Education of

Children. Yet Ferrer was not content to await the distant fruit of his painstaking educational initiatives. Privately, he continued to dedicate a significant portion of the fortune he inherited from his former pupil to funding the growing revolutionary syndicalist movement. Just as he had founded and funded *La Huelga General* earlier in the decade, Ferrer financed *Solidaridad Obrera*, the newspaper of the new labor federation of the same name and lent the union money for a headquarters. Ferrer's objective was not simply to bankroll a gradualist union movement but to spark a revolutionary general strike that would topple the monarchy. To dethrone the Bourbons, which was all-important in his eyes, Ferrer continued to count on the revolutionary potential of the followers of Alejandro Lerroux, recently grouped into his new Radical Republican Party. All that was needed (from Ferrer's perspective) to trigger a conjuncture of radical republicans, anarchists, and revolutionary syndicalists in an insurrectionary general strike against the Crown was a spark. On the heels of the successful campaign against Prime Minister Maura's proposed terrorism law, Ferrer and his allies believed that resurrecting the campaign to liberate the six remaining workers in prison for their role in the Alcalá del Valle insurrectionary general strike of 1904 could capitalize on recent momentum to provide such a revolutionary spark. As it turned out, he was wrong. The kind of spark that Ferrer envisioned would, in fact, ignite the kindling of popular discontent, but not for another a year—with "tragic" consequences for this indefatigable revolutionist. But such turns of events remained in the future for Ferrer and his allies when the Alcalá del Valle campaign resumed over the summer of 1908.

Less than two months after the victory of the campaign against the proposed terrorism law, the Barcelona anarchist newspapers *Tierra y Libertad* and *Solidaridad Obrera* reignited the "humanitarian campaign" for the six remaining Alcalá del Valle prisoners in July 1908.[3] Both papers were funded by Francisco Ferrer, who seems to have been the campaign's primary facilitator. Much of the information we have about Ferrer's machinations during this period comes from José Sánchez González, better known as Miguel Villalobos Moreno (aka Constant Leroy), a former rationalist teacher who had belonged to Ferrer's inner circle before turning against him by publishing a tell-all account of Ferrer's alleged scheming in 1913 titled *Los secretos del anarquismo*. Although Moreno sought to portray Ferrer as having been the ultimate mastermind of all things revolutionary in the wake of the Tragic Week of 1909, his account of Ferrer's work on the Alcalá del Valle campaign is largely plausible since Moreno was part of the campaign's central committee and the editorial group behind *Solidaridad Obrera*.[4] According to Moreno, Ferrer had been preparing the ground for Franco-Spanish revolutionary cooperation in Paris over the spring of 1908 before a key meeting of Solidaridad Obrera organizers and Barcelona anarchists in June to launch the campaign. Against a proposal to expand the proposed campaign to demand the liberation of "all political prisoners," Ferrer argued that such a call would fail to win the support of "foreign agitators . . . because there are political prisoners in all countries." Instead, by reinvigorating recent memories of the "inquisitorial torments of black Spain," Ferrer allegedly explained, "then we can take advantage of this intense agitation to attempt a revolutionary general strike to abolish the regime."[5]

In the fall of 1908, Ferrer financed the voyage of one of his collaborators, José Miquel Claspés, to Marseille to secure the support of the French CGT for the Alcalá del Valle campaign on behalf of Solidaridad Obrera. Miquel's statement, which was drafted by Ferrer and Anselmo Lorenzo, emphasized the expected role of Lerrouxistas in a potential general strike.[6] After the tenuous unity between Alejandro Lerroux and his anarchist collaborators in the Montjuich campaign was fractured by Lerroux's entrance into electoral politics, the prospect of radical republican-anarchist collaboration on defense campaigns was heavily fraught. In *Tierra y Libertad*'s very first issue promoting the new campaign, it published a manifesto warning workers about "the clear opportunism of the false radicals," clearly referring to Lerrouxistas, "who put the possibility of the exercising of human rights beneath the interest of so-called acquired rights."[7] Similarly, by the fall *Solidaridad Obrera* was calling out "the bourgeois press, as radical as it may be," even though in its pursuit of the Alcalá del Valle campaign it called on the support of "all men in whose hearts dwell sentiments of equity and humanitarianism."[8] Tensions between Lerroux's radicals and the syndicalists of Solidaridad Obrera were only aggravated when, after an initial agreement of terms, Lerroux's *El Progreso* ultimately refused to part ways with two of its typographers who had established a rival typographers' union to avoid the critiques of the official Solidaridad Obrera union for having converted their anarchist cooperative typographers' business into a top-down, "bourgeois enterprise." The Lerrouxistas and syndicalists tore each other apart in the press in the midst of what Francisco Ferrer hoped would be a joint campaign of solidarity with the remaining Alcalá del Valle prisoners. Or at least the leadership of both sides ripped into each other. Beneath the polemics there were a significant number of Solidaridad Obrera members who voted Radical.[9] Ferrer was well aware of this dynamic. That is why the statement he helped draft to present to the French CGT in Marseille emphasized the revolutionary potential of the Radical Party rank and file "even if the leadership of the party may refuse to support an anarchist movement."[10] In late 1908 Lerroux's *El*

Progreso published an article from Ferrer explaining his vision of revolutionary hybridity: "We are organizing as far as it is possible to do so, forming syndicates and federations in order to achieve the establishment of the General Confederation of Spanish Labor, so that when the republican party decides [to act], we may take part in the struggle and exert the weight of our force, so that the Spanish republic will be, as far as possible, a social, communist, and libertarian republic."[11]

Ferrer's anarchist comrades bristled at any mention of a "republic." They dedicated a significant amount of their propaganda to publicizing the alleged atrocities of exemplary republics such as France and the United States to emphasize that substituting a republic for a monarchy would not truly liberate workers. Yet Ferrer, whose early political training occurred in Manuel Ruiz Zorrilla's insurrectionary republican movement in exile, continued to hold out hope for the ability of Lerroux's Radicals to open a breach in Spain's political stalemate that anarchists and syndicalists could push in a more libertarian direction. Ferrer seemed to have appeased (some of) his anarchist comrades by focusing on the rank and file of the Radical Party while also maintaining contact with the party's leadership.

Despite ongoing sectarian conflict, the campaign to liberate the six workers languishing in prison in Valencia for their role in the 1903 insurrectionary general strike in Alcalá del Valle gained some momentum moving into 1909. Within Spain, campaign solidarity committees formed in Barcelona, Zaragoza, Bilbao, and Valencia. Abroad, they formed in London, Lisbon, Paris, Brussels, Tangier, Dowlais (Wales), and unspecified locations in Italy and Argentina.[12] Yet the series of "sociological-literary-musical soiree" fundraisers and generic protest meetings of the standard coalitions of rationalist educators, Freemasons, republicans, unionists, and anarchists did not manage push this "humanitarian campaign" out of its usual circles.[13] For anarchist campaigners this dynamic was nothing new. *Tierra y Libertad* reminded readers that "the bourgeois press, as radical as it claims to be, does not make the effort to do anything in favor of these campaigns until they are common knowledge."[14]

The profile of the Alcalá del Valle campaign did not reach popular proportions until the spring of 1909 in response to the government's proposed amnesty law for those convicted of political print or speech crimes. Building on the momentum of the *bloque de izquierdas*, a coalition of left Liberals and republicans united against Maura that was formed in November 1908 out of the momentum of the anti–terror law campaign, republican deputies Juan Sol y Ortega and Félix Azzati called for the Alcalá del Valle prisoners to be included in the proposed amnesty. Sol y Ortega demanded that all workers convicted for striking be amnestied, with the "exception of those [crimes] involving explosives," and that "all those charged with crimes of a social character, such as the Alcalá del Valle prisoners," be released. Antonio Maura rejected this request because the Alcalá del Valle prisoners had, in his mind, committed "common crimes," not political crimes. Maura blamed the commotion on foreign agitators, claiming that "the legend of Spanish terror that circulates abroad" in favor of the Alcalá del Valle prisoners "did not originate in Spain."[15] The anarchist campaigners "were always sickened by every pardon . . . because the pardon supposes clemency, forgiveness, that rejects our dignity, even more when a crime has not been committed." Nevertheless, "in this special case . . . understanding that a review of the case and a just sentence would be impossible," amnesty was considered satisfactory.[16]

Anarchist acceptance of a potential pardon may have been facilitated by the death of the anarchist Salvador Mulero, one of the six remaining Alcalá del Valle prisoners, in May 1909. His funeral became a mass protest as workers walked off the job to attend and wagons, carriages, and trams that continued to operate were assaulted. In the wake of Mulero's death, *Tierra y Libertad* clarified, however, that "we accept liberty, but we never ask for it: a pardon is imposed, not requested." Indeed, unionists across Europe and the Americas attempted to impose a pardon with threats of general strikes and promises to boycott Spanish goods at foreign ports. The editors of *Tierra y Libertad* took matters a step further. "Let the government interpret our words however it chooses," the anarchist paper warned. "If the prisoners of Alcalá del Valle are not liberated, they will be avenged." The paper argued that it was legitimate for comrades to skip Alcalá del Valle meetings "in order to carry out a more practical action with undoubtedly better results," a veiled allusion to propaganda by the deed.[17]

Ultimately unions did not have to lead their members off of the shop floor, would-be assassins did not have to fabricate any bombs, and dockworkers did not have to turn away any Spanish ships, for on June 22, 1909, Queen Victoria Eugenia gave birth to the Infanta Beatriz. To mark the occasion, pardons were issued for three of the five remaining Alcalá del Valle prisoners while the other two had their life sentences reduced to nine years (with about three left to serve).[18] The combination of media pressure, political pressure, and threats of boycotts, strikes, and assassinations largely succeeded. It is unclear exactly which factors were decisive in obtaining the pardon, but certainly the campaign managed to elevate the political cost of keeping five Andalusian workers behind bars to such a point that by the spring of 1909 acquiescence prevailed over intransigence on the part of the Spanish government. In mid-July Francisco Ferrer accompanied the three recently liberated

Alcalá del Valle prisoners on a small, poorly attended victory tour of Catalonia hosted by Solidaridad Obrera. Although the revolutionary general strike that Ferrer had desired failed to materialize, a completely unexpected series of events originating across the sea was about to make the specter of an insurrectionary rupture a reality.

Among the many proposals put forward for the national regeneration of Spain after *El Desastre* of 1898, one of the most influential had been an expanded Spanish imperial presence in Morocco. By the first few years of the twentieth century, European powers had carved up most of the African continent, but Spain only controlled several tiny enclaves in Morocco, such as Ceuta and Melilla, left over from the legacy of the Reconquest of the fifteenth century. In 1859 and again in 1893, the Spanish military ventured out to put down Rif attacks on Spanish positions, but Spain had no more territory to show for it. In 1904 the Spanish sphere of influence in Morocco finally expanded as a result of Spain's weakness rather than military prowess. In the course of negotiations between Britain and France to maintain their imperial equilibrium, it was agreed to allocate approximately one-fifth of Morocco (22,000 km²) to Spain as a way to keep this territory out of the hands of one of the major powers.[19]

Despite the Spanish presence, all of Morocco was still under the official control of the sultan. Yet the sultan had only minimal control over the Berber tribes in the Spanish sphere. Spanish authorities managed to maintain stability in their region for a while by working with the local chieftain, El Rogui, who arranged meetings with mining and railroad companies. Yet the influx of the arms trade and mining companies disrupted regional stability, eventually putting El Rogui at odds with the sultan. With El Rogui out, the chieftain who filled the power vacuum was El Sharif Mohammed Amzian, who gathered five thousand soldiers to wage jihad against Spain. On July 9, 1909, the guerrillas of El Sharif Mohammed Amzian attacked the railroad that connected Spanish mines to the port near Melilla.[20] The Spanish government mobilized an inexperienced and woefully underresourced conscript army for a campaign of counterinsurgent warfare for which it was completely unprepared.

Fed by memories of the futility and bloodshed of the colonial wars of a decade earlier and years of antimilitarist propaganda, support among the popular classes for the latest military adventure was low. Anti-war sentiment found its villain in the form of Claudio López Bru, the second Marquis of Comillas, who was identified with the conflict because of his family's significant investments in Moroccan ports, industry, and mining, but even more symbolically by the role his ships played in the transport of conscripts across the sea starting two days after the attack. Since Comillas wielded his family's fortune—made in large part through the illicit trafficking of slaves in Cuba—to spearhead a new era of militant Catholic activism, and he oversaw the finances of the Jesuits in Spain, anti-war and anti-clerical sentiment fused against what was coming to be known as the Bankers' War.[21]

Within weeks, 24,000 working-class and peasant conscripts were shipped across the sea to defend Spanish colonial interests while the rich could pay their way out of military service. The situation came to a head back home at an embarkation of conscripts in Barcelona on July 18, 1909. As a group of upper-class women started to distribute medals and cigarettes to the reluctant soldiers, some of them threw the gifts into the water, inciting the crowd to shout, "Throw down your weapons" and "Let the rich go; all or none!" The police fired into the air and pulled back the gangway to the ship before matters could escalate further. That night, Amzian's forces attacked again, dealing Spanish imperial forces three hundred casualties.[22] A similar incident occurred in Madrid where the civil guard unleashed their sabers on protesters blocking the railroad tracks, leaving Atocha to prevent the deployment of soldiers.[23]

The week of July 19, 1909, began with popular outrage spilling out into the streets of Barcelona. Despite the government's announcement that no further departures would occur from Barcelona, over the next several evenings groups of angry young workers marched through the city shouting, "Down with the war!" Under the direction of Governor Ossorio, the police made many arrests and even fired their guns into the air to disperse spontaneous anti-war protests, which, along with formal meetings and printed protests, were declared officially illegal by the end of the week. On Wednesday night some anti-war protesters responded to police repression by returning fire, injuring one officer.[24]

With tensions mounting and the Spanish state foreclosing outlets for the expression of anti-war sentiment, a group of revolutionaries and labor leaders at the nexus of anarchist-syndicalist relations met to create a strike committee to organize a general strike on Monday, July 26. Though preparations for the proposed strike were spearheaded by the leadership of Solidaridad Obrera with the tacit support of the Radicals, Catalan socialists, and leftist Catalanists, no party or union would put their name on an illegal mass strike. As word of the imminent strike spread, city officials had sand scattered across major avenues on Sunday to prevent horses from slipping in any potential cavalry charges. Though Governor Ossorio had suspended an attempted strike planning meeting on Friday, he refused to authorize mass preventative arrests or shut down union offices in order to avoid blame for "having provoked the strike" or discarding "the rights of citizens." Against Ossorio's somewhat measured response—no doubt influenced by popular protests against the abuse of state power over the previous decade—stood Interior Minister Juan de la Cierva, who was running the national government with Prime Minister Maura out of town. La Cierva urged Ossorio to take any measures necessary to squelch what he was convinced would be a revolutionary strike. Ossorio maintained confidence in his moderate preparations.[25]

Looking back a year later, Ossorio wrote that "the revolution . . . did not explode like a bomb; it crackled like fireworks."[26] In the hot early morning hours of Monday, July 26, 1909, strike leaders filed out to industries across the province to spread word of the strike. "Like a train of powder the news spread from one factory to another," Anselmo Lorenzo recalled. Women wearing white ribbons symbolizing the work stoppage often led the way in pressuring, shaming, and threatening workers and bosses into halting production. María Llopis Berges, a notorious sex worker nicknamed "Forty Cents," marched at the head of a rowdy group of strikers in the working-class Paralelo district that smashed up windows and destroyed the furniture of businesses that refused to close before attacking a civil guard patrol. Most employers quickly caved in when confronted by the fury of the strikers. In Mataró strikers ended the workday by shutting down the power plant. Elsewhere, strikers set fire to tax booths, cut telegraph wires, and tore up railroad tracks to impede the continuation of the workday and the ability of the authorities to respond with force. By late morning, the strike had largely succeeded throughout the province of Barcelona and parts of neighboring Girona. To propel the momentum further and escalate the stakes of the conflict, anarchists organized strikers to attack police stations to liberate imprisoned comrades. Three strikers were killed and nine police officers injured that afternoon when Carmen Alauch Jérida of the Radical Party's women's organization led a group of strikers armed with revolvers and knives on an attack of a police station in the neighborhood of Clot.[27]

The final hurdle impeding a complete work stoppage was the nonparticipation of the tram workers, whose support had been considered essential to the fortunes of any general strike for years. The strike committee called in reinforcements from the industrial suburb of Pueblo Nuevo to act as "the vanguard of the attack on the trams." Led by women in white ribbons carrying banners reading "Down with the war," the workers of Pueblo Nuevo blocked the tracks with their bodies in the center of Barcelona. Sensing that he had lost the initiative, Governor Ossorio drastically escalated matters by authorizing the use of Mauser rifles for the defense of the tracks. Strikers stoned, burned, and opened fire on uncooperative trams, damaging thirty-four and destroying two more. Shortly thereafter, the tram company ceased operations.[28] Vindicated in his initial alarm, Juan de la Cierva pushed to declare a state of war in Barcelona. Despite his objections in favor of the maintenance of civil jurisdiction, Governor Ossorio was overruled during a midday meeting of authorities and promptly issued his resignation. He was replaced by General Luis de Santiago, who enacted a more defensive strategy to protect key buildings while waiting for reinforcements.[29]

But a key event that evening presaged the unprecedented destruction that would earn the last week of July 1909 the ignominious title of the Tragic Week. Just after midnight on July 27, a group of radicals and strikers set fire to the school of the Marist Brothers in the working-class, heavily Lerrouxista district of Pueblo Nuevo. The plot seems to have originated in the Lerrouxista Casa del Pueblo social center, possibly backed by affiliates of the local Ferrerian rationalist school. Ire against the Catholic school owed to the unfounded rumor that it was funded by the Marquis of Comillas, its relationship with Catholic workers' circles that served as wellsprings of scab labor during strikes, its French foreign origins, and broader anti-clerical sentiment.[30]

As opposed to premodern forms of anti-clericalism that developed from within Catholic ranks, many strains of modern anti-clericalism that emerged toward the end of the eighteenth century and flourished into the nineteenth (when the term was coined) directly targeted the institution of the church and its doctrine. In Spain, anti-clericalism animated liberal defense of the legacy of the Constitution of 1812 before taking a more radical turn by the end of the century in republican and anarchist circles. Though merely a distraction for the socialists of the PSOE, anti-clericalism provided an important bedrock to radical republicanism and anarchism in Spain. As the Liberal Party shifted farther to the left in the new century, it became increasingly anti-clerical in an effort to win working-class support away from the radical republicans. Much of the power of anti-clerical discourse, historian Enrique Sanabria explains, could be found in "its ability to transcend material issues that divided the middle and working classes."[31]

Anti-clericalism's ability to elude class struggle factored significantly in the Tragic Week. Though the attack of the Marist school seemed like an isolated incident to many, the events of the next day would show otherwise as the general strike's initial revolutionary anti-war orientation dissipated into anti-clerical insurrection. Uncertainty reigned on the morning of Tuesday, July 27, 1909. With the newsstands absent of the daily papers, telegraph wires cut, railroad tracks torn up, and only silence from the captain general and the strike committee, Barcelona workers and shopkeepers woke up to rumors about whether the strike had ended or spread like wildfire across the entire country. While many small business owners were eager to reopen, in heavily radical working-class districts like the Paralelo many were shut down by roving groups of strikers, vagrants, and sex workers who were "eager to find a spark that would allow them to unleash a rebellion."[32]

Indeed, in such Radical Party strongholds militant lower-class Radical supporters, particularly the party's militant youth organization known as the Young Barbarians, pushed the party leadership to declare the long-awaited Republic so they could take to the barricades. With Alejandro Lerroux exiled in Argentina, active leadership of the Radical Republican Party was assumed by Emiliano Iglesias, Francisco Ferrer's former lawyer. In response to pressure from below, Iglesias turned to the radical populist blueprint that Lerroux had designed over the past decade. It consisted of harnessing the raw power of aggressive street confrontation through the rhetoric of revolution in order to generate muscle around election time and win over radical workers and former anarchists. Yet the mass party that such street militancy produced would then ideally put into practice the late nineteenth-century insurrectionary republican plan of attaining power on the back of a military pronunciamiento. Lerroux may have urged the Young Barbarians to "sack the decadent and miserable civilization of this unfortunate country, destroy its temples, kill its gods . . . [and set a] purifying fire to this vile social organization," but he and Iglesias did not believe they could sack their way to a republic.[33] Decades later, Lerroux drifted to the right as he became a conservative prime minister in the Second Republic and a supporter of Franco during the Civil War. Historian Joan Connelly Ullman argued that Iglesias decided on a "compromise" with the party's militant wing. Since the uprising was confined to Barcelona and was very unlikely to expand or gain sufficient elite support, Iglesias would not declare the republic or support a revolutionary confrontation with the state or capital. But to appease pressure from below, days after his party published an editorial reminiscing about the murder of monks in 1835, Iglesias may have secretly endorsed a coordinated plan of anti-clerical arson.[34] Though other historians have attributed greater significance to a spontaneous mass anti-clericalism than orders from above, both factors may have converged in the summer of 1909.[35]

While impromptu neighborhood construction crews erected barricades by tearing up cobblestones, toppling street lamps, and hurling bed frames into the streets, and masses of strikers turned rebels assaulted police stations and fired on patrolling police in Pueblo Nuevo and Clot, and insurrectionaries in Gracia even attacked soldiers until cannons demolished their barricades later in the day, ten Radical Party youth disguised as Red Cross workers allegedly filed out into the city on bicycles with lists of churches and convents. Though orders to torch Catholic institutions may have come from above, Radical operatives knew they could tap into an ocean of local anti-clerical resentment. As an asylum run by the Sisters of Charity of Saint Vincent de Paul burned to the ground, the Sisters recognized former students and their parents among the crowd. Neighbors resented the asylum because it allegedly exploited the cheap needlework of its students and "wayward" women to undercut local merchants—an allegation of unfair competition leveled against many church institutions. Other attacks, such as the demolition of the four-story Real Colegio de San Antón, owed in large part to the long-standing relationship between the Piarist order and Carlism. Church valuables were not usually stolen but rather heaped into massive bonfires to manifest popular disdain with ecclesiastical opulence. The clergy frequently expected their congregations to come to their defense. Far more often their neighbors were among the most eager of the arsonists. By the end of the night, twenty-three churches and convents had been set ablaze in Barcelona and another eight were targeted in the suburbs.[36]

Paradoxically, the fires actually made the military authorities *less* repressive. While General Santiago restricted his forces to guarding key locations, insurrectionary arsonists were given largely free reign. Several infuriated nuns and monks were convinced that the soldiers had been ordered "to tolerate certain things." Explicitly or implicitly, military authorities may have considered such activities to be an inevitable safety valve—one far preferable to attacks on the state or capital—while awaiting reinforcements. Military manpower was in even shorter supply than usual that day after the army suffered 1,238 casualties in the disastrous battle of Barranco del Lobo in the Moroccan mountains. While Prime Minister Maura focused on the war effort, Interior Minister La Cierva began to disparage the uprising in the press as a disgraceful act of Catalan separatism.[37]

Before reinforcements arrived on Thursday, General Santiago was so fearful of the conflicted loyalties of his troops that he outlawed exclamations of "Long live the army!" As a member of the strike committee wrote weeks later, soldiers passed "their officers without saluting" while "many local women gave food and drink to the soldiers and the men invited them to have coffee or a smoke."[38] Indeed, women played a powerful role as "the very conscience of the community" in early twentieth-century Barcelona, as Temma Kaplan argued through her concept of "female consciousness." As the standard-bearers for family, community, and humanity, working-class women wielded the gendered power to catalyze resistance and destruction by prodding the masculinity of the men in the community. The sex worker Concha Ortiz (aka La Chelito) allegedly accused men who did not take to the barricades of being "bloodless."[39] In the absence of formal leadership, especially as Radical Party partisans began to feel "abandoned by their leaders," the charisma and local social capital of many women rebels placed them in de facto positions of power.[40] That was certainly the case for the leader of the barricade on calle del Conde del Asalto, Josefa Prieto, who was the owner of one of the largest brothels in the red light district with a rap sheet extending miles for repeatedly stabbing police.[41] In part, sex workers revolted against governmental efforts to clamp down on their industry as part of a broader initiative to "sanitize" the Old City as Barcelona's infrastructure failed to keep pace with its growing population.[42] As historian Chris Ealham argues, the Tragic Week was fundamentally a struggle "between rival forms of urbanism" put forth by bourgeois and (lumpen)proletarian strata of Barcelona.[43]

A large group of women took matters a step further by breaking into convents to open the tombs of fifteen interred nuns. Fueled by long-standing urban legends of torture inflicted on hapless young women lured into the clergy, curious insurgent women eagerly seized on one woman's claim that her sister "had been martyred" in a nearby convent to find decisive evidence of church malfeasance. When they found the feet and hands of the cadavers bound, the women believed they had finally discovered the truth, so they hauled the bodies to the town hall for the mayor to see. Other bodies were dragged to the barricades or dropped off in front of the houses of the Marquis of Comillas (who was blamed for the war) and his brother-in-law, Eusebi Güell. A coal miner named Ramón Clemente García engaged in an obscene dance with one of the corpses on its way to Comillas's house—an act for which he was later executed. More church property was torched on Wednesday, though militants were starting to run out of buildings to set alight. Overall, however, news of the isolation of the uprising sapped the spirits of the rebels as Iglesias and the Radicals refused to take ownership for what had transpired and the Strike Committee "disappeared into thin air."[44]

By Thursday, July 29, 1909, General Santiago finally went on the offensive when his outside reinforcements arrived. Believing they were putting down a Catalan separatist revolt, Santiago's soldiers eventually demolished the barricades of Pueblo Nuevo before working their way through the narrow alleys of the rebel strongholds of Atarazanas and Paralelo. Though mass resistance failed to materialize, lone snipers took shots at the soldiers and angry residents threw rocks, flowerpots, and other projectiles at the occupying force. The army had to wheel in artillery to destroy barricades and subdue the resolute revolutionaries of the working-class district of Clot later that afternoon. One sergeant died and six soldiers were wounded in the clash. Though sporadic sniper fire continued through Saturday, businesses began to reopen and workers started to head back to work by the end of the week as bosses offered to pay back wages for days lost to the strike. Occasional arsons were committed on Friday and Saturday, but the revolutionary threat had been suffocated.[45]

Authorities hurriedly ordered a mass cleanup of the city before the scheduled arrival of 170 German tourists.[46] Despite their best efforts, the tourists took photographs of some of the approximately fifty to ninety religious buildings that were set alight in Barcelona (more were attacked in neighboring towns) during the Tragic Week. Despite the mass arson, only three clergy were killed, as were between four and eight police, four Red Cross workers, and about 104 civilians. Though about two thousand people fled to France to avoid conscription and prosecution, hundreds more were exiled, and 1,725 were charged for their participation in the uprising. That is undoubtedly a substantial number. When taken in tandem with the closure of many workers' centers, lay schools, and radical newspapers, it is understandable that *Lliga Regionalista* leader Francesc Cambó would claim that the government "sought to treat the defeated revolution with the spirit and firmness that it lacked in combatting it as it unfolded." Yet given the gravity of the rebellion and its shocking assault on the church, it is noteworthy that about two-thirds of the charges were quickly dropped. Days after the rebellion, the minister of war instructed the captain general of Barcelona to "immediately release prisoners whose seditious complicity cannot be proven and as quickly as possible transfer prisoners out of the military prisons of Atarazanas and Montjuich so as not to give rise to earlier legends." Though severe, the state's repressive appetite seems to have been mitigated by the recent history of resistance to repression and spiraling cycles of reprisals. Moreover, the initial total of seventeen death sentences was dropped to five, including the most notorious of the five, Francisco Ferrer, accused of being the "author and leader of the rebellion."[47]

Though Ferrer very much seemed to have wanted to help direct the course of the rebellion, tragically, he was wrongfully accused of achieving a level of influence that he had failed to acquire. On the morning of Monday, July 26, 1909, Ferrer met with Moreno of the strike committee to share his concerns about the revolutionary commitment of Emiliano Iglesias and the Radical leadership. That afternoon, Iglesias failed to attend an afternoon meeting with his former client, Ferrer. Exasperated about wasting his time waiting,

Ferrer searched for Iglesias at the Radical Party Casa del Pueblo. There, he was told to leave for expressing doubt as to the ability of the strike to stop the war and likely for his past support of Solidaridad Obrera in its conflict with the party. That night at the editorial office of the Radical *El Progreso*, the socialist Fabra Ribas threatened to kick out Ferrer if he attempted to meddle in the Strike Committee. Since Ferrer failed to influence the course of events among the Barcelona leadership, on Wednesday he tried to push the revolution forward in the Barcelona suburbs of Masnou and Premià del Mar. The Radical mayor of the latter town allegedly rebuffed Ferrer's pleas to start burning convents and proclaim the republic, though local revolutionaries did just that.[48]

Ferrer's known public activities during the Tragic Week end there. Far from uniting the various factions of the rebellion, Ferrer consistently foundered on his liminal status in the revolutionary milieu. "To republican politicians, Ferrer was a bothersome anarchist," Charles Malato explained, while "for the working masses, alas, despite his relations with militants of the revolutionary proletariat, he seemed to be a bourgeois!"[49] Though over the years Ferrer had managed to inhabit a unique position at the crossroads of several radical worlds, his notorious reputation and outsider status made it a liability to publicly associate with him.

Though initial press coverage of the rebellion had not mentioned Ferrer, the conservative *La Época* began to pave the way for his prosecution with erroneous accusations in early August. About a week later, Ferrer's home was searched. His partner Soledad Villafranca claimed that Ferrer was abroad in Paris, but in fact Ferrer was hiding out nearby. He laid low for thirty-four days as the press constructed a public case against the "sinister criminal" behind the rebellion. On August 31, 1909, Ferrer attempted to cross the border to Perpignan by hiding under a pile of sacks in the cart of a friendly book vendor. The fact that they traveled late at night raised the suspicion of local law enforcement near Ferrer's hometown of Alella who recognized Ferrer beneath the sacks despite Ferrer having shaved to change his appearance.[50]

After a five-hour military show trial where Ferrer was not allowed to call any witnesses or select his own lawyer, the founder of the Modern School was sentenced to death. Over the coming days, Ferrer longed for word of a pardon from Prime Minister Antonio Maura, who had issued 119 pardons over the previous two years (fifty-four of them for murder), but he would not be so fortunate. Instead, he spent his final day in the prison chapel where he rejected religious council. When asked if he believed in an afterlife, Ferrer replied, "No, señor. I believe that everything ends here; that everything terminates with the life of a man. Since I acquired this conviction many years ago I have adapted all of my actions to it." And so, having spent his life adapting his revolutionary actions to the belief that nothing mattered beyond life on earth, he stared down the barrels of the rifles pointed in his direction in the moat of Montjuich Castle on the morning of October 13, 1909. "Muchachos," Ferrer cried out, "aim well and fire without fear! I am innocent! *Viva la Escuela Moderna!*" Amid his final words, the firing squad pulled their triggers.[51]

The campaign for the liberation of Ferrer had begun with his arrest and had built momentum moving into the fall of 1909. Support for the imprisoned pedagogue developed among anti-clerical militants in historically Catholic countries, including France, Belgium, and Italy, and in historically Protestant countries, among them England and the United States, by tapping into long-standing anti-Catholic sentiments. As in 1906, the campaign was strongest in France where Ferrer had lived for fifteen years. Not long after his arrest, Ferrer's Parisian comrades formed the Comité de défense des victimes de la répression espagnole to coordinate pro-Ferrer activities. The *comité* united the same constellation of political forces as the solidarity campaigns of the past decade. The Ligue des droits de l'homme and the CGT labor federation endorsed the campaign, and pro-Ferrer intellectuals organized a petition of university professors that obtained 152 signatures, including that of Émile Durkheim. Captain Alfred Dreyfus of the Dreyfus affair supported Ferrer as well. Labor demonstrations and innovative motorcade protests were organized across France over the following weeks, in addition to sporadic attempts at coordinating a boycott of Spanish goods.[52] The political breadth of pro-Ferrer organizers in France was equivalent in other national movements, yet many moderate and liberal elements only supported Ferrer after his death.[53] The night of the execution, a riot broke out at the Spanish embassy in Paris, where protesters tore up benches and trees, extinguished streetlamps, smashed bank windows, and mounted barricades, and one protester fatally shot a police officer.[54] Days later, the largest pro-Ferrer event of the campaign occurred when Parisian socialists organized a peaceful procession of fifty to sixty thousand, which drew the ire of some anarchists for its disavowal of conflict.[55] After France, the most dynamic protests occurred in Italy where general strikes, demonstrations, protest resolutions, boycotts, and sporadic anti-clerical violence gripped seemingly every city in the country for a week. Similarly raucous protests were organized across Belgium, the Netherlands, and Portugal.[56]

Demonstrations were also organized in London and across England, such as a protest of ten thousand people in Trafalgar Square. Eleven thousand people marched through the streets of Berlin, and thousands more organized demonstrations and protest meetings in cities across Germany and in Copenhagen and Bucharest. In Russia, the Socialist Revolutionary Party called for a one-day general strike and students protested in Saint Petersburg. Protests also occurred in Sofia, Athens, and Thessaloniki. Attempts by the Young Turks to organize a protest in Istanbul were thwarted by authorities. Demonstrations, general strikes, attacks on Spanish consulates, and protest resolutions also spread across the Austro-Hungarian Empire in present-day Austria, Hungary, Czech Republic, Slovakia, Ukraine, Slovenia, and Croatia, as well as German-controlled Poland. The protest movement even extended as far as Cairo and Tehran, where several thousand marched for Ferrer, and Beirut, where the playwright Daud Muja'is cowrote a play about Ferrer that caused him to flee the country to avoid a seven-month prison sentence.[57] Across the Atlantic, mobilizations, attempted general strikes, and boycotts developed in Mexico, Uruguay, Argentina, Paraguay, Peru, Costa Rica, Chile, Cuba, Panama, Puerto Rico, and Brazil. More protests were held in New York City, Los Angeles, San Francisco, and across the United States.[58] Demonstrations and commemorations for Ferrer continued over the following years before being overwhelmed by the outbreak of the First World War.[59] Ferrer's martyrdom catalyzed not only a massive transnational protest movement but also what came to be known as the Modern School movement of sympathetic educators who created (more or less) Ferrerian institutions around the world, from Poland to Mexico, from China and Japan to Czechoslovakia and the United States.[60]

The Ferrer campaign did not reach mass proportions within Spain, however. In part, this is because Ferrer was actually more well known and highly regarded abroad than at home but also because of the censorship and repression that immobilized any potential campaign. With thousands in and out of jail or in exile in the wake of the most serious insurrection Spain had witnessed since the start of the Restoration, it was not easy to organize a massive campaign in a matter of weeks before Ferrer's rushed execution. Moreover, a number of radical leaders were anxious to distance themselves from the Tragic Week after their cases were thrown out. Despite frequent predictions and threats of retaliatory violence against Alfonso XIII, such as headlines from Charles Malato like "Ferrer's Life or the King's Head," the king emerged from the affair unscathed. The same could not be said for Prime Minister Maura.[61] When the dust settled from the Tragic Week, momentum developed among republican and Liberal politicians for a revision of Ferrer's case and especially for the ouster of the Maura government. After some heated debates in Parliament, Maura offered his resignation to the king, thinking he would be turned down. To his utter surprise, the king accepted his resignation in order to diffuse tensions. Years later the king told Maura's son that he had been forced to "sacrifice" Maura, because it was impossible to "prevail against half of Spain and more than half of Europe."[62] While the fall of the Maura government pleased Liberal and republican politicians, the king's amnesty for all Tragic Week prisoners in February 1910 appeased popular indignation, effectively ending the turmoil.[63] Though Ferrer met his fate in Montjuich Castle, the suffering of the castle's prisoners thirteen years earlier helped set the dominoes in motion for people across the world to honor the legacy of the Modern School and its martyred founder.

Epilogue
"Neither Innocent nor Guilty"

         Human rights and state sovereignty have shared an uneasy coexistence. Tensions between the two were evident during each of the Spanish prisoner campaigns of the turn of the twentieth century. Those who defended Ferrer's execution, such as the conservative *La Época*, emphasized that Ferrer was "judged in accordance with the existing laws of the Kingdom," while the *Times* of London considered the international protests to be "unwarrantable interference by outsiders in a matter which does not concern them."[1] In contrast, the Ferrer campaign followed in the footsteps of earlier campaigns by framing their appeal across borders and political tendencies to "all who have human sentiment" to rouse "the conscience of the civilised world" in defense of Ferrer "who committed no other crime in that country of obscurantism than being a man of free thought."[2] It was not "a question of the internal affairs of a country, but of an affair of all humanity," the *Berliner Tageblatt* argued, echoing the sentiments of the transnational protest movement.[3] In a similar vein, the Municipal Council of Paris argued that the execution was "a violation . . . against the rights of the human person." French unionists argued that the actions of the Spanish monarchy "are the most flagrant violation of individual liberty and human law."[4] The Belgian *Le Peuple* argued that protesters around the world formed a "universal conscience" familiar with "the rights of humanity."[5] The Hungarian *Pester Lloyd* argued that as with the Dreyfus affair, "the moral conscience of all Europe" would not allow "human rights [to] be brutally by-passed."[6]

Although the term "human rights" was not commonly used in these campaigns, their arguments for natural, equal, universal rights, their efforts to forge broad apolitical coalitions, and their attempts to leverage widely shared affinities for the "modern" values of "humanity" merit inclusion in the history of human rights. Including the Montjuich campaign and the other Spanish prisoner campaigns and the anarchist activists behind them not only challenges standard human rights periodization, which has generally overlooked the turn of the twentieth century, but expands our understanding of how human rights have coexisted with and within a wide variety of political formations. This book argues that the success of these and other campaigns of the era relied on their ability to leverage the widely shared notion of civilizational morality that I call the ethics of modernity. Yet just as the ethics of modernity were attaining near unanimity, newly developing intellectual and political forces were gnawing away at its hegemonic status. The work of figures such as Friedrich Nietzsche, Émile Durkheim, Sigmund Freud, Gustave Le Bon, and others presented a "constant play of lights and shadows instead of an outright division between the light of reason and medieval darkness" that characterized the ethics of modernity.[7] Ultranationalist and protofascist political formations such as the *Action française* pushed back against the abstraction of humanity in the name of the circumscribed nation.

The prevalence of the ethics of modernity was definitively destroyed by the era of the two world wars. As historian Walter Laqueur has argued, prior to 1914 "human rights were increasingly respected, and few dared dismiss them as of no consequence. . . . World War I, with its hecatombs of victims and its enormous destruction, changed all this and had lasting consequences. The chauvinist orgies led to a brutalization of public life. . . . The moral breakdown after World War I was more profound even than the economic crisis."[8] In 1921 humanitarian writer Lilian Brandt lamented how "tragic photographs of starved children and skeleton babies fail now to bring the response which could have been counted on a few years ago."[9]

As opposed to the purported repugnance at the "uncivilized" nature of brutality at the heart of the ethics of modernity, Fascism embraced violence as a sacred, generative force without limits. From a different direction Bolshevism disdained the liberal Enlightenment foundation of the ethics of modernity. Although some scholars have argued that Marx's critiques of bourgeois rights did not necessarily preclude some sympathy for rights in general or what we now refer to as human rights, Marx and Engels generally had no use for ahistorical notions of justice. Following in the Marxist tradition, Lenin argued in 1920 that "our morality is entirely subordinated to the interests of the proletariat's class struggle. Our morality stems from the interests of the class struggle of the proletariat. . . . Morality is what serves to destroy the old exploiting society."[10] Bolsheviks had no interest in the turn-of-the-century anarchist project of reclaiming the universal individuality of classical liberalism that stemmed from "natural law."

Shortly after World War II, the German anarcho-syndicalist, Anarchist Red Cross organizer, and Montjuich campaign supporter Rudolf Rocker reflected on the massive shifts that popular consciousness of human rights had undergone since the turn of the twentieth century:

> When I compare that time to now, the difference is profoundly evident. Then it was still possible that a notorious crime, regardless of what country it was committed in, could put ample layers of the population into movement against abuses of human law. But today, after entire peoples have been swept away by the fires of the totalitarian regime, and after the most criminal war of all times threw the world into an abyss of hunger, misery, and devastation, human beings barely react to the most horrific crimes that are committed daily and that ridicule all human sentiment.[11]

Similarly in 1945 the Catalan journalist Tomás Caballé y Clos wrote that the Liceo attack of 1893, which he had personally survived, elicited "such intense emotion" at the time that contemporary readers could hardly understand in retrospect considering how "multiple later local, and above all global, events have hardened our hearts, weakening individual and collective sensibility."[12]

Samuel Moyn convincingly argues that the "human rights" promoted by the United Nations after World War II amounted to "just another way of arguing for one side in the Cold War" and a stopgap for empire rather than a (re)birth of universalism beyond the state. Such politics developed under different circumstances than those of a half century earlier. The Enlightenment legacy of optimism in the superiority of "civilization" and the perfectibility of society at the core of the ethics of modernity had been shaken by the world wars and decolonization. Those still committed to radical social change in the postwar period, many of whom were Marxists, rarely framed their struggles in terms of human rights, while the "minimalism" of the new discourse of "human rights" that developed over the postwar decades was grounded in skepticism about the prospects for "utopian" transformation.[13] The synergy that had existed at the turn of the twentieth century between the advocacy of universal individual and collective rights and revolutionism among many Spanish prisoner campaigners (but not among the Congo campaigners, in contrast) had been snapped. When anarchism returned as a significant force in radical politics at the end of the twentieth century its confidence in science, logic, reason, and nature as infallible political guides had eroded significantly as a result of feminist, decolonial, and poststructuralist influences. The anarchist emphasis on natural rights was a casualty of this transformation.

This was evident when a new campaign against state repression in response to alleged propaganda by the deed emerged in Spain between 2013 and 2017. In October 2013 a bomb exploded in the Basilica del Pilar in Zaragoza, injuring one woman in the eye. A group calling itself the Comando Insurreccional Mateo Morral (Insurrectionary Mateo Morral cell) after the would-be assassin of Alfonso XIII in 1906 took responsibility for the *atentado* in addition to the placement of a bomb in the Almudena Cathedral in Madrid.[14] Over the next several years the Spanish state arrested dozens of anarchists for allegedly belonging to a group that was suspected of being affiliated with the insurrectionary Informal Anarchist Federation.[15] Founded in 2003 in Italy, this loose network has claimed responsibility for attacks across Europe, Latin America, and Indonesia.[16] Yet Spanish prosecutors failed to demonstrate any link between the arrested anarchists and any such conspiracy, and those arrested were acquitted (although two Chilean anarchists were convicted for the El Pilar *atentado*). Yet the anarchists and their allies who protested state repression did not do so in the name of the "rights of humanity" in 2014. Instead of attempting to appeal to broad societal standards of justice, anarchist campaigners refused to engage with the state's juridical terms. They aimed to target the legitimacy of state violence and promote prison abolitionist politics, which, in their eyes, apply to all human beings whether framed in terms of "rights" or not. A banner at the head of a Madrid anarchist protest march read "Neither innocent nor guilty, neither walls nor bars."[17]

NOTES

Introduction

1. David C. Rapoport, "The Four Waves of Modern Terrorism," in Audrey Kurth Cronin and James M. Ludes, eds., *Attacking Terrorism: Elements of a Grand Strategy* (Washington, D.C.: Georgetown University Press, 2004), 47; Richard Bach Jensen, "The International Campaign against Anarchist Terrorism, 1880–1930s," *Terrorism and Political Violence* 21, no. 1 (2009): 89–109.

2. "El proceso de Montjuich," *El Imparcial*, June 25, 1899. I use Castilian names for places in Catalonia in accord with most maps and newspapers of the era. All translations are by the author unless otherwise indicated.

3. Kirwin R. Shaffer, *Anarchism and Countercultural Politics in Early Twentieth-Century Cuba* (Gainesville: University Press of Florida, 2005); Dongyoun Hwang, "Korean Anarchism before 1945: A Regional and Transnational Approach," in Steven Hirsch and Lucien van der Walt, eds., *Anarchism and Syndicalism in the Colonial and Postcolonial World, 1870–1940* (Leiden: Brill, 2010); Carl Levy, "Anarchism, Internationalism and Nationalism in Europe, 1860–1939," *Australian Journal of Politics and History* 50, no. 3 (2004): 330–42.

4. Ilham Khuri-Makdisi, *The Eastern Mediterranean and the Making of Global Radicalism, 1860–1914* (Berkeley: University of California Press, 2013), 27; Constance Bantman, *The French Anarchists in London, 1880–1914: Exile and Transnationalism in the First Globalisation* (Liverpool: Liverpool University Press, 2013); Kenyon Zimmer, *Immigrants against the State: Yiddish and Italian Anarchism in America* (Urbana: University of Illinois Press, 2017); Kirwin R. Shaffer, "Havana Hub: Cuban Anarchism, Radical Media and the Trans-Caribbean Anarchist Network, 1902–1915," *Caribbean Studies* 37, no. 2 (2009): 45–81; Anthony Gorman, "Anarchists in Education: The Free Popular University in Egypt (1901)," *Middle Eastern Studies* 41, no. 3 (2005): 303–20.

5. Vallina correspondence and address book, Archives nationale (hereafter AN), F7/12510; Pedro Vallina, *Mis memorias* (Seville: Libre Pensamiento, 2000), 77–80.

6. Tom Goyens, "Social Space and the Practice of Anarchist History," *Rethinking History* 13, no. 4 (2009): 442.

7. Constance Bantman, "Internationalism without an International? Cross-Channel Anarchist Networks, 1880–1914," *Revue belge de philologie et d'histoire* 84, no. 4 (2006): 974.

8. James Michael Yeoman, *Print Culture and the Formation of the Anarchist Movement in Spain, 1890–1915* (New York: Routledge, 2020), 19; Raymond Craib, "Sedentary Anarchists," in Constance Bantman and Bert Altena, eds., *Reassessing the Transnational Turn: Scales of Analysis in Anarchist and Syndicalist Studies* (Oakland: PM Press, 2017).

9. Dilip K. Das, *Financial Globalization: Growth, Integration, Innovation and Crisis* (New York: Palgrave Macmillan, 2010), 8.

10. Javier del Valle-Inclán, *Biografía de La Revista Blanca 1898–1905* (Barcelona: Sintra, 2008).

11. Susana Tavera, "Soledad Gustavo, Federica Montseny i el periodisme acrata ¿Ofici o militancia?" *Annals del periodisme Català* 6, no. 14 (1988): 11.

12. Antonio Prado, *Matrimonio, familia y estado: escritoras anarco-feministas en La Revista Blanca (1898–1936)* (Madrid: Fundación Anselmo Lorenzo, 2011).

13. José Álvarez Junco, *La ideología política del anarquismo español (1868–1910)* (Madrid: Siglo XXI, 1991), 479; Pedro Vallina, *Fermín Salvochea: crónica de un revolucionario* (Seville: Renacimiento, 2012).

14. Yeoman, *Print Culture*, 129.

15. "Correspondance et communications," *Les Temps nouveaux*, December 26, 1896–January 1, 1897.

16. Richard Griffiths, *The Use of Abuse: The Polemics of the Dreyfus Affair and Its Aftermath* (New York: Berg, 1991), xii–17.

17. Gonzalo Capellán de Miguel and Aurora Garrido Martín, "'Los intérpretes de la opinión.' Uso, abuso y transforamción del concepto opinión pública en el discurso político durante la Restauración (1875–1902)," *Ayer* 80, no. 4 (2010): 83–114.

18. Gary J. Bass, *Freedom's Battle: The Origins of Humanitarian Intervention* (New York: Alfred A. Knopf, 2008); Claudio Lomnitz, *The Return of Comrade Ricardo Flores Magón* (Brooklyn: Zone, 2014); Kevin Grant, *A Civilised Savagery: Britain and the New Slaveries in Africa, 1884–1926* (New York: Routledge, 2004); Jordan Goodman, *The Devil and Mr. Casement: One Man's Battle for Human Rights in South America's Heart of Darkness* (New York: Farrar, Straus & Giroux, 2010).

19. Michael Barnett, *Empire of Humanity: A History of Humanitarianism* (Ithaca, NY: Cornell University Press, 2011), 16.

20. Lynn Hunt, *Inventing Human Rights: A History* (New York: W. W. Norton, 2007), 20.

21. Samuel Moyn, *The Last Utopia: Human Rights in History* (Cambridge, MA: Belknap Press of Harvard University Press, 2010).

22. Moyn, *Last Utopia*, 41.

23. Mark Bray, "Beyond and Against the State: Anarchist Contributions to Human Rights History and Theory," *Humanity* 10, no. 3 (2019): 323–38; Jesús López Santamaría, "El anarquismo español y derechos humanos," *Studia historica. Historia contemporánea* 26 (2008): 19–52.

24. J. Montseny, *El Proceso de un Gran Crimen* (La Coruña: Tipografía la Gutenberg, 1895), 13.

25. Jean Grave, "The Artist as Equal, not Master," in Robert Graham, ed., *Anarchism: A Documentary History of Libertarian Ideas. Volume 1: From Anarchy to Anarchism (300CE to 1939)* (Montreal: Black Rose, 2005), 218.

26. Stefan-Ludwig Hoffman, "Human Rights and History," *Past and Present* 232 (2016): 308–10.

27. Timothy Shanahan, "The Definition of Terrorism," in Richard Jackson, ed., *Routledge Handbook of Critical Terrorism Studies* (London: Routledge, 2016), 228.

28. "Pallás," *El Imparcial*, October 5, 1893.

29. "Nuestra campaña," *Tierra y Libertad*, April 30, 1908.

30. Shanahan, "Definition of Terrorism," 235; R. Bittner, "Morals in Terrorist Times," in G. Meggle, ed., *Ethics of Terrorism and Counter-Terrorism* (Frankfurt: Ontos/Verlag, 2005), 207.

31. Christopher J. Finlay, "How to Do Things with the Word 'Terrorist,'" *Review of International Studies* 35, no. 4 (2009): 754.

32. Richard Jackson, "Introduction," in Jackson, *Routledge Handbook of Critical Terrorism Studies*, 20.

33. Richard Jackson, "An Argument for Terrorism," *Perspectives on Terrorism* 2, no. 2 (2008): 29.

34. Dominic Bryan, Liam Kelly, and Sara Templer, "The Failed Paradigm of 'Terrorism,'" *Behavioral Sciences of Terrorism and Political Aggression* 3, no. 2 (2011): 80–96.

35. Claudia Verhoeven, *The Odd Man Karakozov: Imperial Russia, Modernity, and the Birth of Terrorism* (Ithaca, NY: Cornell University Press, 2011).

36. Alexandre Skirda, *Facing the Enemy: A History of Anarchist Organization from Proudhon to May 1968* (Oakland: AK Press, 2002), 55.

37. Caroline Cahm, *Kropotkin and the Rise of Revolutionary Anarchism, 1872–1886* (Cambridge: Cambridge University Press, 1989), 207.

38. Siegfried Nacht, "Ce que je pense de Maura" and "Les mésaventures de M. Antonio Maura," *L'Espagne inquisitoriale*, May–June 1904; Ch. Malato, "Lettre ouvert à Monsieur Bourbon," *L'Espagne inquisitoriale*, September 1904.

39. Federico Urales, *Mi Vida*, vol. 1 (Barcelona: Publicaciones de la Revista Blanca, 1932), 232.

40. Anselmo Lorenzo, *El banquete de la vida: Concordancia entre la naturaleza, el hombre y la sociedad* (Barcelona: Imprenta Luz, 1905).

41. Errico Malatesta, "Anarchists Have Forgotten Their Principles," in Graham, *Anarchism*, 287.

42. Archives de la Préfecture de Police (hereafter APP), Ba 77, Anarchistes 1892, flier for meeting on August 6, 1892.

43. Moyn, *Last Utopia*, 172–73.

44. "Protest Meeting in London," *Freedom*, February 1897.

45. Moyn, *Last Utopia*, 121.

46. Alfred Naquet, "Une lettre d'Alfred Naquet," *L'Espagne inquisitoriale*, May–June 1904.

47. Moyn, *Last Utopia*, 146; Bernard Harcourt, *Exposed: Desire and Disobedience in the Digital Age* (Cambridge, MA: Harvard University Press, 2016).

48. Susan Maslan, "The Anti-Human: Man and Citizen before the Declaration of the Rights of Man and of the Citizen," *South Atlantic Quarterly* 103, nos. 2/3 (2004): 358.

49. Hannah Arendt, *On Revolution* (London: Penguin, 1990), 71–72.

50. Barnett, *Empire of Humanity*, 49.

51. Oscar Wilde, *The Picture of Dorian Gray* (New York: Barnes & Noble, 2003), 43.

52. Karen Halttunen, "Humanitarianism and the Pornography of Pain in Anglo-American Culture," *American Historical Review* 100, no. 2 (1995): 319–20; Hunt, *Inventing Human Rights*.

53. F. Urales, *Mi Don Quijote* (Barcelona: Biblioteca de La Revista Blanca, 1932), 12; Marisa Siguán, "Federico Urales: un programa de literatura popular libertaria," *Anthropos* 78 (1987): 36.

54. Federico Urales, "Por humanidad," *El País*, January 5, 1897; Federico Urales, *El Castillo maldito* (Toulouse: Presses Universitaires du Mirail, 1992).

55. Lynn Festa, "Humanity without Feathers," *Humanity* 1, no. 1 (2010): 10, 17.

56. "El entierro," *Las Noticias*, June 9, 1896; Giorgio Agamben, *Sovereign Power and Bare Life* (Stanford, CA: Stanford University Press, 1998).

57. Hannah Arendt, *The Origins of Totalitarianism* (San Diego: Harcourt, 1973), 297.

58. Wilde, *Picture of Dorian Gray*, 43.

59. "El Crimen de Barcelona," *La Época*, September 25, 1893.

60. Bruce Mazlish, *Civilization and Its Contents* (Stanford, CA: Stanford University Press, 2004), 69. Although a not insignificant number of anarchists believed that propaganda by the deed was justifiable, those that held this position tended to support it because they considered the actions of state and capital to be so "barbarous" as to justify anarchist violence in response.

61. Ole Birk Laursen, "Anti-Imperialism," in Carl Levy and Matthew S. Adams, eds., *The Palgrave Handbook of Anarchism* (Cham: Palgrave Macmillan, 2019).

62. Edward Said, *Orientalism* (New York: Vintage, 1979), 206.

63. J. Prat, "Fetichismo," *Tierra y Libertad*, April 9, 1903.

64. Cosmo, "En Espagne," *L'Intransigeant*, July 21, 1897.

1. "With Fire and Dynamite"

1. The celebration of the Virgin of Mercy had not previously included a military parade. Temma Kaplan, *Red City, Blue Period: Social Movements in Picasso's Barcelona* (Princeton, NJ: Princeton University Press, 1992), 30; AN, F7 12725, "Attentats de Barcelone 1893–1908," Report from Commissariat Spécial Thiellement to Director of the Sûreté Générale, September 25, 1893.

2. "Atentado contra el General Martínez Campos," *La Época*, September 25–26, 1893.

3. Nine of the seventeen victims were military. Antoni Dalmau, *El Procés de Montjuïc: Barcelona al Final del Segle XIX* (Barcelona: Editorial Base, 2010), 63–64.

4. "Dinamita en Barcelona," *El Imparcial*, September 27, 1893.

5. Kaplan, *Red City*, 30.

6. "Atentado contra el General Martínez Campos," *El País*, September 29, 1893; Ramon Sempau, *Los victimarios: notas relativas al proceso de Montjuich* (Barcelona: García y Manent, 1900), 277.

7. Dalmau, *El Procés de Montjuïc*, 52, 69; "Atentado contra el General Martínez Campos," *La Época*, September 26, 1893; "Pallás," *El Imparcial*, October 4, 1893.

8. "Atentado contra el General Martínez Campos," *La Época*, September 30, 1893; "Atentado contra el General Martínez Campos," *El País*, October 2, 1893; Ángel Herrerín López, *Anarquía, dinamita y revolución social: violencia y represión en la España de entre siglos (1868–1909)* (Madrid: Catarata, 2011), 96; Dalmau, *El Procés de Montjuïc*, 52–53.

9. "Atentado contra el General Martínez Campos," *La Época*, September 26, 1893.

10. Dalmau, *El Procés de Montjuïc*, 65–70.

11. James A. Baer, *Anarchists and Immigrants in Spain and Argentina* (Urbana: University of Illinois Press, 2017), 3.

12. Dalmau, *El Procés de Montjuïc*, 70; Herbert S. Klein, "The Social and Economic Integration of Spanish Immigrants in Brazil," *Journal of Social History* 25, no. 3 (Spring 1992): 505–6.

13. Dalmau, *El Procés de Montjuïc*, 70–72. *Ravachol: periódico anarquista* published two editions out of Sabadell before changing its name to *El Eco de Ravachol* for one more.

14. "Atentado contra el General Martínez Campos," *La Época*, September 26 and 30, 1893; "Crónica diaria," *El Diluvio*, ed. mañana, September 30, 1893; Dalmau, *El Procés de Montjuïc*, 72–73.

15. "Atentado contra el General Martínez Campos," *La Época*, September 25, 1893; "La dinamita en Barcelona," *El Imparcial*, September 27, 1893.

16. "El crimen de Barcelona," *La Época*, September 25, 1893.

17. "La dinamita en Barcelona," *El Imparcial*, September 25, 1893.

18. "Los crímenes anarquistas," *La Época*, September 26, 1893.

19. "Castigo, no leyes," *El Imparcial*, September 26, 1893.

20. "Republicanos y anarquistas," *El País*, October 2, 1893.

21. "Atentado contra el general Martínez Campos," *El País*, September 26, 1893; "Dinamita en Barcelona," *El Imparcial*, September 28, 1893; Herrerín López, *Anarquía*, 94.

22. Dalmau, *El Procés de Montjuïc*, 76–77; Herrerín López, *Anarquía, dinamita y revolución social*, 93–94; "Atentado contra el general Martínez Campos," *La Época*, September 27, 1893.

23. The police called the group "Benvenuto Salud," but Herrerín López argues that the real name was likely Benvenuto. The "Salud" at the bottom of the letter the police found was a common anarchist way to say goodbye, and so they mistakenly tacked it onto the name of the group. Herrerín López, *Anarquía*, 111.

24. Ángel Herrerín López, "Anarchist Sociability in Times of Violence and Clandestinity," *Bulletin for Spanish and Portuguese Historical Studies* 38, no. 1 (2013): 170; Teresa Abelló Güell, "El Proceso de Montjuïc: la condena internacional al régimen de la Restauración," *Historia Social* 14 (1992): 51.

25. Dalmau, *El Procés de Montjuïc*, 71–72.

26. "La dinamita en Barcelona," *El Imparcial*, September 25, 1893.

27. "Atentado contra el general Martínez Campos," *El País*, September 30, October 2 and 8, 1893; "El proceso Pallás," *El Imparcial*, September 30, 1893; "Atentado contra el general Martínez Campos," *La Época*, September 30, 1893.

28. "Letter from Paulino Pallás," *El País*, October 8, 1893.

29. "Atentado contra el general Martínez Campos," *La Época*, September 30, 1893; "Crónica diaria"; *El Imparcial*, October 4, 1893; *El País*, September 30 and October 2, 1893.

30. "Pallás," *El Imparcial*, October 6–7, 1893; "Paulino Pallás en capilla," *El Diluvio*, October 6, 1893.

31. Eduardo González Calleja, *La razón de la fuerza: orden público, subversión y violencia política en la España de la Restauración (1875-1917)* (Madrid: Consejo Superior de Investigaciones Científicas, 1998), 272.

32. "Pallás en capilla," *El País*, October 6, 1893; "Pallás," *El Imparcial*, October 2 and 5, 1893.

2. Propaganda by the Deed and Anarchist Communism

1. Nunzio Pernicone, *Italian Anarchism, 1864–1892* (Princeton, NJ: Princeton University Press, 1993), 121.

2. Pernicone, *Italian Anarchism*, 121–26; George Richard Esenwein, *Anarchist Ideology and the Working-Class Movement in Spain, 1868–1898* (Berkeley: University of California Press, 1989), 60–62; Claudia Verhoeven, "The Making of Russian Revolutionary Terrorism," in Isaac Land, ed., *Enemies of Humanity: The Nineteenth-Century War on Terrorism* (New York: Palgrave Macmillan, 2008), 99.

3. Paul Thomas, *Karl Marx and the Anarchists* (New York: Routledge, 1980), 293.

4. Mark Leier, *Bakunin: The Creative Passion* (New York: St. Martin's Press, 2006), 111.

5. Though the FRE officially lasted until 1881 when it was disbanded to form the Federación de Trabajadores de la Región Española (FTRE), repression forced it underground in 1874. Esenwein, *Anarchist Ideology*, 44.

6. According to Max Nettlau, the phrase "anarchist communism" was first written in the 1876 "Aux travailleurs manuels partisans de l'action politique" by Francois Dumartheray, an associate of Élisée Reclus. Esenwein, *Anarchist Ideology*, 107. Cafiero was influenced by the hybrid collectivist-communist pamphlet of 1876 *Ideas on Social Organization* by Bakunin's disciple James Guillaume. Pernicone, *Italian Anarchism*, 111–12. Joseph Déjacque developed "a kind of anarchist communism" in the 1850s. Graham, *We Do Not Fear Anarchy, We Invoke It: The First International and the Origins of the Anarchist Movement* (Oakland: AK Press, 2015), 52.

7. Leier, *Bakunin*, 110.

8. Ricardo Flores Magón, *Dreams of Freedom: A Ricardo Flores Magón Reader*, ed. Chaz Bufe and Mitchell Cowen Verter (Oakland: AK Press, 2005), 216.

9. Esenwein, *Anarchist Ideology*, 56, 109.

10. Juan Avilés, "Propaganda por el hecho y regicidio en Italia," in Juan Avilés and Ángel Herrerín, eds., *El nacimiento del terrorismo en occidente: anarquía, nihilismo y violencia revolucionaria* (Madrid: Siglo XXI, 2008), 2–5.

11. Paul Brousse, "Propaganda by the Deed," in Graham, *Anarchism*, 150–51.

12. Verhoeven, *Odd Man Karakozov*, 178. Some argue that Karl Heinzen was the "first to provide a full-fledged doctrine of modern terrorism." Benjamin Grob-Fitzgibbon, "From the Dagger to the Bomb: Karl Heinzen and the Evolution of Political Terror," *Terrorism and Political Violence* 16, no. 1 (2010): 99.

13. Ana Siljak, *Angel of Vengeance: The "Girl Assassin," the Governor of St. Petersburg, and Russia's Revolutionary World* (New York: St. Martin's Press, 2008), 1, 9.

14. Avilés, "Propaganda por el hecho y regicidio," 5.

15. Francisco Otero also tried to assassinate Alfonso XII in December 1879. Rafael Núñez Florencio, *El terrorismo anarquista 1888–1909* (Madrid: Siglo Veintiuno Editores, 1983), 38.

16. Pyotr Kropotkin, *Memoirs of a Revolutionist* (New York: Houghton Mifflin, 1899), 304–16.

17. González Calleja, *La razón de la fuerza*, 255; Avilés, "Propaganda por el hecho y regicidio," 5.

18. Avilés, "Propaganda por el hecho y regicidio," 6; Kropotkin, *Memoirs*, 436–37.

19. John Merriman, *The Dynamite Club: How a Bombing in Fin-de-Siècle Paris Ignited the Age of Modern Terror* (Boston: Houghton Mifflin Harcourt, 2009), 75–76.

20. Richard Bach Jensen, *The Battle against Anarchist Terrorism: An International History, 1878–1934* (Cambridge: Cambridge University Press, 2014), 17.

21. Skirda, *Facing the Enemy*, 43–45.

22. Louis Patsouras, *Jean Grave and the Anarchist Tradition in France* (Middletown, NJ: Calson, 1995), 22.

23. Jensen, *Battle against Anarchist Terrorism*, 45–46.

24. Skirda, *Facing the Enemy*, 44–45.

25. Walter Laqueur, *The Age of Terrorism* (Boston: Little, Brown, 1987), 135. Some Italian anarchist papers were founded by a police agent. Jensen, *Battle against Anarchist Terrorism*, 46.

26. George Woodcock, *Anarchism: A History of Libertarian Ideas and Movements* (Cleveland: Meridian, 1962), 462–63.

27. González Calleja, *La Razón de la Fuerza*, 227; Temma Kaplan, *Anarchists of Andalusia, 1868–1903* (Princeton, NJ: Princeton University Press, 1977), 58.

28. At the Andalusian regional conferences of the FRE in 1876 and 1880, the necessity of reprisals against class enemies was accepted. González Calleja, *La Razón de la Fuerza*, 228.

29. Esenwein, *Anarchist Ideology*, 83; González Calleja, *La Razón de la Fuerza*, 229–33.

30. Lida and Herrerín López argue that Mano Negra existed, while Joll, Waggoner, Esenwein, and Kaplan deny its existence. Álvarez Junco refers to it as a "miniscule, if not imaginary, conspiracy." Esenwein, *Anarchist Ideology*, 88–89; Herrerín López, *Anarquía*, 58; Kaplan, *Anarchists of Andalusia*, 133–34; José Álvarez Junco, *El Emperador del Paralelo: Lerroux y la Demagogia Populista* (Madrid: Alianza, 1990), 142.

31. Herrerín López, *Anarquía*, 59; González Calleja, *La Razón de la Fuerza*, 233–36; Juan Avilés Farré, *Francisco Ferrer y Guardia: pedagogo, anarquista y mártir* (Madrid: Marcial Pons, 2006), 135.

32. Esenwein, *Anarchist Ideology*, 87.

33. Álvarez Junco, *El Emperador*, 142.

34. Antoni Dalmau i Ribalta, "Martí Borràs i Jover (1845–1894) o el primer comunisme llibertari," *Revista d'Igualada* 26 (2007): 20–21.

35. Dalmau, "Martí Borràs i Jover," 22; Esenwein, *Anarchist Ideology*, 111–13.

36. "Organización y revolución," *Ravachol*, October 22, 1892.

37. Dalmau, "Martí Borràs i Jover," 23.

38. "Organización y revolución."

39. "Motus in fine velocior," *La Controversia*, October 7, 1893.

40. Esenwein, *Anarchist Ideology*, 124.

41. Dalmau, *El Procés de Montjuïc*, 38–50.

42. Miguel Íñiguez, ed., *Enciclopedia histórica del anarquismo español* (Vitoria: Asociación Isaac Puente, 2008), 940–41.

43. "Consideracions," *La Tramontana*, October 6, 1893.

44. "No, No Lloramos," *La Revancha*, October 14, 1893.

45. "Letter from Paulino Pallás," *El País*, October 8, 1893.

46. Papers that raised money for Pallás's family: *La Tramontana*, *La Revancha*, *El Corsario* (La Coruña), *Bomba Pallás* (Buenos Aires), and *El Despertar* (New York). Dalmau, *El Procés de Montjuïc*, 90.

47. Dalmau, *El Procés de Montjuïc*, 41–50, 75.

48. Italics added. "Consideracions."

49. Richard D. Sonn, *Anarchism and Cultural Politics in Fin de Siècle France* (Lincoln: University of Nebraska Press, 1989), 260.

3. The Birth of the Propagandist by the Deed

1. Merriman, *Dynamite Club*, 71–72; Charles Malato, "Some Anarchist Portraits," *Fortnightly Review*, September 1, 1894; Michael Burleigh, *Blood and Rage: A Cultural History of Terrorism* (New York: Harper Collins, 2009), 80; Isaac Land, "Men with Faces of Brutes: Physiognomy, Urban Anxieties, and Police States," in Land, *Enemies of Humanity*, 131.

2. Woodcock, *Anarchism*, 307–9; Malato, "Some Anarchist Portraits."

3. Merriman, *Dynamite Club*, 70; Woodcock, *Anarchism*, 307–8; Jean Maitron, *Le Mouvement anarchiste en France: Des origines à 1914* (Paris: Gallimard, 1992), 220.

4. Malato, "Some Anarchist Portraits."

5. Merriman, *Dynamite Club*, 69–70.

6. Malato, "Some Anarchist Portraits."

7. Maitron, *Le Mouvement anarchiste*, 224–25.

8. Merriman, *Dynamite Club*, 70.

9. Merriman, *Dynamite Club*, 79.

10. Some anarchists were upset with his reckless behavior and wished he had been captured while doing something other than running his mouth. Merriman, *Dynamite Club*, 79–80; Burleigh, *Blood and Rage*, 80–81; Maitron, *Le Mouvement anarchiste*, 213, 221.

11. Maitron, *Le Mouvement anarchiste*, 215–16, 227–28; Merriman, *Dynamite Club*, 81; Barbara W. Tuchman, "Anarchism in France," in Irving Louis Horowitz, ed., *The Anarchists* (New York: Dell, 1964), 445.

12. Tuchman, "Anarchism in France," 445; Maitron, *Le Mouvement anarchiste*, 218–19.

13. Maitron, *Le Mouvement anarchiste*, 216.

14. Maitron, *Le Mouvement anarchiste*, 217–18; Woodcock, *Anarchism*, 309.

15. Thierry Lévy, *Plutôt la mort que l'injustice: au temps des procès anarchistes* (Paris: Odile Jacob, 2009), 146; Maitron, *Le Mouvement anarchiste*, 219; Sonn, *Anarchism and Cultural Politics*, 124.

16. Héctor Zoccoli, *La anarquía: las ideas, los hechos* (Barcelona: Henrich y C. A., 1908), 239–40.

17. Merriman, *Dynamite Club*, 84–85; Maitron, *Le Mouvement anarchiste*, 223.

18. Peter Marshall, *Demanding the Impossible: A History of Anarchism* (London: Harper Perennial, 2008), 438–40.

19. David Goodway, *Anarchist Seeds beneath the Snow: Left-Libertarian Thought and British Writers from William Morris to Colin Ward* (Liverpool: Liverpool University Press, 2006), 90–91.

20. Marshall, *Demanding the Impossible*, 438.

21. Merriman, *Dynamite Club*, 86–87.

22. APP, Ba 508, 509, and 510, Anarchistes 1892.

23. Alex Butterworth, *The World That Never Was: A True Story of Dreamers, Schemers, Anarchists and Secret Agents* (New York: Pantheon, 2010), 302; Skirda, *Facing the Enemy*, 56.

24. Merriman, *Dynamite Club*, 86.

25. Merriman, *Dynamite Club*, 83; Woodcock, *Anarchism*, 305.

26. Fred Inglis, *A Short History of Celebrity* (Princeton, NJ: Princeton University Press, 2010), 11.

27. Adam Hochschild, *King Leopold's Ghost: A Story of Greed, Terror, and Heroism in Colonial Africa* (Boston: Houghton Mifflin, 1999), 27.

28. Jean K. Chalaby, *The Invention of Journalism* (New York: St. Martin's Press, 1998), 91.

29. Archivo Histórico Nacional (hereafter AHN), Gobernación, 2A, Exp. 15.

30. J. Llunas, "Sobre anarquismo," *La Tramontana*, June 3, 1892.

31. Tuchman, "Anarchism in France," 446.

32. *La Révolte*, April 23–30, 1892, cited in Maitron, *Le Mouvement anarchiste*, 221.

33. Malato, "Some Anarchist Portraits."

34. Merriman, *Dynamite Club*, 40, 51, 89–90; APP, Ba 77, Report of May 30, 1892, and Ba 1115, report of May 30–31 and June 4, 1892.

35. Merriman, *Dynamite Club*, 89–91; APP, Ba 1115, Report on Émile Henry, February 13, 1894.

36. Merriman, *Dynamite Club*, 25–30; Maitron, *Le Mouvement anarchiste*, 239.

37. Merriman, *Dynamite Club*, 30–42; "L'anarchiste Henry," *Le XIXe siècle*, February 20, 1894; "La vie d'Émile Henry," *Le Rappel*, April 17, 1894; APP, Ba 1115.

38. Malato, "Some Anarchist Portraits."

39. Merriman, *Dynamite Club*, 59–60, 87.

40. Merriman, *Dynamite Club*, 81, 92–94.

41. Avilés, "Propaganda por el hecho y regicidio," 8, 21.

42. Malatesta, "Un peu de théorie," *L'En Dehors*, August 21, 1892.

43. Lucien van der Walt, "Global Anarchism and Syndicalism: Theory, History, Resistance," *Anarchist Studies* 24, no. 1 (2016): 85–106.

44. Marc Sageman, *Turning to Political Violence: The Emergence of Terrorism* (Philadelphia: University of Pennsylvania Press, 2017), 249.

45. Butterworth, *World That Never Was*, 313.

46. Merriman, *Dynamite Club*, 94, 99–101.

47. Merriman, *Dynamite Club*, 101–2.

48. Merriman, *Dynamite Club*, 102–4; Maitron, *Le Mouvement anarchiste*, 242.

49. *Gazette des tribunaux*, April 28, 1894; Merriman, *Dynamite Club*, 104–5. According to Malato, this bombing excited no regret except in high official circles and among the victims' relations. Malato, "Some Anarchist Portraits."

50. Merriman, *Dynamite Club*, 105–20; APP, Ba 1115, Report of April 12, 1894.

51. *Diario de Barcelona*, October 6, 1893, quoted in Herrerín López, *Anarquía*, 97.

52. Dalmau, *El Procés de Montjuïc*, 79–89; "Ejecución de Pallás," *La Época*, October 6, 1893; Miguel López Corral, *La Guardia Civil en la Restauración, 1875–1905: militarismo contra subversión y terrorismo anarquista* (Madrid: Ministerio del Interior, 2004), 574.

4. Introducing the "Lottery of Death"

1. "El Liceo de Barcelona," *La Correspondencia de España*, November 10, 1893; "La catastrofe del Liceo," *La Dinastía*, November 9, 1893.

2. "El atentado del Liceo," *La Correspondencia de España*, November 10, 1893; Archivo General del Palacio (hereafter AGP), Reinados, Alfonso XIII, cajón 7, exp. 2, telegraphic call between Minister of the Interior and Governor of Barcelona, November 8, 1893; "Catástrofe horrible," *La Dinastía*, November 8, 1893; Arxiu de la Corona d'Aragó (hereafter ACA), Sentencias criminales of Santiago Salvador, 186; Dalmau, *El Procés de Montjuïc*, 102–3.

3. "La dinamita," *El País*, November 9, 1893.

4. "Catástrofe horrible," *La Dinastía*, November 8, 1893; Dalmau, *El Procés de Montjuïc*, 105.

5. "El crimen del Liceo," *La Vanguardia*, November 8, 1893.

6. Dalmau, *El Procés de Montjuïc*, 115–19, 135.

7. "El crimen del Liceo," *La Vanguardia*, November 9, 1893.

8. *La Dinastía*, November 8–9, 1893; *La Correspondencia de España*, November 9, 1893; *El País*, November 9, 1893; *La Vanguardia*, November 8, 1893; *El País*, November 9, 1893.

9. "Catástrofe horrible," *La Dinastía*, November 8, 1893.

10. "Otro crimen anarquista en Barcelona," *La Correspondencia de España*, November 9, 1893.

11. "Catástrofe horrible," *La Dinastía*, November 8, 1893; Dalmau, *El Procés de Montjuïc*, 122, 180; AGP, Reinados, Alfonso XIII, cajón 7, exp. 2, telegraphic call between Minister of the Interior and Governor of Barcelona, November 8, 1893; Montseny, *El proceso de un gran crímen*, 27–28.

12. "La dinamita," *El País*, November 9, 1893; "El atentado del Liceo," *La Vanguardia*, November 9, 1893.

13. "El terror anarquista," *La Correspondencia de España*, November 9, 1893.

14. Dalmau, *El Procés de Montjuïc*, 124–28.

15. Manuel Gil Maestre, *El anarquismo en España y el especial de Barcelona* (Madrid: Hernández, 1897), 37.

16. Dalmau, *El Procés de Montjuïc*, 127–30; "Ecos teatrales," *La Dinastía*, November 7, 1893.

17. Tomás Caballé y Clos, *Barcelona de antaño: memorias de un viejo reportero barcelonés* (Barcelona: Aries, 1944), 95. Dalmau cautions that some of Salvador's quotations may have been re-creations made by Caballé y Clos years later. Dalmau, *El Procés de Montjuïc*, 130–31.

18. Caballé y Clos, *Barcelona de antaño*, 95.

19. "El atentado del Liceo," *La Vanguardia*, November 9, 1893.

20. Dalmau, *El Procés de Montjuïc*, 131.

21. Caballé y Clos, *Barcelona de antaño*, 95.

22. "El crimen del Liceo," *La Vanguardia*, November 8, 1893; J. Roca y Roca, "La semana," *La Vanguardia*, November 12, 1893; ¡....!, La Dinastía, November 8, 1893.

23. *Diario Mercantil*, November 8, 1893, cited in *La Dinastía*, November 9, 1893.

24. Roca, "La semana," *La Vanguardia*, November 12, 1893.

25. "El crimen del Liceo," *La Vanguardia*, November 8, 1893.

26. "La anarquía," *El País*, November 9, 1893.

27. "El terror anarquista," *La Correspondencia de España*, November 9, 1893.

28. Timothy Shanahan, "The Definition of Terrorism," in Jackson, *Routledge Handbook of Critical Terrorism Studies*, 232.

29. "El crimen del Liceo," *La Vanguardia*, November 8, 1893.

30. "Notas sueltas," *La Dinastía*, November 9, 1893.

31. "El terror anarquista," *La Correspondencia de España*, November 9, 1893.

32. "Nueva catastrofe," *La Correspondencia de España*, November 8, 1893.

33. "Petardos y Libertad," *La Dinastía*, November 12, 1893.

34. "Notas," *La Dinastía*, November 9, 1893.

35. "La anarquía," *El País*, November 9, 1893.

36. *El Imparcial* cited in "Lo del Liceo en Madrid," *La Vanguardia*, November 11, 1893.

37. "Dentro o fuera de la ley," *La Dinastía*, November 9, 1893.

38. "Día de luto," *La Dinastía*, November 10, 1893.

39. "Dentro," *La Dinastía*, November 9, 1893.

40. "Lo que dice la prensa," *La Dinastía*, November 9, 1893.

41. "El terror anarquista," *La Correspondencia de España*, November 9, 1893.

42. Letter to the editor from D. Ramos, *La Dinastía*, November 12, 1893; Dalmau, *El Procés de Montjuïc*, 144.

43. González Calleja, *La razón de la fuerza*, 43.

44. AN, F7 12725, Report from Commissariat Spécial Thiellement to Director of the Sûreté Générale, November 8, 1893; Martín Turrado Vidal, *Policía y Delincuencia a Finales del Siglo XIX* (Madrid: Dykinson, 2001), 52.

45. Turrado Vidal, *Policía y Delincuencia*, 52, 67, 82–83,.

46. AGP, Reinados, Alfonso XIII, cajón 7, exp. 2, telegraphic call between Martínez Campos, the Interior Minister, and the Minister of War, November 8, 1893.

47. Susan Gilson Miller, *A History of Modern Morocco* (Cambridge: Cambridge University Press, 2013), 56–88.

48. Benedict Anderson, *Under Three Flags: Anarchism and the Anti-Colonial Imagination* (New York: Verso, 2005), 93–94, 103, 146.

49. López Corral, *La Guardia Civil*, 570; González Calleja, *La razón de la fuerza*, 273.

50. Dalmau, *El Procés de Montjuïc*, 149, 221–22.

51. AHN, Asuntos Exteriores, Sección Histórica, 2750, report from Ministerio de Estado, January 8, 1894.

52. NA, Foreign Office (FO), 881/6427, Rosebery to Wolff, November 22, 1893.

53. Dalmau, *El Procés de Montjuïc*, 144–47.

54. Arxiu Nacional de Catalunya (hereafter ANC), 217, Associació de Pares de Família de Catalunya Contra la Immoralitat.

55. Dalmau, *El Procés de Montjuïc*, 152; Dalmau, "Martí Borràs i Jover," 26–27.

56. "Noticias varias," *El Siglo futuro*, March 14, 1894.

57. "El atentado del Liceo," *La Vanguardia*, November 9, 1893; "Ventadas," *La Tramontana*, November 10, 1893.

58. "El atentado del Liceo," *La Vanguardia*, November 10, 1893; "La catastrofe del Liceo," *La Dinastía*, November 10, 1893.

59. Caballé y Clos, *Barcelona de antaño*, 95–96.

60. Sonn, *Anarchism and Cultural Politics*, 32–37.

61. Shanahan, "Definition of Terrorism," 232.

62. Yves Frémion, *Léauthier l'anarchiste: de la propagande par le fait à la révolte des bagnards (1893–1894)* (Montreuil: Éditions L'Échappée, 2011), 11–26.

63. Interview with Faure in *La Petite République française*, November 18, 1893.

64. APP, Ba 141.

65. Vaillant quoted in Emma Goldman, "The Psychology of Political Violence," in Emma Goldman, *Red Emma Speaks: An Emma Goldman Reader*, 3rd ed., ed. Alix Kates Shulman (Amherst, MA: Humanity, 1998), 269.

66. Maitron, *Le Mouvement anarchiste*, 231; Lévy, *Plutôt la mort que l'injustice*, 154–62; Merriman, *Dynamite Club*, 137–38; Goldman, "Psychology of Political Violence," 269.

67. Malato, "Some Anarchist Portraits."

68. Merriman, *Dynamite Club*, 137–38; Tuchman, "Anarchism in France," 451–52; Constance Bantman, "Jean Grave and French Anarchism: A Relational Approach (1870s–1914)," *IRSH* 62 (2017): 451–77.

69. Jean-Paul Brunet, *La Police de l'ombre: indicateurs et provocateurs dans la France contemporaine* (Paris: Seuil, 1990), 264–67; Burleigh, *Blood and Rage*, 81; Maitron, *Le Mouvement anarchiste*, 230. For more on Vaillaint, see AN, F7 12517.

70. Henri Varennes, *De Ravachol a Caserio* (Paris: Garnier Frères, 1894), 115.

71. Brunet, *La Police*, 272.

72. Ernest Raynaud, *Souvenirs de police: La vie intime des commissariats* (Paris: Payot, 1926), 33–46. For more on the Vaillant attentat, see APP, Ba 1289 and Ba 78.

73. Brunet, *La Police*, 270–74.

74. Malato, "Some Anarchist Portraits."

75. "Opinions," *Le Journal*, December 10, 1893; Maitron, *Le Mouvement anarchiste*, 236, 257.

76. "Los anarquistas," *El Imparcial*, December 14, 1893.

77. "Deux documents," *Le Figaro*, July 21, 1894.

78. Goldman, "Psychology of Political Violence," 269.

79. Maitron, *Le Mouvement anarchiste*, 233–34.

80. *Le Parti socialiste*, January 28–February 3, 1894, in Maitron, *Le Mouvement anarchiste*, 235; Varennes, *De Ravachol a Caserio*, 125.

81. *El Imparcial*, December 13, 1893, citing *La Liberté*.

82. Maitron, *Le Mouvement anarchiste*, 233–35.

83. Varennes, *De Ravachol a Caserio*, 130–31; APP, Ba 1289, homages to Vaillant.

84. Varennes, *De Ravachol a Caserio*, 353–55; Patsouras, *Jean Grave*, 32; Merriman, *Dynamite Club*, 139–41.

85. AN, F7 12504, report of April 23, 1894.

86. Merriman, *Dynamite Club*, 125–28.

87. APP, Ba 78, report of May 23, 1893.

88. Malato, "Some Anarchist Portraits."

5. "There Are No Innocent Bourgeois"

1. AN, F7 12508, report of December 31, 1893; Maitron, *Le Mouvement anarchiste*, 251; Merriman, *Dynamite Club*, 142–44.

2. APP, BA 1500, Listes et état des menées anarchists, 1894–1899; Patsouras, *Jean Grave*, 35; Merriman, *Dynamite Club*, 143–44; Maitron, *Le Mouvement anarchiste*, 252.

3. "Les anarchistes," *Le Temps*, January 2, 1894.

4. "Émile Henry aux assises," *L'Intransigeant*, April 30, 1894.

5. Sonn, *Anarchism and Cultural Politics*, 20; Patsouras, *Jean Grave*, 35.

6. "Émile Henry aux assises," *L'Intransigeant*, April 30, 1894.

7. APP, Ba 141, report of May 9, 1894, and APP, Ba 141; Merriman, *Dynamite Club*, 149–52, 157–58; Patsouras, *Jean Grave*, 32–33; Maitron, *Le Mouvement anarchiste*, 239.

8. Merriman, *Dynamite Club*, 149–53.

9. Merriman, *Dynamite Club*, 157, 166.

10. Merriman, *Dynamite Club*, 157–59.

11. APP, Ba 1115, February 19, 1894.

12. Sonn, *Anarchism and Cultural Politics*, 245; Merriman, *Dynamite Club*, 170.

13. APP, Ba 1500, Listes et état des menées anarchistes, 1894–1899; "Les anarchistes," *L'Eclair*, March 17, 1894; Sonn, *Anarchism and Cultural Politics*, 245.

14. Merriman, *Dynamite Club*, 170.

15. Merriman, *Dynamite Club*, 154–57.

16. Frederic S. Zuckerman, *The Tsarist Secret Police Abroad: Policing Europe in a Modernising World* (New York: Palgrave Macmillan, 2003), 12–14.

17. Isaac Land, "Men with the Faces of Brutes," in Land, *Enemies of Humanity*, 128–30.

18. Jensen, *Battle against Anarchist Terrorism*, 173.

19. Turrado Vidal, *Policía y Delincuencia*, 75.

20. Merriman, *Dynamite Club*, 171–72.

21. *Le Soleil*, May 6, 1894, in Merriman, *Dynamite Club*, 171.

22. *Le Journal*, February 19, 1894, in Maitron, *Le Mouvement anarchiste*, 246–47.

23. "L'action anarchiste," *Le Matin*, February 28, 1894.

24. "L'action anarchiste."

25. Merriman, *Dynamite Club*, 160–72.

26. Merriman, *Dynamite Club*, 180–81.

27. Merriman, *Dynamite Club*, 184–86.

28. Mitchell Abidor, ed., *Death to Bourgeois Society: The Propagandists of the Deed* (Oakland: PM Press, 2015), 81.

29. Sonn, *Anarchism and Cultural Politics*, 22.

30. Daniel Guérin, ed., *No Gods No Masters: An Anthology of Anarchism*, book 2, trans. Paul Sharkey (Oakland: AK Press, 1998), 41–42.

31. *La Petite République*, May 7, 1894, in Merriman, *Dynamite Club*, 189.

32. Dalmau, *El Procés de Montjuïc*, 188–90.

33. Dalmau, *El Procés de Montjuïc*, 188–92, 195–96.

34. Sempau, *Los victimarios*, 279; Montseny, *El proceso*, 37, 41–42.

35. Montseny, *El proceso*, 47.

36. Dalmau, *El Procés de Montjuïc*, 156, 179–80, 191–92; *El Nuevo Régimen*, December 16, 1893; Montseny, *El proceso*, 23–25; Caballé y Clos, *Barcelona de antaño*, 88.

37. "A muerte," *El País*, May 21, 1894.

38. "Profecías sobre el anarquismo," *El País*, November 26, 1893.

39. Álvarez Junco, *El Emperador*, 150, 146.

40. Dalmau, *El Procés de Montjuïc*, 202–5; Álvarez Junco, *El Emperador*, 149.

41. Dalmau, *El Procés de Montjuïc*, 206.

42. Montseny, *El Proceso*, 20–23; "Los anarquistas," *El Imparcial*, May 21, 1894.

43. Dalmau, *El Procés de Montjuïc*, 209; "Fusilamiento de los anarquistas," *El País*, May 22, 1894; "Los anarquistas," *El Imparcial*, May 22, 1894.

44. Merriman, *Dynamite Club*, 191.

45. Álvarez Junco, *El Emperador*, 148.

46. Merriman, *Dynamite Club*, 194–99.

47. Maitron, *Le Mouvement anarchiste*, 247–48; Tuchman, "Anarchism in France," 455–56.

48. AN, F7 12511, assassinat du Président Sadi Carnot; Woodcock, *Anarchism*, 313.

49. Varennes, *De Ravachol a Caserio*, 260.

50. AN, F7 12512, Mesures spécialement édictées contre les anarchistes étrangers.

51. Nunzio Pernicone and Fraser M. Ottanelli, *Assassins against the Old Order: Italian Anarchist Violence in Fin de Siècle Europe* (Urbana: University of Illinois Press, 2018), 67–72.

52. Maitron, *Le Mouvement anarchiste*, 248–49; Merriman, *Dynamite Club*, 206.

53. Pernicone and Ottanelli, *Assassins against the Old Order*, 72.

54. Avilés, "Propaganda por el hecho y regicidio," 9.

55. Varennes, *De Ravachol a Caserio*, 355–56; Sonn, *Anarchism and Cultural Politics*, 21.

56. Dalmau, *El Procés de Montjuïc*, 185.

57. González Calleja, *La Razón de la Fuerza*, 282.

58. Merriman, *Dynamite Club*, 67.

59. Sonn, *Anarchism and Cultural Politics*, 26; Maitron, *Le Mouvement anarchiste*, 256; Bantman, *French Anarchists in London*, 25–26.

60. AN, F7 12504, report of April 23, 1894.

61. "Reflexiones saludables," *La Dinastía*, August 30, 1894.

62. Cited in *La Vanguardia*, October 9, 1894.

63. Miguel Sawa, "La conversión de Salvador," *El País*, August 29, 1894.

64. Miguel Sawa, "La conversión," *El País*, September 29, 1894.

65. Álvarez Junco, *El Emperador*, 148–49.

66. *El País*, October 20 and 22, 1894.

67. "Crónica local," *La Dinastía*, October 19, 1894.

68. Cited in Sawa, "La conversión," *El País*, September 29, 1894.

69. "Salvador en Capilla," *La Correspondencia de España*, November 21, 1894; ACA, Santiago Salvador, Sentencias criminales, 186.

70. "El anarquista Salvador," *El Liberal*, November 21, 1894; Dalmau, *El Procés de Montjuïc*, 231–32.

71. "El anarquista Salvador," *El Liberal*, November 21, 1894; "El anarquista Salvador," *El País*, November 21, 1894.

72. "Salvador en Capilla" and "Ejecución de Salvador," *La Correspondencia de España*, November 21–22, 1894; "El anarquista Salvador," *El Liberal*, November 21, 1894; "El anarquista Salvador," *El País*, November 21, 1894; "Santiago Salvador en Capilla," *La Vanguardia*, November 21, 1894.

73. "El anarquista," *El Liberal*, November 21, 1894.

74. "Santiago Salvador," *La Vanguardia*, November 21, 1894.

75. "El anarquista Salvador," *El Liberal*, November 22, 1894.

76. "Ejecución de Salvador," *La Correspondencia de España*, November 22, 1894; "El anarquista," *El Liberal*, November 22, 1894.

77. "Desenllas de una tragedia," *La Campana de Gracia*, November 24, 1894.

78. "Contra el reporterismo," *La Época*, November 27, 1894.

79. Dalmau, *El Procés de Montjuïc*, 244.

6. The Anarchist Inquisition

1. Urales, *Mi Vida*, 1:80–81.

2. Dolors Marín and Salvador Palomar, *Els Montseny Mañé: un laboratori de les idees* (Reus: Les veus del temps, 2010), 31; Montseny, *El proceso*; J. Montseny, *Consideraciones sobre el hecho y muerte de Pallás* (La Coruña: La Gutenburg, 1893).

3. Urales, *Mi Vida*, 1:82–83; Marian Roca, *Records de la meva vida* (Reus: Assaig, 1979), 16.

4. Urales, *Mi Vida*, 1:89–102.

5. Dalmau, *El Procés de Montjuïc*, 254–55; Anderson, *Under Three Flags*, 155.

6. Kaplan, *Red City*, 31–34.

7. "Otro atentado anarquista," *El País*, June 9, 1896.

8. Dalmau, *El Procés de Montjuïc*, 255–57.

9. "Atentado anarquista," *La Época*, June 8, 1896.

10. Biblioteca de Catalunya (hereafter BC), Fondo Pere Coromines, 2637, doc. 23.

11. Álvarez Junco, *El Emperador*, 151; Lawrence Tone, *War and Genocide in Cuba, 1895–1898* (Chapel Hill: University of North Carolina Press, 2006), 230; Dalmau, *El Procés de Montjuïc*, 257; Esenwein, *Anarchist Ideology*, 191; Jensen, *Battle against Anarchist Terrorism*, 32.

12. BC, Fondo Pere Coromines, 2637, doc. 23; "El atentado anarquista," *El País*, June 13, 1896.

13. Herrerín López, *Anarquía*, 148–49.

14. Kaplan lists forty (*Red City*, 34); Núñez Florencio lists forty-two, including some who died shortly thereafter (*El terrorismo anarquista*, 57); Esenwein lists forty-five (*Anarchist Ideology*, 191); Dalmau lists fifty (*El Procés de Montjuïc*, 249); and Herrerin López lists 70 (*Anarquía*, 129). See also *El Imparcial*, June 8, 1896; *Las Noticias*, June 8, 1896.

15. Herrerín López, *Anarquía*, 133; "Otro atentado anarquista," *El País*, June 9, 1896; Dalmau, *El Procés de Montjuïc*, 250.

16. "Crimen anarquista," *El Imparcial*, June 9, 1896; *El Noticiero Universal*, June 11, 1896.

17. "Suspensión de garantias," *Las Noticias*, June 9, 1896.

18. "El entierro," *Las Noticias*, June 9, 1896; "Congreso," *El Imparcial*, June 9, 1896; "Crónica local," *La Dinastía*, June 8, 1896; "Anarquismo indómito" and "Los domadores," *La Época*, June 8–9, 1896.

19. "La propaganda anarquista," *La Época*, June 11, 1896.

20. "Ampliación," *Las Noticias*, June 8, 1896.

21. Cited in *Las Noticias*, June 13, 1896.

22. "Notas sueltas," *La Dinastía*, June 12, 1896.

23. Cited in *Las Noticias*, June 17, 1896.

24. "En estado de anarquía," *El País*, June 9, 1896.

25. "Asuntos del día," *La Dinastía*, June 10, 1896.

26. "Asuntos," *La Dinastía*, June 10, 1896.

27. "Contra la inhumanidad," *El Imparcial*, June 9, 1896.

28. From *El Día*, cited in *La Época*, June 9, 1896.

29. "Otro atentado anarquista," *El País*, June 8, 1896; "En estado de anarquía," *El País*, June 9, 1896.

30. "Ecos de Madrid," *La Dinastía*, June 11, 1896.

31. "Crimen anarquista," *El Imparcial*, June 9, 1896.

32. F. Pí y Arsuaga, "Los anarquistas," *El Nuevo Régimen*, June 13, 1896.

33. "Perder la cabeza," *El Socialista*, June 19, 1896.

34. "Indignación general," *El Imparcial*, June 11, 1896.

35. "¡Venganza!," *El Motín*, June 13, 1896.

36. AHN, Gobernación, 2A exp. 15, law of September 2, 1896.

37. Herrerín López, *Anarquía*, 136–37.

38. Pí y Arsuaga, "Los anarquistas."

39. Dalmau, *El Procés de Montjuïc*, 279.

40. "Crimen anarquista," *El Imparcial*, June 10, 1896; *Las Noticias*, June 11, 1896.

41. "Revista semanal," *El Corsario*, June 11, 1896.

42. "La nueva ley," and "Murmullos barceloneses," *El Corsario*, June 25, 1896.

43. "Revista semanal," *El Corsario*, June 25, 1896.

44. National Archives (hereafter NA), FO 72/2013, British Consul to Barcelona to Secretary of State for Foreign Affairs, June 11, 1896.

45. Dalmau, *El Procés de Montjuïc*, 283; *La Campaña de "El Progreso" en favor de las víctimas del proceso de Montjuich* (Barcelona: Tarascó, Viladot y Cuesta Impresores, 1897–98), 35–36.

46. The commissioner claimed that some "foreign suspects have already left Barcelona," including "Angiolillo." Archives du Ministère des Affaires Étrangers (hereafter AD), La Courneuve, Correspondance politique, 1871–1896, "Espagne," vol. 8, p. 10.

47. Herrerín López, *Anarquía*, 133.

48. Urales, *Mi Vida*, 1:104–5.

49. Íñiguez, *Enciclopedia histórica*, 1676.

50. Fernando Tarrida del Mármol, *Les Inquisiteurs d'Espagne: Montjuich, Cuba, Philippines* (Paris: Stock, 1897), 22–25.

51. Tarrida del Mármol, *Les Inquisiteurs d'Espagne*, 25.

52. Urales, *Mi Vida*, 1:108.

53. Tarrida del Mármol, *Les Inquisiteurs d'Espagne*, 26.

54. Tarrida del Mármol, *Les Inquisiteurs d'Espagne*, 26.

55. María Amalia Pradas Baena, *Teresa Claramunt: La "virgen roja" barcelonesa, biografía y escritos* (Barcelona: Virus Editorial, 2006), 41–46; Íñiguez, *Enciclopedia histórica*, 403–4.

56. "Notas sueltas," *La Dinastía*, June 16, 1896.

57. Sempau, *Los victimarios*, 381–82.

58. *La Campaña de "El Progreso,"* 112–16.

59. *La Campaña de "El Progreso,"* 120–21, 503–6.

60. Herrerín López, *Anarquía*, 134–35.

61. *La Campaña de "El Progreso,"* 506.

62. *La Campaña de "El Progreso,"* 116, 507.

63. Sempau, *Los victimarios*, 382.

64. *La Campaña de "El Progreso,"* 117–18.

65. Urales, *Mi Vida*, 1:109–10.

66. Urales, *Mi Vida*, 1:109–10.

67. Sempau, *Los victimarios*, 382–83.

68. Internationaal Instituut voor Sociale Geschiedenis (hereafter IISG), Salud Borrás Papers, Martín Borrás to Francisco Saperas, May 7, 1894.

69. Dalmau, "Martí Borràs i Jover," 18–19.

70. Íñiguez, *Enciclopedia histórica*, 134, 1595.

71. *La Campaña de "El Progreso,"* 66–69.

72. *La Campaña de "El Progreso,"* 66–69.

73. *La Campaña de "El Progreso,"* 66–69.

74. Dalmau, *El Procés de Montjuïc*, 291, 294, 328; ANC, 217, caja 1, Registry, June 12, 1896.

75. Dalmau, *El Procés de Montjuïc*, 312.

76. *La Campaña de "El Progreso,"* 511; ANC, 217, caja 1, Registry, September 23, 1896.

77. Dalmau, *El Procés de Montjuïc*, 277.

78. *La Campaña de "El Progreso,"* 38.

79. Herrerín López, *Anarquía*, 150; *La Campaña de "El Progreso,"* 71.

80. *La Campaña de "El Progreso,"* 22–23.

81. *La Campaña de "El Progreso,"* 4–6, 23–25, 69–70, 127–28, 143; Íñiguez, *Enciclopedia histórica*, 1667.

82. *La Campaña de "El Progreso,"* 69–70.

83. Urales, *Mi Vida*, 1:111.

84. Urales, *Mi Vida*, 1:111.

85. There are discrepancies in the accounts regarding whether Montseny arrived at Montjuich before or after Suñé. Urales, *Mi Vida*, 1:110–12; *La Campaña de "El Progreso,"* 3–16.

86. Urales, *Mi Vida*, 1:112.

87. José Carlos Mainel, "Apuntes junto al ensayo," in Jesús Gómez, ed., *El ensayo español*, 1: *Los orígenes: siglos XV a XVII* (Barcelona: Crítica, 1996).

88. Carlos Serrano, "El 'nacimiento de los intelectuales': algunos replanteamientos," *Ayer* 40 (2000): 20.

89. Marie Laffranque, "Juan Montseny y los intelectuales: 1898–1905," *Anthropos* 78 (1987): 44.

90. Urales, *Mi Vida*, 1:114–17.

91. BC, Fondo Pere Coromines, 2637, 21; AGP, Reinados, Alfonso XIII, 13104, 1, exp. 1, Ministro de la Gobernación to Ministro de Estado, September 8, 1896.

92. Of the thirty-eight prisoners that Dalmau identified as republican, twenty-four were arrested in August 1896, twenty of them on August 18. Emili Gili was accidentally arrested on August 18 because they confused him with his republican brother. Dalmau, El Procés de Montjuïc, 285–338; Las Noticias, August 19, 1896.

93. According to Coromines's lawyer, "republican politicians were prisoners as a precautionary measure of the Government, against the fear of disturbances, because of the war in Cuba." Amadeu Hurtado, Quaranta anys d'advocat: història del meu temps, vol. 1 (Esplugues de Llobregat: Edicions Ariel, 1968), 23–42.

94. La Campaña de "El Progreso," 16–128.

95. Dalmau, El Procés de Montjuïc, 359.

96. Sempau, Los victimarios, 383–87.

97. Urales, Mi Vida, 1:120.

98. Tarrida del Mármol, Les Inquisiteurs d'Espagne, 51–54; Urales, Mi Vida, 1:120–21; Dalmau, El Procés de Montjuïc, 330.

99. Urales, Mi Vida, 1:120–21.

100. Tarrida del Mármol, Les Inquisiteurs d'Espagne, 30.

101. Urales, Mi Vida, 1:131. Dalmau is skeptical of Montseny's account (El Procés de Montjuïc, 451). Abelló calls his story "bizarre." Teresa Abelló i Güell, Les relacions internacionals de l'anarquisme català (1881–1914) (Barcelona: Edicions 62, 1987), 159.

7. The Return of Torquemada

1. Heather McCrea, "Tentative Testimonies: The Aztecs, Conquest, and the Black Legend," in Louise A. Breen, ed., Converging Worlds: Communities and Cultures in Colonial America (New York: Routledge, 2012), 53.

2. Margaret R. Greer et al., eds., Rereading the Black Legend: The Discourse of Religious and Racial Difference in the Renaissance Empires (Chicago: University of Chicago Press, 2007), 6.

3. Mario Chandler, "Out of Africa: Shifting Places and Faces in Olaudah Equiano's Interesting Narrative," in Joanna Boampong, ed., In and Out of Africa: Exploring Afro-Hispanic, Luso-Brazilian, and Latin American Connections (Newcastle upon Tyne: Cambridge Scholars, 2012), 114.

4. Greer et al., Rereading the Black Legend, 1; Julián Juderías, La leyenda negra: estudios acerca del concepto de España en el extranjero (Barcelona: Arluce, 1914).

5. "La prensa de gran circulación," El Movimiento católico, June 10, 1897; "Dos leyendas," "Nuestro 'affaire,'" and "El suceso del día," La Época, April 20, May 17, and May 22, 1899; "Por el bolsillo," "La carta de Carlos VII," and "Heroes y martires," El Correo Español, April 27, November 17, and December 21, 1899; "Desenlace feliz," El Siglo futuro, June 6, 1899.

6. "El proceso de Montjuich," El Imparcial, June 25, 1899.

7. Charles Malato, "Memoires d'un libertaire," Le Peuple, March 6, 1938.

8. F. Tarrida del Marmol, "Un mois dans les prisons d'Espagne," La Revue Blanche, October 15, 1896.

9. Tarrida del Mármol, Les Inquisiteurs d'Espagne, 32.

10. "Dans les prisons espagnoles," L'Intransigeant, November 27–29, 1896.

11. *La Campaña de "El Progreso,"* 271–72; "El proceso de los anarquistas," *El País*, November 29, 1896; "Más sobre el proceso," *El Nuevo Régimen*, November 28, 1896; "Dans les prisons," *L'Intransigeant*, November 27, 1896.

12. Urales, *Mi Vida*, 1:138–142.

13. Urales, *Mi Vida*, 1:142; *El País*, January–May 1897.

14. Federico Urales, "Por humanidad," *El País*, January 5, 1897.

15. Urales, *Mi Vida*, 1:146.

16. "Noticias," *El País*, November 21, 1896.

17. "Por amor á la justicia," *El País*, December 1, 1896.

18. "Por amor á la justicia," *El País*, December 2, 1896.

19. "El proceso de los anarquistas," *El País*, December 14, 1896.

20. Urales, *Mi Vida*, 1:157–58.

21. Paul A. Kramer, *The Blood of Government: Race, Empire, the United States, and the Philippines* (Chapel Hill: University of North Carolina Press, 2006), 76–81.

22. Urales, *Mi Vida*, 1:196–98; "Deportados en Fernando Poo," *El País*, March 1, 1897.

23. Reports of abuse were printed in *Las Dominicales del Libre Pensamiento* and *La Unión Republicana* in December. Dalmau, *El Procés de Montjuïc*, 459.

24. Urales, *Mi Vida*, 1:128, 135.

25. "Le Meeting," *L'Intransigeant*, December 14, 1896; Tarrida del Mármol, *Les Inquisiteurs d'Espagne*, 166–72.

26. "Le Meeting."

27. Tarrida del Mármol, *Les Inquisiteurs d'Espagne*, 168, 170–71.

28. Archivo General Militar de Madrid (hereafter AGM), legajo 157, Captain General to Minister of War, December 13, 1896.

29. Dalmau, *El Procés de Montjuïc*, 458–59.

30. "El 'meeting' de anoche," *La Época*, June 25, 1899.

31. Capellán de Miguel and Garrido Martín, "'Los intérpretes de la opinión.'"

32. Zuckerman, *Tsarist Secret Police Abroad*, 134; Barry Hollingsworth, "The Society of Friends of Russian Freedom: English Liberals and Russian Socialists, 1890–1917," *Oxford Slavonic Papers* (1970), 52.

33. Zuckerman, *Tsarist Secret Police Abroad*, 136–38.

34. "El proceso de los anarquistas," *El País*, December 12, 1896.

35. "Le drame espagnole," *l'Intransigeant*, December 13, 1896.

36. Dalmau, *El Procés de Montjuïc*, 404.

37. Herrerín López, *Anarquía*, 139–40; Dalmau, *El Procés de Montjuïc*, 403.

38. Herrerín López, *Anarquía*, 141–42; Dalmau, *El Procés de Montjuïc*, 407; "Informaciones," *La Época*, December 23, 1896.

39. Four prisoners got twenty years, fourteen got a little over nineteen years, thirteen got a little over nine years, thirty-five got a little over eight years, and twelve were absolved. "Los anarquistas de Barcelona," *La Dinastía*, January 3, 1897. Coromines got eight years. Dalmau, *El Procés de Montjuïc*, 408; Herrerín López, *Anarquía*, 142–43.

40. "The Anarchists of Barcelona," *Freedom*, April 1897.

41. "'Meeting' socialista en Madrid," *El Socialista*, December 25, 1896.

42. Joseph E. Wisan, *The Cuban Crisis as Reflected in the New York Press (1895–1898)* (New York: Octagon Books, 1965), 66–67, 88.

43. Richard Gott, *Cuba: A New History* (New Haven, CT: Yale University Press, 2005), 93; William R. Everdell, *The First Moderns: Profiles in the Origins of Twentieth-Century Thought* (Chicago: University of Chicago Press, 1997), 118.

44. Tone, *War and Genocide*, 113–14, 223; Ada Ferrer, *Insurgent Cuba: Race, Nation, and Revolution, 1868–1898* (Chapel Hill: University of North Carolina Press, 1999), 152.

45. Tone, *War and Genocide*, 121, 164.

46. Wisan, *Cuban Crisis*, 153–54, 194–95.

47. Tone, *War and Genocide*, 219.

48. Wisan, *Cuban Crisis*, 220–22; *Les Temps nouveaux*, December 1896–January 1897; *L'Intransigeant*, December 14 and 30, 1896; Tarrida del Mármol, *Les Inquisiteurs d'Espagne*, 179.

49. "Telegrammes et correspondances," *Le Figaro*, October 16, 1896; "Cuba libre," *L'Intransigeant*, October 16, 1896; "Los filibusteros en Francia," *El País*, November 3, 1896.

50. "Correspondance et communications," *Les Temps nouveaux*, December 26, 1896–January 1, 1897; "Le meeting de la Salle Pétrelle," *L'Intransigeant*, December 31, 1896; Tarrida del Mármol, *Les Inquisiteurs d'Espagne*, 177.

51. "Correspondence," *Les Temps nouveaux*, December 26, 1896–January 1, 1897.

52. Tone, *War and Genocide*, 92, 173–74.

53. "Manifestación anárquico-filibustera en Paris," *La Época*, January 6, 1897.

54. "Réunions et conférenciers," *Les Temps nouveaux*, January 16–22, 1897; "Le Meeting du Tivoli-Waux-Hall," *L'Intransigeant*, January 7, 1897.

55. "Le Meeting du Tivoli-Waux-Hall"; Cosmo, "Les arrestations d'hier," *L'Intransigeant*, January 8, 1897; Tarrida del Mármol, *Les Inquisiteurs d'Espagne*, 172–76; *Freeman's Journal*, January 5, 1897; *The Standard*, January 6, 1897; Avilés, *Francisco Ferrer*, 77; Dalmau, *El Procés de Montjuïc*, 477; APP, Ba 138, Explosions en Espagne; "Reunión anarquista en Paris," *La Época*, January 6, 1897.

56. "El meeting anarquista," *La Dinastía*, January 7, 1897.

57. "Anarquistas franceses," *El País*, January 8, 1897; "La réunion de la Salle du Commerce" and "Cuba libre," *L'Intransigeant*, January 15 and 24, 1897.

58. "Contre les tortionnaires," *L'Intransigeant*, January 20, 1897; Tarrida del Mármol, *Les Inquisiteurs d'Espagne*, 181–82; AHN, Asuntos exteriores, Sección histórica, 2750, various telegrams from the Spanish legation in the Hague from 1897.

59. Tarrida del Mármol, *Les Inquisiteurs d'Espagne*, 33–36, 165.

60. "Protest Meeting in London," *Freedom*, February 1897.

61. "Protest Meeting in London"; Woodcock, *Anarchism*, 202, 216; Bantman, *French Anarchists in London*, 15.

62. F. M. Leventhal, *The Last Dissenter: H. N. Brailsford and His World* (Oxford: Oxford University Press, 1985), 52.

63. *Free Russia*, November 1, 1892.

64. *Free Russia*, February 1 and March 1, 1894; Hollingsworth, "Society of Friends," 49–50.

65. Anat Vernitski, "Russian Revolutionaries and English Sympathizers in 1890s London: The Case of Olive Garnett and Sergei Stepniak," *Journal of European Studies* 35, no. 3 (2005): 303, 307.

66. Hollingsworth, "Society of Friends," 51–54; Emma Goldman, *Emma Goldman: A Documentary History of the American Years*, vol. 2: *Making Speech Free, 1902–1909*, ed. Candace Falk, Barry Pateman, and Jessica Moran (Berkeley: University of California Press, 2005), 555–56.

67. "The Anarchists of Barcelona," *Freedom*, April 1897; *Morning Post*, February 23, 1897. Days later the British consul in Barcelona asked whether British subjects were imprisoned. He was told that none were. *Edinburgh Evening News*, February 25, 1897.

68. Davide Rodogno, *Against Massacre: Humanitarian Interventions in the Ottoman Empire, 1815–1914: The Emergence of a European Concept and International Practice* (Princeton, NJ: Princeton University Press, 2012), 7.

69. Susan Denene Hinley, "Charlotte Wilson: Anarchist, Fabian, and Feminist" (PhD diss., Stanford University, 1987), 300–301.

70. George Woodcock, "Introduction," in Peter Kropotkin, *The Conquest of Bread* (Montreal: Black Rose Books, 1990), xiii–xiv.

71. N. F. Dryhurst and Robert Lynd, *Nationalities and Subject Races: Report of Conference Held in Caxton Hall, Westminster, June 28–30, 1910* (London: P. S. King & Son, 1911); Gerard Keown, *First of the Small Nations: The Beginnings of Irish Foreign Policy in the Inter-War Years, 1919–1932* (Oxford: Oxford University Press, 2016), 27.

72. Bass, *Freedom's Battle*, 56–77.

73. Rodogno, *Against Massacre*, 188–209.

74. Bass, *Freedom's Battle*, 317.

75. *L'Intransigeant*, February 27 and April 23, 1897.

76. *L'Intransigeant*, February–March 1897.

77. "Les manifestations d'hier soir," *L'Intransigeant*, February 19, 1897.

78. "Le meeting du Tivoli-Waux-Hall," *L'Intransigeant*, February 24, 1897.

79. George R. Whyte, *The Dreyfus Affair: A Chronological History* (New York: Palgrave Macmillan, 2005), 91.

80. James F. Brennan, *The Reflection of the Dreyfus Affair in the European Press, 1897–1899* (New York: Peter Lang, 1998), 31; "Le traitre Dreyfus," *L'Intransigeant*, February 21, March 2, and July 31, 1897.

81. *El País*, December 30 and 31, 1896, January 24 and 28, February 7 and 16, 1897.

82. "La opinión europea," *El País*, January 29, 1897.

83. "Los Presos en Montjuich," *El País*, March 16, 1897.

84. "Noticias," *El País*, March 26, 1897.

85. "Cruel é ilegal," *El País*, March 29, 1897.

86. "The Anarchists of Barcelona," *Freedom*, March 1897; "En Espagne," *L'Intransigeant*, March 22, 1897.

87. "Anarchists of Barcelona"; "Correspondance et communications," *Les Temps nouveaux*, May 1–7, 1897; AHN, Asuntos exteriores, Sección histórica, 2750, Spanish ambassador to Berlin, March 4, 1897.

88. Gustav Landauer, *Revolution and Other Writings: A Political Reader*, ed. and trans. Gabriel Kuhn (Oakland: PM Press, 2010), 22.

89. "The Anarchists of Barcelona," *Freedom*, March and April 1897; Paul Avrich, *An American Anarchist: The Life of Voltairine de Cleyre* (Princeton, NJ: Princeton University Press, 1978), 112.

90. "Por la propaganda" and "En pro de la revisión del proceso de Montjuich," *La Nueva Humanidad*, June 1 and August 1, 1899; *El Rebelde* (Buenos Aires), July 16 and

August 14, 1899; "Pueblo muerto" and "Solidaridad para las víctimas de la inquisición española," *El Nuevo Ideal*, December 14, 1899, and May 23, 1900; "La inquisición en España," *La Verdad*, March 6, 1898; *La Inquisición fin de siglo* (Buenos Aires: Librería Sociológica, 1899).

91. Cosmo, "Les Bêtes féroces de Madrid," *L'Intransigeant*, April 23, 1897.

92. Herrerín López, *Anarquía*, 143; "El proceso anarquista," *El País*, April 21, 1897.

93. "Proceso anarquista," *El País*, May 2, 1897; Dalmau, *El Procés de Montjuïc*, 411–12.

94. "Los anarquistas," *El País*, May 4, 1897; "Los anarquistas en capilla," *La Correspondencia de España*, May 4, 1897.

95. "Los anarquistas de Barcelona," *El Imparcial*, May 4, 1897.

96. Herrerín López, *Anarquía*, 144; IISG, Salud Borrás Papers, Mas to Borrás, December 29, 1896.

97. Sempau, *Los Victimarios*, 389.

98. "Los anarquistas," *El Imparcial*, May 4, 1897.

99. Sempau, *Los Victimarios*, 389; Teresa Claramunt, "Recuerdos," *Suplemento a la Revista Blanca*, May 19, 1900.

100. "The Tortured Spaniards," *Freedom*, August 1897.

101. "El final de una trajedia," *El País*, May 5, 1897; "Los anarquistas de Barcelona," *La Correspondencia de España*, May 5, 1897; "La ejecución," *El Imparcial*, May 5, 1897; "Ejecución de los anarquistas," *La Vanguardia*, May 5, 1897; "Tortured Spaniards"; *Daily News*, May 5, 1897.

8. Germinal

1. "Mass Meeting," *Freedom*, July 1897; "Le meeting de Londres," *L'Intransigeant*, June 1, 1897.

2. *El País*, May 6 and 23, June 10 and 28, and July 6, 7, and 13, 1897.

3. "Le meeting," *L'Intransigeant*, June 1, 1897; Tarrida del Mármol, *Les Inquisiteurs d'Espagne*.

4. Similar pamphlets existed in German, Dutch, Bohemian, and French. Brooklyn's *El Despertar* published a special issue on Spanish abuses. "The Anarchists," *Freedom*, July 1897; NA, FO 72/2048, "Revival of the Inquisition"; "Le meeting," *L'Intransigeant*, June 1, 1897.

5. AHN, Asuntos exteriores, Sección histórica, 2750, report from Italian ambassador, August 11, 1897; Francesco Tamburini, "Michele Angiolillo el anarquista que asesinó a Cánovas del Castillo," *Historia* 16 (1997): 28–29; Pernicone and Ottanelli, *Assassins against the Old Order*, 91–92.

6. "El asesino de Cánovas," *El Imparcial*, August 12, 1897; Abel Paz et al., *La Barcelona rebelde: guía de una ciudad silenciada* (Barcelona: Octaedro, 2008), 253; Tamburini, "Michele Angiolillo el anarquista," 30; Pernicone and Ottanelli, *Assassins against the Old Order*, 92.

7. Esenwein, *Anarchist Ideology*, 190; González Calleja, *La razón de la fuerza*, 293.

8. Archives diplomatiques du Ministère des Affaires Étrangères, La Courneuve (hereafter AD), Correspondance politique et commerciale, series A, "Nouvelle série," vol. 8, "Question catalane." He was on the Parisian *sûreté*'s list of dangerous anarchists in May 1896. APP, Ba 1511, Affaires liées a l'anarchisme en Espagne.

9. Esenwein, *Anarchist Ideology*, 193. The French consul to Barcelona listed Angiolillo among anarchists who escaped Spain after the bombing. "Question catalane."

10. Tamburini, "Michele Angiolillo el anarquista," 30.

11. González Calleja, *La razón de la fuerza*, 290; Herrerín López, *Anarquía*, 168; Dalmau, *El Procés de Montjuïc*, 373.

12. González Calleja, *La razón de la fuerza*, 293.

13. Tamburini, "Michele Angiolillo el anarquista," 30.

14. Tamburini, "Michele Angiolillo el anarquista," 30; Rudolf Rocker, *En la borrasca: años de destierro*, trans. Diego A. De Santillan (Buenos Aires: Editorial Tupac, 1949), 62.

15. Rocker, *En la borrasca*, 62.

16. Avilés, *Francisco Ferrer*, 158; Tamburini, "Michele Angiolillo el anarquista," 30. Rocker lists Cayetano Oller as having participated in this meeting, but he arrived in England later. Rocker seems to have confused Cayetano with Juan Bautista Oller. Rocker, *En la borrasca*, 63.

17. Rocker, *En la borrasca*, 63.

18. González Calleja, *La Razón de la fuerza*, 293; Herrerín López, *Anarquía*, 158.

19. Luis Bonafoux, *Betances* (San Juan: Instituto de Cultural Puertorriqueña, 1970), xx. Anderson speculates that this story was concocted by Betances to make himself feel important. Anderson, *Under Three Flags*, 192.

20. APP, Ba 894, Projets d'attentats anarchistes, 1893–1904 et 1906–1914, report from informant, August 17, 1897.

21. Montseny claimed he was funded by Betances and Rochefort. Urales, *Mi Vida*, 1:229. Coromines claimed he was funded by "Rochefort and the insurgent Cubans." Pere Coromines, *Diaris i records I, Els anys de Joventut i El Procés de Montjuïc* (Barcelona: Cural, 1974), 226. Bonafoux claimed he was funded by Betances (*Betances*, xx). Others point to Malato or Betances. Tamburini, "Michele Angiolillo el anarquista," 34. In 1907 Juan de la Cierva implicated Ferrer. This accusation seems to have more to do with the suspicion shrouding Ferrer after the attempt on Alfonso XIII. González Calleja, *La Razón de la Fuerza*, 293–94. The Spanish embassy in London implicated Lorenzo Portet. AHN, Asuntos exteriores, Sección histórica, 2755, Spanish embassy in London, January 28, 1899. Piqueras denies that Angiolillo's actions were part of a larger plot. José A. Piqueras, *Cánovas y la derecha española: Del magnicidio a los neocon* (Barcelona: Ediciones Peninsula, 2008), 72. Avilés doubts that the assassination was "a purely individual initiative." Avilés, *Francisco Ferrer*, 80.

22. Francesco Tamburini, "Michele Angiolillo e l'assassinio di Cánovas del Castillo," *Spagna contemporanea* 9 (1996): 118; Tamburini, "Michele Angiolillo el anarquista," 35.

23. "Política del día," *El País*, May 28, 1897; "Lettre des acquittés de Montjuich," *Le Libertaire*, July 9–15, 1897.

24. "Contra la inhumanidad" and "Los anarquistas de Barcelona," *El Imparcial*, June 9, 1896, and May 5, 1897.

25. "La deportación de los anarquistas," *El Imparcial*, May 6, 1897.

26. AD, Correspondence politique et commerciale, series A, "Nouvelle série," vol. 10, "Agitation révolutionnaire," 47–48, 53; González Calleja, *La razón de la fuerza*, 287.

27. AHN, Asuntos exteriores, Sección histórica, 2750, report on deportations, July 24, 1897.

28. González Calleja, *La razón de la fuerza*, 288; NA, FO 72/2035, Wolff to Salisbury, July 30, 1897; for profiles of passengers on the *Isla de Luzón* and correspondence between the Home Office and Foreign Office (July 17, 1897), see NA, HO 144/587/B2840C; AGA, Asuntos exteriores, Embajada en Londres, 7011, correspondence between Conde de Casa Valencia and the Ministro de Estado, July 1897.

29. González Calleja, *La razón de la fuerza*, 288.

30. "The Spanish Anarchists," *Times*, May 11, 1897.

31. González Calleja, *La razón de la fuerza*, 288.

32. Urales, *Mi Vida*, 1:211. Urales writes "God Save the King" but he misremembers because Queen Victoria sat on the throne.

33. "Lo que dice Cánovas," *El País*, July 29, 1897.

34. González Calleja, *La razón de la fuerza*, 288–89.

35. "The Anarchists of Barcelona," *Times*, July 26, 1897; NA, FO 72/2034, report from minister of Sweden and Norway, June 28, 1897.

36. "The Anarchists of Barcelona," *Times*, August 7, 1897.

37. AD, Correspondence politique et commerciale, series A, "Nouvelle série," vol. 1, "Dossier général 1897–1900," 93.

38. Joseph Perry, "Spain and the Torture," *Times*, August 3, 1897.

39. AGA, Asuntos exteriores, Embajada en Londres, 7016, correspondence between the Ministro de Estado and Conde de Casa Valencia, August 23, 1897; "The Tortured," *Freedom*, August 1897; *Daily Chronicle*, July 27, 1897.

40. Perry, "Spain and the Torture."

41. *Times*, August 11, 1897.

42. "The Tortured," *Freedom*, August 1897.

43. "The Spanish Anarchists," *Times*, July 30, 1897.

44. Urales, *Mi Vida*, 1:212–16; AGA, Asuntos exteriores, Embajada en Londres, 7011, correspondence between the Ministro de Estado and Conde de Casa Valencia, July and August 1897.

45. Bantman, *French Anarchists in London*; Pietro di Paola, *Knights Errant of Anarchy: London and the Italian Anarchist Diaspora (1880–1917)* (Liverpool: Liverpool University Press, 2013).

46. Enrique A. Sanabria, *Republicanism and Anticlerical Nationalism in Spain* (New York: Palgrave Macmillan, 2009), 4.

47. José Nakens, "De mis recuerdos," *El Imparcial*, October 24, 1901.

48. Nakens, "De mis recuerdos."

49. Piqueras, *Cánovas y la derecha española*, 49.

50. "Relato del crimen," *El Imparcial*, August 9, 1897; AGP, Reinados, Alfonso XIII, 13104, 1, exp. 1, Ministro de Ultramar, August 8, 1897.

51. "Más sobre el asesinato del señor Cánovas," *El Imparcial*, August 9, 1897.

52. "El asesinato de Cánovas," *El Imparcial*, August 10, 1897.

53. "Desde Santa Águeda," *El Imparcial*, August 10, 1897.

54. Piqueras, *Cánovas y la derecha española*, 13–14; "Asesinato de Cánovas," *El País*, August 9, 1897; "Asesinato de D. Antonio Cánovas del Castillo," *El Imparcial*, August 9, 1897.

55. Tamburini, "Michele Angiolillo el anarquista," 36; NA, FO 72/2035, Wolff to Salisbury, August 9, 1897; "El asesinato," *El País*, August 9, 1897.

56. "El asesinato," *El País*, August 9, 1897; "Asesinato del señor Cánovas," *La Época*, August 8, 1897.

57. "Asesinato"; Piqueras, *Cánovas y la derecha española*, 14.

58. "Asesinato de Cánovas," *El País*, August 10, 1897.

59. AD, Correspondence politique et commerciale, series A, "Nouvelle série," vol. 8, 130–32 and vol. 10, 60; González Calleja, *La razón de la fuerza*, 294.

60. "El asesinato," *El País*, August 9, 1897; "En Madrid," *La Época*, August 9, 1897.

61. AN, F7 12725, Attentats et complots en Espagne contre le roi et la reine régente, 1893–1914; AD, Correspondence politique et commerciale, series A, "Nouvelle série," vol. 8, 130–32, and vol. 10, 60.

62. AD, Correspondence politique et commerciale, series A, "Nouvelle série," vol. 8, 132.

63. Jensen, *Battle against Anarchist Terrorism*, 109–10.

64. For growing interest in how heads of state navigated the dangers of travel, see "Como viajan los soberanos," *El País*, August 28, 1897.

65. "Asesinato de D. Antonio Cánovas del Castillo," *El Imparcial*, August 9, 1897.

66. "El asesino de Cánovas," *El Imparcial*, August 13, 1897.

67. "El asesino," *La Época*, August 11, 1897.

68. Antonio María Fabié, *Cánovas del Castillo. Su juventud. Su edad madura. Su vejez. Estudio biográfico* (Barcelona: Gustavo Gili, 1928), 368.

69. Dalmau, *El Procés de Montjuïc*, 467.

70. "Mouvement social," *Les Temps nouveaux*, August 14–20, 1897.

71. Urales, *Mi Vida*, 1:233.

72. "El asesino de Cánovas," *El Imparcial*, August 12, 1897.

73. NA, FO 72/2035, Wolff to Salisbury, August 21, 1897; "El asesino de Cánovas," *El Imparcial*, August 17, 1897.

74. "El asesino de Cánovas"; "Contra el anarquismo," *El País*, August 15, 1897.

75. "El asesino," *La Época*, August 12, 1897.

76. "Desde Santa Águeda," *El Imparcial*, August 10, 1897.

77. Nakens, "De mis recuerdos," *El Imparcial*, October 25–26, 1901.

78. Tamburini, "Michele Angiolillo el anarquista," 38.

79. Piqueras, *Cánovas y la derecha española*, 75.

80. Émile Zola, *Germinal* (Paris: G. Charpentier, 1885), 591. The association between the last line of *Germinal* and Angiolillo from "In Memory of Michael Angiolillo," *Freedom*, September 1897.

81. "The Spanish Anarchist Exiles" and "The Anarchists in London," *Times*, August 13 and 16, 1897.

82. "The Alleged Torture of Spanish Prisoners," *Times*, August 23, 1897; *Standard*, August 23, 1897.

83. "The Anarchists," *Times*, August 16, 1897.

84. "The Alleged Torture," *Times*, August 23, 1897; *Standard*, August 23, 1897.

85. "Alleged Torture"; *Standard*, August 23, 1897.

86. Urales, *Mi Vida*, 1:227–29; "Mouvement social," *Les Temps nouveaux*, August 14–20, 1897; APP, Ba 138, Explosions en France, August 9, 1897.

87. "Alleged Torture"; *Standard*, August 23, 1897.

88. AGA, Asuntos exteriores, Embajada en Londres, 7016, "Spanish Tortures! Official Tortures!"

89. F. Tarrida del Mármol, "A la barre," *La Revue blanche*, June 1897; Marcos Zunino, "Subversive Justice: The Russell Vietnam War Crimes Tribunal and Transitional Justice," *International Journal of Transitional Justice* 10, no. 2 (2016): 211–29.

90. Tarrida, "A la barre" and "Pour la justice," *La Revue blanche*, June and second half of 1897; *Daily Chronicle*, June 3, 1897.

91. "La cuestión anarquista," *El País*, August 15, 1897.

9. Montjuich, Dreyfus, and *el Desastre*

1. Bantman, *French Anarchists in London*, 27, 63.

2. Urales, *Mi Vida*, 1:233–45; "Los presos de Barcelona," *El País*, September 10, 1897; Dalmau, *El Procés de Montjuïc*, 303, 315.

3. Urales, *Mi Vida*, 1:232.

4. AHN, Asuntos exteriores, Sección histórica, 2750, Sanderson to Spanish ambassador to London, October 8, 1897; AGA, Asuntos exteriores, Embajada en Londres, 7011, 7016, Casa Valencia to Ministro de Estado, October 8, 1897.

5. Urales, *Mi Vida*, 1:232.

6. Urales, *Mi Vida*, 1:239–49.

7. Urales, *Mi Vida*, 1:250–53.

8. Piqueras, *Cánovas y la derecha española*, 114–15.

9. Tone, *War and Genocide*, 49, 234.

10. Tone, *War and Genocide*, 223, 234–38.

11. Tarrida del Mármol, "Autour de Montjuich," *La Revue blanche*, November 1, 1897.

12. "Comunicado" and "Los presos de Montjuich," *El País*, October 17–18, 1897.

13. Dalmau, *El Procés de Montjuïc*, 441–42.

14. Álvarez Junco, *El Emperador*, 116–20.

15. Urales, *Mi Vida*, 2:5–7.

16. Federico Urales, "Sobre la verdad en marcha," *La Publicidad*, September 14, 1907.

17. Brennan, *Reflection of the Dreyfus Affair*, 31–32.

18. Martin P. Johnson, *The Dreyfus Affair: Honour and Politics in the Belle Époque* (New York: St. Martin's Press, 1999), 156; David Drake, *French Intellectuals and Politics from the Dreyfus Affair to the Occupation* (New York: Palgrave Macmillan, 2005), 16; Sébastien Faure, *Les Anarchistes et l'affaire Dreyfus* (Paris: Lafont, 1898).

19. Lazare broke with Herzl over his advocacy of a "bourgeois" Jewish state. In 1899 he abandoned the official Zionist movement despite maintaining his belief in Jewish autonomy. Jean-Marc Izrine, *Les Libertaires dans l'affaire Dreyfus* (Paris: Éditions d'Alternative libertaire, 2012), 61–64.

20. Izrine, *Les Libertaires*, 65.

21. Guillaume Davranche, "Préambule: Quand le racisme n'était ni 'de gauche' ni 'de droite,'" in Izrine, *Les Libertaires*, 8.

22. Griffiths, *Use of Abuse*, 24.

23. Johnson, *Dreyfus Affair*, 84; Izrine, *Les Libertaires*, 74–75.

24. Robert L. Hoffman, *More than a Trial: The Struggle over Captain Dreyfus* (New York: Free Press, 1980), 128.

25. Wendy Ellen Perry, "Remembering Dreyfus: The Ligue des Droits de l'Homme and the Making of the Modern French Human Rights Movement" (PhD diss., University of North Carolina, 1998), xvi, 13.

26. Perry, "Remembering Dreyfus," xvi; Izrine, *Les Libertaires*, 75.

27. Max A. Likin, "Defending Civil Society and the State: The Ligue des Droits de l'Homme in French and European Politics, 1898–1948" (PhD diss., Rutgers University, 2004), 20–21; Hoffman, *More than a Trial*, 165.

28. Émile Zola, "J'accuse," *L'Aurore*, January 13, 1898.

29. Johnson, *Dreyfus Affair*, 88–90; Hoffman, *More than a Trial*, 117.

30. Izrine, *Les Libertaires*, 73, 76.

31. "La revisión de un proceso," *El País*, September 18, 1898.

32. "Los presos de Montjuich," *El Imparcial*, January 21, 1898.

33. "El proceso de Montjuich," *El País*, February 14, 1898; "La manifestación de ayer," *La Publicidad*, edición de la mañana, February 14, 1898; "Manifestación de protesta," *La Correspondencia de España*, February 14, 1898; "La manifestación de ayer," *La Vanguardia*, February 14, 1898; Dalmau, *El Procés de Montjuïc*, 497.

34. "El proceso de Montjuich," *El País*, February 14, 1898; Dalmau, *El Procés de Montjuïc*, 495.

35. *El Progreso*, February–April 1898; *Progreso*, September 30, 1900; Álvarez Junco, *El Emperador*, 163.

36. *La Campaña de "El Progreso,"* 286–92.

37. Dalmau, *El Procés de Montjuïc*, 498.

38. "La manifestación de ayer," *El País*, April 4, 1898; "La manifestación de ayer," *El Imparcial*, April 4, 1898.

39. *La Campaña de "El Progreso,"* 720–32; Sempau, *Los Victimarios*, 357–62.

40. Tone, *War and Genocide*, 241–43, 257, 278–80.

41. Tone, *War and Genocide*, 239–40.

42. Álvarez Junco cites thirteen pro-Weyler articles in *El Progreso* during its first year. Álvarez Junco, *El Emperador*, 127.

43. Urales, *Mi Vida*, 2:31–32.

44. A. Lerroux, "Caciquismo," *La Revista Blanca*, July 1, 1898; Urales, *Mi Vida*, 2:35.

45. Urales, *Mi Vida*, 2:33.

46. "Otro atentado anarquista," *El Imparcial*, September 4, 1897.

47. "El atentado de Barcelona," *El Imparcial*, September 5, 1897; "Atentado en Barcelona," *El País*, September 5, 1897; Urales, *Mi Vida*, 2:80.

48. Anderson, *Under Three Flags*, 5, 198.

49. Dalmau, *El Procés de Montjuïc*, 375.

50. Urales, *Mi Vida*, 2:80.

51. William Henry Scott, *The Unión Obrera Democrática: First Filipino Trade Union* (Quezon City: New Day, 1992), 14–15.

52. Anderson, *Under Three Flags*, 201, 227–29.

53. Urales, *Mi Vida*, 2:81.

54. AD, Correspondence politique et commerciale, series A, "Nouvelle série," vol. 1, 140.

55. Urales, *Mi Vida*, 2:81.

56. N. S., "Sempau y Montjuich," *La Revista Blanca*, January 1, 1899; ACA, Sentencias criminales, 205, Ramón Sempau.

57. Dalmau, *El Procés de Montjuïc*, 377.

58. NA, FO 881/7179, report on 1898 Rome Conference, 10.

59. For more on the Rome Conference, see AHN, Asuntos exteriores, Sección histórica, 2750; Francesco Tamburini, "La conferenza internazionale di Roma per la difesa sociale contro gli anarchici (24 Novembre–21 Dicembre 1898)," *Clio* 2 (1997): 227–65; Jensen, *Battle against Anarchist Terrorism*, 131–82; Hsi-Huey Liang, *The Rise of Modern Police and the European State System from Metternich to the Second World War* (New York: Cambridge University Press, 1992), 156–65.

10. "All of Spain Is Montjuich"

1. "El 'meeting' de revisión," *El País*, June 25, 1899.

2. "Comité republicano de Cette," *La Publicidad*, May 15, 1899 (edición de la mañana).

3. Álvarez Junco, *El Emperador*, 139.

4. Brennan, *Reflection of the Dreyfus Affair*, 42–53.

5. Álvarez Junco, *El Emperador*, 164–65.

6. Urales, *Mi Vida*, 2:32–36.

7. "El proceso de Montjuich," *La Correspondencia de España*, May 15, 1899; "Meeting revisionista," *La Vanguardia*, May 15, 1899; "La revisión del proceso de Montjuich," *La Publicidad*, May 15, 1899 (edición de la mañana).

8. "Los procesos de Barcelona," *El Imparcial*, May 15, 1899; Dalmau, *El Procés de Montjuïc*, 499–500.

9. *Vida Nueva*, May 28, 1899; Dalmau, *El Procés de Montjuïc*, 473.

10. Dalmau, *El Procés de Montjuïc*, 504–5.

11. "Nuestro 'affaire,'" *La Época*, May 17, 1899.

12. "El proceso de Montjuich," *El Nuevo régimen*, May 20, 1899.

13. *Vida Nueva*, May 14, 1899; *La Campana de Gracia*, May 20, 1899; *Suplemento a la Revista Blanca*, June 24, 1899. Drawings from the *Suplemento* were reprinted in the pamphlet *La Inquisición fin de siglo* printed in Buenos Aires.

14. Heide Fehrenbach and Davide Rodogno, eds., *Humanitarian Photography: A History* (Cambridge: Cambridge University Press, 2015).

15. "Meeting revisionista," *La Vanguardia*, May 15, 1899.

16. Katherine Lee Bates, *Spanish Highways and Byways* (Chautauqua, NY: Chautauqua Press, 1905), 208–10; "El proceso de Montjuich," *El Imparcial*, June 25, 1899.

17. "El proceso de Montjuich," *La Época*, June 25, 1899; Whyte, *Dreyfus Affair*, 242.

18. "El proceso de Montjuich"; "El 'meeting,'" *El País*, June 25, 1899; "El proceso," *La Época*, June 25, 1899.

19. Bates, *Spanish Highways*, 210.

20. "El proceso de Montjuich"; "El proceso."

21. "Insurrecciones, asesinatos, incendios y complots," *Suplemento a la Revista Blanca*, July 1, 1899.

22. "El proceso"; "Lo de Montjuich" and "Meetings revisionistas," *El Imparcial*, July 2 and 3, 1899; "Cataluña y la revisión," *El País*, July 3, 1899; Dalmau, *El Procés de Montjuïc*, 501, 521.

23. "Cataluña," *El País*, July 3, 1899.

24. *Progreso*, July 9, 1899, cited in Álvarez Junco, *El emperador del Paralelo*, 167.

25. "Cataluña"; Álvarez Junco, *El emperador*, 168.

26. "Cataluña"; *La Dinastía*, July 3, 1899.

27. "Cataluña"; "Meeting revisionista," *La Correspondencia de España*, July 3, 1899.

28. "Lo de ayer," *La Dinastía*, July 3, 1899.

29. "Lo de ayer"; "Cataluña"; *El Imparcial*, June 25 and July 3, 1899; *Suplemento a la Revista Blanca*, June 24 and July 1, 1899; Dalmau, *El Procés de Montjuïc*, 495–501.

30. Dalmau, *El Procés de Montjuïc*, 510–13.

31. *La Campaña de "El Progreso,"* 3.

32. Dalmau, *El Procés de Montjuïc*, 522–23.

33. AHN, Asuntos Exteriores, Sección Histórica, 2751, Ministro de Estado to Wolff, May 2, 1900.

34. Urales, *Mi Vida*, 2:61–62.

35. González Calleja, *La razón de la fuerza*, 297; Dalmau, *El Procés de Montjuïc*, 527.

36. NA, FO 638/20, British consul in Barcelona to Salisbury, April 28, 1900; NA, HO 144/587/B2840C, Sanderson to Under Secretary of State, April 28, 1900.

37. AHN, Asuntos exteriores, Sección histórica, 2751, Letter from Wolff, May 1, 1900, and response May 2, 1900.

38. Kropotkin, "Los mártires de Montjuich en Londres," *Suplemento a la Revista Blanca*, May 19, 1900.

39. "Los extrañados," *Suplemento a la Revista Blanca*, June 16, 1900; *Gaceta de Madrid*, July 15, 1900.

40. "El proceso de Cambios Nuevos," *Suplemento a la Revista Blanca*, February 3, 1900.

41. *La Campaña*, January 25, 1898; Dalmau, *El Procés de Montjuïc*, 378.

42. Kropotkin, "Los mártires." Dalmau thinks this is exaggerated (*El Procés de Montjuïc*, 377).

43. AGP, Reinados, Alfonso XIII, 13177, José Alsó Valls, June 15, 1906; Avilés, *Francisco Ferrer y Guardia*, 71.

44. *El Corsario*, June 25 and July 2, 1896.

45. J. M., "Dos fechas," *Suplemento a la Revista Blanca*, May 19, 1900; Urales, *Mi Vida*, 1:78.

46. Malato and Rocker said his name was François. Bonafoux said it was Jean. Malato, "Les martyrs de Montjuich," *L'Aurore*, May 3, 1900; Rocker, *En la borrasca*, 61; Dalmau, *El Procés de Montjuïc*, 429.

47. Rocker, *En la borrasca*, 61.

48. Luís Bonafoux, "Como viven los anarquistas," *La Publicidad*, June 21, 1901 (edición de la noche). Mella and Prats paint a similar picture of a French anarchist in London. Núñez Florencio, *El terrorismo anarquista*, 163.

49. Diego Abad de Santillán, *Memorias 1897–1936* (Barcelona: Planeta, 1977), 98–100.

50. J. Romero Maura, "Terrorism in Barcelona and Its Impact on Spanish Politics, 1904–1909," *Past and Present* 41 (December 1968): 131; Herrerín López, *Anarquía*, 151; Álvarez Junco, *El emperador*, 152; Avilés, *Francisco Ferrer*, 84; Pradas Baena, *Teresa Claramunt*, 50; López Corral, *La Guardia Civil*, 589; Dalmau, *El Procés de Montjuïc*, 431; Tone, *War and Genocide*, 230; Jensen, *Battle against Anarchist Terrorism*, 50.

51. "El despertar," *El Progreso*, February 14, 1898.

52. Álvarez Junco, *El emperador*, 170–71.

53. Álvarez Junco, *El emperador*, 170–71.

54. Urales, *Mi Vida*, 2:66.

11. The General Strike and the Montjuich Template of Resistance

1. Kaplan, *Anarchists of Andalusia*, 172–84; González Calleja, *La razón de la fuerza*, 238–39; Herrerín López, *Anarquía*, 76–78.

2. Herrerín López, *Anarquía*, 76–78.

3. González Calleja, *La Razón de la Fuerza*, 240; Herrerín López, *Anarquía*, 78.

4. Herrerín López, *Anarquía*, 80; Kaplan, *Anarchists of Andalusia*, 179–80.

5. For reports from Spanish embassies on international Jerez demonstrations in 1892, see AHN, Asuntos exteriores, Sección histórica, 2750.

6. Urales, *Mi Vida*, 1:66, 2:66.

7. "Montjuich y Jerez," *Suplemento a La Revista Blanca*, February 3, 1900.

8. "Al pueblo" and "Los tormentos de Jerez," *Suplemento a La Revista Blanca*, February 10 and April 28, 1900; Urales, *Mi Vida*, 2:66.

9. *Suplemento a La Revista Blanca*, February 10–May 25 and July 28, 1900.

10. "Los tormentos de Jerez," *Suplemento a La Revista Blanca*, May 25, 1900.

11. Federico Urales, "Justicia," *Suplemento a La Revista Blanca*, November 3, 1900.

12. Spanish papers that supported the campaign: *Progreso, La Publicidad, La Redención Obrera, La Unión Republicana* (Mallorca), *La Lucha* (Vigo), *El Demócrata* (Jerez), *El Coriano* (Coria del Río), *El Clamor Público* (Ferrol). *Suplemento a La Revista Blanca*, March 3, March 24, and June 30, 1900. In Buenos Aires: *El Rebelde, L'Avenire*, and *La Protesta Humana*. *Suplemento a La Revista Blanca*, August 11, 1900. In New York: *El Despertar. Les Temps nouveaux* mentioned the campaign.

13. Teresa Claramunt, "La mano negra," *Suplemento a La Revista Blanca*, September 1, 1900.

14. "Los tormentos de Jerez," *Suplemento a La Revista Blanca*, June 2, 1900.

15. "Los tormentos," *Suplemento a La Revista Blanca*, March 10 and June 9, 1900.

16. Soledad Gustavo, "Por la libertad de los presos," *Suplemento a La Revista Blanca*, June 9, 1900.

17. Demonstrations also occurred in Buenos Aires. *Suplemento a La Revista Blanca*, February 17, April 14, June 30, July 28, August 11, September 1, October 20, December 29, 1900.

18. *Suplemento a La Revista Blanca*, September 22–October 20, 1900.

19. "Los tormentos de Jerez," *Suplemento a La Revista Blanca*, September 29, 1900.

20. Soledad Gustavo, "Los tormentos de Jerez," *Suplemento a La Revista Blanca*, November 24, 1900.

21. "Groupe de solidarité internationale," *Les Temps nouveaux*, November 24, 1900–February 1, 1901.

22. "Consejo de ministros," *El Imparcial*, February 7, 1901.

23. "El indulto," *La Época*, February 5, 1901.

24. Gustavo, "Los tormentos," and "Más sobre la muerte de Humberto," *Suplemento a La Revista Blanca*, August 11, 1900.

25. R. M. and J. P., *La barbarie gubernamental en España* (Brooklyn: Imp. de *El Despertar*, 1897), 93.

26. "Movimiento social," *Suplemento a La Revista Blanca*, October 20, 1900; Íñiguez, *Enciclopedia histórica*, 1257; Álvarez Junco, *El Emperador*, 270.

27. Montseny quit the FSORE because he believed the federation should only include "manual workers," not intellectual workers. Federico Urales, "Después del congreso," *Suplemento a La Revista Blanca*, October 27, 1900.

28. Herrerín López, *Anarquía*, 204; Xavier Cuadrat, *Socialismo y anarquismo en Cataluña (1899–1911): Los orígenes de la C. N. T.* (Madrid: Ediciones de la Revista de Trabajo, 1976), 65.

29. González Calleja, *La razón de la fuerza*, 308; Temma Kaplan, "The Social Base of Nineteenth-Century Andalusian Anarchism in Jerez de la Frontera," *Journal of Interdisciplinary History* 6 (Summer 1975): 62–63.

30. Álvarez Junco, *La ideología política*, 552, 549–51; Íñiguez, *Enciclopedia histórica*, 1257.

31. Álvarez Junco, *La ideología política*, 555, 566; Maitron, *Le Mouvement anarchiste*, 271–72.

32. González Calleja, *La Razón de la Fuerza*, 312; Herrerín López, *Anarquía*, 207.

33. Joan Connelly Ullman, *La semana trágica: Estudio sobre las causas socioeconómicas del anticlericalismo en España (1898–1912)* (Barcelona: Ediciones Ariel, 1968), 126, 76; Juan Gómez Casas, *Historia del anarco sindicalismo español* (Madrid: Editorial ZYX, 1968), 76; Joaquín Romero Maura, *"La rosa de fuego": El obrerismo barcelonés de 1899 a 1909* (Barcelona: Ediciones Grijalbo, 1975), 206.

34. González Calleja, *La razón de la fuerza*, 311.

35. Kaplan, *Red City*, 60; Herrerín López, *Anarquía*, 201; Romero Maura, *"La rosa de fuego,"* 204.

36. Sebastian Balfour, "Riot, Regeneration and Reaction: Spain in the Aftermath of the 1898 Disaster," *Historical Journal* 38, no. 2 (1995): 406; Adrian Shubert, *A Social History of Modern Spain* (London: Routledge, 1990), 15; Ullman, *La semana trágica*, 119, 130; Romero Maura, *"La rosa de fuego,"* 156–58.

37. Angel Smith, "From Subordination to Contestation: The Rise of Labour in Barcelona, 1898–1918," in Angel Smith, ed., *Red Barcelona: Social Protest and Labour Mobilization in the Twentieth Century* (London: Routledge, 2003), 25–26; Romero Maura, *"La rosa de fuego,"* 145.

38. Smith, "From Subordination to Contestation," 33.

39. Romero Maura, *"La rosa de fuego,"* 60, 206–7; "Movimiento social," *Suplemento a La Revista Blanca*, October 20, 1900; NA, FO 72/2149 and 638/22, Reports from Roberts to Lansdowne from April and May 1901.

40. Herrerín López, *Anarquía*, 205; Miguel Rodríguez, "Una tragedia obrera olvidada," *La Opinión a Coruña*, May 30, 2013.

41. "Los sucesos de La Coruña," *Suplemento a La Revista Blanca*, July 6 and August 3, 1901.

42. "Solidaridad internacional," *Suplemento a La Revista Blanca*, August 31, 1901.

43. "Solidaridad obrera internacional," *Suplemento a La Revista Blanca*, July 27, 1901; *El Nuevo Ideal*, June 12, 1901.

44. Ullman, *La semana trágica*, 119–22; Stanley Payne, "Catalan and Basque Nationalism," *Journal of Contemporary History* 6, no. 1 (1971): 15–51; Francisco Bergasa, *¿Quién mató a Ferrer i Guardia?* (Madrid: Aguilar, 2009), 55, 73.

45. Ullman, *La semana trágica*, 122–23.

46. González Calleja, *La Razón de la Fuerza*, 316; Romero Maura, *"La rosa de fuego,"* 207; NA, FO 638/22, Roberts to Lansdowne, January 1902.

47. Urales, *Mi Vida*, 2:74; Pradas Baena, *Teresa Claramunt*, 24, 64.

48. Ullman, *La semana trágica*, 132; Romero Maura, *"La rosa de fuego,"* 215; González Calleja, *La razón de la fuerza*, 317.

49. González Calleja, *La razón de la fuerza*, 317; Kaplan, *Red City*, 64–66; Romero Maura, *"La rosa de fuego,"* 211–17; Ullman, *La semana trágica*, 132; Herrerín López, *Anarquía*, 206; NA, FO 638/22, Roberts to Lansdowne, February 1902.

50. NA, FO 638/22, Roberts to Lansdowne, February 20, 1902.

51. González Calleja, *La razón de la fuerza*, 317.

52. Herrerín López, *Anarquía*, 207; Romero Maura, *"La rosa de fuego,"* 230; Ferran Aisa, *La cultura anarquista a Catalunya* (Barcelona: Edicions de 1984, 2006), 31–32; González Calleja, *La razón de la fuerza*, 320.

53. Álvarez Junco, *El Emperador*, 202, 288.

54. Álvarez Junco, *El Emperador*, 127.

55. Urales, *Mi vida*, 2:86.

56. Álvarez Junco, *El Emperador*, 228, 246, 271–72.

57. *Tierra y Libertad*, January 25–August 16, 1902.

58. *Les Temps nouveaux*, January 10–30, 1903; *Tierra y Libertad*, October 25, 1902–March 5, 1903; *La Voz del Pueblo*, January 17, 1903; Constance Bantman, "La culture de la campagne médiatique dans le mouvement anarchiste de la Belle Époque: Jean Grave et 'les atrocités espagnoles' (1885–1909)," *Printemps* 33 (2020): 40–55.

59. Urales, *Mi Vida*, 2:118–38.

60. Johnson, *Dreyfus Affair*, 144–45.

61. "Mouvement social," *Les Temps nouveaux*, January 10–16, 1903.

62. Urales, *Mi Vida*, 2:120–21; Abelló, *Les relacions internacionals*, 178–80.

63. Urales, *Mi Vida*, 2:118–38; *La "mano negra" et l'opinion française* (Paris: Temps Nouveaux, 1903).

64. Urales, *Mi Vida*, 2:127–29.

65. Perry, "Remembering Dreyfus," 69.

66. Pressensé, "Mano negra," *L'Aurore*, December 31, 1902.

67. AHN, Asuntos exteriores, Sección histórica, 2751, Ministro de Estado to Subsecretario de Orden Público, January 15, 1903.

68. "Consejo de ministros," *El País*, March 5, 1903.

69. "Solidaridad internacional," *Tierra y Libertad*, March 12, 1903.

70. Romero Maura, *"La rosa de fuego,"* 224–30; Ullman, *La semana trágica*, 134; González Calleja, *La razón de la fuerza*, 318.

71. *Tierra y Libertad*, April 16–August 9, 1903.

72. AHN, Gobernación, 2A, exp. 15, report on "Sucesos de Alcalá del Valle"; Herrerín López, *Anarquía*, 209–12.

73. *Tierra y Libertad*, August 8–October 12, 1903.

74. "El parto de los montes" and "La persecución gubernativa a Urales," *Tierra y Libertad*, August 15, 1903; Urales, *Mi Vida*, 2:160–80.

75. *Tierra y Libertad*, September 3–October 31, 1903; *El Rebelde*, August 11, 1904.

76. Gustavo, "Los tormentos de Alcalá," *Tierra y Libertad*, November 19, 1903.

77. AHN, Asuntos exteriores, Sección histórica, 2751, Leon y Castillo to Spanish embassy in Paris, February 19, 1904.

78. Fehrenbach and Rodogno, "The Morality of Sight," in Fehrenbach and Rodogno, *Humanitarian Photography*, 5.

79. *El Rebelde*, August 18, 1904; AHN, Asuntos exteriores, Sección histórica, 2751, *Auto de sobreseimiento libre* . . . con motivo de los sucesos de Alcalá del Valle el 1 de agosto de 1903, IX.

80. AHN, Asuntos exteriores, Sección histórica, 2751, Ordre du jour of Union des Syndicats ouvriers de la Ville de Mèze, March 10, 1904.

81. *Tierra y Libertad*, February 11–July 26, 1904; *El Rebelde*, March 11–24, 1904; AGA, Asuntos exteriores, Embajada en Paris, 5882, reports from Sannois, 1904.

82. *El Rebelde*, March 11–24, 1904; P. Delesalle, "Pour les torturés d'Alcala," *Les Temps nouveaux*, March 19–25, 1904; *Tierra y Libertad*, February 4–April 21, 1904; reports on international protests from Spanish foreign service at AHN, Asuntos exteriores, Sección histórica, 2751; "Informaciones," *El Obrero*, August 1, 1904; *La Protesta*, January 16, 1904.

83. AHN, Asuntos exteriores, Sección histórica, 2751, Spanish legation in Buenos Aires to Ministro de Estado, October 17, 1904.

84. "Los mitins del 13 de Marzo," *El Rebelde*, March 18, 1904; "Pout les Torturés d'Alcala et d'ailleurs," *Les Temps nouveaux*, March 26–April 1, 1904; "Alcalá del Valle en el extranjero," *Tierra y Libertad*, March 24, 1904.

85. "Barcelona," *El País*, June 23, 1904.

86. *El Rebelde*, March 18–24 and June 30, 1904.

87. Rafael Núñez Florencio, "El terrorismo," in Julián Casanova, ed., *Tierra y libertad: cien años de anarquismo en España* (Barcelona: Critica, 2010), 78.

88. J. Miguel Artal, "A los anarquistas," *El Rebelde*, July 28, 1904.

89. ATSJC, Criminal, Sentencias de jurados, 1904, Artal.

90. ANP, F7/12725, Bonnecarrère to Sûreté Générale, June 12, 1904.

91. AN, BB18, 2311, Confidential Report.

92. AGA, Asuntos exteriores, Embajada en Paris, 5882, Sannois, November 28 and December 12, 1904.

93. AHN, Asuntos exteriores, Sección histórica, 2751, Spanish legation in Lisbon, July 17, 1904, and *Auto de sobreseimiento libre*, II.

94. *Tierra y Libertad*, October 9–25, 1903.

95. Urales, *Mi Vida*, 2:234–44; Antonio Apolo, "Tirando de la Manta," *El Rebelde*, October 13, 1904; Antoni Dalmau, *El Cas Rull: viure del terror a la Ciutat de les Bombes (1901–1908)* (Barcelona: Columna, 2008), 123.

96. Romero Maura, *"La rosa de fuego,"* 233–34; Eduard Masjuan, *Un héroe trágico del anarquismo español: Mateo Morrall, 1879–1906* (Barcelona: Icaria, 2009), 169; Pradas Baena, *Teresa Claramunt*, 71–72; "La protesta de Barcelona liberal," *La Publicidad*, June 8, 1905; AGP, Reinados, Alfonso XIII, 13177, José Barbará to Alfonso de Aguilar, June 6, 1906.

12. The Iron Pineapple

1. "L'arrivée de S. M. Alphonse XIII a Paris" and "La deuxième journée de S. M. Alphonse XIII a Paris," *Le Figaro*, May 31 and June 1, 1905.

2. "L'arrivée" and "La deuxième journée"; Melchor Fernández Almagro, *Historia del Reinado de Alfonso XIII* (Barcelona: Montaner y Simón, 1977), 63–64; AN, F7 12513, Attentat de la rue de Rohan.

3. "Ecos políticos," *La Correspondencia de España*, June 2, 1905.

4. Vallina, *Mis memorias*, 77–85; Nicolás Estévanez, *Fragmentos de mis memorias* (Madrid: Hijos de R. Álvarez, 1903); González Calleja, *La razón de la fuerza*, 356; José Álvarez Junco, "Un anarquista español a comienzos del siglo XX: Pedro Vallina en Paris," in Bert Hofmann, Pere Joan i Tous, and Manfred Tietz, eds., *El anarquismo español y sus tradiciones culturales* (Madrid: Iberoamericana, 1995), 16–17.

5. Sanabria, *Republicanism and Anticlerical Nationalism*, 164–65.

6. Vallina, *Mis memorias*, 52–54.

7. Constance Bantman, "The Dangerous Liaisons of Belle Epoque Anarchists: Internationalism, Transnationalism, and Nationalism in the French Anarchist Movement (1880–1914)," in Bantman and Altena, *Reassessing the Transnational Turn*, 186–88; Patsouras, *Jean Grave*, 31; Davide Turcato, *Making Sense of Anarchism: Errico Malatesta's Experiments with Revolution, 1889–1900* (Oakland: AK Press, 2015), 106, 116–17.

8. Vallina, *Mis memorias*, 77–85; Álvarez Junco, "Un anarquista español," 20; Urales, *Mi Vida*, 1:248–49; for documents confiscated from Vallina, see AN, F7 12510.

9. AN, F7 12510; Álvarez Junco, "Un anarquista español," 20–25; Vallina, *Mis memorias*, 81.

10. Vallina, *Mis memorias*, 81–87.

11. *Tierra y Libertad*, February 25–March 4, 1904; P. Vallina, "Correspondencia de Paris," *El Rebelde*, March 11, 1904; Vallina, *Mis memorias*, 89; Álvarez Junco, *El Emperador*, 294–95; González Calleja, *La razón de la fuerza*, 361; AGA, Asuntos exteriores, Embajada en Paris, 5882, Sannois, June 14, 1904, list of Spanish anarchists in Paris, and "A los revolucionarios españoles."

12. Ch. Malato, "Lettre ouvert a Monsieur Bourbon," *L'Espagne inquisitoriale*, September 1904; For more on the committee and *L'Espagne inquisitoriale*, see AGA, Asuntos exteriores, Embajada en Paris, 5882.

13. AHN, Asuntos exteriores, Sección histórica, 2751, French embassy in Madrid, August 3, 1904.

14. "A los revolucionarios españoles"; F. Domela Nieuwenhuis, "Lettre de F. Doméla Nieuwenhuis," *L'Espagne inquisitoriale*, September 1904.

15. AGA, Asuntos exteriores, Embajada en Paris, 5881; Jordi Pons Pujol, "Imatge oficial i política francesa respecte la Catalunya espanyola, 1895–1914" (PhD diss., Universitat Autònoma de Barcelona, 2015), 205.

16. AGA, Asuntos exteriores, Embajada en Paris, 5882, Sannois, April 4 and November 26, 1904.

17. AGA, Asuntos exteriores, Embajada en Paris, 5882, 5884, Sannois, January 4, 6, and 9, 1905, and two reports from January 8, 1905.

18. Vallina, *Mis memorias*, 79.

19. "Campaña humanitaria," *El Rebelde*, July 21, 1904.

20. AGA, Asuntos exteriores, Embajada en Paris, 5884, Sannois, August 22, 1904, and February 15, 1905.

21. AGA, Asuntos exteriores, Embajada en Paris, 5884, Sannois, February 1905.

22. AGA, Asuntos exteriores, Embajada en Paris, 5884, Sannois, February and March 1905; Vallina, *Mis memorias*, 92–93; APP, Ba 1511, Anarchistes en Espagne, Vallina to Cornelissen, January 8, 1905.

23. AFAM, Correspondencia oficial, leg. 165, carp. 13, 18, Ossorio to la Cierva, January 4, 1908, and Ossorio on anarchism, 1907; APP, Ba 1511, report from informant, June 5, 1905; Romero Maura, "Terrorism in Barcelona," 139; Álvarez Junco, *El Emperador*, 297; Vallina, *Mis memorias*, 79; González Calleja, *La razón de la fuerza*, 364–67.

24. Alejandro Lerroux, *Mis memorias* (Madrid: Afrodisio Aguado, 1963), 449–51; Romero Maura, "Terrorism in Barcelona," 139.

25. On Malatesta: Vallina, *Mis memorias*, 93; AGA, Asuntos exteriores, Embajada en Paris, 5884; González Calleja, *La razón de la fuerza*, 364.

26. AGA, Asuntos exteriores, Embajada en Paris, 5884, Sannois, March 25 and April 8, 1905.

27. AGA, Asuntos exteriores, Embajada en Paris, 5884, Sannois, April 3, 1905.

28. AN, F7 12513, Commissaire spécial de Cerbère to Directeur de la Sûreté Générale, June 5, 1905, report from Ambassador to Spain, June 13, 1905, report on Malato and Vallina, May 18, 1905, copy of Ferrer's check, April 13, 1905; APP, Ba 1317, copy of Ferrer's check, April 14, 1905, and report to Prefecture of Police, April 14, 1905; *Gazette des tribunaux*, November 27–28, 1905; *Gazette du Palais*, December 5, 1905.

29. AGA, Asuntos exteriores, Embajada en Paris, 5884, Sannois, March 28, 1905.

30. AGA, Asuntos exteriores, Embajada en Paris, 5884, Sannois, May 3, 1905.

31. W. Y. Carman, *A History of Firearms: From Earliest Times to 1914* (New York: Routledge, 2016), chapter 10.

32. *Gazette des tribunaux*, November 27–28, 1905; *Gazette du Palais*, December 5, 1905; AGA, Asuntos exteriores, Embajada en Paris, 5884, Sannois, April 3, 1905; Romero Maura, "Terrorism in Barcelona," 144; AN, F7 12513, report on Malato and Vallina, May 18, 1905.

33. AGA, Asuntos exteriores, Embajada en Paris, 5858 and 5884, Sannois, May 1905; *Gazette des Tribunaux*, November 27–28, 1905.

34. AGA, Asuntos exteriores, Embajada en Paris, 5884, Sannois, May 13, 1905; APP, Ba 1317, report on May 10 protest, May 11, 1905, report on May 24 protests, May 25, 1905, Prefect of Police to Minister of the Interior, May 24, 1905; "Paris a la bourse du travail," *L'Aurore*, May 25, 1905; "Le voyage d'Alphonse XIII," *Le Matin*, May 20, 1905; Avilés, *Francisco Ferrer*, 150–51.

35. AN, F7 12513, report dated May 23, 1905; APP, Ba 1319, report dated May 18, 1905; Herrerín López, *Anarquía*, 222–23.

36. Vallina, *Mis memorias*, 95.

37. AGA, Asuntos exteriores, Embajada en Paris, 5858, Sannois, May 26, 27, 30, and 31, 1905; APP, Ba 1317, Voyage en France du roi d'Espagne.

38. "Ante el atentado," *La Época*, June 1, 1905.

39. AGA, Asuntos exteriores, Embajada en Paris, 5858, report from Spanish embassy in Paris, June 3, 1905; AHN, Gobernación, 2A, exp. 15, report on rue de Rohan *attentat*.

40. *Gazette des tribunaux*, November 27–December 2, 1905; J. Avilés, "Contra Alfonso XIII," in Avilés and Herrerín, *El nacimiento del terrorismo*, 146.

41. *Gazette des tribunaux*, November 27–December 2, 1905; AGA, Asuntos exteriores, Embajada en Paris, 5858, Spanish embassy in Paris, November 28, 1905; Álvarez Junco, *El Emperador*, 299; "Les complots policiers," *L'Action*, November 28, 1905.

42. *Gazette des tribunaux*, December 2, 1905; Malato, "Memoires," *Le Peuple*, March 25, 1938.

43. AGA, Asuntos exteriores, Embajada en Paris, 5858, Sannois, August 28 and December 1, 1905; Malato, "Memoires," *Le Peuple*, March 25, 1938; Vallina, *Mis memorias*, 96.

44. Avilés, *Francisco Ferrer*, 162; Romero Maura, "Terrorism in Barcelona," 138; Bergasa, *¿Quién mató a Ferrer i Guardia?*, 120.

45. Malato, "Memoires," *Le Peuple*, March 24, 1938.

46. AN, BB18, 2311, Procureur Général to Ministre de la Justice, December 9, 1905, January 25 and March 8, 1906; AGA, Asuntos exteriores, Embajada en Paris, 5883, Sannois, June 23, 1906.

47. Romero Maura, "Terrorism in Barcelona," 144; AN, F7 12513, attentat de la rue de Rohan; AGA, Asuntos exteriores, Embajada en Paris, 5883, Spanish embassy in Paris, December 27, 1907; González Calleja, *La razón de la fuerza*, 367.

48. Arguments for Aviño: Avilés, *Francisco Ferrer*, 156–57; Herrerín López, *Anarquía*, 223; Maitron et al eds., *Dicionnaire biographique du mouvement ouvrier français. 10, P. 3. 1871–1914, de la Commune à la Grande Guerre* (Paris: Ed. Ouvrières, 1973), 334–35. Arguments for Morral: Romero Maura, "Terrorism in Barcelona," 141–44; Masjuan, *Un héroe trágico*, 178–83. Argument for Morral as bomb mailer: Núñez Florencio, *El terrorismo anarquista*, 147.

49. Romero Maura, "Terrorism in Barcelona," 141–44; Masjuan, *Un héroe trágico*, 71–87, 171; Francisco Ferrer Guardia, *Anarchist Education and the Modern School: A Francisco Ferrer Reader*, ed. Mark Bray and Robert H. Haworth (Oakland: PM Press, 2018), 186; Mateo Morral, *Pensamientos revolucionarios de Nicolás Estévanez* (Barcelona: José J. de Olañeta, 1978); Lerroux, *Mis memorias*, 185–86, 462.

50. Romero Maura, "Terrorism in Barcelona," 141–44; Masjuan, *Un héroe trágico*, 178–83; *Gazette des tribunaux*, November 27–28, 1905; AGA, Asuntos exteriores, Embajada en Paris, 5882, Sannois, October 31, 1904; Albano Rosell, *Vidas trágicas: Mateo Morral, Francisco Ferrer* (Montevideo, 1940) in Francisco J. Romero Salvadó, *¿Quién mató a Eduardo Dato?: comedia política y tragedia social en España, 1892–1921* (Granada: Comares, 2020), 105.

51. Malato, "Memoires," *Le Peuple*, March 24, 1938; Vallina, *Mis memorias*, 95–96; Pedro Vallina, "El tirano y el tiranicida," *Solidaridad obrera*, August 31, 1961.

13. Tossing the Bouquet at the Royal Wedding

1. Ricardo de la Cierva, *Alfonso y Victoria: Las tramas íntimas, secretas y europeas de un reinado desconocido* (Madrid: Editorial Fénix, 2001), 170–71; Carlos Seco Serrano, *Alfonso XIII* (Madrid: Arlanza Ediciones, 2001), 19.

2. Serrano, *Alfonso XIII*, 22, 130; de la Cierva, *Alfonso y Victoria*, 149.

3. de la Cierva, *Alfonso y Victoria*, 145, 173–80.

4. Masjuan, *Un héroe trágico*, 183.

5. Masjuan, *Un héroe trágico*, 61–69.

6. Ferrer, *Anarchist Education*, 9, 26–27.

7. Sylvain Wagnon, *Francisco Ferrer: une éducation libertaire en héritage* (Lyon: Atelier de création libertaire, 2013), 44–45; Maitron, *Le mouvement anarchiste*, 353–56; Salvador Canals, *Los sucesos de España en 1909: Crónica documentada Tomo II* (Madrid: Impr. Alemana, 1911), 53–54; Ferrer, *Anarchist Education*, 29–30.

8. Ferrer, *Anarchist Education*, 213–15.

9. Masjuan, *Un héroe trágico*, 71–76.

10. Masjuan, *Un héroe trágico*, 76–78; "Una excursión escolar al país de la industria," *Boletín de la Escuela Moderna*, September 30, 1903.

11. Masjuan, *Un héroe trágico*, 81–103.

12. Masjuan, *Un héroe trágico*, 105–14; Sol Ferrer, *Le véritable Francisco Ferrer: d'après des documents inédits* (Paris: L'Écran du monde, 1948), 126.

13. Masjuan, *Un héroe trágico*, 126–27, 193; Avilés, *Francisco Ferrer*, 168.

14. Paul Avrich, *The Russian Anarchists* (Princeton, NJ: Princeton University Press, 1967), 38–48; Anna Geifman, *Thou Shalt Kill: Revolutionary Terrorism in Russia, 1894–1917* (Princeton, NJ: Princeton University Press, 1996), 127; Zimmer, *Immigrants against the State*, 115.

15. Avrich, *Russian Anarchists*, 47–49, 72.

16. Masjuan, *Un héroe trágico*, 126–27.

17. Masjuan, *Un héroe trágico*, 127–41, quotation on 141; Urales, *Mi vida*, 2:77–79.

18. Morral, *Pensamientos revolucionarios*, 16, 52; Masjuan, *Un héroe trágico*, 174.

19. Masjuan, *Un héroe trágico*, 202.

20. Serrano, *Alfonso XIII*, 39–40.

21. Masjuan, *Un héroe trágico*, 202–10; Sanabria, *Republicanism and Anticlerical Nationalism*, 105–6; *Regicidio frustrado 31 Mayo 1906 I. Causa contra Mateo Morral* (Madrid: Sucesores de J. A. García, 1911), 540–42.

22. Masjuan, *Un héroe trágico*, 204–8; *Regicidio frustrado 31 Mayo 1906 I*, 63.

23. AHN, Asuntos exteriores, Sección histórica, 2751, Almodovar, May 16, 1906, Spanish embassy in Italy, May 11, 1906, Spanish embassy in London, May 16, 1906, Ministro de la Gobernación, May 12, 1906; AGA, Asuntos exteriores, Embajada en Paris, 5882, Ministro de la Gobernación to Spanish embassy in Paris, March 22, 1906; NA, FO 371/136; González Calleja, *La razón de la fuerza*, 370–72.

24. AN, F7 12823, Bonnecarrère, May 17 and 23, 1906.

25. de la Cierva, *Alfonso y Victoria*, 199–200.

26. Masjuan, *Un héroe trágico*, 212–14, 235–36; *Regicidio frustrado*, 414; González Calleja, *La razón de la fuerza*, 374.

27. "Fiestas reales," *El Liberal*, May 29, 1906; *Regicidio frustrado*, 266–67, 278–82, 488–89; José Esteban, *Mateo Morral el anarquista: causa por un regicidio* (Madrid: Vosa, 2011), 75–85.

28. *Regicidio frustrado*, 469–87.

29. Álvarez Junco, *El Emperador*, 104–6.

30. *El proceso Ferrer en el Congreso: recopilación de los discursos pronunciados por varios diputados durante el debate* (Barcelona: Impr. Lauria, 1911), 140.

31. Lerroux, *Mis memorias*, 460–63.

32. Lerroux, *Mis memorias*, 464–66.

33. AN, F7 12725, report of June 14, 1906; Álvarez Junco, *El Emperador*, 306; AGA, Asuntos extertiores, Embajada en Paris, 5883, Sannois, July 11, 1906.

34. AGA, Asuntos exteriores, Embajada en Paris, 5883, Sannois, April 28, 1906; AHN, Asuntos exteriores, Sección histórica, 2751, Spanish embassy in Paris, May 3, 1907.

35. Charles Malato, *L'Assassinat de Ferrer: Eclaircissements* (Geneva: Édition du Réveil, 1911), 5.

36. González Calleja, *La razón de la fuerza*, 374.

37. "Atentado anarquista," *La Época*, June 1, 1906.

38. Masjuan, *Un héroe trágico*, 127–28; "Atentado," *La Época*, June 1, 1906.

39. *Regicidio frustrado*, 190–91; Esteban, *Mateo Morral*, 92–95.

40. Masjuan, *Un héroe trágico*, 224–39.

41. "Monumento del 31 de Mayo de 1906," *El Imparcial*, November 5, 1908.

42. S. Sueiro, "El asesinato de Canalejas y los anarquistas españoles en estados unidos," in Avilés and Herrerín, *El nacimiento del terrorismo*, 160.

43. Masjuan, *Un héroe trágico*, 244, 264–68.

14. "Truth on the March" for Francisco Ferrer

1. University of California San Diego (UCSD), Special Collections, Francisco Ferrer Collection (hereafter Ferrer Collection), MS 248, box 1, folder 4, Ferrer to Malato, September 23, 1906.

2. Peter Anderson, *The Francoist Military Trials: Terror and Complicity, 1939–1945* (New York: Routledge, 2010), 13, 19.

3. Ferrer to Malato, September 23, 1906.

4. Ferrer Collection, MS 248, box 1, folder 4, Ferrer to Malato, September 19, 1906.

5. Herrerín López, *Anarquía*, 226–27; Avilés, *Francisco Ferrer*, 176.

6. Conde de Romanones, *Notas de una vida*, vol. 2 (Madrid: Renacimiento, 1929), 164; Sanabria, *Republicanism and Anticlerical Nationalism*, 104; Urales, *Mi Vida*, 3:15–16; Masjuan, *Un héroe trágico*, 231, 248.

7. Real Academia de Historia (hereafter RAH), Archivo Romanones, leg. 53, exp. 12, Urales to Romanones, July 9, 12, and 16, 1906.

8. Urales, *Mi Vida*, 3:17–23.

9. Urales, *Mi Vida*, 1:111–12, 2:235–6; Angel Cunillera, "El ideal en peligro," *Suplemento a la Revista Blanca*, August 24, 1901.

10. Urales, *Mi Vida*, 1:206, 2:77–78.

11. AGA, Asuntos exteriores, Embajada en Paris, 5883, Sannois, August 15–17, 1906; APP, Ba 1075, report of August 17, 1906; Malato, "Memoires," *Le Peuple*, March 26–27, 1938.

12. Avilés, *Francisco Ferrer*, 41; *Proceedings of the M. W. Grand Lodge of Free and Accepted Masons of the District of Columbia from November 4, A. L. 5845 to January 21, A. L. 5847* (Washington, DC: T. Barnard, 1847), 50.

13. Bergasa, *¿Quién mató a Ferrer i Guardia?*, 88; Avilés, *Francisco Ferrer y Guardia*, 46–47; Ferrer, *Anarchist Education*, 22.

14. Malato, *L'Assassinat de Ferrer*, 4.

15. APP, Ba 1075, report of July 24, 1907; AHN, Asuntos exteriores, Sección histórica, 2757, report of February 26, 1907, and 2759, report of February 24, 1907; Avilés, *Francisco Ferrer*, 183–84.

16. APP, Ba 1075, report of January 6, 1907.

17. "Pour Francisco Ferrer," *L'Humanité*, January 6, 1907.

18. Georges Dangon, "Francisco Ferrer," *Le XIXe siècle*, December 25, 1906.

19. Ferrer, *Anarchist Education*, 218, 221.

20. *España Nueva*, November 14, 1906, in William Heaford, "Some Side-Lights on Ferrer's Personality," in *Francisco Ferrer: His Life, Work, and Martyrdom* (New York: Francisco Ferrer Association, 1910), 24–25.

21. "Pour Francisco Ferrer," *L'Humanité*, January 6, 1907.

22. AGA, Asuntos exteriores, Embajada en Paris, 5883.

23. "La presse radicale sous Clemenceau," *Le Libertaire*, May 26–June 2, 1907.

24. AGA, Asuntos exteriores, Embajada en Paris, 5883, Sannois, July 20, 1906.

25. *El Rebelde* (Rosario de Santa Fe), January 1, 1907.

26. AGA, Asuntos exteriores, Embajada en Paris, 5882, Sannois, September 28, various from October 1906, October 8, 1906, December 17, 1906; NA, FO 371/136, Bunsen, October 24 and November 3, 1906; "Une fête," *Le Libertaire*, December 23–30, 1906.

27. Joan Connelly Ullman, *The Tragic Week: A Study of Anticlericalism in Spain, 1875–1912* (Cambridge, MA: Harvard University Press, 1968), 100.

28. AGA, Asuntos exteriores, Embajada en Paris, 5883, Sannois, August 21, 1906.

29. Álvarez Junco, *El Emperador*, 307–8; Ullman, *Tragic Week*, 100; Avilés, *Francisco Ferrer*, 183; Canals, *Los sucesos de España*, 134–35; Malato, *L'Assassinat de Ferrer*, 6; Archivo de la Fundación Antonio Maura (hereafter AFAM), Correspondencia oficial, 165, carp. 3.

30. Rafael Salillas, "La celda de Ferrer," *Revista Penitenciaria*, año IV, tomo IV, entrega 1a (June 1907), 321–47.

31. AGA, Asuntos exteriores, Embajada en Paris, 5882 and 5883, Sannois, December 17, 1906; AHN, Asuntos exteriores, Sección histórica, 2757, report of March 5, 1907.

32. AHN, Asuntos exteriores, Sección histórica, 2757, report of February 23, 1907; Ch. Malato, "Le procès de Sept," *Le Libertaire*, January 20–27, 1907.

33. Ferrer Collection, MS 248, box 1, folder 6, Ferrer, February 6, 1907.

34. *Regicidio frustrado*, 317–20; Masjuan, *Un héroe trágico*, 121–25; Vallina, "El tirano," *Solidaridad Obrera*, August 31, 1961.

35. Herrerín López, *Anarquía*, 227; Álvarez Junco, *El Emperador*, 308.

36. Herrerín López, *Anarquía*, 229.

37. AFAM, Corespondencia oficial, 165, carp. 6, Gobernador to Ministro de la Gobernación, June 16, 1907; Ferrer Collection, MS 248, box 1, folder 4, Ferrer, November 18, 1906.

15. The Birth of the "City of Bombs"

1. "Carlistas en Barcelona," *El País*, Jan. 21, 1907; Dalmau, *El cas Rull*, 199–200.

2. "Graves sucesos en Barcelona," *El País*, Jan. 21, 1907.

3. Ullman, *La semana trágica*, 21 and 60.

4. Ibid., 60; *La Vanguardia*, Jan. 21, 1907; Javier Moreno-Luzón, *Modernizing the Nation: Spain during the reign of Alfonso XIII, 1902–1931* (Brighton: Sussex Academic Press, 2016), 14.

5. Alvarez Junco, *El Emperador del Paralelo*, 307–08.

6. "El mitin católico," *La Publicidad*, Jan. 21, 1907; "Graves sucesos en Barcelona," *El País*, Jan. 21, 1907.

7. Ibid.

8. "Jornada sangienta: Batalla campal en la Granvía," *La Publicidad*, Jan. 21, 1907.

9. "Una bomba en la Rambla," *El País*, Jan. 21, 1907.

10. José María Marco, *Antonio Maura: La política pura* (Madrid: Fundación FAES, 2013), 124.

11. "Jueves de Gedeón," *Gedeón*, Dec. 30, 1906.

12. Dalmau, El procés de Montjuïc, 42.

13. AN, F7/12725, Attentats et complots en Espagne; coverage in *La Publicidad*, August-September, 1903; Núñez Florencio, *El terrrorismo anarquista*, 194–95.

14. Núñez Florencio, *El terrorismo anarquista*, 194–95.

15. Dalmau, *El cas Rull*, 143.

16. "Lo de Barcelona," *El Porvenir del Obrero*, Sept. 29, 1905.

17. AN, F7/12725, "Nuestra protesta," November, 1904.

18. *El Porvenir del Obrero*, Sept. 29, 1905; AN, F7/12725.

19. AGP, Reinados, Alfonso XIII, 13163, "Basta de farsa"; González Calleja, *La razón de la fuerza*, 351.

20. "Jornada sangienta: Batalla campal en la Granvía," *La Publicidad*, Jan. 21, 1907.

21. Dalmau, *El cas Rull*, 70–3, 102, 106, 122–6; Urales, *Mi Vida* vol. 2, 240–1; AN, F7/12725; AGA, Asuntos exteriores, Embajada en Paris, 5884.

22. González Calleja, *La razón de la fuerza*, 354–55.

23. *El Imparcial*, March 26, 1908; Dalmau, *El cas Rull*, 154.

24. *El Liberal*, Feb. 14–15, 1906.

25. Dalmau, *El cas Rull*, 158–61.

26. Gary Wray McDonogh, *Good Families of Barcelona: A Social History of Power in the Industrial Era* (Princeton: Princeton University Press, 1986), 86–7; Jaume Genís Terri, *Gaudí, entre l'arquitectura cristiana i l'art contemporani* (Barcelona: Publicacions de l'Abadia de Montserrat, 2009), 144–6, 200.

27. Dalmau, *El cas Rull*, 161–2.

28. Dalmau, *El cas Rull*, 164–84; NA, FO, 371/136.

29. Dalmau, *El cas Rull*, 163–92.

30. "Explosion de una bomba," *La Publicidad*, edición de mañana Dec. 27, 1906; Dalmau, *El cas Rull*, 193–94.

31. Dalmau, *El cas Rull*, 200–01 and 209; "Jornada sangienta: Batalla campal en la Granvía" and "Otra infamia," *La Publicidad*, edición de mañana, Jan. 21, 1907; "Indignación pública," *El País*, Jan. 21, 1907.

32. "Estaba previsto," and "Ayuntamiento," *La Publicidad*, edición de mañana December 28, 1906 and Jan. 22, 1907.

33. Rhiannon McGlade, "The 'fets de Cu-Cut!' Cartooning Controversy in Catalonia" *Romance Quarterly* 62, no. 4 (2015): 199–211.

34. Alvarez Junco, *El Emperador del Paralelo*, 316–25; González Calleja, *La razón de la fuerza*, 384–85.

35. AN, F7/12725; AGP, Reinados, Alfonso XIII, 15458, exp. 3; Dalmau, *El cas Rull*, 201–02; "La reunion de anoche," *La Publicidad*, edición de mañana January 29, 1907.

36. AHDB, Lligall 897 and 3545.

37. "Tiros en un mitin," *La Correspondencia Militar*, Aug. 12, 1907; Charles Arrow, *Rogues and Others* (London: Duckworth, 1926), 196–97.

38. AHDB, Lligall 897 & 3545; NA, FO, 185/1078; Arrow, *Rogues and Others*, 197–98.

39. AN, F7/12725; AHN, Gobernación, 2A exp. 15; González Calleja, *La razón de la fuerza*, 352–53.

40. Miguel Ángel Cabrera, *El reformismo social en España (1870–1900)* (Valencia: Publicacions de la Universitat de València, 2014).

41. Ullman, *La semana trágica*, 67; Marco, *Antonio Maura*, 88–94; Álvaro Soto Carmona, *El trabajo industrial en la España contemporánea (1874–1936)* (Barcelona: Anthropos, 1989), 418.

42. Francisco J. Romero Salvadó, "Antonio Maura: From Messiah to Fireman," in Alejandro Quiroga and Miguel Ángel del Arco eds., *Right-Wing Spain in the Civil War Era: Soldiers of God and Apostles of the Fatherland, 1914–45* (London: Continuum, 2012), 3.

43. González Calleja, *La razón de la fuerza*, 394–98.

44. NA, FO, 185/1078.

45. Dalmau, *El cas Rull*, 213–26; AN, F7/12725; Kaplan, *Red City*, 95.

46. Dalmau, *El cas Rull*, 239–43.

47. Ibid., 310–21; "Se va viendo claro," *Tierra y Libertad*, July 25, 1907; González Calleja, *La razón de la fuerza*, 400; AFAM, Correspondencia official, leg. 165, carp 15.

48. "Servicio telegráfico," *La Publicidad*, ed. Noche, Sept. 14, 1907, ed. mañana Dec. 24, 1907; AN, F7/12725; Dalmau, *El cas Rull*, 255–56.

49. AFAM, Correspondencia official, leg. 165, carp. 1 & 12; "El terrorismo en Barcelona," *El Imparcial*, Jan. 4, 1908.

50. González Calleja, *La razón de la fuerza*, 407 & 410; AFAM, Correspondencia official, leg. 149, carp. 1, Ossorio to Maura, May 28, 1907 & leg. 440, carp. 5, "Notas autógrafas."

51. For the text of the proposed law, see AFAM, Correspondencia official, leg. 443, carp. 14, Diario de las sesiones de Cortes: Senado, January, 24, 1908; Ullman, *La semana trágica*, 92; González Calleja, *La razón de la fuerza*, 353.

52. AFAM, Correspondencia privada, leg. 80, carp. 9; AHN, Gobernación, 2A, exp. 15; AN, F7/12725.

53. "Madrid contra la suspension," *Tierra y Libertad*, Jan. 24, 1908; AFAM, Correspondencia official, leg. 165, carp. 13, Telegram from governor of Barcelona to minister of the Interior, January 25, 1908.

54. Ullman, *La semana trágica*, 190–202; Romero Maura, *La rosa de fuego*, 465; Francisco Madrid, *Solidaridad Obrera y el periodismo de raíz ácrata* (Badalona: Solidaridad Obrera, 2007) 87–88.

55. "Nuestra campana," *Tierra y Libertad*, April 30, 1908; "La Prensa y la Ley," *El Heraldo de Madrid*, May 5, 1908 and "Bloque de prensa," *El Heraldo de Madrid*, May 6, 1908; Marco, *Antonio Maura*, 120–22; Margarita Márquez Padorno, "El liberalismo en la prensa: Miguel Moya" *Historia Contemporánea* 43 (2011): 688–94; Romanones, *Notas*, 221–24.

56. "Contra el Terrorismo," "Los anarquistas patriotas," and "Campaña," *Tierra y Libertad*, April 30, May 7, and June 18, 1908; "Atropello máximo," *El Heraldo de Madrid*, May 4, 1908.

57. "Los mitins," *El Heraldo de Madrid*, May 31, 1908; "Granos de arena," *Solidaridad Obrera*, June 5, 1908; Romero Maura, *La rosa de fuego*, 471; AHN, Gobernación, 60A exp. 14.

58. "Contra un proyecto de Ley," "Discurso de Iglesias contra el ley," and "El bloque de las izquierdas," *El Socialista*, May 22, May 29, and June 5, 1908.

59. Ullman, *La semana trágica*, 95–6.

16. Francisco Ferrer and the Tragic Week

1. Charles Bertram Black, *South-France; or, France beyond the Loire* (Edinburgh: Adam & Charles Black, 1885), 573.

2. William Archer, *The Life, Trial, and Death of Francisco Ferrer* (New York: Moffat, Yard and Company, 1911), 20.

3. "Alcalá del Valle," *Tierra y Libertad*, July 30, 1908; "Campaña humanitaria por los de Alcalá del Valle," *Solidaridad Obrera*, July 31, 1908.

4. Constant Leroy, *Los Secretos del anarquismo* (Mexico: Renacimiento, 1913), 169, 232; Report on Moreno, Asuntos exteriores, Sección histórica, 2757, AHN.

5. Leroy, *Los Secretos*, 225–32.

6. Ibid., 243–44.

7. "Manifiesto á los trabajadores," *Tierra y Libertad*, July 30, 1908.

8. "A la prensa burguesa por radical que sea," and "Por los de Alcalá del Valle," *Solidaridad Obrera*, September 25, 1908.

9. *Solidaridad Obrera*, August 28, 1908–January 8, 1909; Ullman, *La semana trágica*, 225–28; Romero Maura, *"La rosa de fuego,"* 488–89.

10. Leroy, *Los Secretos*, 244.

11. Ullman, *La semana trágica*, 121.

12. *Tierra y Libertad*, October 8, 1908–June 24, 1909; Leroy, *Los Secretos*, 234.

13. "Alcalá del Valle," *Tierra y Libertad*, March 25, 1909; "Notas sueltas," *Solidaridad Obrera*, August 7, 1908.

14. "Alcalá," *Tierra y Libertad*, October 8, 1908.

15. "La amnestía," *El País*, April 15, 1909; María Marco, *Antonio Maura*, 124; "Crónicas parlamentarias," *El Globo*, April 18, 1909; "Informaciones," *La Época*, April 22, 1909; "Cortes," *El Siglo Futuro*, April 22, 1909.

16. "Alcalá del Valle," *Tierra y Libertad*, May 20, 1909.

17. *Tierra y Libertad*, May 13–June 17, 1909; "Barcelona," *El Liberal*, April 17, 1909.

18. "Indultos plausibles," *El País*, June 25, 1909; "Sección de noticias," *El Imparcial*, June 26, 1909; Antonio Loredo, "Alcalá," *Tierra y Libertad*, July 1, 1909.

19. David S. Woolman, *Rebels in the Rif: Abd El Krim and the Rif Rebellion* (Stanford, CA: Stanford University Press, 1968), 31–33; Eloy Martín Corrales, "El nacionalismo catalán y la expansión colonial española en Marruecos: de la guerra de África a la entrada en vigor del Protectorado (1860–1912)," in Eloy Martín Corrales, ed., *Marruecos y el colonialismo español (1859–1912): De la guerra de África a la "penetración pacífica"* (Barcelona: Edicions Bellaterra, 2002), 167–70; Víctor Morales Lezcano, *El colonialismo Hispanofrances en Marruecos (1898–1927)* (Madrid: Siglo veintiuno de España, 1976), 21–46; Sebastian Balfour, *Deadly Embrace: Morocco and the Road to the Spanish Civil War* (Oxford: Oxford University Press, 2002), 4–11; Miller, *A History of Modern Morocco*, 72.

20. Balfour, *Deadly Embrace*, 17–19; Woolman, *Rebels in the Rif*, 38–41.

21. Enrique Faes Díaz, *Claudio López Bru: Marqués de Comillas* (Madrid: Marcial Pons Historia, 2009), 15, 208–9; Kaplan, *Red City*, 94.

22. Leopoldo Bonafulla, *La revolución de julio* (Barcelona: T. Taberner, 1910), 11–12; Ullman, *La semana trágica*, 295–302; Kaplan, *Red City*, 94–95; González Calleja, *La razón de la fuerza*, 427; Gobernador to Ministro de la Gobernación, July 18, 1909, Reinados, Alfonso XIII, 15458, exp. 5, AGP.

23. Alvarez Junco, *El Emperador*, 376.

24. Josep Benet, *Maragall i la Setmana Tràgica* (Barcelona: Edicions 62, 1965), 38; Ullman, *La semana trágica*, 302–12; Angel Ossorio y Gallardo, *Barcelona, Julio de 1909 (Declaración de un testigo)* (Madrid: R. Rojas, 1910), 32–43.

25. Ullman, *La semana trágica*, 322–39; "El terror en Barcelona," *El País*, November 2, 1909.

26. Ossorio, *Barcelona*, 52.

27. Ossorio, July 26, 1909, 151, carp. 1 and 4, AFAM; Bergasa, *Quién mató a Ferrer i Guardia?*, 161–62; Ullman, *La semana trágica*, 344–75; "International Notes," *Freedom*, September 1909.

28. "El terror," *El País*, November 2, 1909; Ullman, *La semana trágica*, 352, 364–65; Kaplan, *Red City*, 95; Alvarez Junco, *El Emperador*, 377.

29. González Calleja, *La razón de la fuerza*, 429; Bergasa, *¿Quién mató a Ferrer i Guardia?*, 164–65.

30. Ullman, *La semana trágica*, 381–84.

31. Sanabria, *Republicanism and Anticlerical Nationalism*, 2, 9, 20, 152.

32. Ullman, *La semana trágica*, 385–88; Antoni Dalmau, *Set dies de fúria: Barcelona i la Setmana Tràgica (juliol de 1909)* (Barcelona: Columna, 2009), 40.

33. A. Lerroux, "¡Rebeldes, rebeldes!" *La Rebeldía*, September 1, 1906.

34. Ullman, *La semana trágica*, 392–93.

35. Joan B. Culla i Clarà, *El republicanisme lerrouxista a Catalunya (1901–1923)* (Barcelona: Curial, 1986), 212.

36. Ullman, *La semana trágica*, 395–438.

37. Ibid., 390–408.

38. Bonafulla, *La revolución de julio*, 27; Vidal y Ribas, "En pleine révolution," *L'Humanité*, August 15, 1909.

39. Kaplan, *Red City*, 106. She was listed as both "Ortiz" and "Ruiz." "La represión en Cataluña," *El País*, October 8, 1909.

40. Vidal, "En pleine," *L'Humanité*, August 15, 1909.

41. Ullman, *La semana trágica*, 448.

42. David Martínez Fiol, *La Setmana Tràgica* (Barcelona: Pòrtic, 2009), 36–45.

43. Chris Ealham, "The Struggle for Barcelona during the 'Tragic Week': The Clash between Two Urban Models and Two Antithetical Ways of Understanding the City," in José Álvarez Junco et al., *Tràgica, roja i gloriosa: una setmana de 1909* (Barcelona: Ajuntament de Barcelona, 2010), 31.

44. Ullman, *La semana trágica*, 455–76.

45. Ibid., 480–91; Romero Salvadó, *¿Quién mató a Eduardo Dato?*, 136.

46. Arrow, *Rogues and Others*, 202–6; "De Barcelona," *El País*, August 2, 1909.

47. Romero Maura, *"La rosa de fuego,"* 515; Ullman, *La semana trágica*, 508–14; Dalmau, *Set dies de fúria*, 59; *Causa contra Francisco Ferrer Guardia: instruida y fallada*

por la Jurisdicción de Guerra en Barcelona, año 1909 (Madrid: Sucesores de J. A. García, 1911), 645; 151, carp. 2 and 8, AFAM; Bergasa, *¿Quién mató a Ferrer i Guardia?*, 194.

48. Archer, *The Life,Trial, and Death* 143–4; Ferrer, *Le véritable Francisco Ferrer*, 181–84; Bergasa, *¿Quién mató a Ferrer i Guardia?*, 181–87; Ullman, *La semana trágica*, 346–471.

49. Malato, *L'Assassinat de Ferrer*, 9.

50. Bergasa, *¿Quién mató a Ferrer i Guardia?*, 199–242.

51. Ibid., 516–28; Ferrer, *Anarchist Education*, 1.

52. Reports of September–November 1909, Ba 1075, APP; *L'Humanité*, September 10, 12, and October 9, 1909; Peter Tiidu Park, "The European Reaction to the Execution of Francisco Ferrer" (PhD diss., University of Virginia, 1970), 224–26; *Le Journal*, September 10, 1909; *Le Libertaire*, September 12, 1909; F7 13066, AN; Vincent Robert and Eduard J. Verger, "'La protesta universal' contra la ejecución de Ferrer: las manifestaciones de octubre de 1909," *Historia Social* 14 (Autumn 1992): 61–82.

53. Pedro Voltes Bou, *La semana trágica* (Madrid: Espasa Calpe, 1995), 199–206.

54. *L'Humanité*, October 14, 1909; *L'Intransigeant*, October 14, 1909; *Le Temps*, October 15, 1909; F7 13066, AN; Asuntos exteriores, Embajada en Paris, 5892, AGA.

55. Park, "European Reaction," 266–69; Juan Avilés, *Francisco Ferrer*, 253; Sol Ferrer, *La vie et l'oeuvre de Francisco Ferrer: un martyr au XXe siècle* (Paris: Librairie Fischbacher, 1962), 175–84; Madeleine Rebérioux, "Manifester pour Ferrer Paris Octobre 1909," in Francine Best et al., *L'affaire Ferrer* (Castres, France: Centre national et Musée Jean Jaurès, 1991), 79–100.

56. Park, "European Reaction," 312–29, 570–82; Ferrer, *La vie et l'oeuvre*, 185–99.

57. Avilés, *Francisco Ferrer*, 256–58; Park, "European Reaction," 414–592; Ferrer, *La vie et l'oeuvre*, 192–99; di Paola, *Knights Errant*, 114–15; Khuri-Makdisi, *Eastern Mediterranean*, 60–62; *Times*, October 14, 1909; Asuntos Exteriores, Sección Histórica, 2752, AHN.

58. Asuntos Exteriores, Sección Histórica, 2752 and Gobernación, 2A exp. 15, AHN; Asuntos exteriores, Embajada en Washington D.C., 8090, AGA; Pere Solà i Gussinyer, "Los grupos del magisterio racionalista en Argentina y Uruguay hacia 1910 y sus actitudes ante la enseñanza laica oficial," *Historia de la Educación* 1 (1982): 236–37; Avilés, *Francisco Ferrer*, 258; Park, "European Reaction," 591; Ferrer, *La Vie et l'oeuvre*, 199–202; Amparo Sanchez Cobos, *Sembrando ideales: anarquistas españoles en Cuba, 1902–1925* (Seville: Consejo Superior de Investigaciones Científicas, 2008), 234–35; Frank Fernández, *Cuban Anarchism: The History of a Movement*, trans. Charles Bufe (Tucson: See Sharp Press, 2001), 47; Leoncio Lasso de la Vega, *El asesinato de Ferrer: la protesta del Uruguay* (Montevideo, 1909); Maria del Mar Araus Segura, "La escuela moderna en Iberoamérica: repercussion de la muerte de Francisco Ferrer Guardia," *Boletín americanista* 52 (2002): 13–22.

59. Daniel Laqua, "Freethinkers, Anarchists and Francisco Ferrer: The Making of a Transnational Solidarity Campaign," *European Review of History/Revue européenne d'histoire* 21, no. 4 (2014): 471.

60. See Ferrer, *Anarchist Education and the Modern School*.

61. Ch. Malato, "La vie de Ferrer ou la Tête du roi!" *Le Libertaire*, October 17, 1909.

62. Gabriel Maura y Gamazo and Melchor Fernández Almagro, *Por qué cayó Alfonso XIII? Evolución y disolución de los partidos históricos durante su reinado* (Madrid: Ediciones Ambos Mundos, S.L., 1948), 154–56.

63. Eduardo González Calleja, *La razón de la fuerza*, 438; *El proceso Ferrer en el Congreso.*

Epilogue

1. "Después de la ejecución," *La Época*, October 13, 1909; "The Execution of Señor Ferrer," *Times*, October 14, 1909.

2. "Comité de defense sociale" and "Francisco Ferrer," *Le Libertaire*, September 12 and 19, 1909; "Shall Ferrer Be Shot?" *Freedom*, October 1909.

3. *Berliner Tageblatt*, November 1, 1909, in Park, "European Reaction," 493.

4. "Pour Ferrer" and "La reprobation," *Le Libertaire*, September 19 and October 24, 1909.

5. *Le Peuple*, October 8, 1909, in Park, "European Reaction," 307.

6. *Pester Lloyd*, October 16, 1909 (morning edition), in Park, "European Reaction," 422–23.

7. Gal Gerson, *Margins of Disorder: New Liberalism and the Crisis of European Consciousness* (Albany: State University of New York Press, 2004), 15.

8. Walter Laqueur, *Fascism: Past, Present, Future* (New York: Oxford University Press, 1997), 17–18.

9. Kevin Rozario, "'Delicious Horrors': Mass Culture, the Red Cross, and the Appeal of Modern American Humanitarianism," *American Quarterly* 55, no. 3 (2003): 420.

10. V. I. Lenin, "The Tasks of the Youth Leagues," in V. I. Lenin, *On Culture and Cultural Revolution* (Rockville, MD: Wildside Press, 2008), 134–35; Justine Lacroix, Jean-Yves Pranchère, and Sarah-Louise Raillard, "Was Karl Marx Truly against Human Rights? Individual Emancipation and Human Rights Theory," *Revue française de science politique (English Edition)* 62, no. 3 (2012): 47–65.

11. Rocker, *En la borrasca*, 59.

12. Tomás Caballé y Clos, *La criminalidad en Barcelona* (Barcelona: Ariel, 1945), 95–96.

13. Moyn, *Last Utopia*, 45, 121.

14. R. Pérez, "El grupo que atentó en La Almudena reivindica el ataque en El Pilar," *ABC*, November 4, 2013.

15. Marcos Pinheiro, "Pandora, Piñata y Ice," *El Diario*, August 25, 2018, https://www.eldiario.es/politica/pandora-pinata-ice-operaciones-terrorismo_1_1968745.html.

16. Michael Loadenthal, *The Politics of Attack: Communiqués and Insurrectionary Violence* (Manchester: Manchester University Press, 2017).

17. Mercedes Domenech, "Tres detenidos en la marcha anarquista en Madrid," *El Diario*, December 16, 2014, https://www.eldiario.es/sociedad/detenidos-anarquista-madrid-operacion-pandora_1_4456890.html.

Bibliography

Archives

France

Archives de la Préfecture de Police (APP)
Archives diplomatiques du Ministère des Affaires Étrangères, La Courneuve (AD)
Archives nationales (AN)
Bibliothèque nationale de France

Netherlands

Internationaal Instituut voor Sociale Geschiedenis (IISG)

Spain

Archivo de la Fundación Antonio Maura (AFAM)
Archivo del Tribunal Superior de Justicia de Cataluña (ATSJC)
Archivo General de la Administración (AGA)
Archivo General del Palacio (AGP)
Archivo Histórico Nacional (AHN)
Arxiu de la Corona d'Aragó (ACA)
Arxiu Històric de la Diputació de Barcelona (AHDB)
Arxiu Nactional de Catalunya (ANC)
Ateneu Enciclopèdic Popular (AEP)
Biblioteca de Catalunya (BC)
Biblioteca Nacional de España (BNE)
Biblioteca Pública Arus
Centre de Documentació- Fundació Francesc Ferrer i Guàrdia
Hemeroteca Municipal de Madrid
Real Academia de Historia (RAH)

UK

British Library
National Archives (NA)

USA

New York Public Library
Tamiment Library, New York University
University of California, San Diego Special Collections (UCSD)

Newspapers

Barcelona

Boletín de la Escuela Moderna
La Campana de Gracia
El Diluvio
La Dinastía
Las Noticias
El Noticiero Universal
El Productor
La Publicidad
La Rebeldía
Solidaridad obrera
Tierra y Libertad
La Tramontana
La Vanguardia

Latin America

La Nueva Humanidad (Rosario de Santa Fe)
El Nuevo Ideal (Havana)
El Obrero (Montevideo)
La Protesta (Buenos Aires)
El Rebelde (Buenos Aires)
El Rebelde (Rosario de Santa Fe)
La Verdad (Montevideo)
La Voz del Pueblo (Córdoba, Argentina)

London

Fortnightly Review
Freedom
Free Russia
Morning Post
Standard
Times

Madrid

    ABC
    El Correo Español
    La Correspondencia de España
    La Época
    España Nueva
    Gaceta de Madrid
    Gedeón
    El Globo
    El Heraldo de Madrid
    El Imparcial
    El Liberal
    El Motín
    El Movimiento católico
    El Nuevo Régimen
    El País
    El Progreso
    Progreso
    El Rebelde
    La Revista Blanca
    Revista Penitenciaria
    El Siglo futuro
    El Socialista
    Suplemento a la Revista Blanca
    Tierra y Libertad
    Vida Nueva

Paris

    Le XIXe siècle
    L'Action
    L'Aurore
    La Campaña
    L'Eclair
    L'En dehors
    L'Espagne inquisitoriale
    Gazette des tribunaux
    Gazette du palais
    L'Humanité
    L'Intransigeant
    Le Figaro

Le Journal

Le Libertaire

Le Matin

La Petite république française

Le Peuple

Le Rappel

La Révolte

La Revue blanche

Le Soleil

Solidaridad Obrera

Le Temps

Les Temps nouveaux

Elsewhere in Europe

La Controversia (Valencia)

El Corsario (La Coruña)

El Eco de Ravachol (Sabadell)

Freemans Journal (Dublin)

El Porvenir del Obrero (Mahón)

Ravachol (Sabadell)

La Revancha (Reus)

Published Primary Sources

Abad de Santillán, Diego. *Memorias 1897–1936*. Barcelona: Planeta, 1977.

Abidor, Mitchell, ed. *Death to Bourgeois Society: The Propagandists of the Deed*. Oakland: PM Press, 2015.

Archer, William. *The Life, Trial, and Death of Francisco Ferrer*. New York: Moffat, Yard and Company, 1911.

Arrow, Charles. *Rogues and Others*. London: Duckworth, 1926.

Bates, Katherine Lee. *Spanish Highways and Byways*. Chautauqua, NY: Chautauqua Press, 1905.

Bonafoux, Luis. *Betances*. San Juan: Instituto de Cultural Puertorriqueña, 1970.

Bonafulla, Leopoldo. *La revolución de julio*. Barcelona: T. Taberner, 1910.

Caballé y Clos, Tomás. *Barcelona de antaño: memorias de un viejo reportero barcelonés*. Barcelona: Aries, 1944.

———. *La criminalidad en Barcelona*. Barcelona: Ariel, 1945.

La Campaña de "El Progreso" en favor de las víctimas del proceso de Montjuich. Barcelona: Tarascó, Viladot y Cuesta Impresores, 1897–1898.

Canals, Salvador. *Los sucesos de España en 1909: Crónica documentada Tomo II*. Madrid: Impr. Alemana, 1911.

Causa contra Francisco Ferrer Guardia: instruida y fallada por la Jurisdicción de Guerra en Barcelona, año 1909. Madrid: Sucesores de J. A. García, 1911.

Coromines, Pere. *Diaris i records I, Els anys de Joventut i El Procés de Montjuïc.* Barcelona: Cural, 1974.

Dryhurst, N. F., and Robert Lynd. *Nationalities and Subject Races: Report of Conference Held in Caxton Hall, Westminster, June 28–30, 1910.* London: P. S. King & Son, 1911.

Estévanez, Nicolás. *Fragmentos de mis memorias.* Madrid: Hijos de R. Álvarez, 1903.

Goldman, Emma. *Emma Goldman: A Documentary History of the American Years.* Vol. 2: *Making Speech Free, 1902–1909.* Edited by Candace Falk, Barry Pateman, and Jessica Moran. Berkeley: University of California Press, 2005.

———. *Red Emma Speaks: An Emma Goldman Reader.* 3rd ed. Edited by Alix Kates Shulman. Amherst, NY: Humanity Books, 1998.

Graham, Robert, ed. *Anarchism: A Documentary History of Libertarian Ideas.* Vol. 1: *From Anarchy to Anarchism (300 CE to 1939).* Montreal: Black Rose, 2005.

Guérin, Daniel, ed. *No Gods No Masters: An Anthology of Anarchism.* Translated by Paul Sharkey. Oakland: AK Press, 1998.

Faure, Sébastien. *Les Anarchistes et l'affaire Dreyfus.* Paris: Lafont, 1898.

Fehrenbach, Heide, and Davide Rodogno, eds. *Humanitarian Photography: A History.* Cambridge: Cambridge University Press, 2015.

Ferrer, Sol. *Le véritable Francisco Ferrer: d'après des documents inédits.* Paris: L'Écran du monde, 1948.

———. *La Vie et l'oeuvre de Francisco Ferrer: un martyr au XXe sie`cle.* Paris: Librairie Fischbacher, 1962.

Ferrer Guardia, Francisco. *Anarchist Education and the Modern School: A Francisco Ferrer Reader.* Edited by Mark Bray and Robert H. Haworth. Oakland: PM Press, 2018.

Flores Magón, Ricardo. *Dreams of Freedom: A Ricardo Flores Magón Reader.* Edited by Chaz Bufe and Mitchell Cowen Verter. Oakland: AK Press, 2005.

Francisco Ferrer, His Life Work and Martyrdom. New York: Francisco Ferrer Association, 1910.

Gil Maestre, Manuel. *El anarquismo en España y el especial de Barcelona.* Madrid: Hernández, 1897.

Hurtado, Amadeu. *Quaranta anys d'advocat: història del meu temps,* vol. 1. Esplugues de Llobregat: Edicions Ariel, 1968.

La Inquisición fin de siglo. Buenos Aires: Librería Sociológica, 1899.

Juderías, Julián. *La leyenda negra: estudios acerca del concepto de España en el extranjero.* Barcelona: Arluce, 1914.

Kropotkin, Pyotr. *The Conquest of Bread.* Montreal: Black Rose Books, 1990.

———. *Memoirs of a Revolutionist.* New York: Houghton Mifflin, 1899.

Landauer, Gustav. *Revolution and Other Writings: A Political Reader.* Edited and translated by Gabriel Kuhn. Oakland: PM Press, 2010.

Lasso de la Vega, Leoncio. *El asesinato de Ferrer: la protesta del Uruguay.* Montevideo, 1909.

Lenin, V. I. *On Culture and Cultural Revolution.* Rockville, MD: Wildside Press, 2008.

Leroy, Constant. *Los Secretos del anarquismo.* Mexico: Renacimiento, 1913.

Lerroux, Alejandro. *Mis memorias.* Madrid: Afrodisio Aguado, 1963.

Lorenzo, Anselmo. *El banquete de la vida: Concordancia entre la naturaleza, el hombre y la sociedad.* Barcelona: Imprenta Luz, 1905.

M., R., and J. P. *La barbarie gubernamental en España*. Brooklyn: Imp. de *El Despertar*, 1897.

Malato, Charles. *L'Assassinat de Ferrer: Eclaircissements*. Geneva: Édition du Réveil, 1911.

———. "Some Anarchist Portraits." *Fortnightly Review*, September 1, 1894.

Montseny, J. *Consideraciones sobre el hecho y muerte de Pallás*. La Coruña: Tipografia la Gutenberg, 1893.

———. *El proceso de un gran crímen*. La Coruña: Tipografia la Gutenberg, 1895.

Morral, Mateo. *Pensamientos revolucionarios de Nicolás Estévanez*. Barcelona: José J. de Olañeta, 1978.

Ossorio y Gallardo, Angel. *Barcelona, Julio de 1909 (Declaración de un testigo)*. Madrid: R. Rojas, 1910.

El proceso Ferrer en el Congreso: recopilación de los discursos pronunciados por varios diputados durante el debate. Barcelona: Impr. Lauria, 1911.

Raynaud, Ernest. *Souvenirs de police: La vie intime des commissariats*. Paris: Payot, 1926.

Regicidio frustrado 31 mayo 1906. Causa contra Mateo Morral. Madrid: Sucesores de J. A. García, 1911.

Roca, Marian. *Records de la meva vida*. Reus: Assaig, 1979.

Rocker, Rudolf. *En la borrasca: años de destierro*. Translated by Diego A. De Santillan. Buenos Aires: Editorial Tupac, 1949.

Conde de Romanones. *Notas de una vida*, vol. 2. Madrid: Renacimiento, 1929.

Rosell, Albano. *Vidas trágicas: Mateo Morral, Francisco Ferrer*. Montevideo, 1940.

Sempau, Ramon. *Los victimarios: notas relativas al proceso de Montjuich*. Barcelona: García y Manent, 1900.

Tarrida del Mármol, Fernando. *Les Inquisiteurs d'Espagne: Montjuich, Cuba, Philippines*. Paris: Stock, 1897.

Urales, Federico. *El Castillo maldito*. Toulouse: Presses Universitaires du Mirail, 1992.

———. *Mi Don Quijote*. Barcelona: Biblioteca de La Revista Blanca, 1932.

———. *Mi Vida*. 3 vols. Barcelona: Publicaciones de la Revista Blanca, 1932.

Vallina, Pedro. *Fermín Salvochea: crónica de un revolucionario*. Seville: Renacimiento, 2012.

———. *Mis memorias*. Seville: Libre Pensamiento, 2000.

Varennes, Henri. *De Ravachol a Caserio*. Paris: Garnier Frères, 1894.

Wilde, Oscar. *The Picture of Dorian Gray*. New York: Barnes & Noble, 2003.

Zoccoli, Héctor. *La anarquía: las ideas, los hechos*. Barcelona: Henrich y C. A., 1908.

Zola, Émile. *Germinal*. Paris: G. Charpentier, 1885.

Secondary Sources

Abelló i Güell, Teresa. "El proceso de Montjuïc: la condena internactional al régimen de la Restauración." *Historia Social* 14 (1992): 46–60.

———. *Les Relacions internacionals de l'anarquisme Català (1881–1914)*. Barcelona: Edicions 62, 1987.

Agamben, Giorgio. *Sovereign Power and Bare Life*. Stanford, CA: Stanford University Press, 1998.

Aisa, Ferran. *La cultura anarquista a Catalunya*. Barcelona: Edicions de 1984, 2006.

Álvarez Junco, José. *El Emperador del Paralelo: Lerroux y la Demagogia Populista*. Madrid: Alianza, 1990.

——. *La ideología política del anarquismo español (1868–1910)*. Madrid: Siglo XXI, 1991.

Álvarez Junco, José, et al. *Tràgica, roja i gloriosa: una setmana de 1909*. Barcelona: Ajuntament de Barcelona, 2010.

Anderson, Benedict. *Under Three Flags: Anarchism and the Anti-Colonial Imagination*. New York: Verso, 2005.

Anderson, Peter. *The Francoist Military Trials: Terror and Complicity, 1939–1945*. New York: Routledge, 2010.

Araus Segura, Mª del Mar. "La escuela moderna en Iberoamérica: repercussion de la muerte de Francisco Ferrer Guardia." *Boletín americanista* 52 (2002): 7–22.

Archer, William. *The Life, Trial, and Death of Francisco Ferrer*. New York: Moffat, Yard and Company, 1911.

Arendt, Hannah. *On Revolution*. London: Penguin, 1990.

——. *The Origins of Totalitarianism*. San Diego: Harcourt, 1973.

Avilés Farré, Juan. *Francisco Ferrer y Guardia: pedagogo, anarquista y mártir*. Madrid: Marcial Pons, Ediciones de Historia, S.A., 2006.

——. "Propaganda por el hecho y regicidio en Italia." In Avilés and Herrerín, *El nacimiento del terrorismo en occidente*, 2–5.

Avilés, Juan, and Ángel Herrerín eds. *El nacimiento del terrorismo en occidente: anarquía, nihilismo y violencia revolucionaria*. Madrid: Siglo XXI, 2008.

Avrich, Paul. *An American Anarchist: The Life of Voltairine de Cleyre*. Princeton, NJ: Princeton University Press, 1978.

——. *The Russian Anarchists*. Princeton, NJ: Princeton University Press, 1967.

Baer, James A. *Anarchists and Immigrants in Spain and Argentina*. Urbana: University of Illinois Press, 2017.

Balfour, Sebastian. *Deadly Embrace: Morocco and the Road to the Spanish Civil War*. Oxford: Oxford University Press, 2002.

——. "Riot, Regeneration and Reaction: Spain in the Aftermath of the 1898 Disaster." *Historical Journal* 38, no. 2 (1995): 405–23.

Bantman, Constance. "La Culture de la campagne médiatique dans le mouvement anarchiste de la Belle Époque: Jean Grave et 'les atrocités espagnoles' (1885–1909)." *Printemps* 33 (2020): 40–55.

——. *The French Anarchists in London, 1880–1914: Exile and Transnationalism in the First Globalisation*. Liverpool: Liverpool University Press, 2013.

——. "Internationalism without an International? Cross-Channel Anarchist Networks, 1880–1914." *Revue belge de philologie et d'histoire* 84, no. 4 (2006): 961–81.

——. "Jean Grave and French Anarchism: A Relational Approach (1870s–1914)." *IRSH* 62 (2017): 451–77.

Bantman, Constance, and Bert Altena, eds. *Reassessing the Transnational Turn: Scales of Analysis in Anarchist and Syndicalist Studies*. Oakland: PM Press, 2017.

Barnett, Michael. *Empire of Humanity: A History of Humanitarianism*. Ithaca, NY: Cornell University Press, 2011.

Bass, Gary J. *Freedom's Battle: The Origins of Humanitarian Intervention*. New York: Alfred A. Knopf, 2008.

Benet, Josep. *Maragall i la Setmana Tràgica*. Barcelona: Edicions 62, 1965.

Bergasa, Francisco. *¿Quién mató a Ferrer i Guardia?* Madrid: Aguilar, 2009.

Best, Francine, et al. *L'affaire Ferrer*. Castres, France: Centre national et Musée Jean Jaure's, 1991.

Black, Charles Bertram. *South-France; or, France beyond the Loire.* Edinburgh: Adam & Charles Black, 1885.

Boampong, Joanna, ed. *In and Out of Africa: Exploring Afro-Hispanic, Luso-Brazilian, and Latin American Connections.* Newcastle upon Tyne: Cambridge Scholars, 2012.

Bray, Mark. "Beyond and Against the State: Anarchist Contributions to Human Rights History and Theory." *Humanity* 10, no. 3 (2019): 323–38.

Breen, Louise A., ed. *Converging Worlds: Communities and Cultures in Colonial America.* New York: Routledge, 2012.

Brennan, James F. *The Reflection of the Dreyfus Affair in the European Press, 1897–1899.* New York: P. Lang, 1998.

Brunet, Jean-Paul. *La Police de l'ombre: indicateurs et provocateurs dans la France contemporaine.* Paris: Seuil, 1990.

Bryan, Dominic, Liam Kelly, and Sara Templer. "The Failed Paradigm of 'Terrorism.'" *Behavioral Sciences of Terrorism and Political Aggression* 3, no. 2 (2011): 80–96.

Burleigh, Michael. *Blood and Rage: A Cultural History of Terrorism.* New York: Harper Collins, 2009.

Butterworth, Alex. *The World That Never Was: A True Story of Dreamers, Schemers, Anarchists, and Secret Agents.* New York: Pantheon, 2010.

Cahm, Caroline. *Kropotkin and the Rise of Revolutionary Anarchism, 1872–1886.* Cambridge: Cambridge University Press, 1989.

Capellán de Miguel, Gonzalo, and Aurora Garrido Martín. "'Los intérpretes de la opinión.' Uso, abuso y transforamción del concepto opinión pública en el discurso político durante la Restauración (1875–1902)." *Ayer* 80, no. 4 (2010): 83–114.

Carman, W. Y. *A History of Firearms: From Earliest Times to 1914.* New York: Routledge, 2016.

Casanova, Julián, ed. *Tierra y libertad: cien años de anarquismo en España.* Barcelona: Critica, 2010.

Chalaby, Jean K. *The Invention of Journalism.* New York: St. Martin's Press, 1998.

Cronin, Audrey Kurth, and James M. Ludes, eds. *Attacking Terrorism: Elements of a Grand Strategy.* Washington, DC: Georgetown University Press, 2004.

Cuadrat, Xavier. *Socialismo y anarquismo en Cataluña (1899–1911): Los orígenes de la C.N.T.* Madrid: Ediciones de la Revista de Trabajo, 1976.

Culla i Clarà, Joan B. *El republicanisme lerrouxista a Catalunya (1901–1923).* Barcelona: Curial, 1986.

Dalmau i Ribalta, Antoni. *El Cas Rull: viure del terror a la Ciutat de les Bombes (1901–1908).* Barcelona: Columna, 2008.

——. *El Procés de Montjuïc: Barcelona al final del segle XIX.* Barcelona: Editorial Base, 2010.

——. "Martí Borràs i Jover (1845–1894) o el primer comunisme llibertari." *Revista d'Igualada* 26 (2007): 15–31.

——. *Set dies de fúria: Barcelona i la Setmana Tràgica (juliol de 1909).* Barcelona: Columna, 2009.

Das, Dilip K. *Financial Globalization: Growth, Integration, Innovation and Crisis.* New York: Palgrave Macmillan, 2010.

de la Cierva, Ricardo. *Alfonso y Victoria: Las tramas íntimas, secretas y europeas de un reinado desconocido.* Madrid: Editorial Fénix, 2001.

del Valle-Inclán, Javier. *Biografía de La Revista Blanca 1898–1905.* Barcelona: Sintra, 2008.

di Paola, Pietro. *Knights Errant of Anarchy: London and the Italian Anarchist Diaspora (1880–1917).* Liverpool: Liverpool University Press, 2013.

Drake, David. *French Intellectuals and Politics from the Dreyfus Affair to the Occupation.* New York: Palgrave Macmillan, 2005.

Esenwein, George Richard. *Anarchist Ideology and the Working-Class Movement in Spain, 1868–1898.* Berkeley: University of California Press, 1989.

Esteban, José. *Mateo Morral el anarquista: causa por un regicidio.* Madrid: Vosa, 2011.

Everdell, William R. *The First Moderns: Profiles in the Origins of Twentieth-Century Thought.* Chicago: University of Chicago Press, 1997.

Fabié, Antonio María. *Cánovas del Castillo. Su juventud. Su edad madura. Su vejez. Estudio biográfico.* Barcelona: Gustavo Gili, 1928.

Faes Díaz, Enrique. *Claudio López Bru: Marqués de Comillas.* Madrid: Marcial Pons Historia, 2009.

Fernández Almagro, Melchor. *Historia del Reinado de Alfonso XIII.* Barcelona: Montaner y Simón, 1977.

Fernández, Frank. *Cuban Anarchism: The History of a Movement.* Translated by Charles Bufe. Tucson: See Sharp Press, 2001.

Ferrer, Ada. *Insurgent Cuba: Race, Nation, and Revolution, 1868–1898.* Chapel Hill: University of North Carolina Press, 1999.

Festa, Lynn. "Humanity without Feathers." *Humanity* 1, no. 1 (2010): 3–27.

Finlay, Christopher J. "How to Do Things with the Word 'Terrorist.'" *Review of International Studies* 35, no. 4 (2009): 751–74.

Frémion, Yves. *Léauthier l'anarchiste: de la propagande par le fait à la révolte des bagnards (1893–1894).* Montreuil: Éditions L'Échappée, 2011.

Geifman, Anna. *Thou Shalt Kill: Revolutionary Terrorism in Russia, 1894–1917.* Princeton, NJ: Princeton University Press, 1996.

Gerson, Gal. *Margins of Disorder: New Liberalism and the Crisis of European Consciousness.* Albany: State University of New York Press, 2004.

Gómez, Jesús, ed. *El ensayo español, 1: Los orígenes: siglos XV a XVII.* Barcelona: Crítica, 1996.

Gómez Casas, Juan. *Historia del anarco sindicalismo español.* Madrid: Editorial ZYX, 1968.

González Calleja, Eduardo. *La razón de la fuerza: orden público, subversión y violencia política en la España de la Restauración (1875–1917).* Madrid: Consejo Superior de Investigaciones Científicas, 1998.

Goodman, Jordan. *The Devil and Mr. Casement: One Man's Battle for Human Rights in South America's Heart of Darkness.* New York: Farrar, Straus & Giroux, 2010.

Goodway, David. *Anarchist Seeds beneath the Snow: Left-Libertarian Thought and British Writers from William Morris to Colin Ward.* Liverpool: Liverpool University Press, 2006.

Gorman, Anthony. "Anarchists in Education: The Free Popular University in Egypt (1901)." *Middle Eastern Studies* 41, no. 3 (2005): 303–20.

Gott, Richard. *Cuba: A New History.* New Haven, CT: Yale University Press, 2005.

Goyens, Tom. "Social Space and the Practice of Anarchist History." *Rethinking History* 13, no. 4 (2009): 439–57.

Graham, Robert. *We Do Not Fear Anarchy, We Invoke It: The First International and the Origins of the Anarchist Movement.* Oakland: AK Press, 2015.

Grant, Kevin. *A Civilised Savagery: Britain and the New Slaveries in Africa, 1884–1926.* New York: Routledge, 2004.

Greer, Margaret R. et al., eds. *Rereading the Black Legend: The Discourse of Religious and Racial Difference in the Renaissance Empires.* Chicago: University of Chicago Press, 2007.

Griffiths, Richard. *The Use of Abuse: The Polemics of the Dreyfus Affair and Its Aftermath.* New York: Berg, 1991.

Grob-Fitzgibbon, Benjamin. "From the Dagger to the Bomb: Karl Heinzen and the Evolution of Political Terror." *Terrorism and Political Violence* 16, no. 1 (2010): 97–115.

Halttunen, Karen. "Humanitarianism and the Pornography of Pain in Anglo-American Culture." *American Historical Review* 100, no. 2 (1995): 303–34.

Harcourt, Bernard. *Exposed: Desire and Disobedience in the Digital Age.* Cambridge, MA: Harvard University Press, 2016.

Herrerín López, Ángel. "Anarchist Sociability in Times of Violence and Clandestinity." *Bulletin for Spanish and Portuguese Historical Studies* 38, no. 1 (2013): 155–74.

——. *Anarquía, dinamita y revolución social: violencia y represión en la España de entre siglos (1868–1909).* Madrid: Catarata, 2011.

Hinley, Susan Denene. "Charlotte Wilson: Anarchist, Fabian, and Feminist." PhD diss., Stanford University, 1987.

Hirsch, Steven, and Lucien van der Walt, eds. *Anarchism and Syndicalism in the Colonial and Postcolonial World, 1870–1940.* Leiden: Brill, 2010.

Hochschild, Adam. *King Leopold's Ghost: A Story of Greed, Terror, and Heroism in Colonial Africa.* Boston: Houghton Mifflin, 1999.

Hoffman, Robert L. *More than a Trial: The Struggle over Captain Dreyfus.* New York: Free Press, 1980.

Hoffman, Stefan-Ludwig, ed. "Human Rights and History." *Past and Present* 232 (2016): 279–310.

——. *Human Rights in the Twentieth Century.* New York: Cambridge University Press, 2011.

Hofmann, Bert, Pere Joan i Tous, and Manfred Tietz, eds. *El anarquismo español y sus tradiciones culturales.* Madrid: Iberoamericana, 1995.

Hollingsworth, Barry. "The Society of Friends of Russian Freedom: English Liberals and Russian Socialists, 1890–1917." *Oxford Slavonic Papers* 3 (1970): 46–64.

Horowitz, Irving Louis, ed. *The Anarchists.* New York: Dell, 1964.

Hunt, Lynn. *Inventing Human Rights: A History.* New York: W. W. Norton, 2007.

Inglis, Fred. *A Short History of Celebrity.* Princeton, NJ: Princeton University Press, 2010.

Íñiguez, Miguel, ed. *Enciclopedia histórica del anarquismo español.* Vitoria: Asociación Isaac Puente, 2008.

Izrine, Jean-Marc. *Les libertaires dans l'affaire Dreyfus.* Paris: Éditions d'Alternative libertaire, 2012.

Jackson, Richard. "An Argument for Terrorism." *Perspectives on Terrorism* 2, no. 2 (2008): 25–32.

——, ed. *Routledge Handbook of Critical Terrorism Studies*. London: Routledge, 2016.

Jensen, Richard Bach. *The Battle against Anarchist Terrorism: An International History, 1878–1934*. Cambridge: Cambridge University Press, 2014.

——. "The International Campaign against Anarchist Terrorism, 1880–1930s." *Terrorism and Political Violence* 21, no. 1 (2009): 89–109.

Johnson, Martin P. *The Dreyfus Affair: Honour and Politics in the Belle Époque*. New York: St. Martin's Press, 1999.

Kaplan, Temma. *Anarchists of Andalusia 1868–1903*. Princeton, NJ: Princeton University Press, 1977.

——. *Red City, Blue Period: Social Movements in Picasso's Barcelona*. Princeton, NJ: Princeton University Press, 1992.

——. "The Social Base of Nineteenth-Century Andalusian Anarchism in Jerez de la Frontera." *Journal of Interdisciplinary History* 6 (Summer 1975): 47–70.

Keown, Gerard. *First of the Small Nations: The Beginnings of Irish Foreign Policy in the Inter-War Years, 1919–1932*. Oxford: Oxford University Press, 2016.

Khuri-Makdisi, Ilham. *The Eastern Mediterranean and the Making of Global Radicalism, 1860–1914*. Berkeley: University of California Press, 2013.

Klein, Herbert S. "The Social and Economic Integration of Spanish Immigrants in Brazil." *Journal of Social History* 25, no. 3 (Spring 1992): 505–29.

Kramer, Paul A. *The Blood of Government: Race, Empire, the United States, and the Philippines*. Chapel Hill: University of North Carolina Press, 2006.

Lacroix, Justine, Jean-Yves Pranchère, and Sarah-Louise Raillard. "Was Karl Marx Truly against Human Rights? Individual Emancipation and Human Rights Theory." *Revue française de science politique (English Edition)* 62, no. 3 (2012): 47–65.

Laffranque, Marie. "Juan Montseny y los intelectuales: 1898–1905." *Anthropos* 78 (1987): 42–46.

Land, Isaac, ed. *Enemies of Humanity: The Nineteenth-Century War on Terrorism*. New York: Palgrave Macmillan, 2008.

Laqua, Daniel. "Freethinkers, Anarchists and Francisco Ferrer: The Making of a Transnational Solidarity Campaign." *European Review of History/Revue européenne d'histoire* 21, no. 4 (2014): 467–84.

Laqueur, Walter. *The Age of Terrorism*. Boston: Little, Brown, 1987.

——. *Fascism: Past, Present, Future*. New York: Oxford University Press, 1997.

Leier, Mark. *Bakunin: The Creative Passion*. New York: St. Martin's Press, 2006.

Leventhal, F. M. *The Last Dissenter: H. N. Brailsford and His World*. Oxford: Oxford University Press, 1985.

Levy, Carl. "Anarchism, Internationalism and Nationalism in Europe, 1860–1939." *Australian Journal of Politics and History* 50, no. 3 (2004): 330–42.

Levy, Carl, and Matthew S. Adams, eds. *The Palgrave Handbook of Anarchism*. Cham, Switzerland: Palgrave Macmillan, 2019.

Lévy, Thierry. *Plutôt la mort que l'injustice: au temps des procès anarchistes*. Paris: Odile Jacob, 2009.

Liang, Hsi-Huey. *The Rise of Modern Police and the European State System from Metternich to the Second World War*. New York: Cambridge University Press, 1992.

Likin, Max A. "Defending Civil Society and the State: The Ligue des Droits de l'Homme in French and European Politics, 1898–1948." PhD diss., Rutgers University, 2004.

Loadenthal, Michael. *The Politics of Attack: Communiqués and Insurrectionary Violence.* Manchester: Manchester University Press, 2017.

Lomnitz, Claudio. *The Return of Comrade Ricardo Flores Magón.* Brooklyn: Zone, 2014.

López Corral, Miguel. *La Guardia Civil en la Restauración, 1875–1905: militarismo contra subversión y terrorismo anarquista.* Madrid: Ministerio del Interior, 2004.

López Santamaría, Jesús. "El anarquismo español y derechos humanos." *Studia histórica. Historia contemporánea* 26 (2008): 19–52.

Madrid, Francisco. *Solidaridad Obrera y el periodismo de raíz ácrata.* Badalona: Solidaridad Obrera, 2007.

Maitron, Jean. *Le mouvement anarchiste en France: Des origines à 1914.* Paris: Gallimard, 1992.

Maitron, Jean, et al., eds. *Dictionnaire biographique du mouvement ouvrier français. 10, P. 3. 1871–1914, de la Commune à la Grande Guerre.* Paris: Ed. Ouvrières, 1973.

Marín, Dolors, and Salvador Palomar. *Els Montseny Mañé: un laboratori de les idees.* Reus: Les veus del temps, 2010.

Márquez Padorno, Margarita. "El liberalismo en la prensa: Miguel Moya." *Historia Contemporánea* 43 (2011): 688–94.

Marshall, Peter. *Demanding the Impossible: A History of Anarchism.* London: Harper Perennial, 2008.

Martín Corrales, Eloy, ed. *Marruecos y el colonialismo español (1859–1912): De la guerra de África a la "penetración pacífica."* Barcelona: Edicions Bellaterra, 2002.

Martínez Fiol, David. *La Setmana Tràgica.* Barcelona: Pòrtic, 2009.

Masjuan, Eduard. *Un héroe trágico del anarquismo español: Mateo Morral, 1879–1906.* Barcelona: Icaria, 2009.

Maslan, Susan. "The Anti-Human: Man and Citizen before the Declaration of the Rights of Man and of the Citizen." *South Atlantic Quarterly* 103, nos. 2/3 (2004): 357–74.

Maura y Gamazo, Gabriel, and Melchor Fernández Almagro. *Por qué cayó Alfonso XIII? Evolución y disolución de los partidos históricos durante su reinado.* Madrid: Ediciones Ambos Mundos, S.L., 1948.

Mazlish, Bruce. *Civilization and Its Contents.* Stanford, CA: Stanford University Press, 2004.

Meggle, G., ed. *Ethics of Terrorism and Counter-Terrorism.* Frankfurt: Ontos/Verlag, 2005.

Merriman, John. *The Dynamite Club: How a Bombing in Fin-de-Siècle Paris Ignited the Age of Modern Terror.* Boston: Houghton Mifflin Harcourt, 2009.

Miller, Susan Gilson. *A History of Modern Morocco.* Cambridge: Cambridge University Press, 2013.

Morales Lezcano, Víctor. *El colonialismo Hispanofrances en Marruecos (1898–1927).* Madrid: Siglo veintiuno de España, 1976.

Moyn, Samuel. *The Last Utopia: Human Rights in History.* Cambridge, MA: Belknap Press of Harvard University Press, 2010.

Núñez Florencio, Rafael. *El terrorismo anarquista 1888–1909*. Madrid: Siglo Veintiuno Editores, 1983.

Park, Peter Tiidu. "The European Reaction to the Execution of Francisco Ferrer." PhD diss., University of Virginia, 1970.

Patsouras, Louis. *Jean Grave and the Anarchist Tradition in France*. Middletown, NJ: Calson, 1995.

Payne, Stanley. "Catalan and Basque Nationalism." *Journal of Contemporary History* 6, no. 1 (1971): 15–51.

Paz, Abel, et al. *La Barcelona rebelde: guía de una ciudad silenciada*. Barcelona: Octaedro, 2008.

Pernicone, Nunzio. *Italian Anarchism, 1864–1892*. Princeton, NJ: Princeton University Press, 1993.

Pernicone, Nunzio, and Fraser M. Ottanelli. *Assassins against the Old Order: Italian Anarchist Violence in Fin de Siècle Europe*. Urbana: University of Illinois Press, 2018.

Perry, Wendy Ellen. "Remembering Dreyfus: The Ligue des Droits de l'Homme and the Making of the Modern French Human Rights Movement." PhD diss., University of North Carolina, 1998.

Piqueras, José A. *Cánovas y la derecha española: Del magnicidio a los neocon*. Barcelona: Ediciones Peninsula, 2008.

Pons Pujol, Jordi. "Imatge oficial i política francesa respecte la Catalunya espanyola, 1895–1914." PhD diss., Universitat Autònoma de Barcelona, 2015.

Pradas Baena, María Amalia. *Teresa Claramunt: La "virgen roja" barcelonesa, biografia y escritos*. Barcelona: Virus Editorial, 2006.

Prado, Antonio. *Matrimonio, familia y estado: escritoras anarco-feministas en La Revista Blanca (1898–1936)*. Madrid: Fundación Anselmo Lorenzo, 2011.

Robert, Vincent, and Eduard J. Verger. "'La protesta universal' contra la ejecución de Ferrer: las manifestaciones de octubre de 1909." *Historia Social* 14 (Autumn 1992): 61–82.

Rodogno, Davide. *Against Massacre: Humanitarian Interventions in the Ottoman Empire, 1815–1914: The Emergence of a European Concept and International Practice*. Princeton, NJ: Princeton University Press, 2012.

Romero Maura, Joaquín. *La Romana del Diablo: Ensayos Sobre la Violencia Política en España*. Madrid: Marcial Pons, 2000.

——. *"La Rosa de Fuego": El obrerismo barcelonés de 1899 a 1909*. Barcelona: Ediciones Grijalbo, 1975.

——. "Terrorism in Barcelona and Its Impact on Spanish Politics, 1904–1909." *Past and Present* 41 (December 1968): 130–83.

Romero Salvadó, Francisco J. *¿Quién mató a Eduardo Dato?: comedia política y tragedia social en España, 1892–1921*. Granada: Comares, 2020.

Rozario, Kevin. "'Delicious Horrors': Mass Culture, the Red Cross, and the Appeal of Modern American Humanitarianism." *American Quarterly* 55, no. 3 (2003): 417–55.

Sageman, Marc. *Turning to Political Violence: The Emergence of Terrorism*. Philadelphia: University of Pennsylvania Press, 2017.

Said, Edward. *Orientalism*. New York: Vintage, 1979.

Sanabria, Enrique A. *Republicanism and Anticlerical Nationalism in Spain*. New York: Palgrave Macmillan, 2009.

Sanchez Cobos, Amparo. *Sembrando ideales: anarquistas españoles en Cuba, 1902–1925*. Seville: Consejo Superior de Investigaciones científicas, 2008.

Scott, William Henry. *The Unión Obrera Democrática: First Filipino Trade Union*. Quezon City: New Day, 1992.

Serrano, Carlos. *Alfonso XIII*. Madrid: Arlanza Ediciones, 2001.

——. "El 'nacimiento de los intelectuales': algunos replanteamientos." *Ayer* 40 (2000): 11–23.

Shaffer, Kirwin R. *Anarchism and Countercultural Politics in Early Twentieth-Century Cuba*. Gainesville: University Press of Florida, 2005.

——. "Havana Hub: Cuban Anarchism, Radical Media and the Trans-Caribbean Anarchist Network, 1902–1915." *Caribbean Studies* 37, no. 2 (2009): 45–81.

Shubert, Adrian. *A Social History of Modern Spain*. London: Routledge, 1990.

Siguán, Marisa. "Federico Urales: un programa de literatura popular libertaria." *Anthropos* 78 (1987): 35–41.

Siljak, Ana. *Angel of Vengeance: The "Girl Assassin," the Governor of St. Petersburg, and Russia's Revolutionary World*. New York: St. Martin's Press, 2008.

Skirda, Alexandre. *Facing the Enemy: A History of Anarchist Organization from Proudhon to May 1968*. Oakland: AK Press, 2002.

Smith, Angel, ed. *Red Barcelona: Social Protest and Labour Mobilization in the Twentieth Century*. London: Routledge, 2003.

Solà i Gussinyer, Pere. "Los grupos del magisterio racionalista en Argentina y Uruguay hacia 1910 y sus actitudes ante la enseñanza laica official." *Historia de la Educación* 1 (1982): 229–46.

Sonn, Richard D. *Anarchism and Cultural Politics in Fin de Siècle France*. Lincoln: University of Nebraska Press, 1989.

Tamburini, Francesco. "La conferenza internazionale di Roma per la difesa sociale contro gli anarchici (24 Novembre–21 Dicembre 1898)." *Clio* 2 (1997): 227–65.

——. "Michele Angiolillo e l'assassinio di Cánovas del Castillo." *Spagna contemporanea* 9 (1996): 101–30.

——. "Michele Angiolillo el anarquista que asesinó a Cánovas del Castillo." *Historia* 16 (1997): 28–39.

Tavera, Susana. "Soledad Gustavo, Federica Montseny i el periodisme acrata: ¿Ofici o militancia?" *Annals del periodisme Català* 6, no. 14 (1988): 9–20.

Thomas, Keith. *Man and the Natural World: A History of the Modern Sensibility*. New York: Pantheon Books, 1983.

Thomas, Paul. *Karl Marx and the Anarchists*. New York: Routledge, 1980.

Tone, Lawrence. *War and Genocide in Cuba, 1895–1898*. Chapel Hill: University of North Carolina Press, 2006.

Tuchman, Barbara W. "Anarchism in France." In Horowitz, *The Anarchists*, 440–62.

Turcato, Davide. *Making Sense of Anarchism: Errico Malatesta's Experiments with Revolution, 1889–1900*. Oakland: AK Press, 2015.

Turrado Vidal, Martín. *Policía y Delincuencia a Finales del Siglo XIX*. Madrid: Dykinson, 2001.

Ullman, Joan Connelly. *La semana trágica: Estudio sobre las causas socioeconómicas del anticlericalismo en España (1898–1912)*. Barcelona: Ediciones Ariel, 1968.

——. *The Tragic Week: A Study of Anticlericalism in Spain, 1875–1912*. Cambridge, MA: Harvard University Press, 1968.

van der Walt, Lucien. "Global Anarchism and Syndicalism: Theory, History, Resistance." *Anarchist Studies* 24, vol. 1 (2016): 85–106.

Verhoeven, Claudia. *The Odd Man Karakozov: Imperial Russia, Modernity, and the Birth of Terrorism*. Ithaca, NY: Cornell University Press, 2011.

Vernitski, Anat, "Russian Revolutionaries and English Sympathizers in 1890s London: The Case of Olive Garnett and Sergei Stepniak." *Journal of European Studies* 35, no. 3 (2005): 299–314.

Voltes Bou, Pedro. *La semana trágica*. Madrid: Espasa Calpe, 1995.

Wagnon, Sylvain. *Francisco Ferrer: une éducation libertaire en héritage*. Lyon: Atelier de création libertaire, 2013.

Whyte, George R. *The Dreyfus Affair: A Chronological History*. New York: Palgrave Macmillan, 2005.

Wisan, Joseph E. *The Cuban Crisis as Reflected in the New York Press (1895–1898)*. New York: Octagon Books, 1965.

Woodcock, George. *Anarchism: A History of Libertarian Ideas and Movements*. Cleveland: Meridian, 1962.

Woolman, David S. *Rebels in the Rif: Abd El Krim and the Rif Rebellion*. Stanford, CA: Stanford University Press, 1968.

Yeoman, James Michael. *Print Culture and the Formation of the Anarchist Movement in Spain, 1890–1915*. New York: Routledge, 2020.

Zimmer, Kenyon. *Immigrants against the State: Yiddish and Italian Anarchism in America*. Urbana: University of Illinois Press, 2017.

Zuckerman, Frederic S. *The Tsarist Secret Police Abroad: Policing Europe in a Modernising World*. New York: Palgrave Macmillan, 2003.

Zunino, Marcos. "Subversive Justice: The Russell Vietnam War Crimes Tribunal and Transitional Justice." *International Journal of Transitional Justice* 10, no. 2 (2016): 211–29.

INDEX

Page numbers in *italic* refer to illustrations.

De los Reyes, Isabelo, 150
Los Descamisados, 232
Los Desheredados, 37
Despujol, Eulogio, 90, 94, 95, 111, 123, 155
Diario Universal, 228
La Dinastía, 59, 61, 81, 92, 93
El Diluvio, 61, 98, 104, 126
Dreyfus, Alfred, 2, 121, 145–47, 183; Ferrer campaign, 265; *La Revue blanche* and, 5; verdict annulment, 158, 160
Dreyfus, Mathieu, 145
Dreyfus affair, 7, 73, 139, 145–47, 154, 156, 183, 265; Ferrer campaign and, 230; Sébastien Faure and, 65, 145–46; "Spanish edition," 159; "truth and justice," 6; Zola and, 102
Drumont, Édouard, 139
Dryhurst, Nannie Florence, 119–20
Durkheim, Émile, 146, 265

Ealham, Chris, 262
Elisabeth, Empress of Austria, 152
L'Endehors, 51, 52
Engels, Friedrich, 176, 270–71
La Época, 16, 24–25, 81, 91, 112, 116, 155, 156; Ferrer prosecution role, 264; on rue de Rohan bombing, 202; view of Ferrer execution, 268
Escuela Moderna. *See* Modern School
L'Espagne inquisitoriale, 11, 12, *12*, 186, 195–96
España Nueva, 231
Esquerdo, José María, 144, 148
Esterhazy, Ferdinand Walsin, 146
Estévanez, Nicolás, 103, 192, 207, 208, 218, 222, 223
Esteve, Juan, 130
ethics of modernity, 14–18, 60, 107, 171, 270, 271

Fabbri, Luigi, 216
Falk, Nora, 216–17, 224
Farrás, Alejandro, 200
Farrás, Alejandro (pseudonym), 200, 202–4, 207, 208
Faure, Félix, 80, 84, 129, 130
Faure, Sébastien, 51, 65–66, 80, 116, 129, 230; Dreyfus affair, 145–46, 154
Federación de Sociedades Obreras de la Región Espanõla (FSORE), 165, 175–76, 178, 184, 208, 214; dissolution, 248
Federación de Trabajadores de la Región Española (FTRE), 36–37, 39, 175, 176, 177

Federación Regional Española (FRE), 31, 35–36, 39, 176, 177
Fénéon, Félix, 51, 80
Fernando Po (African penal colony), 92, 110, 130
Ferrer, Francisco, 2, 6, 11, 199, 212–14, 263–65; Alcalá del Valle campaign, 252, 254; Angiolillo and, 129; Calle Mayor bombing arrest, imprisonment, and acquittal, *225*, 226, 227–34, 251; as Cero, 214, 231, 234; *La Huelga General*, 208, 214, 231, 234, 252; Lerroux and, 198; Montseny and, 228–29; Morral and, 208, 218, 221–23, 234; Nakens and, 221–22, 234; Nora Falk and, 217; Portas encounter, 163; rue de Rohan bombing, 204, 207, 208; Tragic Week arrest, trial, and execution, 252, 264–65
Festa, Lynn, 15
Figueroa y Torres, Álvaro, 228
Filipinos. *See* Philippine Revolution
First International. *See* International Workingmen's Association (IWMA)
Flores Magón, Ricardo, 32
France, Anatole, 146, 183, 231
Franco, Francisco, 225, 260
Franz Ferdinand, Archduke of Austria, 220
Freedom, 113, 117, 118, 120, 132
Freemasonry, 207, 229–30
Free Russia, 118
Freixa, Daniel, 100–101
French Revolution, 8, 13, 67, 155
French Trial of the Thirty. *See* "Trial of the Thirty" (France)
FSORE. *See* Federación de Sociedades Obreras de la Región Espanõla (FSORE)
FTRE. *See* Federación de Trabajadores de la Región Española (FTRE)

Gana, Francisco, 101, 103, 104, 124, 128, 132, 148, 204; deportation and exile, 130, 138–39
García de Polavieja, Camilo. *See* Polavieja, Camilo García de
Garrison, William Lloyd, 118
Gasset, Rafael, 159
Gedeón, 249
Gente Joven, 214
German Club, London, 136, 137, 140, 162
German press, 122
Germinal (Zola), 72, 137
Gladstone, William, 119, 120, 139
Goldman, Emma, 118, 123
González Calleja, Eduardo, 177